Never Givin' Up

NEVER GIVIN' UP

The Life and Music of Al Jarreau

KURT DIETRICH

WISCONSIN HISTORICAL SOCIETY PRESS

Published by the Wisconsin Historical Society Press
Publishers since 1855

The Wisconsin Historical Society helps people connect to the past by collecting, preserving, and sharing stories. Founded in 1846, the Society is one of the nation's finest historical institutions.
Join the Wisconsin Historical Society: wisconsinhistory.org/membership

Photographs identified with WHI or WHS are from the Society's collections; address requests to reproduce these photos to the Visual Materials Archivist at the Wisconsin Historical Society, 816 State Street, Madison, WI 53706.

Front cover image: Al Jarreau at the Performing Arts Center in Milwaukee, 1980. © Milwaukee Journal Sentinel - USA TODAY NETWORK
Back cover image: Al Jarreau in the choir room at Ripon College's Rodman Center for the Arts, 1982. Courtesy of Ripon College
Back cover quote: *Al Jarreau L'enchanteur: Un Documentaire Musical de Thierry Guedj*, directed by Thierry Guedj (France: Portrait & Company, aired January 1, 2016, on French O).

All images of Al Jarreau album covers, unless otherwise noted, were provided courtesy of RHINO Entertainment Company.

Printed in Canada
Typesetting by Wendy Holdman

27 26 25 24 23   1 2 3 4 5

Library of Congress Cataloging-in-Publication Data
Names: Dietrich, Kurt, author.
Title: Never givin' up : the life and music of Al Jarreau / Kurt Dietrich.
Other titles: Never giving up
Description: [1st.] | Madison : Wisconsin Historical Society Press, 2023. | Includes index.
Identifiers: LCCN 2022061303 (print) | LCCN 2022061304 (e-book) |
    ISBN 9781976600197 (hardcover) | ISBN 9781976600203 (epub)
Subjects: LCSH: Jarreau, Al. | Singers—Wisconsin—Biography. | Singers—
    United States—Biography. | Jazz Musicians—Wisconsin—Biography. |
    Jazz musicians—United States—Biography.
Classification: LCC ML420.J2707 D54 2023 (print) | LCC ML420.J2707 (e-book) |
    DDC 782.42165092 [B]—dc23/eng/20221223
LC record available at https://lccn.loc.gov/2022061303
LC e-book record available at https://lccn.loc.gov/2022061304

♾ The paper used in this publication meets the minimum requirements of the American National Standard for Information Sciences—Permanence of Paper for Printed Library Materials, ANSI Z39.48-1992.

To the family, friends, and fans of Al Jarreau

Contents

Preface   ix

Introduction   1

1 The Jarreau Family   5

2 Early Days   15

3 Ripon   24

4 Milwaukee   33

5 Iowa   39

6 California   45

7 Duo   51

8 Moving Up   66

9 The First Three Albums   76

10 Transition   95

11 Breakin' Through   107

12 Touring and Homecomings   127

13 Changing Course   140

14 Working It Out   163

15 Searching   170

16 Guest Appearances   187

17 More Touring   204

18 Plugging Away   212

19 Looking Back   224

20 Taking Stock   239

21 Back to the Studio   253

22 Coming Full Circle   270

23 Late Career   286

24 Finale   301

25 Legacy   318

Acknowledgments   330
Notes   333
Index   375

PREFACE

This biography was written in large part because Al Jarreau attended Ripon College in Ripon, Wisconsin. He earned a degree in psychology at the school in 1962. Prior to beginning my teaching career at Ripon College in 1980, I was completely unaware of this. Once there, however, I was soon clued in to one of Ripon's most celebrated alumni. Because I taught at the college, I was able to meet Al on campus on three separate occasions. As an ambassador for the college, I interacted with him a fourth time at the 2016 gala celebration in Milwaukee when he received a Lifetime Achievement Award from the Wisconsin Foundation for School Music.

The first time I saw Al on campus was in 1982, when he returned for homecoming weekend just as his career was beginning to explode with success. Immediately apparent was his amazingly charismatic aura. I doubt anyone in the choir room at the Rodman Center for the Arts that Friday evening will ever forget it. And he created that aura without singing a single note!

In 2006, Al returned to campus and gave an unforgettable concert. Every concertgoer was surely struck with his personal magnetism, his joy in performance, and his love of Ripon and Wisconsin.

Al snuck onto campus unannounced in 2012, crashing his class's fiftieth reunion. I had been tipped off to his attendance ahead of time and had been set up to interview him, but conducting an interview in this space was a nearly impossible task. Almost every person at the reunion wanted to visit with their beloved friend and classmate.

The college sent me and two of my music students to the Lifetime Achievement Award festivities in October 2016, which turned out to be just months before Al's death. It was a joyous occasion, as no one had any premonition of how little time Al had left. That evening, I had the privilege of meeting Al's sister, Rose Marie Freeman, who became an absolutely crucial collaborator in the creation of this book. I also reconnected with Al's musical director, Milwaukee native Joe Turano (whom I had briefly met decades earlier), who proved to be another invaluable contributor to the book.

A couple of years after Al's death, I realized that no one was planning to write his biography. Understanding that his life story needed to be recorded, I respectfully decided to give it a shot. However, I would not undertake the project without the permission and cooperation of Joe Gordon, Al's last manager. Communication with Joe made it clear that the approval I really needed was from the head of the family: Rose Marie. She and I met again in Milwaukee in the fall of 2019 and forged a working relationship that has, in the years since, turned into a deep friendship. There is no way this book would be in your hands had not Rose Marie given so freely of herself and her wisdom. Ultimately, many of Al's friends, family, and fellow musicians made invaluable contributions to this book, for which I am deeply grateful. I thank them in greater detail in this book's acknowledgments. Several of Al's friends read early drafts of this book and encouraged me to refer to him by Al, rather than Jarreau, as the nickname epitomized his down-to-earth demeanor. As a result, I have primarily used his first name throughout the book.

Throughout this process, I have been inspired and humbled by such towering jazz biographies as Robin D. G. Kelley's *Thelonious Monk: The Life and Times of an American Original* and the late Mark Tucker's *Ellington: The Early Years*. I have wrestled with problematic works such as Miles Davis's autobiography and Ross Russell's *Bird Lives!: The High Life and Hard Times of Charlie (Yardbird) Parker*. And I have read and reread many other biographies of musicians and nonmusicians.

Writing a biography is a challenge from many standpoints, but one of the biggest issues is writing to a target audience. I hope that the readership of this story will be broad and inclusive. Al's fans want to know about his life, and I believe they want to read about his music, too—specifically, the records that they have loved for years. The music needs to be addressed and discussed seriously, but not using language that excludes those fans. This book is for the lay reader, and while I have written it, in part, to be a valuable historical document, I also hope that Al's fans think of it as a gift.

Because I am American, I wrote from an American perspective. But many would argue that Al was more of a star in Europe than here in his own country. Someone else will have to do the deeper documentation of that remarkable aspect of his career. Because I am a Wisconsinite, I also wrote specifically about Al Jarreau's connection with Wisconsin, which was certainly crucial to his whole life.

I started my research with Ripon College's Al Jarreau archive, and the almost puzzling variety of sources and materials from all over the country in that small collection inspired me to follow that eclectic model throughout. While this book includes opinions on Al and his music from *Down Beat*, the *New York Times*, and *People* magazine, it also includes what was written about him in Fremont, California's *The Argus*; Allentown, Pennsylvania's *The Morning Call*; and *The Black Collegian*, based in New Orleans. Since Al is no longer here to speak for himself, I quoted him as often as possible.

May Al Jarreau's spirit and his music live on.

INTRODUCTION

"**M**y name is Al Jarreau, I'm from Milwaukee, I sing jazz and I sing pop and I sing R&B, and sometimes I mix the things, and they come out sounding like Al Jarreau from Milwaukee."

These are the first words spoken by Al Jarreau in the 2016 French documentary film *Al Jarreau L'enchanteur*. By this late point in his career, Al was truly a citizen of the world, possibly more famous in Europe than in the United States. Nonetheless, he identified with the place where he grew up: a midwestern industrial city where his family had moved just a few years before Al was born in 1940. Al spent the first eighteen years of his life in Milwaukee. He left to attend college in little Ripon, Wisconsin, then returned to the city after graduation. By the time he left Milwaukee again in 1962, for graduate school at the University of Iowa, he had already started his professional career as a singer. Although he returned to Milwaukee to perform both during and after his two years in Iowa City, he was never again a resident of Wisconsin's largest city. He left for California in 1964 and lived there for the rest of his life. Yet, it seems he never really thought of himself as a Californian.

More than fifty years after moving away, Al described himself as "Al Jarreau from Milwaukee." His hometown had influenced his values and provided him with a musical foundation; his school, his church, and especially his family shaped him into the man and artist we know today.

When Al returned to Milwaukee in 2016 to receive a Lifetime Achievement Award from the Wisconsin Foundation for School Music, the honor and the event that accompanied it meant a great deal to him. He was returning to a venue—the Pfister, downtown Milwaukee's signature hotel—where he had entertained Milwaukeeans more than a half-century earlier, at the beginning of his career, before anyone could have guessed that he would someday be recognized around the world as a jazz, pop, and R&B

icon. At the Pfister event, a surprisingly large number of people in the crowd had attended Milwaukee's public schools with Al in the 1950s and 1960s. Also present were family members, professional associates, fans, and, much to Al's delight, Milwaukee public school students playing and singing music.

During this visit, Al took a drive through his old neighborhood, something he often did when he returned to Milwaukee.[1] But on this occasion, he was driven by the executive director of the Wisconsin Foundation for School Music, Tim Schaid, and accompanied by Wisconsin Public Television producer Steven Doebel and a camera operator. Filming was underway for a documentary about Al that would end up being released in 2017, shortly after his death. Al had suggested the tour, and the producers were easily persuaded that it would be a good idea. Although almost none of the footage made it into the final documentary, Al's observations and reflections on the recording reveal the influence his Milwaukee upbringing had on his work ethic, his passion for music, and his selfless desire to uplift others.[2]

One of Al's early remarks on this day served as a prelude to everything that he talked about on the tour. "The connections between me and this city just continue to deepen," he said, "between me and this city, and my life as it went out of here on this yellow brick road." His deep gratitude for his life's successes went hand in hand with his unfailingly positive outlook on life. Al was always looking for and expecting the best. "I'm such a silly, sappy, sentimental so-and-so," he conceded. "I'm a Pollyanna, and I believe in dreams." Indeed, many of the memories he shared on the car tour were sweet remembrances of things from his past. He admitted that some of his memories were probably rosier than the reality had been.

As soon as the car left the Pfister, Al began reacting to his surroundings in a free-flowing stream of consciousness. Near two significant landmarks on Third Street—the old Schlitz brewery and the former Schuster's Department Store—Al stated, with some pride, "This is the neighborhood I grew up in." He described Schlitz, A. O. Smith (the manufacturing company that employed his father for many years), and Allis-Chalmers Manufacturing Company as the "foundation of the city," where parents could earn enough to send their kids to the University of Wisconsin–Madison or Ripon College. Al had a clear grasp of the engine that drove the city of Milwaukee: a working-class ethos that mirrored the diligence he had shown to his craft for decades. And he was a font of knowledge when it came to Milwaukee history, providing anecdotes on everything from the stately mansions on the bluff overlooking Lake Michigan to the former site of the Weyenberg Shoe Factory. "I can smell the leather now," he mused as they drove by.

Al also recalled the sounds of his old neighborhood. From over the fence in his backyard, he used to hear the clatter of pins falling at the CYO bowling alley where he occasionally worked as a pinsetter. All through the night, polkas and the sounds of people dancing would drift in through his bedroom window from Mike Blahowski's Polka Tavern next door.[3] "I know more polkas than Frankie Yankovic," he joked.[4] When asked how he was able to sleep with the noise of bowling and polkas in the air, Al replied that he slept "like a baby." "Families with six children were not disturbed by a little outside noise," he said. "We were families who were not rich; I'm not sure what you would call it. Not even middle class—we were approaching middle class. . . . People worked hard and felt good about themselves, and so, yeah, we slept pretty darn good."

Al teared up upon seeing the building that once housed his grade school—Henry L. Palmer School on North First Street. "My mother would bring me and I would sing a little song at PTA meetings," he remembered. And he talked about Lincoln High, where deaf and blind students, as well as those with other mental and physical disabilities, received special instruction on the top floor of the school. "[They were] sent here to go to school with Blacks, Italians, kids from the other side of the tracks," he said. "It doesn't get talked about very much, but [this is] an important part of the history of that building."

Upon being asked how this affected him, Al responded, "I'm a master-degreed rehabilitation counselor. It got in me: helping professions. I'm in a helping profession right now. My music is a small little ministry. It has to do with 'You are okay.' We are okay; we're children of God. You're okay; don't let anybody tell you that you're less than a child of God. Come on, let's sing together and have some fun, and wake up in the morning and feel better."[5] For a second time on the car trip, Al teared up. "People, when they hear me say, 'I can, like any other man, reach out and touch the face of God.'[6] Hey, man, that's part of this training that I got here in these classrooms, and in my church that just has me realizing there are some things that we owe each other as children of God trying to do as well as we can on this planet."

Al was pleased that what had been Lincoln High was now the Lincoln Center of the Arts, a middle school focused on arts education. He called it a "wonderful evolution of my old school." A couple of days after the car tour, he would work and talk with the jazz students at the Milwaukee High School for the Arts, where many Lincoln Center students go on to continue their schooling, prior to the high school students' performance at his award event at the Pfister Hotel.

The tour footage portrays Al as the upbeat, generous, and compassionate soul that he was—nostalgic about his childhood, full of stories, quick to laugh and quick to cry. His life would take him far from the modest home where he was raised on Reservoir Avenue, but he would always think of himself as "Al Jarreau from Milwaukee."

1

THE JARREAU FAMILY

A l Jarreau grew up in a strong, nuclear family that was held in high regard in its community. Surprisingly little is known, however, of the generations that preceded his parents. Al's father, Emile Jarreau Jr. (or "Emile the Second," as Al's older sister, Rose Marie, called him), was born in New Orleans, Louisiana, on September 24, 1902.[1] Somewhere in the family's past, a male ancestor had been a white plantation owner of French descent in the New Orleans area, thus the French surname. Al's immediate family identifies as African American.[2] Emile Jr.'s father was Emile Alphonse Jarreau ("Emile the First"), and his mother was Ida Perry Jarreau.

Al's mother, Pearl Walker, also born in 1902, was an only child. She grew up in Punta Gorda, Florida. Her mother died at a young age, and Pearl never talked with her children about her father; she learned of his death by telegram when she was in her adulthood.[3]

Emile and Pearl both attended Oakwood Junior College in Huntsville, Alabama, a historically Black Seventh-day Adventist school.[4] Founded in 1896 on 380 acres of a former plantation where enslaved people labored, and where Dred Scott once resided, the college had as its stated mission "to educate the recently-freed African-Americans of the South" based on the belief that "'all people are created equal' and deserved the opportunity to learn a trade."[5] Al's understanding of his parents' college was that it "trained especially ministers and teachers and missionaries to go abroad in third-world countries and bring the good news of Jesus."[6] Pearl's aunt Isabella Cunningham was the dean of girls at Oakwood and talked her niece into attending the college.

Al Jarreau's parents, Emile Jarreau II (center) and Pearl Walker (right), with Emile's sister Edythe Jarreau (left) at Oakwood Junior College in the 1920s. COURTESY OF ROSE MARIE FREEMAN

Emile studied theology at Oakwood. He also participated in a school gospel quartet that toured the United States, reportedly singing in thirty-eight of the forty-eight states that made up the country at that time. On one 1927 tour, the group performed at the Pabst Theater in Milwaukee.[7] Participation in the group earned Emile's tuition, allowing him to attend college. Pearl received training at Oakwood to become a teacher, though family obligations prevented her from going on to teach.[8]

According to Rose Marie, Emile's sister Edythe knew that Emile had his eye on a different woman in college. But Edythe apparently told him, "Nope, Pearl Walker is the one for you." She took credit for bringing the two together and did not let Emile forget it.[9]

After Emile and Pearl graduated in 1927 (a year in which total enroll-ment at Oakwood reached an all-time high of two hundred) and married in 1928, Emile decided that he was not going to raise a family in the segregated South.[10] The young couple headed north to Chicago for his first ministry, and their first child, Emile III, was born there in 1929. The elder Emile's next assignment brought the family to Flint, Michigan, where son Alphaeus and daughter Joyce were born in 1930 and 1932, respectively. After moving to Indianapolis for Emile's next posting, their daughter Rose Marie was born in 1934.

Around 1935, the growing family moved to its final destination— Milwaukee, Wisconsin—where Emile served the Sharon Seventh-day Adventist congregation. Six years passed between the births of Rose Marie and her younger brother Al—a gap she refers to as "six years of intermittent silence." According to Rose Marie, her mother had at least one miscarriage during this time.[11] Eventually, though Emile may not have been thrilled by the news, another child was on the way. Alwin Jarreau—now known universally as Al—was born on March 12, 1940. The youngest sibling, Marshall, was born in 1942, bringing the total to six children. According to Rose Marie, despite the size of the family, the children never felt a lack of love in their home. "[Emile and Pearl] were always loving and very dedicated parents, and attentive to us. And we were never hungry," she claimed, even during the difficult years of the Great Depression.

Baby Al with his mother, Pearl, circa 1940.
COURTESY OF ROSE MARIE FREEMAN

The Jarreau family lived at 336 West Reservoir Avenue in central Milwaukee during Al's youth.[12] St. Michael's Hospital stood kitty-corner across the street from their house, and the Catholic youth hall, complete with a gym and bowling alley, jutted into the Jarreaus' backyard. Alphaeus, Al, and Al's good friend Maxwell Carter set pins there when they were teenagers, coming home with a couple of dollars after about three hours of pinsetting.[13] Next to the house was Mike Blahowski's Polka Tavern. Al, who slept in the bedroom along that side of the house, could hear polkas playing all night long. He remembered going into the tavern during the day to buy Geiser's potato chips and Ambrosia chocolate for his mother.[14]

Down the street, the priests and sisters of St. Francis had a residence. With some of her Catholic friends, Rose Marie would sometimes go into the church to sit in the pews and admire the windows, soaking up the rarified air of the place. As Al explained in the footage for the Wisconsin Public Television documentary in 2016, St. Francis Church "had a monumental influence on the immediate community." Not everybody in the area was Catholic, but people felt an association with the parish. Al remembered that his family was moved by the sight of the nuns, who lived in the nearby convent, walking by in their habits, as well as the priests and brothers from the monastery in their brown robes and white belts. The nuns taught at the church's grade school where about three hundred neighborhood children attended. "There was just kind of a connection between that Christianity and love of God and principles of Christianity . . . that still is with me," Al said in 2016. "I'm not Catholic, but seeing all that, and the devotion [of] these members of the church, including the nuns and priests, just affected me. . . . My dad was a minister, so any connection to the church in our house was a very sacred thing."

The neighborhood, now known as Halyard Park, had been settled in the 1850s and "filled to capacity by 1890."[15] Like so many Milwaukee neighborhoods of that era, it was primarily inhabited by German immigrants. They established St. Francis Church in 1877 at Fourth and Brown Streets, just down the street from what would later become the Jarreaus' home. As the Germans moved into other parts of the city at the turn of the twentieth century, Halyard Park became "one of the most diverse [neighborhoods] in Milwaukee's history," housing African Americans, Hungarians, Italians, Czechs, Slovaks, Poles, and Jews from eastern Europe. Among the Jewish residents was Goldie Mabowehz, who later became the prime minister of Israel as Golda Meir. (Fourth Street School, which she attended, just blocks away from the Jarreau home, was renamed Golda Meir School in 1979.)

By 1930, according to Milwaukee historian John Gurda, the "neighborhood was well on its way to becoming the core of Milwaukee's African-American community."[16] The Jarreaus' neighborhood bordered the area known as Bronzeville, an African American center of business and entertainment for many years before it was broken up in part by the building of Interstate Highway 43, which destroyed many homes and businesses in the 1960s. The neighborhood only became known as Halyard Park in the mid-1970s when it was chosen for an urban renewal project.

When the Jarreaus bought the house on Reservoir, between Third and Fourth Streets, they were the first Black family in the neighborhood.[17] Al recalled it as an area where everyone got along, but his siblings' memories were more mixed. Rose Marie remembered a white neighbor girl whose family did not allow her to play with Rose Marie. But, other than this incident, Rose Marie said she "never felt segregated growing up" and described the neighborhood as tolerant. Alphaeus recalled one frightening incident with five people being attacked with a baseball bat, a scene that "stuck with [him] for a long time," yet his memories of the neighborhood were otherwise overwhelmingly positive. He said people looked out for one another and lived by the ethos "Love your neighbor as thyself."

Even before the last two boys were born, Emile realized he could not support his growing family solely on his salary from the Sharon Seventh-day Adventist Church. He decided to find a second job. Soon, he was working as a consultant for a funeral director named Emile O'Bee, providing spiritual help to families processing the loss of a loved one.[18] Eventually, he took on more tasks, helping with the nuts and bolts of the funeral process, joining entourages going to the cemetery, and assisting in any way he was needed.[19] Pastor Jarreau's new employment, however, was not appreciated by some members of his congregation, who felt that a minister's full attention should be on the considerable needs of his flock. The ensuing disagreement about his duties led to Emile's resigning from his position at the church.

Years later, Al said he believed that when his father was hired at Sharon it marked the first time that the congregation had an ordained minister "of the cloth" who was formally trained in the ministry. As Al recalled, this was "frowned upon by that group of families who had been the organizers of that church. Here comes an outsider to be the head of their church. It was their thing, and so it didn't work out for them. It didn't work out for my dad; it didn't work out for those founding families of the Black church."[20]

Because of his father's leaving the ministry, Al told *Down Beat*'s Lee Underwood in 1976, "I never got to hear my father preach in church. . . . But he preached at home—he preached everywhere! . . . And I'm seeing that happen to me. I'm doing the same thing, taking up the ministry, only my pulpit is the barroom and the stage. My church is the world."[21]

Emile needed to make yet more money to support his family of eight. At many places where he applied for work, he was told that despite his college degree, Black men were being hired only for caretaking or janitorial jobs. In order to get a better-paying job, Emile started attending a technical school at night, where he was trained in acetylene welding. With this training, he was hired at A. O. Smith Corporation, a prominent Milwaukee manufacturer known for its production of automobile frames and glass-lined brewery tanks. During World War II, when Emile was first hired, the company shifted all production to wartime purposes, making landing gear, propeller blades, and components for the atomic bomb project, among other items.[22] Alphaeus remembered his father going to work every day "with torch in hand." Emile worked for A. O. Smith until he retired, after twenty-five years, in 1967.

When Emile left his position at the church, he stopped attending regularly, but he did not allow his children's attendance to lapse. "He made sure that we got up and went to church," Rose Marie remembered. Despite his split from the church, Emile "believed in the religion. [Leaving the church] didn't destroy his faith."

At home, Emile dominated the household. "[My father] used to use the statement, 'Walk the chalk line,'" Rose Marie explained. "He was very dedicated to proper conduct and attention to detail and 'do it right the first time.' . . . To say he was driven would not be exaggerating." Marshall simply described him as a "disciplinarian." Corporal punishment was relatively common in families of the era, including in the Jarreau household. Alphaeus related, "You'd be at the end of some of those whippings and you'd wonder whether you're going or coming." Al's close friend Maxwell

Carter remembered both his parents and Al's as being very strict: "[When we were] fourteen, fifteen years old, we had to be in front of our house at eight o'clock. Now, that's unheard of. Eight o'clock at night, you had to be 'where I can see you.'"

Another important focus for Emile was education. One of his favorite expressions was: "If you prepare yourself, your chance will come." This philosophy made it possible for the children to pursue higher education. "From grade school through graduate school . . . I missed less than three days of school," Al said. He mimicked his father's words: "Go to school. Get to school. If you don't do anything else, go to school."[23] And Emile made sure that his children studied. "Every day," said Carter, "when Al and I came home, three or four or five days a week, we would stop by this pastry shop and buy a lemon pie, and come home, and go downstairs in his basement and do our homework, and eat lemon pie and [drink] milk. It was almost a ritual."[24] Whether it was right after school or after a sports practice, schoolwork was done whenever they got home. "Al is probably the reason why I graduated with the grades that I had," Carter said. "Al took care of business first, because that's what his parents put on his shoulders."

In addition to their studies, Emile expected his kids to do chores and contribute to domestic duties. The boys were tasked with keeping coal in the basement furnace. "Shoveling coal, that's what I did," Al remembered. "A big furnace and clothes hanging on a line, because it was wintertime. My mother had washed clothes and they were drying in the basement, with a lot of that heat from a big furnace."[25]

Al at age seven in 1947. COURTESY OF ROSE MARIE FREEMAN

Despite the fact that money was tight, none of the Jarreau kids remembered wanting for anything. "We had everything. . . . We didn't even know we were poor," said Marshall. Rose Marie, too, described these early years in glowing terms: "We had a wonderful childhood. Never starved to death, were always clothed, always had a roof over our heads." "We Got By," the touching and popular song from Al's first major album, describes a childhood of hardly having a "bellyful," "hand-me-down books and shoes," and "strolling for miles to a movie show." While Al claimed it was not a literal recounting of his life as a child, he said it did reflect that reality. Marshall called the story in the song "very real" and recalled his father giving him one dollar as an allowance. Emile would "take the dollar between his fingertips . . . and then blow on it. He did a whole routine with that," Marshall said.

Peter Bock, Al's close friend from Ripon College, remembered that Emile didn't trust banks and kept all of his money in cash, "on him, or under his mattress, rolled up in rolls with rubber bands." When the young Bock once cautioned Mr. Jarreau about handling his money that way, "he patted [Peter] on the cheek and said, 'Well, I think I'll be okay.'"[26]

With a tight budget and a family of eight, the Jarreaus made the most of the space in their house. The main floor comprised a parlor, a living room, and Pearl and Emile's bedroom. The parlor became the bedroom for the girls, Joyce and Rose Marie. For years, Al and Marshall slept together in a fold-up rollaway bed stored in the living room. The older boys, Emile III and Alphaeus, slept on the third floor, in the attic. Alphaeus recalled it being "a little chilly" in the winter, but he added, using lyrics from Al's famous song, "we got by." The second floor had a kitchen, bathroom, and bedrooms, which were rented out to a succession of roomers to help subsidize the payments on the house. The most notable roomers, at least for Al, were Al's close friend in his teen years, Maxwell Carter, and his parents.

The Jarreau children were raised strictly, but lovingly, in a family that cared about others. From Carter's perspective, the Jarreaus stood apart from other families. "The Jarreaus were not one of the pack," he said. "Not that they were better than anybody else, but it was just their way of life. And [they were] very nice people. If there was anybody in this world that I would want to live next door to me, it would be the Jarreaus." Peter Bock, who visited frequently—sometimes for days at a time—during his college days with Al, described "a warm household [where] everything moved like clockwork, everybody knew what was going on, and [he] never saw a stitch happen."[27]

Balancing Emile's authoritarian ways in the Jarreau household was his wife, Pearl. A loving, tolerant, and kind mother, she was also a patient and understanding wife. Al laughingly remembered the way his aunt Edythe used to tell Pearl, "You are an angel, child. You've put up with my brother all these years."[28] Rose Marie, too, recalled how her mother "had a very quiet, smooth way of keeping [Emile] . . . calm, and having the ability to proceed with whatever the challenges were."[29]

During her college years, Pearl had become ill during the Spanish flu epidemic of 1918. She survived, but the illness left her with a heart murmur. Years after recovering, when she had two children less than a year and a half apart, her doctor recommended that she not have any more children. But, as Rose Marie said, "Apparently, they trusted in the Lord, or some divine feeling, and they went on having kids."

Pearl worked for some time as a third-shift nurse at St. Michael's Hospital. At other times, she also did seasonal work at the post office.[30] After coming home from her hospital shift in the morning, she would cook breakfast for her kids and send them off to school. And when she woke up later that evening, she would cook supper.[31] Although she often looked tired, Rose Marie said, "she seemed to have an energy, and make the day seem like it had thirty or forty hours in it." Reflecting on lines from one of his songs (that was seemingly never recorded)—"My mother, she loved my wounded father" and "those white Christmas dinners with neighbors and friends and unwed mothers"—Al marveled at his mother's kindness: "That was the kind of person she was; she took care of people."[32]

Al seems to have inherited his father's drive and his mother's caring nature, but his parents also provided him with a passion for making music. Although he was sometimes the stern ruler of the household, Emile had a beautiful tenor voice. Al described him as "a brilliant singer."[33] ("Al [got] his voice from my dad," Rose Marie said.) Pearl played piano and organ at the Sharon church for twenty-seven years, and this had a profound influence on Al. He had fond memories of sitting by her side at the church piano. "For as long as I ever knew her, that was her gig," he joked.[34] Every Saturday, for many years of his life, he soaked up music in this setting.

Emile also played the musical saw.[35] ("That saw was something you'd have to hear," Alphaeus recalled. "Sounds like somebody whistling."[36]) Together, Emile and Pearl performed classical, gospel, and spiritual music. "I can close my eyes and see them rehearsing in the living room at 336 West Reservoir," said Rose Marie. "I can almost hear him playing 'Ave Maria,' [and] a song called 'Tonight We Love.'"

On occasion, Emile would display his skills in area talent contests, including some that took place in Milwaukee theaters between the movies of a double feature. "The winner of the talent show would take home a gold watch or a hundred dollars," Al remembered. "My dad augmented [his] seventy-five dollars a week salary with several occasions during the year when he would go and sing 'I am an American, I am every part of me.' And people would go crazy."[37] According to Rose Marie, some of these contests were associated with the nationally known Major Bowes competitions popular on radio and later folded into Ted Mack's *Amateur Hour* on television. Marshall, too, remembered his father going to Chicago to do "one of those Ted Mack shows."[38]

Not only did Emile and Pearl pursue their own artistic interests, but they also supported their children's passions. Alphaeus said his family taught him that "your parents want you to do well . . . so they're there to guide you and to help you achieve the goals that you might have." And when it came to Al's specific passion, Marshall remembered that his father "worked with Alwin a lot on [singing] and was very supportive." The Jarreau parents' talents and their encouragement of their children's deep involvement in music most certainly had a crucial impact on the direction of their son Al's life.

2

EARLY DAYS

A l once said that he was hearing music before he was born.[1] He could hear his family playing music while his mother was pregnant with him, and once he was out in the world, he would sit on the piano bench next to her and listen. Her music making was a constant, and since all of her children sang in the choir, they heard her play in church on the Sabbath (Saturdays for Seventh-day Adventists) and at choir rehearsals on Wednesdays.[2]

According to his older sister Rose Marie, Al "had rhythm and loved music [from birth]; it obsessed his whole being."[3] At six or seven months old, she claimed, "he could keep a beat, keep time to the music, and he would rock when the music was playing [in church]."[4] Once he started singing, with his mother accompanying on piano, Rose Marie said he "took to it like a fish to water." As kids, Rose Marie and Al would lie on the floor of their living room, listening to music on the family's old wind-up Victrola record player.

A June 1944 performance by "boy singer" Alwin Jarreau at a "garden fair" on North Fifth Street became a noted event in family lore. Four-year-old Al, in a sailor's suit, was the featured performer at an all-day affair that also included an appearance by a "Chicago Girls Trio." Accompanied by his mother, Al presented his "Summer Varieties" at three and seven o'clock at the home of a neighbor, Mrs. Owens, who had a grand piano. For a dollar, attendees could take part in an open house complete with free food. Commenting on that photo years later, Al said, "[The poster] says age four, but I had to have been singing before that. I don't know who told me to put my hand on my hip, but I do think the Garden Fair was held in the yard of one of our more well-to-do church members. I really think that they found chairs and brought them to the yard; I think I performed in this garden."[5] Rose Marie remembered her mother and father "putting [Al] through his paces" in rehearsal and recalls that at the event, "the people came to see *him.*"

Three years later, the whole Jarreau family performed a concert at Calvary Baptist Church, a pillar of Milwaukee's Black community, on Fourth Street.[6] Sisters Joyce and Rose Marie sang a duet, the old hymn "Fairest Lord Jesus." The older brothers, Emile III and Alphaeus, also sang a duet. Al sang, of course. And the youngest brother, Marshall, who was only about five years old, sang "Jesus Wants Me for a Sunbeam." (Marshall said in 2020 that he could "hardly remember" singing at this event.) Father Emile was prominently featured on the musical saw, possibly presenting a couple of his standbys—"Tonight We Love" and the Charles Gounod classic "Ave Maria"—and probably some hymns. Pearl accompanied everyone.

Al also made music with his brothers, Emile, Alphaeus, and Marshall. In the car on the way to church, or even when just walking around, Alphaeus would sing bebop and scat or mimic horn riffs, and his three brothers would repeat the sounds back to him. They'd harmonize and trade solos. "Following what he did made me realize there were really fun things to do with vocalizing," Al said. "[Alphaeus] was the free spirit of the family and a big influence, but there was also [my brother] Emile, who had an incredible lyric tenor voice.[7] I learned a lot from him—ballads and tunes that jazz singers used to sing at the time."[8]

Al's brothers also brought music into the home when they practiced singing in quartets with their peers. "They were my first examples of a quartet of people singing together," Al said—something that encouraged him to join and form quartets later.[9] One of his brothers' quartets, known as the Counts of Rhythm (made up of Alphaeus, Emile, and two non–family members, Charles Lawrence and Gerald Mack) would rehearse in the family living room, singing standards like "What Is This Thing Called Love?" and "Once in a While."[10] During these rehearsals, Alphaeus remembered, little Alwin was "very, very attentive. [He] had a good ear . . . for the music. So he would sit on the floor by the couch and listen. [He had] a very keen sense of what would go together."[11] "I wanted to *do* that," Al

The Jarreau family poses in their living room prior to their concert performance at Milwaukee's Calvary Baptist Church in 1947. From left to right are Al's parents, Emile II and Pearl, and his siblings Emile III, Marshall (in front), Alphaeus, Rose Marie, and Joyce. Al is at far right. COURTESY OF ROSE MARIE FREEMAN

remembered thinking as he watched them sing jazz and bebop lines. "I wanted to *be* like that."[12]

Besides what he was hearing in church, on the Victrola, and live in his living room, Al was also absorbing plenty of other music. He listened to pioneering Black deejay Daddy-O Daylie on Chicago radio, and there and elsewhere he heard the popular music of the day, ranging from 1950s singers Patti Page, Perry Como, Dean Martin, Frankie Laine, and the Four Freshmen to the pioneers of rock and roll: Little Richard, Chuck Berry, and Bill Haley and the Comets. Nat King Cole, and later on, Johnny Mathis and Harry Belafonte, were also family favorites.[13] Al also learned the music of Broadway. Though he went on to sing doo-wop, a popular style of the day, he said that "never was as exciting as singing [jazz songs like] 'How

High the Moon' or 'Red Top' or something else that was just so much more consuming."[14]

Some of Al's first jazz singing was with the Mel Marcus Trio. Led by pianist Mel Marcus, who attended Washington High School, the trio performed at the Jewish Center, now known as the Jewish Museum Milwaukee. In 1977, Al told jazz critic and columnist Leonard Feather: "During my high school years, there was a little jazz scene happening in Milwaukee—thanks largely to the Jewish Community Center. They had a couple of festivals each year, and whenever they had an affair or dance of some kind, they'd bring in a real jazz-oriented band. So this involvement with the musicians around 1955 really brought jazz into my life."[15]

Throughout his years at Lincoln High, Al was a member of the choirs led by choral director Bob Beduhn (including the All-City Choir in 1956), but his real time to shine in school music was in the Follies. These shows, led by Beduhn and band director Ron DeVillers at the time, took place on two consecutive nights each spring. When Al was in seventh grade, he heard a student named Ramon Levy sing the great Rodgers and Hart standard "Where or When," and he remembered saying to himself, "I want to sing like that on stage here at Lincoln in the Follies. It's something to look forward to. This semiprofessional life of singing."[16]

In the 1957 show, called "Fun and Fancy," songs from *Carousel*, *My Fair Lady*, *Porgy and Bess*, and *State Fair*, among others, were performed by the school's show band and chorus and by soloists (including future Milwaukee jazz icon Penny Goodwin). A square dance, pantomime, and ventriloquist were also on the docket. In addition to singing in the chorus, seventeen-year-old Alwin Jarreau had featured spots on two hits from *Porgy and Bess*: "I Got Plenty o' Nuttin'" and "It Ain't Necessarily So." As part of the vocal group The Hi Fis, a quintet of two young men and three young women, Al was featured singing "Up on a Mountain." The group also sang the doo-wop Del-Vikings hit "Come Go With Me" and the standard "Red Sails in the Sunset." Marshall Jarreau, who played trombone in the show's band, was moved by Al's soulful rendition of "Red Sails," recalling, "It was like a prayer. It was too much."[17]

In 1958, when Al was a senior, the Follies show "Two on the Aisle" again largely featured show tunes. Al was featured on two selections from *Guys and Dolls*: "I've Never Been in Love Before" and, with Veatrice DeWalt, "A

Bushel and a Peck." He was spotlighted again as a soloist on "This Much I Know," from the then-recent Broadway show *Happy Hunting*. Al also sang with the Beltones, another five-voice group (with one other member from The Hi Fis).

Al's older brother Alphaeus attended these shows when Al was a participant, and he recalled that the Follies performed "on a professional level. . . . They had a lot of talent . . . in [that] school."[18] Al referred to the Follies shows as "the beginning and the foundation and the catapult as I felt those things and got . . . the feedback that said, 'Somebody likes what I do. I'm going to keep doing this.'"[19]

Al also approached his schoolwork with dedication. Education was a priority in the Jarreau household, and Al developed a strong work ethic in his youth. When asked if his parents pressured him to get his homework done, he once said, "Oh, I was tough on me. . . . When you get brought up a certain kind of way, you're tougher on yourself than they could be. But I don't remember them ever having to encourage me to do homework. I can see me now studying in the basement, where there was a big furnace, that coal-burning furnace in the wintertime . . . with a little card table that unfolded. . . . Me and Maxwell Carter Jr."[20] Al also remembered putting in extra efforts to succeed as early as kindergarten: "I wasn't an especially good student, and so my mom would get me to school early in the morning and I would get in forty-five minutes to an hour on vowels and ABCs and 123s."

Every weekday morning of his youth, Al would walk to Henry L. Palmer School on North First Street. One of the landmarks they passed on their route was Kilbourn Reservoir Park. Years later, Al would name his music publishing company Reservoir, Inc., and he remarked that the name stood for "spare water, good water." Al also recalled that one "could get blown off the [nearby Holton Street] bridge in the winter."[21] One of Al's fondest memories from his grade-school days was the iconic Milwaukee Santa Claus who visited schools around the city at Christmastime. The children at Palmer took a break at ten in the morning and came out to see Santa arrive on a big flatbed truck along with his assistant, Me-Tik, a "real Alaskan Eskimo" who tended the reindeer.[22] As Al recalled, "Santa would say 'Ho, ho, ho' and sing a few Christmas carols. But it was a highlight of the season if you were a student."

In their teenage years, Al and Maxwell Carter walked a bit farther to attend Lincoln High School—past a fish market as well as the house of Jim Catania, whose parents owned Mortell's Cocktail Lounge.[23] Once, Maxwell remembered, Jim Catania's mom stopped him and Al on their way to school and asked if they could help with her son, who was in a wheelchair. From that day on, for at least a couple of years, Al and Maxwell would bring Jim down the stairs in his wheelchair, where a school bus would pick him up.[24] According to Al's brother Marshall, the boys carried out this task without any problems, never dropping the chair. It was something "very special," Marshall recalled, proving that even at that age, the boys were capable of handling a lot of responsibility.[25]

Also on their walks to school together, Carter listened to Al develop the sounds that would become a signature of his early career. "Like young men, we talked about everything," Carter said. "And then Al [would] be off into his thing [*imitates musical instruments*]. And I'm looking at this guy and thinking to myself, *What the hell's wrong with him?* But he's beginning to compose these musical instruments [in] his head. And he's beginning to sound like instruments."[26]

In addition to high school music activities, Al served on the student council and the Senior Boys Club and, perhaps most significantly, was president of his class in his freshman, sophomore, and junior years.[27] He was also one of the high school students approved to serve for one day as a temporary legislator for the Milwaukee Common Council.[28] "In high school I was probably a nerd of sorts," he said. "I didn't know anything about cutting class or skipping school. . . . I guess I was a booker of a sort."[29]

Nerd, booker, or whatever else, Al was well liked and popular. Thomas Cheeks, a revered teacher at Lincoln, said he couldn't remember anyone saying a negative thing about Al in high school: "He was a natural-born leader. He stood out as a person coming down the corridor, in the classroom, in the contributions he would make." Cheeks credited those traits and Al's positive outlook to his family and the atmosphere he grew up in.[30]

An influential experience for Al came during the summer before his senior year in high school when he attended Badger Boys State, the American Legion–sponsored week of mock government for Wisconsin high school student leaders held annually at Ripon College. According to Al's brother Marshall, there was some question in the family, particularly in the mind of their father, as to whether Al should attend Badger Boys. His concern was related to Al's safety, or at least his comfort level, as an African American at an event that would be attended almost exclusively by white people in a small town in the middle of rural Wisconsin in 1957. In the end, Emile must have been persuaded to let Al attend. And once he arrived, Al broke one of the first of many barriers in his life—his charisma led him to a leadership position, and he was elected governor, the highest elected office in the weeklong exercise.[31] Some residents of little Ripon, Wisconsin, may have been shocked to see a young Black man sitting on the back of a convertible driven down the main street by members of the American Legion as the new governor of Boys State.

Al was also a gifted athlete. Besides running cross-country, he was a star high school basketball player, and a baseball player talented enough to be invited to a summer training camp by the Milwaukee Braves.

Al's brother Marshall fondly remembered Al taking on the role of his

Al rides in a parade down the main street of Ripon, Wisconsin, as the elected governor of Badger Boys State in 1957. COURTESY OF RIPON COLLEGE

cross-country coach and mentor the summer before Marshall started at Lincoln. The brothers laid out a route through the neighborhood and used it for training throughout the summer. It ended with a challenging four-block run up the hill of North Palmer Street. Al taught Marshall about pacing, breathing, relaxing, sprinting, and other fine points of running. Later that year, the Jarreau brothers both ran in the state cross-country meet. They stayed together for much of the race, but on the brink of being outmaneuvered near the end, they took off. Marshall, only a freshman, made a big splash by finishing second in the race—something practically unheard of for a first-year runner. He believes that Al must have finished in third or fourth place. Marshall went on to be a top runner for the rest of his high school career, setting city and various meet records in the half-mile and mile races in track. He modestly attributed his success to his brother, saying, "Alwin made me a star."[32]

In 2016, during his tour around the city for the Wisconsin Public Television documentary, Al remembered his high school cross-country team's practice route. He directed the car past St. Catherine's Residence, where the Lincoln High choir would sing Christmas carols every year; past the Jewish Center, where Al did some early jazz singing; and along Milwaukee's lakefront, where he claimed the runners experienced "the severest weather in the city." As they passed ducks that day, Al quacked at them, sounding remarkably like a duck himself, and said, "If I made that sound for Marshall or Maxwell, they'd be like, 'Al, that's what those ducks sounded like when we were running cross-country down there.'" Finally, as the group drove along Lincoln Memorial Drive, Al pointed out where the runners would sprint to the finish line. "Having a goal, keeping it in mind, and heading toward it with passion, intention. You learn that as a cross-country runner," he said.

But as much as he loved running, baseball may have been Al's strongest sport. In his youth, he played "strike out," a modified version of baseball or stickball, on a cement wall of the St. Francis grade school. On Sundays when the weather was good, he, Marshall, and Maxwell Carter were regulars in the game, which could be played by as few as two boys: one "throwing strikes" and the other batting. Hitting a distant building across the way was considered a home run. Al remembered that Carter, who went on to be a pitcher in high school and even briefly in minor league baseball, had a wicked pitch that Marshall, who hated to bat against him, called a "curve-drop."

Al played second base on the Lincoln High team along with Marshall, a third baseman, and Maxwell Carter, a formidable pitcher. Al made several all-city baseball teams, as named by both of the city's newspapers, the *Journal* and the *Sentinel*. He may have even entertained thoughts of playing baseball professionally.[33] Marshall remembered accompanying Al to a session held by the hometown Milwaukee Braves to which Maxwell Carter had also been invited.[34] Al began attending Silver Sluggers camps hosted by the Braves after his sophomore year in high school. At these camps, selected players from around the state would train, scrimmage, and play games. Though Al attended several of these training camps, the *Oshkosh Daily Northwestern* reported that he "declined to discuss a contract when he realized that a professional baseball career would force his college education to be spread over a seven year period."[35]

When Al attended Ripon College, he played baseball for just one year, but stuck with basketball, for which he received financial help, throughout his four years in school. "When the Braves thing didn't work out," Marshall remembered, Al "settled into a more singular thing." Singular in sports, at least.[36] Academics and music continued to become increasingly important to Al's life in college.

Regardless of his many other interests, young Al knew where he was headed: "I was destined to be a singer, you know, by the time I was ten. Destined to be a singer. I didn't know how it was going to come about, but I was going to sing. By the time I was nine or ten years old, I knew that I was going to sing. And if I got paid for it, great. But I'm gonna sing."[37]

3

RIPON

H ad it not been for Al Jarreau's participation in Badger Boys State, he probably would not have ended up as a student at Ripon College. Lowell Weber, a 1957 graduate of Ripon, was working in the college's admissions department the year after he graduated. Weber reported, "When I was in admissions at Ripon College . . . Al was elected Governor of Badger Boys State. An automatic $700 scholarship to Ripon always went with it. Anyway, Al dropped out of sight and wasn't planning to go to any college when I remembered the scholarship and went down to Milwaukee and dragged him to campus. I'm going to include this in my small list of good things I've done in my life."[1]

After his matriculation in the fall of 1958, the first mention of Jarreau in the school newspaper, the *Ripon College Days*, came in November 1958 in an article called "Frosh Elect." He was announced as president of the freshman class. It was reported that "Al Jarreau immediately took over his position and led a meeting on the bonfire and other homecoming activities."[2]

Although Al obviously dove right into student life at Ripon, initially college life was not easy for him. In a number of interviews, he mentioned the big step that was necessary to translate success in academics at Lincoln High School into success at Ripon College. Al said he not only "flagged," or flunked, his French and European history courses, but he "*red*-flagged" them.[3] This led to his losing the Badger Boys scholarship, which surely created a financial hardship for his family. However, the young basketball coach, Kermit "Doc" Weiske, encouraged Al to stay on the team and helped

24

him find a job on campus. As Al described it, "I had a tipping point when I was at Ripon. I lost that scholarship that I got from Boys State like that [*snaps fingers*]. I wasn't ready for a high-powered little [liberal] arts school in the middle of Wisconsin with kids with four years of language and five years of math and science. I mean the curve was kicking my butt."[4]

When Al returned home for a break, he had a discussion with his mentor and former teacher, Tom Cheeks. Al remembered telling him, "I don't know, maybe I'm going to come home. I'm not making it there." Without speaking sharply, Cheeks responded, "You know, we've had this discussion before. In our classroom, you know what we used to say about quitters and winners[?] . . . You get yourself up and brush yourself off and you keep on going. Your mother and dad would be so disappointed if you just stopped."[5]

Al returned, and he did top the curve, but school was always a struggle for him. He claimed his education and psychology professor, Don Thomann, had to hold his hand through statistics to help him graduate.[6] Twenty years after Al's graduation, when he returned to the Ripon campus in 1982, the *College Days* reported this story that Al told a group during his visit: "One of his clearest memories of Ripon is of a History mid-term exam. 'I walked into the mid-term,' he said, 'and when I looked at the test, the only thing I could recognize was the directions: now open the blue book.' About one-half hour into the exam period, he said, he turned in his test and 'walked out like a genius,' fooling his classmates into thinking that he had finished early."[7]

Even later in his college career there were challenges. Although Al never spoke about it, very few students of color attended Ripon during his tenure there. There was one student from Korea and another from Hawaii. However, there appear to have been almost no other Black students at the college during Al's four years there, excepting one from the Panama Canal Zone during Al's first year, and two African students: one from Nigeria and one from Uganda. Incidentally, Ulysses Doss, a Black man from Racine who went on to become head of Black Studies at the University of Montana, graduated from Ripon College in 1957, but his time at the college did not overlap with Al's. To use his sister Rose Marie's expression, Al was "a fly in the buttermilk."

Ripon is tucked in the northwest corner of Fond du Lac County, a half hour from the small city of Fond du Lac and eighty-five miles from Milwaukee. As one of Al's fellow students from Ripon College recalled, "Al used to hitchhike home from time to time, going east to Fond du Lac and then south on Highway 41 to the Milwaukee area. He once said that to put motorists more at ease about the possibility of his presence in their cars, he used to hold up a sign that read: UNARMED. Humor was but one of his many charms."[8] It could not have been easy to be in a racial minority in small-town Wisconsin in the early 1960s.

Al's name occasionally appeared in the college paper over the next four years, mostly due to his success on the basketball team. Al was never a star, but he was a respected member of the squad and had a few standout moments. In January 1960, a rare front-page sports headline blazed in large letters "Ripon Wins First Game As Jarreau Sinks Final Points."[9] "After ten discouraging losses," the article stated, "the Ripon College Redmen finally snapped their long losing streak as they upset Carleton College, 73-66." In March, the headline on the sports page read "Mullen, Jarreau Lead Way to Win" in the last game of the team's season.[10] Early in his senior year season, the *Days* spotlighted Al as that week's "Sports Personality," in an article titled "Jarreau, One of Stalwarts": "A swinging senior smoothly nicknamed 'Gyro' gets the ball for this week's Sports Personality. This, however, as we all know is nothing new for Al Jarreau, who has been described by some as the best sixth man in the Midwest conference. By this is meant that Al is called in when the team needs a spark to incite momentum or raise team spirit if the going gets rough. This is a rare quality in a basketball player, but Al seems to be one of the best 'spot men' to be found."[11]

Although the four years Al spent at Ripon College were formative to his life in many ways, a significant chapter in his singing career also played out during this time, as Al became one of the founders of the quartet the Indigos. In an article for the college's alumni magazine in 1993, Indigos member Peter Bock detailed the vocal group's beginnings: "'God rest ye, merry gentlemen . . . ,' I sang softly against the jazz harmony I was arranging at the piano in the student lounge. As I transitioned into the next phrase, a strong tenor voice (Thomas 'Duffy' Ashley-Farrand '62) joined in. A few moments later a countertenor voice filled in a high part (Alwin 'Al' Jarreau '62). As the three of us searched for appropriate harmonies, a so-

Al, pictured here in the early 1960s, played on the Ripon College basketball team for all four years of his college career.
COURTESY OF RIPON COLLEGE

prano voice took the melody (Donna Oberholtzer '63). And as I descended to a more comfortable bass line, the Indigos were born."[12]

Bock (also class of '62), who grew up in the Chicago area, had just transferred to Ripon after a year at Purdue University. Ashley-Farrand and Oberholtzer likewise were from the Chicago suburbs. Oberholtzer remained with the group for only a year (1959–60). When she left, she was replaced by Gail Jensen (1960–61), who was succeeded by Ann Hassler (1961–62). The three men remained members of the group for its three-year existence.

The Indigos took their name from Duke Ellington's immortal "Mood Indigo," and their musical inspiration came largely from the then-popular jazz vocal group Lambert, Hendricks & Ross.[13] While the Indigos had four

The original
members of the
Ripon College
quartet, the
Indigos, were
(left to right)
Peter Bock, Al
Jarreau, Thomas
"Duffy" Ashley-
Farrand, and
Donna Ober-
holtzer. COURTESY
OF RIPON COLLEGE

voices as opposed to Lambert, Hendricks & Ross's three, it was not difficult
to adapt the great trio's arrangements to fit the young college quartet.
Al has cited the Double Six of Paris as another influence. Bock had hopes
that the Indigos could combine classical music, specifically that of Johann
Sebastian Bach, with jazz, which was being done by the Swingle Singers
at this time; but the group never did go in that direction. Some of Lambert, Hendricks & Ross's hits became core repertoire for the Indigos; a
special favorite was Annie Ross's brilliant setting of lyrics to a Wardell Gray
saxophone solo, "Twisted." The Indigos also "borrowed" the arrangement
Lambert, Hendricks & Ross crafted of Bobby Timmons's instrumental
hit for Art Blakey and the Jazz Messengers, "Moanin'," with lyrics by Jon
Hendricks. The Indigos remade such standards as "Moonlight in Vermont"
and jazz classics like "Mood Indigo," and they also performed originals,
including an Ashley-Farrand composition titled "Sonar," with lyrics by Al.

While Bock, Ashley-Farrand, and Oberholtzer all had some formal musical training, which Al did not (outside of what he learned in high school

choir), Bock said that Al had the musical knowledge and musical ear. Thus, most of the arrangements were figured out by ear, not written out, with Al singing each note of the chords and assigning them to the singers.

The Indigos performed on their campus with some frequency, at dances and other functions, such as Upperclass Stunt Night, Union Board gatherings, and Spring Sing. A photo of the quartet performing at an annual "Night on the Town" event appears in the 1960 Ripon College yearbook, the *Crimson*. The event was described as "designed to simulate an evening of nightclubbing (and is in every way successful)."[14] The group also sang at one school dance at which the Stan Kenton Orchestra was the featured band, an event that took place with considerable fanfare in May of 1960.[15] The 1961 college yearbook praised the Indigos "and their progressive sound" as "truly a new and welcome innovation in music on Ripon's campus."[16]

Local gigs off campus included frequent appearances at Ripon's Republican House restaurant and a bar in nearby Berlin, as well as a regular Saturday night engagement eight miles away at Green Lake's Tuscumbia Country Club, after which the group would sing for their breakfast at a local eatery. Eventually, they traveled farther, to Fond du Lac, Green Bay, and Milwaukee.

In fact, one of the group's very first jobs was at the Driftwood Lounge in Milwaukee, where Jarreau worked with Les Czimber during some summers in his college years. Bock related a story that remained part of the Indigos' treasured history:

Early in our career, Al arranged a gig for us at the Driftwood Lounge in Milwaukee. In the first set, we sang four songs. As we took our bows, a more-than-slightly inebriated man standing at the bar called out, "If you kids are so great, how about singing my favorite song?" The four of us exchanged nervous glances and then Duffy asked, "And what might that be, sir?" "*Mood Indigo*," the man replied. "Do you college kids know *Mood Indigo*?" Our nervousness relaxed instantly into glee. "Well, we don't usually do encores," I intoned with dignity, "But we'll make an exception this time." *Mood Indigo* just happened to be the fifth and *only other* song in our repertoire at that time.[17]

The Indigos were a significant enough presence on the Ripon College campus by November 1961 that an article was printed in the college newspaper to announce that Ann Hassler, "a freshman alto from Kirkwood, Missouri, was chosen from the field of fifteen talented candidates who sought to fill the position recently vacated by the departure of Gail Jensen." In the quaint language of the day, the group was referred to as "Ripon College's cool and soothing vocal foursome."[18]

Despite its small size, the town of Ripon (population 6,163 in 1960) was close enough to Wisconsin's Fox Cities (45 miles), Madison (75 miles), Milwaukee (85 miles), and Chicago (175 miles) to support a somewhat sophisticated jazz-based music group. While Ripon students of this era mostly stayed on campus, they certainly attended events in these nearby cities. And the college also brought music to campus. During Jarreau's four years at Ripon, the Minneapolis, St. Louis, and Cincinnati orchestras played on campus, as did two of the hottest groups in jazz at that time: the Dave Brubeck Quartet and the Ahmad Jamal Trio. It was announced that Duke Ellington's great orchestra would appear on campus in May of 1959, but the show was apparently canceled.[19]

The climax of the Indigos' career was a performance at the Notre Dame Collegiate Jazz Festival in South Bend, Indiana, April 6 and 7, 1962. The festival, which was primarily a showcase for instrumental groups, apparently invited the Indigos to appear as a showcase group, not a group that would compete before the judges, which included the distinguished composer-arrangers Quincy Jones and Henry Mancini.[20] (A big band from Ripon College, the Falconaires, also performed at the festival that year.) Bock believes that someone from Columbia Records, the biggest record label in the country at that time, heard the Indigos perform somewhere, possibly in the Chicago area, and chose them for the festival.

The Indigos realized that despite their success for three years as a strictly vocal a cappella group, it might be a good idea at Notre Dame to have a backing rhythm section. Al secured a drummer and pianist, probably from his contacts in Milwaukee. The Indigos met these players for the very first time the day before the festival. As they practiced, bassist Jim Higgins walked into their rehearsal space and said, "You guys are really good. Do you need a bassist?" Of course they did, so Higgins joined them.

He not only supplied a crucial aspect to the group's sound at the festival, but he also maintained contact with the Indigos after the event and eventually wrote out arrangements of all of their tunes.[21]

By all accounts, the Indigos were a huge hit at the jazz festival. They performed in a late Saturday afternoon slot, immediately preceding the announcement of the groups who would "play off" for the prizes later in the evening, so the venue was packed. In recordings of the performance, the audience sounds enthusiastic, almost to the point of ecstatic. "The audience was just wild," Bock recalled. *College Days* reported (with an accompanying photo of the group) that "the 'Indigoes' [sic] received a standing ovation from the crowd."[22]

Later that spring, someone from Columbia Records contacted the group and offered them the opportunity to record an album for the label. As was standard in those days, the release of an album would require the group to follow up with a tour. It was, as Bock called it, "a crisis." Al was completely on board with the idea of recording an album. Ashley-Farrand, having been in the Reserve Officer Training Corps at Ripon, would soon owe the United States several years of his life, and Bock was planning to attend graduate school. But both of them were willing to entertain the possibility of a career in music beyond Ripon. Hassler, however, had only just completed her first year at Ripon, and she said she could not do it. The men consulted with Gail Jensen, who was living in the Chicago area, but she, too, did not feel that she could make the commitment. So, Bock said, "We all hugged each other and went to the four winds."[23] In retrospect, it's hard to imagine that it would be more than ten years before Al would have another opportunity to sign a record deal.

As his graduation from Ripon approached, Al was the subject of a rare feature in the school newspaper: "Al Jarreau Closes Out Illustrious Ripon Career." In it, reporter Joan Howard summed up Al's time at the college.

This June many a Riponite's eyes will turn "misty" as we lose one of the nicest guys ever to attend Ripon.

This senior is also proof that the old adage, "nice guys never win" is pure whimsy. Al Jarreau manages to finish first in anything he undertakes. . . .

Al was quite thankful at being given the chance to attend college. He also felt that this privilege entailed a great responsibility. So, upon his arrival on campus, he set out to prove himself.

In his freshman year he ran cross-country, played baseball, and was a standout on the basketball squad. Since then Al has decided to concentrate on basketball. He has been awarded three varsity letters in this sport. Due to his very busy schedule he has been unable to compete in any other sports.

High on the list of activities which help Al to while away his leisure time is singing. He entertains at most of the campus social events, and also is the founder and a member of the [Indigos], a singing group of great renown.

Al has also served on the Homecoming Committee for the past two years and is a member of Student Court. The gravity and responsibility of this latter position hangs especially heavy on his shoulder[s]. In his own words, "any organization which is dealing with other people's . . . lives is always a ticklish operation." . . .

As for the future Al would like a career in one of two fields. He would either like to utilize his undergraduate training here for a career in clinical psychology, or look to singing for his daily bread. To this end, Al will be working at the Driftwood Lounge in Milwaukee next year.

In his four years here at Ripon, Al has found his own special spot in our hearts. He has also assumed more than his fair share of the responsibility of being a Ripon College student.[24]

Al was changed by his years at this small midwestern liberal arts school. As an impressionable young student, he was challenged both academically and socially. But he overcame those challenges thanks in large part to the college's nurturing culture. This culture, combined with the friends and musical opportunities he found at Ripon, enriched his life and forged his lifelong loyalty to his alma mater.

4

─────■─■─■─────

MILWAUKEE

A l had a performing career, outside of the performances with his
family, before he left Milwaukee, both during and after his time
at Ripon College. A significant part of that career was intertwined with
pianist Lazlo "Les" Czimber.

Czimber, who was still going strong until shortly before his death in
2020 at age eighty-six, lived in Wisconsin for only a few years, but he
made a strong impression on the Milwaukee jazz scene, and particularly
on Al Jarreau.[1]

Czimber was born in Budapest, Hungary, in 1934 and grew up in the
area around that city. He played piano at an early age and, hearing a great
deal of jazz on Willis Conover's radio broadcasts for Voice of America, was
drawn to the largely American art form. He formed a popular jazz group in
Budapest while still a teenager. Czimber was a member of the Hungarian
army during the uprising of 1956—he survived a harrowing capture by
the Soviet army, a long walk to freedom in Yugoslavia, and a severe injury
in a car accident before heading for the United States. By 1957, Czimber
had made it to Milwaukee. He quickly integrated himself into the jazz
scene, becoming the pianist in the house trio at the Driftwood Lounge on
Capitol Drive, right across the street from the WTMJ radio and television
building.[2] The Driftwood was run by two young entrepreneurs, Abe Totah
and Bill Gillan. Totah first hired Czimber to clean the bar and play piano
at night. "He was a worker," Totah recalled. "You come from the old country, what're you going to do, you know?"[3] But Czimber soon set himself
apart as a talented musician. Not long after arriving in Milwaukee, he set

33

One of Al's first gigs in Milwaukee was singing with the house trio at the Driftwood Lounge on Capitol Drive, pictured here in the mid-1950s. COURTESY OF ABE TOTAH

a record for "marathon" piano playing by playing for seventy-eight consecutive hours, with fifty minutes of playing and ten minutes of rest per hour.[4] After he landed the Driftwood engagement, around 1959, Czimber remembered a young singer arriving and sitting in with the band.[5]

According to Totah, Al Jarreau didn't just sit in—he came into the club and told Totah that he was working with a quartet at Ripon College, but that he also wanted to start working solo.[6] Totah invited him to audition and recalled, "If you just closed your eyes and sat there and listened—he sang 'Maria' from *West Side Story*—he sounded just like Johnny Mathis." Al was hired on the spot, establishing a musical partnership with Czimber that continued for years.[7]

Once Al became a part of the music scene at the Driftwood, Totah claimed, "he came in, and he starts singing, and you could hear a pin drop with one hundred and fifty, two hundred people in there. It was just jammed." Among the guests who showed up at the Driftwood during its glory years in the late 1950s and early 1960s were John F. Kennedy (then a US senator), comedian/actor Jerry Lewis, Los Angeles Dodgers Hall of Fame pitcher Don Drysdale, and jazz singer Carmen McRae, whom Totah brought to the club when she was appearing at the Brass Rail downtown. McRae even sat in and sang a couple of songs with Czimber, probably during a time when Al was at school.[8] Many employees and guests from WTMJ would cross the street and visit the club after work. Because the Mafia ran many of the entertainment venues in the city, Totah added that due to the club's success after Al started working there, "every Italian guy, every Italian club owner wanted the place."

The owners were proud of their racially diverse clientele, which was at that time somewhat unusual for a venue in a primarily white neighborhood like the one on Capitol Drive. Among the musicians, the trio's sometime bassist Jimmy Johnson was African American. And one white musician who sat in with the band was future Milwaukee trumpet star Kaye Berigan.[9]

Czimber said that during the day Al would come over to his house, and the two of them "set up his library . . . a big library of show tunes [and] jazz standards." As Al put it, "I was two years out of high school when Les threw me over his shoulder and plopped me down in his living room to listen to the stuff that influenced the musical framework of what I do today . . . letting me try it out on his bandstand."[10] Immediately, Czimber says, Al "sounded terrific." And, he added, "His scatting was probably hipper than the scatting he used on the pop stuff later on."

Al and Les would work together every summer during Al's years in school, both at Ripon and, later on, when Al was in graduate school at the University of Iowa. In 1962, the Driftwood "mysteriously" burned down.[11] Czimber took a job at the newly refurbished Pfister Hotel, which had been taken over by the Marcus family. The house trio, with Al joining in the summers, worked in the Columns, the upscale bar adjacent to the lobby of the classy and historic hotel. "One of the most beautiful hotels . . . anywhere," Al said years later, describing the Pfister's big marble columns. "And hey man, for me to be hired by the Marcus family to go and sing there and see my name on the marquee outside—I was twenty, twenty-one [years old]—it [was] very important stuff."[12]

As Al remembered it, the trio was Czimber on piano, Lee Burrows on bass, and Lou Lalli on drums during much of the band's time at the Columns. Bassist George Welland and drummer Jack Carr also played with Les and Al during this period. Both were just starting out in the city.

Welland, an Appleton, Wisconsin, native, was a nineteen-year-old student at UW–Milwaukee. Carr had just finished college at Notre Dame; he had played with Czimber at the Driftwood before moving downtown to the Pfister in the summer of 1962.[13] Soon after Al left for Iowa in the fall of 1962, Carr entered the armed forces for a two-year stint. After his return to Milwaukee, he and Welland both became first-call players in the city— positions they held for decades.

Years later, Carr related a story about his friendship with Al that spoke to race relations in the Milwaukee area in the early 1960s:

> Al used to come out to our family house in [suburban] Elm Grove . . . I remember one Sunday, Al was visiting and we were playing Lawn Darts . . . and with Elm Grove being a very conservative community at the time, I think it was also somehow associated with the John Birch Society. So being the smart ass drummer I am, I made a comment to Al that since we had been playing in plain sight on our front lawn, two "For Sale" signs had gone up in the neighborhood. Fortunately, he found it funny and really laughed; I further went on to depict a supposed neighbor with binoculars up to their eyes saying, "Who do those Carrs have over there now? Damn, I knew we shouldn't have let any Irish people start living here, it's just the start of trouble!" As I said, Al liked it![14]

Besides the work with Czimber at the Driftwood and the Pfister Hotel, Al played at Sardino's, on the East Side, as well as at the Holiday House, one of Milwaukee's top night spots for some years. The Holiday House, a downtown supper club that was reportedly run by a Milwaukee branch of the Mafia from the 1940s into the 1960s, brought in such name acts as Tony Bennett, Andy Williams, Dean Martin, and Milwaukee native Liberace. The band director at Al's high school, Ron DeVillers, was a member of the house band at the Holiday House for a few years in the late 1950s and early 1960s, and he recalled Al's engagement there.[15] The core band at the time was small—just a trumpet, alto saxophone, and three-piece rhythm section, with more musicians hired as necessary for some of the acts. They would play for the headliners when necessary or, as in Al's case, for the warm-up acts before the headliners.

For a string of nights, Al opened for a comedian known as Professor Backwards. Prior to the gig, Al called DeVillers, letting him know that he was booked for the club (for perhaps two weekends and the week in between) and asking for a special new musical arrangement. Specifically, Al wanted an arrangement of "Something's Coming" from the recent Broadway blockbuster *West Side Story*. DeVillers came up with something Al liked so much that he continued to use a version of the arrangement for years afterward. When Al's brother Marshall heard him do that song and a medley from *West Side Story*, he was blown away. "I knew Alwin was good," Marshall recalled, "but he really just blew that [arrangement] up."[16]

While Czimber was at least partly responsible for Al's gig at the Pfister, Marshall "Gus" Azinger also deserves some credit for the booking. Marshall Jarreau referred to Gus as Al's first manager, describing him as "a very nice guy, with a very nice family." As Al told it, Gus had the looks of a "young fifteen-year-old, but [he] had four kids [*laughs*]. But [he] had such a great smile. He had a little newspaper, a magazine called the *Milwaukee Magazine*, and it talked about things that were going on, including the [Milwaukee Braves] and whatever theater was going on, [such as] the Pabst [Theater] . . . and he distributed it to the hotels in Milwaukee. Well, he heard me sing and said, 'Hey, Al, let me help you. I know some people.' And so, between him and Les Czimber, I came and sang my first notes in the Pfister."[17] Al continued to work at the Pfister with Les when he was back in Milwaukee on breaks from school in Iowa, right up until the two of them left to play on the West Coast in the mid-1960s.

As the perennial master of ceremonies at the Miss Wisconsin and Miss Milwaukee pageants, Azinger was also instrumental in getting Al the featured performances at the 1962 Miss Oshkosh Pageant and the 1963 Miss Wisconsin Pageant.[18] As the contestants for both pageants were overwhelmingly white during this era, it must have been noteworthy for a Black man to have appeared onstage at these events.

Upon the announcement that Al had been chosen to perform at the Miss Wisconsin pageant, a lengthy article appeared in the *Oshkosh Daily Northwestern* in April 1963.[19] The article included a great deal of information about Al's career up to that point, which was likely supplied by the resourceful Gus Azinger. After mentioning that Jarreau "thrilled a capacity crowd at the 1962 Miss Oshkosh Pageant," the article went on to talk about his "fascinating background," noting that he was "a very popular entertainer in the area."

Describing his successful appearances at the Columns for a week around Thanksgiving and two weeks near Christmas, the article also included catchy quotes from the Milwaukee papers: "He has everything it takes to be a great star. You are only conscious of a grand young entertainer, and nothing, and no one else" from the *Sentinel*, and "tremendous range . . . personable . . . from [Billy Eckstine] to . . . [Nat King] Cole-type treatment" from the *Journal*. The piece emphasized that Al had been flown (not driven!) from Iowa for the grand opening of the new club, the Boom-Boom Room, at the "plush" Red Carpet Inn in Milwaukee, and that on the two nights he was there, "not a seat was available for any one of the six performances." He was booked to return in the spring for a stint at the club, "capped by a big show on Easter Sunday." Al was scheduled to come to Oshkosh a couple of days before the pageant to "do some radio and TV promotional work" and to rehearse with the musical director.

Capping off the article, Jack Erkilla, chairman of Miss Wisconsin, contributed this quote: "The 1963 Miss Wisconsin Pageant promises to be the most exciting show of the year, and Al Jarreau, who is destined to become one of America's biggest singing sensations of this decade, will bring a great talent to it." Clearly, Al's four years playing in and around Milwaukee had already brought him a considerable amount of notoriety.

5

IOWA

During Al's years of playing around Milwaukee—both while he attended college and in the summers in between—and as he established himself as a working musician, he experienced a tragic loss in his personal life. In February of 1962, Al's beloved mother passed away. As his sister Rose Marie recalled, Pearl's health "took a toll on her, and she died at fifty-nine, not quite sixty years old."[1] Years later, Al's close friend Peter Bock remembered going home with Al when his mother died. "That was a serious event," Bock reported. "It was not a joyous affair. . . . They were such a close knit group."[2]

Later that spring, the Indigos had their triumph at the Notre Dame Jazz Festival, followed by the offer of a record contract. Then Al graduated from Ripon College and began singing at the Pfister and other spots around Milwaukee. All of this had to have been enough to make his head spin, and he surely wondered what he would do next. In a move that must have surprised some of his fellow working musicians, Al decided to go to graduate school. In the summer of 1962, he received a federal grant allowing him to pursue a master's degree in vocational rehabilitation—what Gus Azinger colorfully described as "rehabilitative therapeutics"—at the University of Iowa, which he accepted, "turning down some $3,600 in advance bookings." "After serious thought and discussion with his personal manager," the Oshkosh Daily Northwestern reported, Al "decided that his master's degree was worth an 18-month delay in his singing career."[3]

So, in the fall of 1962, Al began a master's program in vocational rehabilitation, inspired in part by his older brother Emile, who was employed

as a social worker. "When [Emile] found an interest in social studies and
the helping professions, I thought that was one of the greatest things in
the world to be able to do," Al said years later. "Don't you think that would
be a nice job? To be helping people to do better?"[4] Al continued to take his
studies seriously, as he had done in high school and college, apparently
spending most of his time "at the library."[5] But he also continued to nur-
ture his musical talents, performing at least a couple of nights a week.[6]

A significant portion of those performances took part at the Tender
Trap, a club in nearby Cedar Rapids named for a song popularized by Frank
Sinatra.[7] The club was variously billed as "the only jazz club in Iowa," a
venue "'Where Modern American Music Is Heard'—Not Rock 'n Roll," and
as a place "Where Friends Meet" during the time when Al performed there.[8]

Shortly after moving to Iowa, Al met pianist Bill Bell, who was working
at the Tender Trap. Al visited the club and was soon invited to sing Friday
and Saturday nights. According to Al, he was singing at what he later identified as "an open mike thing" on campus when Bell heard him for the first
time. It's possible that this was the same event mentioned in a 2017 article
by University of Iowa archivist David McCartney as the performance that
introduced Al to the wider university community. The star of this November 30, 1962, concert was Simon Estes, an African American singer
from Centerville, Iowa, who went on to become a major star in the world
of opera.[9] Managing editor of *The Daily Iowan* Larry Hatfield raved about
Estes's performance, reporting that "Estes received one of the rare standing ovations for his dramatic and sympathetic interpretation of 'Ol' Man
River.'"[10] But, as McCartney points out, Al also made an impression that
night: "The fact that Mr. Jarreau was not majoring in music or wouldn't
perform onstage professionally for several years didn't prevent him from
appearing in a program to benefit a campus charity on the night of Friday,
Nov. 30, 1962, only three months after he arrived in Iowa City."[11] Hatfield
reported that Al sounded like "a combination of Johnny Mathis and a 1947
Billy Eckstine."[12]

Al began performing regularly at the Tender Trap. He was recorded
there in 1963 with a group that featured tenor saxophonist J. R. Monterose, a talented journeyman musician active in the wider jazz scene in
the 1950s.[13] Monterose was immortalized by his participation in Charles
Mingus's landmark 1956 album *Pithecanthropus Erectus*. But after cutting
an album as a leader for Blue Note Records just months later and remaining

During his graduate school years at the University of Iowa, Al performed regularly at the Tender Trap in Cedar Rapids. *THE DAILY IOWAN*, OCTOBER 8, 1964

on the East Coast scene for several more years, Monterose's career lost momentum. In 1963, he moved to Iowa, where he stayed for some months, at least. Years later, Al diplomatically said that Monterose went to Iowa "to take a rest; he needed a rest. He had some habits he needed to rest from."[14] Monterose, for his part, later said, "I spent a year in Iowa and I had a ball there."[15] In any case, Monterose was a skilled and experienced jazzman, and Al learned a great deal from him. Al is featured on three tunes on Monterose's 1963 album: the standard "Summertime," Duke Ellington's "Sophisticated Lady," and a Monterose original. Even this early recording includes traces of Al's signature sound and style, which he would further develop on his next recording in 1965. Dale Oehler, the pianist on Monterose's album, was also a student at Iowa; he later contributed some of the arrangements on Al's 1976 album *Glow*.[16]

Along with Bell and Monterose, Al performed at the Tender Trap with

Joe Abodeely, the drummer for the house trio, who also ran the club. "It was a pretty broad community of family who came to the Tender Trap to hear this music that Joe Abodeely was making available," Al said. He recalled Abodeely "as a force of nature who booked some of the biggest names in jazz and played drums with his house band while serving as maître d' for his popular nightclub, pointing to open tables with his drumsticks." Abodeely had also been a member of the world-famous University of Iowa wrestling team. "He weighed 260 pounds and was about six feet tall," Al remembered. "He was a handful, and he played drums so amazingly. He skipped like a ballerina on the drums."[17]

Star saxophonist David Sanborn also played regularly at the Tender Trap when he was a student at the University of Iowa, though he and Al never performed together at that time.[18] Years later, Sanborn humorously described the way Abodeely and Jarreau interacted in the club: "[Joe] would try to run the club from behind the drums. So he'd be looking around, . . . you know, he'd be playing the drums [and then he'd say,] 'Gloria, table 6, table 6.' And the tempo would go up like that, and slow down. And you know, it was challenging. And Al played with this, you know, it was a house band. So the legend of Al Jarreau lived on in Cedar Rapids, Iowa. He had a huge audience there; he was a very charismatic performer even then."[19]

By the fall of 1964, Al was listed in some of the Tender Trap's advertisements as "one of the country's top vocalists." Some ads also highlighted, in all uppercase letters, "The Vocal Stylings of the Fabulous Al Jarreau." It had taken him only two years to earn this sort of star billing.

Though he almost never spoke of it publicly, Al entered into a serious relationship during his time in Iowa. He married Phyllis Hall, a white woman who had grown up in the small town of Perry, Iowa, and was an undergraduate at the university during Al's time there. In 1963, Phyllis was writing for *The Daily Iowan*, and she eventually became the president of the local chapter of Theta Sigma Phi, a national professional journalism society for women. She graduated, as Al did, in 1964. Remarkably, no record of the date or even place of the wedding seems to exist.[20] None of Al's family members were present at the ceremony, and the marriage ended in divorce in 1968. On the rare occasions when Al mentioned this marriage later in life, he expressed his regrets about it not working out.

Al and his first wife, Phyllis Hall, at a Jarreau family get-together in Milwaukee in 1963. Standing (left to right): Alphaeus, Aunt Edythe, Emile II, Phyllis, and Al. Sitting (left to right): Marshall's wife, Lynda, holding baby Lynette; Alphaeus's wife, Beverly; Marshall (in front); Alphaeus's daughter, Cheryl, holding Rose Marie's daughter Jocelyn; and Rose Marie. COURTESY OF ROSE MARIE FREEMAN

Around this time, Al also made his first record, a single, at Dave Kennedy Studios in Milwaukee on the virtually unknown Raynard label. Appearing on one side of the 45 rpm disc is Al's song "Shake Up," a generic but professional-sounding soul/pop dance tune in the style of the day, complete with a full band, including horns and background vocals; it's sung in almost a doo-wop style.[21] Al's voice is recognizable, but it is not yet distinctive. On the B-side is a tune called "Room-Boom." Despite Al's growing fame in Milwaukee and other Wisconsin cities, this record evidently went nowhere. Jack Erkilla's predictions for Al's future were prescient, but it would take much longer for him to reach those career peaks than some may have imagined.

After receiving his master's degree in vocational rehabilitation in 1964, Al cut an album of much different material in 1965 in nearby Rock Island, Illinois.[22] Along with drummer Joe Abodeely and bassist Gary Allen, the pianist on the album was Cal Bazemer, who grew up in tiny Sully, Iowa.[23]

The album features Al at this early stage of his career singing standards—probably songs that he had been singing for several years with Les Czimber in Milwaukee. Those included "My Favorite Things," "Sophisticated Lady," "Come Rain or Come Shine," and, as a harbinger of one favored slice of Al's future repertoire, the Brazilian standard "One Note Samba."

Decades after this album's original release, after Al had become a star, many bootleg versions of the recording were made and distributed— some by professional labels. Notably, neither Al nor the Jarreau estate ever received royalties from any of these versions. In 1989 in *Down Beat*, Bainbridge Records defended its particular release of this session (called, simply, *Al Jarreau, 1965*). Harlene Marshall, from the record label, claimed that Bainbridge "legally licensed this recording from its producer and present owner."[24] Furthermore, Marshall stated that the label "offered Mr. Jarreau, in a letter to his manager, Patrick Rains, involvement in the release process as well as a royalty. His response came in the form of a lawsuit seeking to prohibit the album's release."[25] Ultimately, Al's team decided not to pursue the lawsuit any further after discovering the nebulous nature of Al's original contract, and requests for royalties to be paid to Al likewise failed.[26]

The performance is a snapshot of Al before he had firmly established his musical personality, yet his golden voice is immediately identifiable, even as it does bear a similarity to Johnny Mathis's. Al is clearly a jazz stylist at this time. In fact, jazz vocal star (and Milwaukee native) Tierney Sutton has talked of learning a great deal from this record about how a vocalist needs to phrase in a jazz style.[27] Both the style and the repertoire from this recording carried over to Al's performances some months later in San Francisco with George Duke's trio.

After several years in Iowa, making some important musical connections and finding his footing as a performer, Al made the consequential decision to leave the Midwest for California. His life and, eventually, his career were about to experience a momentous change.

6

CALIFORNIA

A l's move to California gave him the chance to be part of a much bigger music scene than was available to him in the Midwest. But the opportunity to find his footing in that scene was connected to his longtime Milwaukee piano partner, Les Czimber, and Abe Totah. Totah had been one of the owners of the Driftwood Lounge; he moved to California in the late 1950s and opened a club—the Mecca Lounge—in Santa Clara, forty-five miles south of San Francisco. He offered work to Les and Al, so in the mid-1960s, they moved west as well. According to Czimber, he and Al and a bass player and drummer were hired at the Mecca Lounge for a three-week engagement. They ended up working there for five months.[1]

Shortly after moving west, Al got a day gig in San Francisco as a rehabilitation counselor, the culmination of his studies and training at Ripon College and the University of Iowa. But just as his adjustment to college at Ripon had been difficult a few years earlier, Al's adjustment to work in San Francisco was not easy. He described his job working in rehab for the State of California as "one of the greatest jobs that you might do in life."[2] But it required a level of competency with multitasking and handling bureaucracy that Al admitted he did not have. "At any moment that you would talk to me about my caseload in those days," he said, "I would be talking about upwards of one hundred people that I was trying to serve. I was in overwhelm; constant overwhelm. I didn't do well in that setting. . . . I was a good counselor but terrible about the bureaucratic aspects of the gigs, like filling out reports."[3]

After four years at the job, Al said, "I sat down with my supervisor *again* and said, 'I just ain't getting it.' And we agreed that it wasn't happening and we would look at it for another period of time, and if it still wasn't working for me then we should really talk about parting company."[4] In 1968, Al resigned from his job.

Despite the difficulties, there were rewards to the counseling job. Looking back on it decades later, Al became emotional as he explained, "I think that this work sharpened my ability to understand pain . . . and hard times, and other people. When you sit there across from a guy who's an amputee, when you sit there across from someone who has cerebral palsy, when you sit there across from someone who just got back from rehabilitation because he was on drugs and he's still struggling with that, when you sit across from people like that, it changes you. It changed me."[5]

A change was also coming in Al's life as a musician. Although he may have struggled with his day gig, Al was having a wonderful time in San Francisco. Years later, he riffed on the scene in the Bay Area at that time: "It glowed and shined like a little pearl inside a setting of tie-dye, psychedelic patchouli oil, and frangipani, lava lamps, bell bottoms, make love not war, wow-man, right on, bong, and 'I have a dream!' A special era for which I'm truly grateful. What an experience!"[6]

An enormous part of what made that era special to Al was George Duke. A number of sources have referred to Duke as being little more than a child during his collaborative years with Al in San Francisco. Julio Martinez, Al's musical companion in the late 1960s and early 1970s, said Duke was around sixteen years old at the time. "He had to get his mother's permission to go out there and play in the club," Martinez said, "and he had to be home at 12:30."[7] Longtime Jarreau sideman Chris Walker remembered hearing that George's mother would tell Al, "Now you make sure you have George home in time for him to play in church on Sunday."[8]

Whether or not these statements are completely accurate, the remarkable George Duke was just a teenager when he started making music with Al. Born in 1946 in San Rafael, the county seat of Marin County, across the Golden Gate Bridge from San Francisco, Duke grew up in nearby Marin City and attended high school in Mill Valley.[9] He had training in music, played trombone in his school bands, and eventually received a degree in trombone and composition (with a minor in contrabass) from the San Francisco Conservatory in 1967. Later, he earned a master's degree in

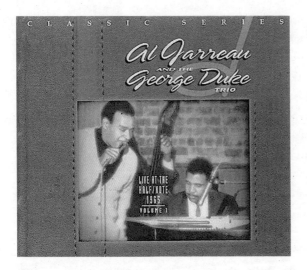

Al played with George Duke at the Half Note in San Francisco during the mid- to late 1960s. This live set was recorded in 1965 but not released until 2011. NAME AND LIKENESS RIGHTS COURTESY OF THE ESTATE OF GEORGE DUKE

music composition from San Francisco State University. He was a student in his late teens and early twenties when he worked with Al at the Half Note, a jazz club on the outskirts of the city's legendary Fillmore District.[10]

With Al, George was playing so-called straight-ahead jazz, although the two were also exploring the popular style of the era known as soul jazz. Duke first came to the notice of the wider jazz community after his time with Al, while playing with the fusion band of French violinist Jean-Luc Ponty in 1969. He became even more well known in 1970 and 1971 as a member of the difficult-to-classify band of Frank Zappa, the Mothers of Invention. He reasserted his more traditional jazz chops between 1971 and 1973 while working and recording with Cannonball Adderley, whose soul-jazz quintet was one of the most popular acts in jazz. But after leaving Cannonball's group, Duke went back to Zappa. By the mid-1970s he was recording successful albums under his own name—a mixture of jazz, soul, funk, pop, and rock that determined Duke's musical direction for the rest of his career. Among his more high-profile acts were bands that he co-led with drummer Billy Cobham and with bassist Stanley Clarke. For much of his career, Duke was active as an album producer, supervising projects by a who's who of R&B, soul, and pop performers. In jazz circles, he resurfaced again in 1986 as a collaborator on Miles Davis's album *Tutu* (although by this time, many in the jazz community were claiming that Davis was no longer a jazz artist).

At the Half Note in the mid- to late 1960s, Duke was the key member of the house trio. However, bassist John Heard and drummer Al Cecchi were also very skilled players. Heard would go on to collaborate with a wide variety of artists. He recorded with Duke and Jean-Luc Ponty in 1969 and was especially active in the 1970s, recording with Cal Tjader, Joe Henderson, and Ahmad Jamal. Through his very visible presence in the rhythm section of the great Count Basie Orchestra in the mid- to late 1970s, Heard also recorded with other mainstream jazz artists, including Zoot Sims, Harry Edison, and Oscar Peterson, who were recording on Pablo Records, the label of Basie's band at the time. Heard also had a career as a visual artist. Al Cecchi was much more than competent on the drums. It was a fine unit.

When Al Jarreau began singing with Duke's trio in the mid-1960s, the two formed a mutually inspirational partnership that would last for decades. Of their friendship, Duke once said, "It's almost like falling in love. You know, you don't pick who you fall in love with really, in many ways. And it's a spiritual thing; it's like it just happens; the chemistry was there from the very beginning. I started playing, [Al] started singing, and it was like, 'Oh, okay, it's like, okay we're home.' That's deep."[11] Al, too, described it in spiritual terms, saying, "We both had prayed this prayer, you know, that we could find something in music to do and find an audience for what we do, and have a career doing music."[12] They found the answer to that prayer in each other.

This experience was certainly heightened by the fact that Al and George were playing in the midst of a musical revolution. In San Francisco's Haight-Ashbury scene, they were surrounded by the sights and sounds of that tumultuous time. "We grew up in Janis Joplin, Big Brother and the Holding Company, Gracie Slick, Grateful Dead, Jefferson Airplane—in their backyard," Al explained. "We grew up with the flower power children. They had burned their bras and burned their draft cards and were walking around naked from [the] waist up and barefoot, and writing home to Mom and Dad: 'Tell our congressman to bring the kids home from Vietnam.' . . . That's what was happening when George and I were doing this other kind of music right there, on the cusp of the Haight-Ashbury. On the way to my counseling job, I passed right through there, through the panhandle of the Golden Gate Park."[13]

The Half Note, which featured a jazz trio with a singer doing straight-ahead jazz, was an anomaly—a throwback of sorts in the wildness of the rock scene that was dominating popular music at that time. In the 2016 French documentary *Al Jarreau L'enchanteur*, Duke went into some depth describing how what he and Al were doing at the club fit into the musical milieu in San Francisco at the time:

> We were a small club in the middle of a musical renaissance in the San Francisco Bay Area. There was Malo and Santana, and those kind of Latin groups.[14] There was the Jimi Hendrix Experience; you had that country rock kind of thing; you had the ultra-rock thing with some of the acid groups. Then there was the ultra-jazz stuff, I mean like what we call "Nutville," where they just, you know . . . nobody's supposed to relate; you just play whatever you want—free jazz. Then there was the funk jazz, like the Ramsey Lewis stuff.
>
> And we were kind of in the middle of all of this, these different musical genres going on at the same time in the Bay Area that had an audience. And so actually, fusion was born out of that. . . . This was pre-fusion, and we just thought, "Look, let's just take the American Songbook"—that's what we did. But we rearranged it. Because [Al] was really at that time into Miles Davis, and Miles used to take these show tunes from, you know, *My Fair Lady* or *Pajama Game* or whatever these musicals were on Broadway, and he would take them and reconstruct them and make a jazz thing out of them and make a hit. So that's what we tried to do is take our little niche there and do something really kind of special with it, not just a normal routine of singing a standard, but we tried to bring something else to it.[15]

In 1984, when he was at the top of his record-producing career, Duke suggested in a *Down Beat* interview that readers would be interested in Al's singing from those early San Francisco days "because he was really singing some straightahead stuff in those days. We did one record as a demo, but everyone said he was too jazz-oriented to sell records."[16]

Indeed, music was in transition in the 1960s, and "traditional" jazz was starting to be overwhelmed by what eventually became known as fusion. The music George Duke's trio was doing was unusual in San Francisco at the time. Record companies during this innovative period were not looking for the next singer to continue the Great American Songbook tradition, no matter how skilled that singer might be. Ultimately, the music Al made with George would not bring him widespread fame, but the Half Note engagement enabled him to get deeply involved in the vital San Francisco music scene, giving him confidence that he could be successful outside of his youthful base in the Midwest.

LIVE AT THE HALF/NOTE *1965*, VOLUME 1
BPM Records, 2011

This set by Al Jarreau and the George Duke Trio contains songs one would expect to hear from other hip young jazz singers in nightclubs across the United States in 1965. The show tunes "I Could Write a Book" and "It Never Entered My Mind" had both been notably interpreted instrumentally by Miles Davis. Al's soulful take on "Come Rain or Come Shine" also appeared on the session Al had recorded in Rock Island, Iowa, just months earlier. The album also includes jazz tunes—Duke Ellington and Billy Strayhorn's "Satin Doll" (already a standard in lounges) and two songs done originally by Art Blakey's Jazz Messengers: a most impressive Jarreau rendering of "Dat Dere," as well as "Moanin'," which Al had sung many times with the Indigos back in Wisconsin, in the song's incarnation created by Lambert, Hendricks & Ross.

Interspersed with the songs on the album are short conversations between Al and Duke as they reminisce, thirty-five years after the fact, about their time together in the mid-1960s. Apparently, plans had been made to release a second volume of material, but due to George Duke's death in 2013, this never transpired.

The album is a fascinating look at what Al and Duke were doing, together and separately, at this particular moment in time. Al's reimagined interpretations and improvisations still sound fresh and inventive. The set reveals a musical direction that either or both of these artists might have followed, probably with solid success, had they so chosen. It seems safe to say, though, that generations of fans have been blessed that they both opted to explore other musical styles. After the release of *Live at the Half/Note 1965* in 2011, Al and George played a number of special gigs together, celebrating their fruitful musical relationship—past and present.

7

Duo

According to Julio Martinez, Al's close musical companion during the late 1960s and first half of the '70s, the two of them met in December 1967. Julio recalled,

> I was a fledgling guitarist; I'd been playing about two years. I was looking to play in front of the public, and I was at the On Broadway Theater as the music director of a play. And I was playing, Al Jarreau walked up, and he was looking for a pianist to sit in with. The owner of the club said, "We don't have a pianist, it's just that kid sitting up there with the guitar." So Al came; we found four songs we knew together. We did the four songs; [the club owner] said, now this was on Dec. 30, the day before New Year's Eve, "Look, I'm having a big party here New Year's Eve, we want you two to play." That was it, that was our first job. New Year's Eve, 1967. . . . I was not a very good guitarist. So when I said I played four songs, I played *the* four songs that I knew.[1]

Martinez had come to San Francisco at roughly the same time as Al in 1964. An interesting path led him there. Julio describes himself as a Nuyorican—born in New York City to Puerto Rican parents who were dancers. They first came to Southern California temporarily, to work on a movie; bitten by the bug of Hollywood and plentiful sunshine, they moved west. Julio grew up in downtown Los Angeles and nearby Montebello. He studied music as a child and played trumpet in bands growing up. He attended Los Angeles City College, then the University of Michigan, receiving a bachelor's degree in music in 1961. He financed some of his schooling by teaching nights at the local Arthur Murray dance studio. At the U of M, he got to know future jazz star keyboardist Bob James, who, coincidentally, heard Al Jarreau sing with Ripon College's Indigos at the Notre Dame Jazz Festival in 1962.[2]

Julio expected to attend graduate school, but the political crisis in Berlin in 1961 led to his being drafted into the service. Because of his musical training, he was assigned to teach music theory at the "band school" at Fort Ord, near Monterey, a couple of hours south of San Francisco. After two years of service, Martinez expected to be discharged, but world events again intervened. Due to the Cuban Missile Crisis, he was kept on— supposedly because of his Spanish-language proficiency. However, his work had nothing to do with the crisis, or speaking or writing Spanish. He managed to "escape" Fort Ord when he was sent to San Francisco to play with the Sixth Army Band. After John F. Kennedy was assassinated in November 1963, Julio was called upon as a trumpet player to play "Taps" more than sixty times in forty-five days. He finally declared that he'd had enough, requesting to be relieved of playing duties. Having passed the typing proficiency exam, he spent the last eight months of his service typing.

In his free time during his years of service, Julio explored the burgeoning Bay Area music scene. Like Al, he heard the cutting-edge music exploding in the area, from Jerry Garcia (about to found the Grateful Dead), Moby Grape, Grace Slick (who would soon join Jefferson Airplane), and members of Canned Heat. Julio, who had been entertaining the idea of playing guitar, picked up a nylon six-string classical instrument and began playing it.

After finally leaving the service, Julio entered graduate school at the University of California–Berkeley and began studying modern European history. He matriculated during the time when the movement that later became known as the Free Speech movement started at Berkeley, arguably the beginning of the wider student protest movement.

Concurrently, Martinez was hired as music director of the San Francisco Mime Troupe. This group was decidedly "left wing, anti-establishment," performing what became known as guerrilla theater. The troupe was managed by Bill Graham, who became a major figure after he started booking music at the Fillmore Auditorium in San Francisco in late 1965. At the university in 1966, the troupe's presentation of *The Minstrel Show: Civil Rights in a Cracker Barrel* "caused a minor riot," in Martinez's words. Employing characteristics of historical minstrel shows, this piece provoked picketing from both Black and white groups from various points on the political spectrum. Martinez was among those arrested for civil disobedience, and as a result, he was kicked out of school. After a long trial, he served fifty-five days in the Alameda County Santa Rita Jail.

Once out of jail, he concentrated on his guitar playing, but he also had to work. He was hired at the On Broadway Theater as the music director for a play.[3] When this show was over, he was at the theater, where he sometimes tried out his guitar skills in the lounge, on the fateful day when Al Jarreau walked in looking for work.

Although he was an inexperienced guitarist, Julio had other musical skills. Of his abilities at the time, he remembered,

> I had studied orchestration and arranging. I could find anything I wanted on the guitar. I could play in any key, I could transpose at will. And even though I didn't know what I was doing, if [Al] said the song was written in D and he wanted to perform it in E-flat, I just transposed it up a half step. And he was very impressed with that, more than the fact that I didn't play like George Benson [*laughs*]. So I worked with him, and I really worked hard. By the time a month had gone by, I knew about two sets I could play with Al. . . . We went around auditioning, and we found this club in Sausalito called Gatsby's. It was a bar. And we auditioned. The owner of it, in his great musical knowledge, said . . . , "You guys play great calypso" [*laughs*]. So we worked two nights a week; we opened the first week . . . by the second night, the line was going out the door to come in.[4]

Going to just a duo, Al had to change his style and repertoire. As Julio explained,

> What happened was, Al had gotten used to singing with the trio, with a great jazz pianist like George Duke, who could improvise. Al would sing a song and George would improvise and Al would come in and do a scooby-doo kind of improvisation; they'd end the song together.

But working with me, I was a six-string classical guitarist, who played
finger style. I didn't strum, I didn't pick, I played pretty much the way
cocktail guitarists would play. I could play full chords, and I played
melodies and chords together. So he found it a very good accompanying instrument. But our musical repertoire was kind of limited. I
[couldn't] get into those really fast driving Lambert, Hendricks & Ross
kind of vocals. And so I said, "Why don't we do other kinds of songs
that work with the guitar?" . . . Al was very open to it. He started in-
vestigating the songs of James Taylor, Joni Mitchell, Carole King, and
since bossa nova worked very well with guitar, we did a lot of bossa
nova.[5] So, going from a . . . jazz singer, Al became more of a pop-jazz
singer. And he became very, very popular.

Al recalled how quickly their music caught on at Gatsby's:

[After the first night,] they said, "Will you come back and play tomorrow?," and by the time we finished that night, "And would you come
back and play next week Thursday?" And we came back and played
on next week Thursday and through the weekend, and by the time
we got through with the weekend, they said, "What about a five-day
week?" All of this happening within fourteen days. And folks were
coming from all over to hear this little duet with the crazy singer
[laughs]. Crazy singer! Now there was all this space; there were no
drums, there was no upright bass, and I began to explore.[6]

During these early days of the duo, Al's marriage to Phyllis ended. No
information about the breakup seems to have been part of the public record; Al did not refer to it in interviews. However, Martinez claimed that
Phyllis was glad he was working with Al, who didn't read or write music.
"She had played piano a little," Julio remembered, and she "had the job of
trying to write chords and notes down for Al, so he could communicate
[those] to a pianist." But Julio could read directly from chord sheets or
piano music, allowing Phyllis to be relieved of that duty. Interestingly,
when Al finally quit his "day job" with the State of California, Phyllis, who
must also have had some training in rehabilitation counseling, took over
his position.[7]

Once the duo took the gig at Gatsby's, Al began commuting to the club, first two nights a week and eventually four or five nights. He was rarely at home. And when he and Julio eventually left Gatsby's to work in Los Angeles, the strain on Al and Phyllis's marriage was too much. Al moved out of the apartment he shared with Phyllis and moved into an apartment with Julio in Southern California. Though Al and Phyllis made periodic attempts to work things out, the marriage could not be saved. Decades later, Al said, "That seems like I was a baby when I was married to Phyllis. Great lady. But sometimes . . . I wasn't ready. I was not ready."[8]

After the duo had spent several months at Gatsby's, Bill Straw, an attorney from Capitol Records (who would go on to become Al's lawyer for many years), heard them and brought them to Los Angeles. Straw lined up a gig for them at Dino's Lodge, a club associated with the big star Dean Martin.[9] While they were in Southern California, it made sense for them to record a demo, a bit of music that would serve as a calling card when being introduced to record company executives. The session took place at the Gold Star Studio in Hollywood in the fall of 1968.[10]

The session included "Love Not Now," a light, Brazilian-influenced song; an imaginative reworking of the Beatles' "A Day in the Life"; "Better Than Anything," which would later appear on Al's Grammy-winning 1977 album *Look to the Rainbow*; and an extended version of Antônio Carlos Jobim's "She's a Carioca." On these tracks, Al rolls out many of his vocal "tricks," including Jon Hendricks–style scatting, vocal "flute" solos, various percussion sounds, and other vocal sound effects. There is no mistaking Al's already singular voice.

The stint at Dino's was another big success; after a week, the duo was held over for another two weeks. At that time—prior to its becoming a tourist trap, according to Martinez—Dino's was a hot spot for celebrities and "Al was bringing in all these Hollywood people." They made one connection with the management company of singer Peggy Lee, which was working on the impending Madison Square Garden debut of the recent Olympic gold medal winner, figure skater Peggy Fleming. The company hired Al and Julio to record a version of Stevie Wonder's hit "You Are the Sunshine of My Life" for a big feature in Fleming's show.[11]

The duo continued to work around Los Angeles, including a stint at Whittinghill's Restaurant in Sherman Oaks, a popular spot then run by one

Al and Julio Martinez performed as a duo during the late 1960s and early 1970s. Here they are at the Bla Bla Café in Southern California. COURTESY OF JULIO MARTINEZ

of the most famous disc jockeys in Southern California history, "Sweet" Dick Whittington. There, Jackie Gayle, who was a top comedian on the Playboy Club circuit, talked them into getting on that circuit, which involved playing Playboy Clubs around the country and in London.[12]

For the next year and a half, the duo went on two separate, long Playboy Club tours. This episode in the duo's career is described at some length in Patty Farmer's book *Playboy Swings*.[13] All the shows were set up similarly, with a comedian as the headliner. Al and Julio would play for twenty minutes, then the comedian would do a forty-minute show. On weeknights, they'd perform two shows a night, with three on Fridays, four on Saturdays, and the occasional Sunday matinee. Although Al sang just twenty minutes each hour, the work was exhausting and especially demanding on his voice on weekends. But it was an exciting time to be on this circuit. Hugh Hefner's Playboy empire was becoming a prominent cultural presence across the country, and sophisticated music—specifically Hefner's favorite, jazz—was a part of his vision of the good life.

This was a period of societal change, and the Playboy Clubs—which employed young women known as "Bunnies" as waitresses in rabbit ears, tails, and skimpy outfits—were Hefner's vision of a revolutionary, modern lifestyle. Though he never spoke of it publicly, Al was reported to have enjoyed the attentions of some of these women, occasionally after work hours.[14] As Julio described it, "Al was six-foot-two, an immensely handsome, all-American, Black, athletic-looking intellectual. . . . So you can see why he was a favorite among the Bunnies. . . . Wherever we went . . . the Bunnies immediately fell in love with Al." Decades later, George Duke made a similar observation about Al's presence in the Half Note, saying, "Ladies loved Al. They just, you know, he was like the young Harry Belafonte who sang jazz."[15]

At the New York Playboy Club, a connection was made that led to Al's first appearance on *The Tonight Show*. Someone had suggested Al and Julio audition for the late-night talk show. They did so, and apparently the producers liked the act. However, they were assured that they wouldn't be scheduled on the show for some time. Al stayed in New York after the audition while Julio went home to California for a short break. But the call came sooner than expected, and Martinez found himself stuck at home when Al was suddenly called for that first appearance. Years later, Julio related: "I was missing out on my big chance to be on *The Tonight Show*! That evening, my wife and I watched from three thousand miles away as my partner sang 'The Look of Love' in the wrong key. He was almost a fourth too high—but Al is such a genius that he kept flipping his register back and forth, and he was great. They gave him a standing ovation and Doc Severinsen, the leader of the orchestra, invited Al to go on tour with him to the New England colleges," though that idea never came to fruition.

"Playboy was like the 'I think I can' engine," Al told Patty Farmer in 2012. "Everyone was young and had dreams and thought anything was possible. Lots of folks were getting big breaks because scouts from TV shows and other clubs would come around to find new and interesting talent. In addition to the scouts, the bigger-name entertainers who played there were on the lookout for good opening acts. . . . Working at Playboy in New York, I felt anything was possible, and I found the music that would define me. It was a wonderful time, filled with good music and good friends."

Also while in New York, Al and Julio played at Rodney Dangerfield's recently opened club, sharing the bill with the comedian. Gigs at

Dangerfield's and at the Improv comedy club led to further appearances
on national television. Besides several spots on *The Tonight Show*, the
duo appeared on the popular shows hosted by Mike Douglas and David
Frost. They occasionally also appeared on television in California, playing
for Steve Allen's show several times and on the show of ex-football-star-
turned-TV-movie-and-recording-personality Rosey Grier.[16]

Al's appearance on Frost's program in November 1969 has become
legendary. Martinez had to write the arrangements that Al would perform
with the show's house band, and he was told that he would also play, and
direct the band, from behind a screen. The band was made up of extremely
skilled musicians—as Julio put it, "half of the Count Basie Orchestra."[17]
He went on,

> The coordinator came out, he said to Al, "After you sing, David Frost
> is going to ask you about your sounds. So, can I have a list of the
> [vocal-instrumental] sounds that you do, so he can ask about it?"
> Al wrote them down, gave them to the guy. So, when it came time,
> David Frost said, "So Al, we hear you do sounds. Do some of them."
> And Al froze. He thought the guy was going to ask him, and Al sort
> of fumbled around; he couldn't think of anything to do. So, I started
> playing a blues riff; that was his cue to do a blues harp. So, he did
> that—so, you hear me playing by myself behind a screen—he did
> that, then he was free. He did them all after that.[18]

In addition to the harmonica, Al could produce the sounds of a flute, a
drum set, congas, and the percussion instrument cuica.

Al returned to his hometown, Milwaukee, in July of 1970 for an extended engagement with Julio.[19] Michael Drew's review in the *Milwaukee
Journal*, "Singer Al Jarreau Displays New Skills," presents an interesting
viewpoint from someone who had known Al as a fledgling singer some
years before.[20] "Since his last visit to the Pfister Hotel," Drew wrote, "singer
Al Jarreau has come up in the world. Twenty-three stories, to be exact,
from the hotel's Columns Lounge to the larger Crown Room, where he
proficiently opened a two week stay Monday night." Drew asserted that
when Al was "jobbing" around Milwaukee in the early 1960s, he was "an
undisciplined, breathy shouter who strained too hard." "But," Drew went

In the summer of 1962, Al played at the Columns in Milwaukee's Pfister Hotel with Les Czimber. When Al returned to Milwaukee in 1970, he moved up to the twenty-third floor and performed in the Crown Room, the Pfister's showcase lounge, pictured here. MARCUS CORPORATION ARCHIVES

on, "after three years as a West Coast pro, with visits to most of the network TV talkathons, he's gained considerable presence and a new style." Indeed, Drew referred to Al's "stage manner" as "bright and articulate, as you might expect from the holder of an M.A. in counseling."

Drew characterized Al's vocal manipulations as "imitations of flute, drum and bass viol, simulated reverberation and frequent falsetto leaps." Although this had not been part of Al's vocal repertoire while working with George Duke's trio, he had developed it during his time with Martinez. Of course, as his childhood friend Maxwell Carter noted, Al had started working on these sounds way back when he was in high school. The Milwaukee audience's reaction to Al's new style seems to have been mixed. Drew suggested that some of it "registered as too precious and overwrought for the average nightclub patron. In fact, one of Monday's ruder clients suggested that Jarreau 'just sing.'" Of course, just a few years later, these "imitations" would become widely known as part of Al's signature sound and style.

The duo's repertoire during this engagement included a jazz standard ("Bluesette"), the Beatles' "Eleanor Rigby," and several originals, which Drew described as being "arranged by [Al's] facile guitarist Julio Martinez." Drew's closing remarks included the somewhat sexist suggestion that Al's stage presence would particularly appeal to female fans: "With his new folkish image, the Pfister's psinging [sic] psychologist enhances his resemblance to Harry Belafonte. And though all the pyrotechnics may turn off a few male customers, our prodigal son should light up their companions."

After leaving the Playboy circuit in late 1969 or early 1970, the duo took an unexpected career turn. According to Martinez, Al and Julio took on a manager: Sheldon "Shelly" Jacobs, a native of the Twin Cities in Minnesota who was working in California for the Jacobs family business.[21] Jacobs said he'd like to start booking the duo at rock clubs and suggested that they get off the Playboy circuit. "Rock clubs were getting very big," Martinez recalled. "The San Francisco Sound people, the Jefferson Airplane, the Grateful Dead, were now expanding and working clubs all over the country. Moby Grape; Three Dog Night; Steppenwolf."[22]

Jacobs was friends with a member of the Fingerhut family, which ran a highly successful mail-order business in the Twin Cities. Singer Danny Stevens had opened a club called the Depot, eventually supported by Allan Fingerhut, in a former bus station in Minneapolis. Stevens and Fingerhut brought Al and Julio to play the club. "When we went down there to rehearse," Julio remembered, "there was a band [Zarathustra] in there, who came in with like two trucks of amplifiers and got all set up. And I walked in with my guitar in one hand and an amp in the other hand [laughs]. And [we] said, 'What is that?' And they said, 'This is the group.'"

Fingerhut and Jacobs then had a short talk and told Al and Julio, "You have to expand. You [two] guys might sound great, but people want to hear the full complement." The duo replied, "We don't know anybody here."

Three members of Zarathustra and one local pro joined Al and Julio to become the band Jarreau. Besides Al and Julio, it consisted of two Twin Cities veteran musicians, bassist Dik Hedlund and highly regarded drummer Dick Bortolussi (who had played with jazz greats Teddy Wilson and Ahmad Jamal); a talented young pianist named Richard "Junior" Dworsky; and a young Hendrix- and Clapton-influenced guitarist, Robert "Kinky" Schnitzer, on lead guitar.

Al said that at the time, "speaking musically, artistically, philosophically, Minneapolis was just bursting at the seams with good stuff." It also became an important time in Al's career because the band started doing new, original music that he had written.[23]

Richard Dworsky had grown up in St. Paul, Minnesota. He began play-

The band Jarreau, formed in Minneapolis–St. Paul in the late 1960s, included (left to right) Dik Hedlund, Richard Dworsky, Bobby Schnitzer, Julio Martinez, Al Jarreau, and Dick Bortolussi. COURTESY OF RICHARD DWORSKY

ing classical piano at age six and was studying piano at the University of Minnesota by age eleven. By the time he was a teenager, he was playing for theatrical productions and in his first rock band.[24] At the time of Dworsky's participation in Jarreau, Martinez said, he was "a sixteen-year-old genius."[25] Although he went on to have a diverse and interesting musical career, Dworsky will always be remembered for his twenty-three-year stint (1993–2016) as pianist and music director for Garrison Keillor's iconic radio show *A Prairie Home Companion*.

Back in the late 1960s, though, Dworsky, Hedlund, and Schnitzer were in the local Twin Cities band Zarathustra. According to Dworsky, it was a "funk-pop" group that played some originals and established "long dance grooves."[26] They had started, more or less, as a house band at a local spot called the Scotch Mist. Then they moved over to the Depot, the new hot spot in the Cities. Dworsky remembered Al coming to the club prior to the formation of the band Jarreau, usually showing up with friends, including Owen Husney, who later became famous for "discovering" the local musician who became known as the superstar Prince, and Marilyn Goodman, who hosted a popular local radio show interviewing touring musicians. Marilyn and Al had met in California thanks to Shelly Jacobs; they became a couple during this time in Minnesota, and they remained friends throughout Al's life.[27]

Once the band Jarreau was established, they worked at the Depot, the Labor Temple (opening there for a name act of the day, Poco), and perhaps some other local clubs. In the winter of 1970–1971, they traveled to frigid Fargo, North Dakota, to play at a showcase for acts vying to work the college circuit. Martinez remembered the Count Basie band being there, and Dworsky recalled that Jarreau shared a showcase bill with comedian Pat Paulsen, a major star at the time who appeared weekly on *The Smothers Brothers Comedy Hour* on national television.[28] Possibly as a result of that showcase, but more likely through Husney, who was, according to Dworsky, running a "one-stop local production company," Jarreau ended up opening concerts for such big-name acts as Steppenwolf and Canned Heat—shows in the equally frigid cities of Winnipeg, Manitoba, and Calgary, Alberta.[29]

Jarreau the band recorded a demo in Minnesota in December 1970. The songs were originals, mostly composed by Al. "Lovely Lady Light Up" is a funky rock/R&B groove with multiple sections, scatting, a full band sound, background vocals, a flashy piano solo by young Dworsky, and a wa-wa guitar solo from Schnitzer. "Something to Lose," a song in a somewhat similar style, is likewise jam-packed with diverse musical ideas and vocal acrobatics. The band made other recordings during this period, both in Minnesota and California, including "Window Well," a song cowritten by Al and Dworsky. This song is more progressive than the earlier material, clearly influenced by trends both in rock and jazz; Al's closing improvisation sounds modern even today.[30]

Somehow (perhaps through Husney), Shelly Jacobs got to know Bruce

The band Jarreau performing at the Twin Cities hot spot the Depot during the winter of 1970–1971. THE BARICH ARCHIVE

Glatman, a West Coast mover and shaker in the business, and Ned Shankman, the manager for Barry White, who was about to break out as a superstar. Sometime in 1971, Glatman and Shankman negotiated a contract for Jarreau to open shows on the West Coast for yet another top group at that time, Three Dog Night. The band was good, and as Dworsky said, Al "was incredibly talented, and . . . just blowing people's minds with his energy and his vocal scatting and imitating of instruments. . . . He was clearly a rock star ready to happen."

But to make this happen, the band would have to go to California. Hedlund and Bortolussi were not willing to leave their lives in Minnesota, but Schnitzer and Dworsky, who was only seventeen years old and still in high school, jumped at the opportunity. Dworsky told his parents that the band would "spend two weeks, do a showcase, and then get a record deal," assuming that "then you go out on tour, and then you make a million dollars, and then you buy a house in Beverly Hills." As Al said later, "We *had* to think that what we were doing was valid, and we all returned to L.A."[31]

When what was left of the group arrived in California in the spring of 1971, the showcase did not happen as scheduled. It kept getting delayed, by weeks, then months. What's more, the opportunity to open for Three Dog Night fell through. But the members of Jarreau were living the dream, being put up by their financial backers in a house in Laurel Canyon, a hot spot in the late 1960s and early 1970s for the musicians living and creating music there—Joni Mitchell, Linda Ronstadt, members of Crosby, Stills & Nash, and many others.[32] Al and Dworsky continued to write new material and rehearse, and they cut more demos in several studios in California, using different drummers and bass players. Not your "normal pop band," as Dworsky put it, they were being influenced by cutting-edge music of the time—electric Miles Davis, Frank Zappa, and others. However, in the midst of all the creative music being written, played, and recorded at that time, the mix that Jarreau invented did not get any record executive to bite.

Dworsky's and Schnitzer's mothers flew out and caught the band (with drummer Joe Correro and bassist Dave Parlato) at Jazz West, and, surprisingly, they approved of the boys' youthful experiment. But shortly after they had arrived in California, the band parted ways with their managers due to disagreements about the musical direction of the band. Rich, whose rent was no longer being paid by his former managers, was forced to move out of the digs in Laurel Canyon, finally landing in a back shed (and frequent rehearsal space) at Joe Correro's with carpeted walls that smelled like cat urine.[33]

They couldn't keep a steady band together because there was no work for them. The band's hopes that they'd get a record deal and then be able to employ some players was not enough of a guarantee for those players who were looking for work. "It didn't work," Al told the *Minneapolis Star* in 1977. "People in the group needed money."[34] Bobby Schnitzer eventually went on the road with a rock band, while Dworsky remained in California until July 1973. The tremendously talented drummer Joe Correro, who played on some of the demos, began an association with Al that came to fruition a few years later, when he played on Al's first few albums after Al "made it."

Despite the failed attempt to establish the band in California, Al spoke quite favorably of his time in Minnesota with the band: "It was an incredibly important period for me because it represented the first time I was able to have a band that would play music the way I wanted to be accompanied. Those were pivotal years. I wrote my first song in Minneapolis. Everything since then has been an outgrowth of that change of focus. . . . We tried for a recording career for the band; it didn't happen, so one by one the guys left and went back home."[35]

Al and Julio Martinez had achieved some real success in the late 1960s and early 1970s, from popular shows at Gatsby's, in clubs in Southern California, and on the Playboy Club circuit to television appearances on both coasts. The new band, Jarreau, opened shows for major pop acts around the Twin Cities and in Canada, and although they did not land the record deal they'd hoped for, the seeds of Al's major recording career had been planted.

8

Moving Up

Another Minnesota emigrant, Patrick Rains, had moved from Minnesota to California around the same time as Al with two songwriters from the Twin Cities that he hoped would make it big in the music business. Rains met Al a few weeks before Al auditioned at the Bla Bla Café, in the San Fernando Valley area of greater Los Angeles. Rains described the café as "sort of a hang for the musician gay community." Before 10:30 at night, he recalled, "they had no business. So the [owners] were trying to create a sort of coffee house environment where . . . every [musician] would get their twenty-five- or thirty-minute set, at the end of which they'd pass a bucket around the room, and you'd put in whatever you thought you could afford to help support the artist."[1]

After auditioning at an open-mic night at the Bla Bla Café, Al began working there in 1971, performing as a duo with his longtime musical partner Julio Martinez and doing the music they had developed over their years together.[2] However, soon Al started working more frequently at the café as a duo with Rich Dworsky. They became known as "Jarreau and Junior." Occasionally drummer Joe Correro would sit in on congas. The popularity of this duo seemed to hold the promise of a record contract. When Al performed, Dworsky said, the club, which could hold just seventy-five to a hundred people, "became electric . . . not at all like coffee house entertainment. It's like it was . . . an experience. Needless to say, [Al] developed kind of a cult following."[3] The whole audience would sing along with certain tunes. "He'd get the whole Bla Bla Café to be like a chorus,"

Dworsky remembered. "[The] regulars at the club Al jokingly called the Bla-bettes. And they'd sing along, and so the whole place was just rockin'." But a record contract did not materialize. For Dworsky, the West Coast dream did not become a reality, and he went home to Minnesota in 1973. Decades later, he still found it baffling that record executives who came to the club (or heard the demos) could not understand what was going on and see what a special talent was standing right in front of them.

Although Al performed often with Dworsky, his days with Julio Martinez were not over. According to Martinez, after the dissolution of Jarreau the band, Al said, "Let's stay here. I don't want to go on the road again."[4] They continued to work on and off as a duo into 1975, playing at "any club that would hire [them]."[5] Besides the Bla Bla, they played at two Scotch and Sirloin clubs and the Bitter End West, among other spots around L.A. They even played in the lounge of a Cholo, a Mexican restaurant chain. Every summer, Al and Julio would also return to the Bay Area to play a few weeks at Gatsby's.

When Patrick Rains first heard Al play with Julio at the Bla Bla, they had been performing more of Al's originals, as well as jazz standards and songs by contemporary songwriters such as Joni Mitchell and James Taylor. "I just fell in love with what it was that [Al] was doing onstage in this duo situation," said Rains. "And kind of a light bulb went off in my head, 'You know, this is probably the real reason I moved to California.' . . . Al and I kind of bonded very, very quickly for whatever reason. . . . You know, you meet somebody you've never known before and you feel some . . . there's something that you feel draws you. So, we became friends, and we started hanging out together."

Shelly Jacobs had given up managing Al at the end of the Minneapolis period, and the managerial types who had promised the Jarreau band Los Angeles showcases had apparently never signed formal agreements with Al or the band. "And, you know," said Rains, "hanging out over a period of weeks, talking about what [Al's] aspirations and goals might be, what mine were, I started trying to convince him that he really needed a manager, and I was the guy. And that's kind of how it happened."

One of the first things Rains did as Al's new manager was capitalize on his popular shows at the Bla Bla. He explained,

As Al continued to perform at
the Bla Bla Café in the early
1970s—first with Julio Martinez, then with Richard "Junior"
Dworsky, and finally with Tom
Canning—he developed a
loyal local following in Southern California. BARRY SCHULTZ
PHOTOGRAPHY / NETHERLANDS

Once the Bla Bla kind of picked up some steam, and Al began to get
a little bit of attention, he was selling the place out every Friday and
Saturday night. And the club had never had a cover charge before.
So . . . basically I convinced them that if we stayed exclusive to them
in the Valley, that they would start charging a dollar at the door, and
we'd get the door. And then eventually it went up to two dollars,
and . . . [Al] was making enough money between Friday and Saturday
night at that point that he was actually doing okay. I mean he might
have made a hundred and fifty dollars a week. In 1974, 1975, that was
not bad money.

Rains also worked to give Al a "calling card"—a demo recording to
provide to record companies. But this turned out to be a complicated en-
deavor. "I was primarily trying to get people to see Al live," Rains recalled.
"We had some demos that we had made at the gig that were really not
great. But the biggest thing was, some of what Al did doesn't really trans-

late itself to just recording. And without the money to really go into the studio and produce something, you know, the question is, 'Okay, are you better off with a bad demo or a great live show?'"

Finding the funding to record a demo was a challenging process in and of itself. Rains recalled the effort required of a manager in this position:

> What was not an uncommon situation back in those days is [you'd] make a relationship—you know, somebody like me, a would-be manager going around to the various record companies, knocking on the doors, trying to get people's attention. And maybe after a couple of visits, or a half a dozen phone calls that never got returned . . . you would try to befriend the secretary, and eventually the secretary would feel sorry for you, because you kept calling and the boss wouldn't call back; she'd figure out a way to get you in for a meeting, or get the boss to call you back. And if you were lucky you'd make a relationship, and then he might give you five hundred or a thousand dollars as a budget for a demo. [Then] you could actually go into a studio, and you had the money to pay for a couple hours of studio time and an engineer, and you could make a demo.

While continuing the effort to capture the attention of record labels, Al was also looking for musicians who could collaborate and help him further his musical vision. In the spring of 1973, overlapping with the duo's later period, Al began working with pianist Tom Canning. Canning grew up in the Rochester, New York, area, where his father was a professor of music theory and composition at the world-famous Eastman School of Music.[6] From the age of six, Tom took piano lessons at Eastman. When he was nine, he was tapped to play the title character in an Eastman holiday production of the beloved Gian-Carlo Menotti opera *Amahl and the Night Visitors*, giving him a taste of high-level music making at a very young age.[7] He grew to be a fan of many different types of music, from Miles Davis and John Coltrane to the rock and roll of his generation. Besides the "traditional" classical music being played at the Eastman professor's home, Tom also heard avant-garde "art music," such as the music of Karlheinz Stockhausen and Vladimir Ussachevsky, along with ethnic music from around the world. Young Tom did not discriminate between categories;

none of this music seemed "weird" to him, and one kind of music wasn't inherently better than another.

When it was time to go to college, Tom wanted to attend a school where he could study jazz. In the late 1960s, there weren't many schools with great programs for jazz study. Tom ended up attending the most prestigious, the Berklee School (now College) of Music. But there were a couple of problems with Berklee: tuition was very expensive, and at that time, Berklee did not award any traditional undergraduate degrees, which did not sit well with Tom's father, the academic.

So, after less than a year at Berklee, Tom transferred to the country's other top jazz school, North Texas State University (NTSU). One could earn a degree in music at North Texas, and although much of the music faculty had little regard for jazz, the program (which had been fashioned and was run by Leon Breeden) was well on its way to achieving iconic status. There was no jazz pianist on the faculty at NTSU, but Tom would be influenced by his peers, other highly motivated and skilled musicians who came there to study and play. In Tom's case, that included such future jazz luminaries as trumpeters Sal Marquez and Gary Grant, guitarist (and later legendary session player) Dean Parks, saxophonist Lou Marini, and trombonists Bruce Fowler and Tom Malone. Hanging out with these and other jazz-crazed students brought Canning into contact with the exciting contemporary music of the time: everything from standard jazz to Jimi Hendrix to music that Tom already knew, like Stockhausen. NTSU students also played gigs and occasionally recorded in nearby Dallas. In the hallway of a studio at one recording session, Tom met T-Bone Burnett, who would become an important figure in Tom's later career.

At school, Canning formed a quartet with Dean Parks, bassist David Hungate, and drummer Matt Betton that he described as "informed by rock [and] crossover [music]" and was "creatively inspired." The quartet went on tour, but that short-circuited Tom's career at NTSU, leaving him a semester shy of earning a degree.

At the end of the tour in late 1969 or early 1970, Canning found himself in Southern California and decided to stay. One of his first connections there was with T-Bone Burnett, who was just beginning what would become a fabled career as a singer-songwriter and especially producer. Tom soon found himself working with a band led by Burnett. He also connected with saxophonist John Klemmer. Klemmer, in his early twenties, had arrived in California in the late 1960s after cutting a number of albums that combined jazz and other styles—notably rock—in a way that was about to take over a significant share of contemporary music. Klemmer hired Canning, who played on several of Klemmer's albums. Tom's most notable collaboration with Klemmer was at the Montreux Jazz Festival in Switzerland, playing in an adventurous quartet with jazz "heavies" Cecil McBee and Alphonse Mouzon.[8] Canning also had the privilege of hanging out with pianist Chick Corea, who was on the West Coast around this time with a group that became known as Circle.

Occasionally one friend or another would ask Tom if he had heard Al Jarreau. Most could not adequately describe what Al did musically, admitting that Tom needed to hear him in person. But before Tom ever attended a performance, he received a call from Al in the spring of 1973, seemingly out of the blue. Al needed a new pianist (Dworsky was about to head home to Minnesota), and he invited Tom to come down to the Bla Bla to hear a set, check out the music he was doing, and "see if it would be something you'd want to do." So, Canning went to the Bla Bla, which he described as "pretty rough"—a "little place, filled with smoke, and [you] could barely see in there." Al had saved Tom a table right in front, about three feet away from where he was singing and playing his African shaker. Tom remembered looking up at the stage with amazement at Al and Dworsky:

> Al had that cabasa going, too! I'm telling you . . . they started, and I couldn't believe it. I was completely floored. I mean, I couldn't have moved out of my chair. . . . I was absolutely overwhelmed. This guy was unbelievable. . . . It was a very rare and deeply moving experience for me. [At the] end of the set, Al—so charismatic and friendly and handsome, and with that great big smile—comes over to my table, and says, "So, what do you think? Is this something you'd like to do?" Are you kidding? Absolutely!

Other future collaborators of Al's had similar experiences at the Bla Bla. Joe Turano, a fellow Milwaukeean, had just moved to the West Coast when he heard Al and Dworsky play as a duo. "Al [was] standing up with the shekere . . . making percussion sounds with his foot on the base of the microphone stand, and singing. It was a wonderful experience."[9] (Turano would go on to join Al's band in 2000 and serve as Al's music director from 2008 until Al's death.)

Larry Williams, who would play keyboards with Al from the early 1980s until Al's death, met Al at a club in L.A. called the Times. Williams remembered attending the club with his bandmate from Seawind, drummer Bob Wilson:

> I remember Bob and I walking in. . . . When Al opened his mouth and started singing, he was doing all the flute stuff, you know, the [vocal] percussion; the whole thing was there. The Brazilian stuff. . . . We just looked at each other and went, "What the fuck is that?" [We] had never heard anything like that. There was no nomenclature of [singing techniques], up to that point. . . . That was revolutionary. . . . I remember thinking, like every musician did, "I want to play with this guy" [laughs]. Little did I know . . . what the journey would be.[10]

As Al continued to astound patrons at his live performances, Rains continued his quest to bring Al to the attention of someone powerful in the business. Eventually, he found a couple of people willing to help make a demo possible. He developed a relationship with an employee of Epic Records, who provided Al with a small budget for a studio recording. At the same time, Rains made a connection with Al Schmitt, an already-successful engineer, mixer, and producer who would go on to a historic career in recording. Later in his career, Schmitt would be known for both his engineering and producing, working with artists as diverse as Henry Mancini, Steely Dan, George Benson, Toto, and Natalie Cole; along the way he would win twenty Grammy Awards. "We ended up with some decent demos with Al Schmitt," Rains said, "and . . . that gave us a little extra calling card. But the big drama was always, no one could ever figure out what to do with Al." According to Rains, they were turned down once or twice by every single record company, adding, "I think Warner Bros. turned us down three times, maybe even four times."[11]

Perhaps the essence of Al Jarreau could not be captured in a studio recording. Canning, like Rains, always believed, "If the right person hears him, he'll get signed." But when the record people came to hear Al live, they often couldn't figure out how they would market him. One night at the Bla Bla when he was outside during a break, Tom Canning saw "a giant limo—a Rolls-Royce about two blocks long—[and] out steps Ahmet Ertegun." Ertegun was best known for cofounding Atlantic Records, where he and his brother Nesuhi "discovered" and/or promoted such classic blues, R&B, and jazz artists as Big Joe Turner, Ruth Brown, the Coasters, the Drifters, and most importantly, Ray Charles. Ertegun, whom Canning recognized right away, came in and listened to a set. His feedback was, essentially, that Al was fantastic, but Ertegun didn't know what to do with him.

Eventually, the stars aligned for a pivotal event in Al's career. In January of 1975, Rains explained, "we had been playing around town quite a bit, and I'd finally gotten a relationship with the L[os] A[ngeles] Free Press [the most widely distributed underground paper in Southern California during that era] and a couple of the local music rags, and Al had gotten some really great reviews, so his name was starting to bubble." Lorne Saifer, an Epic Records executive who had helped to make possible Al's demos with Al Schmitt, was working with Rains to get a deal with Epic. But they needed to convince higher-ups that Al Jarreau was worth pursuing.

One day, when Rains was at the Epic offices, he happened to overhear a phone call between Saifer and the management at the Troubadour, one of L.A.'s most popular music venues. The Troubadour had just booked Les McCann, a jazz pianist and singer who, along with saxophonist Eddie Harris, had scored a big hit in 1969 with the single "Compared to What." McCann was coming in as a last-minute replacement act, but he refused to play every set, so the club needed an opener. Rains, who had been trying to get Al into the Troubadour for months, raced home and called the club.[12] "I heard a rumor that you're looking for an act for next week," he said. "We're in the process of making a deal with Epic Records, and I can get them to pick up a tab for next week." Rains, of course, didn't know if he could convince Epic to invite guests to the show and pick up their bar charges, but he knew he needed to sell Al first. The Troubadour representative reportedly said, "Geez, it's really coincidental, I'm sitting here reading [the review in the Free Press] from the show you guys did two weeks ago," and he asked for Rains's contact at Epic. After concluding that call, Rains quickly called Saifer. He said, "Lorne, you'll never guess what just happened. Doug from the Troubadour just called me. They're looking for an act, and he's reading the review of Al, and if you'll pick up a tab, they'll put him on a show." Top executives from Epic just happened to be scheduled to come to Los Angeles, Saifer secured the funding, and the show was booked. Al had an opportunity.

The opening moments of the gig were described in detail three years later by Lee Underwood in *Down Beat*:

> In 1975 when the houselights dimmed, an expanding wave of energy whirled through the room as Jarreau walked toward the stage for his debut performance at Hollywood's famed Troubadour club. He was the opening act for Les McCann. A spotlight zeroed in on him as he wove his way through the tables. Fans from the Bla Bla days began clapping as soon as they saw him. The applause spread. Soon, the entire audience was cheering and applauding. Al stopped in mid-aisle and raised his arms in the spotlight to those old and new friends who so energetically welcomed him to the big stage.[13]

The Troubadour show was unique for several reasons. Rather than performing in his normal duo format, Al was backed on this night by a trio of piano, bass, and drums. Surprisingly, the pianist was not Tom Canning. By that point, he had burned out playing weekends for little money and doing free showcases for Al that did not lead to a record deal.[14] With Al that week were pianist Greg Mathieson, bassist Paul Stallworth, and drummer Joe Correro. (Stallworth would go on to play on Al's first two albums; Correro, an indispensable member of Al's bands during this period, would play on the first four; and Mathieson would contribute to several as well.) The lights, too, were notably different from what was normal at the Troubadour. Jerry Levin, who would become an important member of Jarreau's inner circle, had been hired as lighting designer, and he worked hard to make this show special. "I wanted the stage to look like somebody's living room," he said. "So, I bought some old furniture . . . a little small couch, a couple of chairs, a little stand; I found a lamp that looked like a Tiffany lamp, but you know, it was plastic, and . . . the stage was kind of glowing when everybody walked in. . . . I brought in some extra lighting, and we really created an atmosphere that when people walked in, the first thing that they thought was, 'Wow, this is different. This is really different.'"[15]

As it turned out, the Epic executives never showed up. However, on another night early in the week, an A&R (artists and repertoire) man at Warner Bros. Records named Tommy LiPuma came to a show with Al Schmitt, with whom LiPuma had frequently collaborated.[16] LiPuma was so impressed by Al that he talked Warner's chairman, Mo Ostin, into coming to the closing-night gig. Ostin, too, was blown away. Just minutes into Al's set, Rains explained, he and Mo "happened to be sitting at a table together. Mo turned to me, he said, 'Hey, look—I have no idea what we would do with this guy, but we have to sign him. Can you be in my office tomorrow morning at nine o'clock?' Of course, I was there at 8:45. And by 9:30, we had a deal. It wasn't a lot of money, but it was a deal for three guaranteed records, which was very unusual in those days."[17]

Al Jarreau was going to become a star.

9

THE FIRST THREE ALBUMS

After the signing of the Warner Bros. contract in late January 1975, Pat Rains stated, "It [all] happened very quickly."[1] The demo Al had recorded with Al Schmitt had allowed him to develop his material and get a sense of what he sounded like on a record. And Tom Canning returned from his short break to begin playing and writing with Al again.[2] "When the Troubadour event happened," Rains said, "we were ready to go into the studio with Al Schmitt and start recording almost immediately. So I mean literally, within a month we were in the studio recording. [And] in those days . . . it [didn't] take that long to make a record. Particularly given the low budget that we had. It wasn't like we were Fleetwood Mac and could spend a year and a half getting high and gazing at our navels. So the record came out the first week of August, 1975."

That record was *We Got By*. Al wrote all of the songs; many of them had been part of his live act for quite some time. The title track, a beautiful slow tune, became one of Al's most beloved songs with audiences—not to mention family and friends—throughout the entirety of his career. The song opens with images of earlier and simpler (but possibly harder) times: "I hardly had a bellyful / Never knew a new bicycle / Hand-me-down books and shoes / They brought the yule tides in July."[3] Al's brother Marshall said of the song, "Well, it talks about our childhood. Celebrating Christmas in July; it talks about family. [We] loved each other, and we got by."[4] Al had been working on "We Got By" and another track on the album, "Sweet Potato Pie," with Julio Martinez since the two were in Minneapolis together.[5] Rich Dworsky remembered another

Al's debut album, *We Got By* (1975), was his only album to exclusively feature his original songs.

song, "Lock All the Gates," as one of Al's sing-along tunes at the Bla Bla Café that got the place rocking several years earlier.[6]

In his 1975 review of *We Got By* in *High Fidelity* magazine (a high-end magazine of the era, mostly aimed at classical music audiences and audiophiles), Jim Gosa echoed the sentiments of many of Al's supporters: "When you hear this album, you will probably wonder, as I did, why it took so long for someone to put Al Jarreau on record. On-stage he is a vivid, attractive, exciting performer. In his first LP, you get enough of his tremendous talent to more than justify the investment of money, time, and attention."[7] He compares Al's singing style to that of Bill Withers, Al Green, and Oscar Brown Jr., describing his vocal manipulations as "shouts, croons, coos, whines, and scats." This was just the latest attempt to describe in words what Al did vocally, an exercise that had challenged writers for years and would continue to do so for many years to come. But Gosa was most impressed with Al's songwriting skills:

> Those songs! They are the surprise bargain. In these melodies there is not a trace of the familiarity that breeds contempt. Indeed, some of them sound as if they'd been invented on the spot, the singer seeking a melodic line to convey the words and feelings in a sort of musical chain of thought. . . .

In his poetry set to music, there are moments when Jarreau
reminds me of the eloquence and elegance of Langston Hughes.
Sometimes he speaks in a black vernacular and, to some extent, of
black experience. But in the main, he reiterates Hughes and John
Donne and other poets, past and present, in pointing out that the
real experience is the human one that touches us all.

Notable in this album's lyrics are semiautobiographical references,
not just in "We Got By," but also in the album's opening track, "Spirit."
There, Al mentions, "There is a way my father / Taught me how to sing /
And I sing my song every day now / There is a way my father / Taught me
how to live my life / And I do that every day."[8] His Seventh-day Adventist
minister father, a highly skilled singer, was obviously still a strong influence in Al's life. "Susan's Song" was a love song to Susan Player, a woman
Al had met at the Bla Bla Café in the early 1970s who would later become
his wife. Despite many striking images, the lyrics to "Lock All the Gates"
and "Aladdin's Lamp" remain obscure years later, even to Tom Canning,
who played the tunes many, many times.

Al's life changed after the release of *We Got By*, but the album didn't
make a huge splash in the marketplace, at least in the United States. It did
win a Deutscher Schallplattenpreis (later renamed the Echo Award), a prize
presented by the Deutsche Phono-Akademie, an association of German
recording companies formed to recognize outstanding achievement in
the music industry. Al received the Nachwuchskünstler prize for young,
or new, artists. This was the equivalent of winning a Grammy Award in
the United States.[9] Still, Pat Rains estimated that the album had sold just
7,500 copies at the time.

From his days as a promoter in Minneapolis–St. Paul, Rains had friends
in the booking business, and through the efforts of Fred Bolander and
Dan Weiner at International Famous Agency in booking and Carl Scott in
artist relations at Warner Bros., Al was sent on short tours in Los Angeles,
Boston, New York, and Philadelphia. But work was not exactly plentiful.
To supplement the short tours, Rains hustled to book other shows for Al.
He said, "Most of the big gigs that we did in the major markets, like in New
York or L.A. or San Francisco, were things that I ended up putting together,
just like getting on the phone, . . . finding out who the local promoters

were that might be interested, [then] trying to develop a relationship with them, to feel some investment in Al. . . . That's sort of how things happened in those days." Warner Bros. had signed Al to three albums, so regardless of the success of the first album, he had two more to go. Sometime in the early part of 1976, the basic tracks for the second record, *Glow*, were laid down. From the standpoint of repertoire, *Glow* was something of a hybrid. While it featured four of Al's original songs, it also contained his very personal interpretations of songs by other prominent songwriters of the time: Leon Russell, Elton John and Bernie Taupin, Antônio Carlos Jobim, James Taylor, and Sly Stone (Sylvester Stewart). It's possible someone at the record label believed that having songs written by better-known artists (some of them already hits) on the record would result in name recognition that would lead to better sales. These songs weren't necessarily new to Al; according to Tom Canning, half of the record was "stuff that was left over from the Bla Bla days." Some were songs that Julio Martinez had done with Al even earlier, when he helped Al expand his musical scope to become more contemporary.

Other musicians of the era were beginning to experiment with this hybrid style as well. As Pat Rains explained, "In 1975, there were some very hip radio stations around the country. Some of them were basically R&B stations, R&B/soul stations. Some were what became traditional rock FM stations. But there were a number of stations that played this sort of hybrid that was coming onto the scene that was [a] hybrid of R&B, soul, jazz, pop." Musicians working in this hybrid style ranged from groups like Earth, Wind & Fire to artists coming out of the jazz tradition such as the Crusaders and Grover Washington Jr. While some of these stations were in big city markets, college radio stations all over the country provided space for young deejays to experiment with playing a wide variety of musical styles, not just over the course of a day's or week's programming, but within individual shows. These were the types of stations that would broadcast Al Jarreau's new hybrid style.

Not long after some of the first songs for *Glow* had been recorded, Al and Canning appeared on the new hit television show *Saturday Night Live*, then in its first season. They performed with two musicians from the house band: bassist and jazz veteran Bob Cranshaw and drummer Buddy Williams. Al sang "We Got By," and the crowd hooted and hollered in response.

Immediately afterward, another event occurred that would have a profound effect on Al's career in both the short and long term: Al and Canning went on a short European tour. They flew into London without a full rhythm section, planning to pick up a bass player and a drummer once they arrived. This was done, quite simply, because it saved money for Warner Bros., who was providing funding for tour support.

The practice of picking up "local" musicians is still, in the 2020s, not uncommon, though it's unusual for small groups. One never knows what kind of band is going to result—especially in a trio backing up a singer. In this instance, however, good fortune was with Al and Tom. Bassist Jerome Rimson, originally from Detroit, was living in Europe at that time, and he joined Al and Tom along with the British drummer Nigel Wilkinson. Canning claimed, "They were fantastic."[10] Rimson and Wilkinson were both huge Al Jarreau fans, and they already knew most of the tunes that they would need to play on the tour.

In March 1976, the quartet played three evenings at Onkel Pö in Hamburg, Germany. According to Canning, after the first night, "it was an absolute sensation." The performance on the second evening was broadcast live on Norddeutscher Rundfunk (NDR) radio. "That night," Canning recalled, "a guy [from NDR] said, 'You'll have to come do a TV show later. It will go out live to the entire country. Will you be able to do it in a couple of days?' After that show aired, there was an absolute explosion." It is unclear how many Germans, and other Europeans, already knew We Got By, due to Al's Best New Artist award. But the success at Onkel Pö led to considerably more dates being booked than had been originally planned for the tour. What had begun as a tour of only a few weeks ended up being expanded to last between two and three months. And his concerts attracted impressive crowds: 800 in Berlin's "Quartier Latin," 2,000 in the Hamburg music hall, and 4,700 at the Jazz Days festival, among others.[11]

At one of these gigs on April 22, a recording was made in Bremen, Germany, that was not released until years later, in 2017 (without the approval of the Jarreau estate). On the concert recording, Al announces that his version of Elton John's "Your Song" is from "a new album." He goes on, obviously somewhat insecure about his situation at Warner Bros.: "I hope [it] will be available in June, if I'm still with Warner." Referencing the middling sales of *We Got By*, he says, "We didn't sell a million. Enough to let people know we're around, but not enough to impress the statisticians. Those who measure red against black [on the ledgers]."

Despite Al's misgivings, *Glow* was released in the summer of 1976. The review in the mainstream US jazz press—that is to say, *Down Beat*—was a mixed bag. Chuck Mitchell began his review by speculating, "Stardom can't be too far off for Jarreau."[12] But Mitchell also expressed his reservations: "He has talent to burn, but his problem on LP thus far has been what he's burned it on. . . . Neither of his first two albums have been able to communicate the warm, lithe excitement of his in-person performances." While there was at least some truth in this observation, Mitchell could not have known (and neither could Al) that this situation would be rectified with Al's next album.

After describing and comparing some of the material on Al's two albums, Mitchell went on to criticize Al's cover song selections: "His choices from the current pop repertoire are only occasionally appropriate for his admittedly impressive repertory of vocal effects. I don't get the feeling, amidst all the embellishment, that Jarreau really cares about the lyrics to James Taylor's *Fire and Rain* and Elton John's *Your Song*, which are trivial selections to begin with." While fans of those two songs would surely

Glow (1976), Al's second album, featured both originals and covers of others' popular songs.

argue about their triviality—one can now say with certainty that both have enjoyed long, healthy lives—many jazz critics in the 1970s tended to disparage pop material, as they had for decades and, in fact, do to this day. Al certainly seemed to care about the lyrics to those songs based on the expressive way he performed them, even if Mitchell did not appreciate those renditions.

Regardless of his critiques, Mitchell's closing thoughts in his 1976 review demonstrate the positive impression Al was making, even on jazz critics, at the time: "Like any vocalist fresh to the scene who has unique phrasing and scatting powers, Al hasn't quite figured out where they do and don't work—where to let 'em loose and where to sing it straight. It's a hit or miss proposition at this stage. But he's getting there. Obvious ability like Jarreau's only comes along once in a while, and can't be contained for long by mediocre settings."

In addition to *Down Beat*, *Glow* was also reviewed in some unlikely publications. In *Time*, the United States' "weekly newsmagazine," reviewer Joan Downs wrote about the album in a column of short takes on new releases by singers such as Linda Ronstadt, Neil Diamond, and Natalie Cole.[13] Downs began with a debatable statement: "Jarreau is primarily a jazz singer with a scatman's vast repertory of swoops, glides and vocal glissandi." No one would argue about the "vast repertory," but it was not accepted fact that Al was primarily a jazz singer—at this time or any other during his career. In fact, this debate has continued among critics and fans for many years, and it has always depended on the debaters' opinions of what defines a jazz singer—an issue that has never been settled in the hundred-year history of jazz.

Al made an attempt to define his own unique style in 1978 in his first big feature in *Down Beat*, "Al Jarreau: The Amazing Acrobat of Scat." In this article, writer Lee Underwood obviously identified Al as part of the jazz vocal tradition. But Al tried to position his singing in slightly different terms:

> People often describe me as some kind of *Ed Sullivan Show* carnival freak. They say I imitate conga drums, flute sounds, drummers and bass players. They make me sound like a mimic instead of a singer. But except for the occasional visual resemblance, every-

thing is handled in the context of the music in such a way that it's only music.

I scat sing, but I don't use the same vowels and combinations of vowels that the bebop singers used. I use my own sounds—guitar-like, electronic, grunts, hisses, ahhhhh's—I like soft sounds. I don't think of the instrument when I'm doing it. I just take the conga sound or whatever and make it into something different.[14]

Pat Rains had a theory that the public perception of Al as a jazz singer was influenced by deejays who had grown up in postwar Europe.[15] "I don't think anybody thought of Al as a jazz singer," he said. "It wasn't until we went to Europe that the jazz thing started to become obvious. And I think that has more to do with the open acceptance that the jazz community has in Europe in general." According to Rains, deejays on radio stations in Europe in the 1970s had been exposed to jazz in their youths after World War II. At that time, many disc jockeys on stations in Europe were American GIs who played the popular music of Nat King Cole, Ella Fitzgerald, Count Basie, and others from that era. "When Al came along," Rains said, "these European deejays who had grown up listening to jazz said, 'Wow! This is a jazz singer.'" Rains believed that Al had the phrasing of a jazz singer but did not write jazz songs.

European countries, and Germany in particular, were crucial to Al's early commercial success. *Der Spiegel* published a feature on Al in the November 15, 1976, issue based on his 1976 tours. Although he would not become a star in the United States for some time, Al was already a star in Germany. And a rave article like this—in one of Europe's most highly circulated journals—both reflected that new stardom and promoted its growth. Claiming that the Berlin Philharmonie had rarely experienced such applause in thirteen jazz years, the article described Al as having "a whole orchestra in his throat" and, in contrast with Chuck Mitchell's critique in *Down Beat*, praised Al's expressive cover song performances:

Until recently, Ella Fitzgerald was considered the world champion of so-called scat singing, in which a voice improvises wordlessly and virtuosically like an instrument. In the early 1960s, the Lambert, Hendricks & Ross ensemble sang entire orchestral scores and famous instrumental solos—but that was a trio. Jarreau can do it all by himself.

With your eyes closed you can hardly tell whether the respective saxophone, bass or bongo solo comes from a musician or from Jarreau's vocal cords. . . . Often even two souls seem to be making music in his skin: one who performs the lyrics melodically and another who improvises a counter-rhythm using larynx tricks, stamping feet and snapping fingers.

In addition, Al Jarreau tears up the songs, exposes hidden textual content through spontaneous insertions of language, and turns standards like James Taylor's "Fire And Rain" or Dave Brubeck's "Take Five" into complex soul dramas. In a jumble of phrases and syllables, tones become carriers of meaning, words transform into pure sound.[16]

In sync with Rains's claim that it was in Europe where Al was categorized as a jazz artist, the article argues,

While German sound interpreters . . . speculate that this vocal jazz could point into the future as a pop music trend, no one raises an eyebrow in the USA when it comes to such feats. In his home country Jarreau was only allowed to appear in small clubs and in the opening act of prominent rock bands; his two LPs were not even listed in the "Top 100." So many musical elements have fused together in his uncategorizable universal style that none of the rock, jazz, blues, gospel and soul factions in the US music business feels quite responsible for him.

The article concludes: "After many years in the semi-darkness of American nightclubs, Jarreau says he is 'still unable to believe the bright spotlights, the many microphones and television cameras.' That sounds sincere. But when he comes home he's a star."

Both the remarkable success of the 1976 European tour—with a "pickup" band—and the release and expanded sales of Glow led to a second tour in Europe later in the year, including Al's first appearance at the Montreux Jazz Festival in Switzerland in July. Al arrived at the festival with Tom Canning as his only accompanying musician, expecting that they would pick up a drummer and bass player for the performance as they had done on the first European tour that spring. But, at the last minute, the musicians they had lined up backed out. Journalist Lee Underwood described the scene that followed in an article in *Down Beat* later that year: "'I had been ill,' said Jarreau. 'I was weak and feverish from heat stroke, and then, in Europe, caught the flu. There I was, 10,000 miles from home, and sick. Then the musicians didn't arrive, and my performance time was coming up. What to do? The best that I damn well could.' Accompanied only by his pianist, Jarreau received three standing ovations *during* the set."[17]

Due in part to the extensive touring, among other factors, sales of *Glow* far outstripped those of *We Got By*. "I think the first record, we might have sold 7,500 copies," said Rains. "And then the second record, we ended up selling 80,000. That's a pretty significant jump."

As admirable as the first two albums were, hearing Al live was not like hearing Al on a recording. Downs, in the *Time* piece about *Glow*, got to the heart of the matter when she wrote: "In concerts he adds his own million-dollar magic trick: he carries a band in his larynx—or so it seems when Jarreau fills in the melody with vocal imitations of instruments. . . . He can even accompany himself, crooning the words of a sleepy ballad while making rhythmic clicks deep in his throat to provide percussive counterpoint." People who knew Al, including the "brass" at Warner Bros., realized that the wider public needed to hear an album of Al's live performances. With the great success that Al had experienced in Europe, it only made sense to record him in front of large, appreciative audiences on his early 1977 tour there.

The tracks for the third album were recorded in Europe in January and February. On this tour, besides his regulars (Canning and Correro), the basic trio was filled out with the young bassist Abraham "Abe" Laboriel. Lynn Blessing was added on the vibraphone. Jerry Levin, tour director and assistant to Patrick Rains, remembered how Laboriel came to the band: "Al Schmitt tipped me off that this young kid from Cleveland had just moved to Los Angeles and didn't know if he wanted to go out on the road, because he was trying to become one of the 'A' session players. And he gave me [Abe's] number; I called him up. . . . He had just gotten married. I went to his house, I met his wife, Lyn, I convinced him that this was something that could really be great, and [said,] 'Just please come and just play. Just come and play with Joe and Tom and let's see how it works.'"[18]

When Laboriel came in to the SIR studios in Hollywood that the Jarreau team had rented, he and Al had an instant connection, jamming and doing jazz standards with Tom and Joe. Levin remembered watching from the back of the room and thinking that their chemistry was magic. According to Levin, Al said, "Man, I don't know what it's going to take to get this guy; you just have to get him. You have to make sure that this works."

"It was incredible," Levin said. "That day in that room is one of my most amazing musical experiences."

The venues and the crowds on the 1977 tour were considerably larger than those of the previous year. Al's "German Grammy" was an indication of both critical and fan approval. One of the shows took place at the Musikhalle, now known as Laeiszhalle, in Hamburg where Al had played his very first European show in March of 1976.[19] "He had rabid fans there," Jerry Levin remembered. "But they had only seen Al play with a trio; they had never seen this. And what they were playing on that tour was songs from *We Got By* and *Glow*. So everybody knew these songs, but [they were] different arrangements. . . . It was completely different from the record. . . . [That night] in Hamburg, people would not leave the building. He did two encores, went off, and thirty minutes later people were still chanting. It was awesome."

Other performances on the tour were similarly successful. In Berlin, Al opened for Roberta Flack, a big star at the time, and the response to Al's show was so overwhelming that she didn't want to go on after him. Management had to turn the houselights on after extended ovations for Al in order to quiet the crowd for Flack. At the Salle Pleyel in Paris, Al opened for the Manhattan Transfer, and in order to settle the crowd before the "feature act," the club waited an hour before bringing on the main act.[20]

Due to the nature of live recordings, considerable production work must have been required after the fact, yet the album was released in May, a very short turnaround time for a project of this sort. Warner Bros. clearly considered Al a valuable commodity if it was willing to pull this off. And *Look to the Rainbow*, which was a double-LP set, turned out to be a huge success. It went on to win Al's first Grammy Award, for Best Jazz Vocal Album.

On *Look to the Rainbow*, Al really did sound more like a "jazz artist," singing with the freedom that comes with live performance. The live songs tended to be longer, too, giving Al more room to improvise than he had on the previous studio albums. This improvisational element is evident

Al's third album, *Look to the Rainbow* (1978), recorded live in Europe, won a Grammy Award (Al's first) for Best Jazz Vocal Performance.

on almost every track. And even on a song like "We Got By," a ballad that never called for a great deal of improvising, Al could turn up the heat in his live performances, putting more emotion and edge into the rendition than he had on the *We Got By* album.

The cut from *Look to the Rainbow* that made the biggest splash was Al's remake of Dave Brubeck's hugely popular "Take Five," written by Brubeck's saxophonist Paul Desmond and originally appearing on Brubeck's highly successful 1959 album *Time Out*, one of the bestselling jazz albums of all time. "Take Five" may have seemed an unlikely choice almost twenty years after its debut, but it was a triumph for Al, and it foreshadowed his later remakes of Brubeck's "Blue Rondo à la Turk" and Chick Corea's "Spain." In Brubeck's original, "Take Five" is largely a showcase for a long drum solo by Joe Morello; in the Jarreau version, it is Al's feature almost all the way through, beginning with his stunning unaccompanied vocal introduction. His lyrics to the tune are satisfactory, but his extended improvisation completely steals the show.

An innovative bit of marketing may also have helped sales of *Look to the Rainbow*. Pat Rains came up with the idea while the Jarreau team was in Europe:

[In those days,] what was typical in England was you'd go to a movie, and before the movie ran, there would be commercials that would run for ten, fifteen, twenty minutes. Little local commercials. And I

was in a movie theater [in London], and I saw a commercial for Joan
Armatrading, who had just put out her first record. And it was brilliant. And I thought to myself, *Shit, we could do that.* So we got back to
America, and I went to Warner Bros. and I convinced them to give me
ten thousand dollars, and I went and I hired a woman named Penelope
Spheeris, who went on to become a very successful independent film
director.[21] But I hired her—one of her very first projects—to make a
four-minute video, a four-minute movie of Al singing "We Got By." . . .
This was before there were videos. [That is, before MTV hit the airwaves
with music videos in 1981.] So we went in to Chicago, Detroit, Boston,
New York, Philadelphia, Cleveland, Los Angeles, and San Francisco,
and we bought time. I mean, no one had done this before. So it was,
like, really groundbreaking. . . . We went through the movie releases,
what movie was playing in what neighborhood, what did we [think]
were the most appropriate neighborhoods that would be into Al, what
films would be the appropriate ones—and that is what boosted us from
[sales of] seventy, [to] seventy-five thousand on the *Glow* record to over
a quarter of a million on *Look to the Rainbow*. And for many, many,
many people *Look to the Rainbow* was their introduction to Al Jarreau.
And to this day I run into people who tell me, "You know, I was in a
movie theater, and I saw this thing."

There's no way to know whether the video is what pushed *Look to the Rainbow* "over the top," but the album's sales clearly moved Al to a different
level of marketability in the notoriously fickle music business.

Leave it to *Down Beat* to throw some cold water on the album. Mikal
Gilmore awarded *Look to the Rainbow* three and a half stars out of a possible five—not bad, but hardly a rave review.[22] More interesting from a
historical standpoint are some of Gilmore's comments, which shed light
on how one widely read critic in the mainstream jazz press viewed Al and
his work in 1977. He opened the review by focusing his admiration on one
small phrase:

In the opening passage of his new live *Look To The Rainbow*, Al Jarreau delivers a rubbery scat phrase that cuts any other single moment
on the record, or any other exercise in his recorded repertoire, for

that matter. Sounding not unlike the scattering offspring of an un-earthly mating of Johnny Mathis and Daffy Duck, Jarreau transfixes his audience with a liquefied, non-verbal twanging riff, punctuated with an alluring drag-and-push timing. Elsewhere, in the late Paul Desmond's *Take Five*, Al revives the tonality, except this time he injects it with a sinewy Nagaswaram flavor and Yiddish inflection. Huh? A crooning duck that sings with a nasal Jewish accent? Well, not exactly, although like such a chimerical creature, Al Jarreau is hardly typical of any one vocal school, a trait which in the end may prove more detrimental than praiseworthy.

Although Gilmore praises Al's singing, he continues his verbal on-slaught while attempting to explain his songwriting:

As anyone can attest to who has seen him perform live, Jarreau has the makings of a true phenomenon. His fluid talents derive from the elastic contours and contortions of this mouth: sprawling lips that frame a resounding airy cavity, and a tough, adeptly thudding tongue, possessing a remarkable percussive quality. Top that off with a cornet-like tone and his scalar facility—he can turn chromatic slides and tricky minor-key descents with disarming precision—and you have a potentially killer combination.

Unfortunately, Jarreau elects to dilute the package by straining it through a plethora of his own material, an agreeable enough but formless collection of songs built around one or two phrase riffs. That approach, which borrows heavily from the gospel tradition, allows ample room for improvisation bents, but makes for forgettable songwriting.

Jazz singing—by any standards, Jarreau can fit the bill—has always been enhanced by the quality of the song as much as the singer, even in the scat style, and invariably Al is at his best on the non-originals.

Gilmore's closing remarks crystalize this opinion—one that Jarreau would receive repeatedly in the years to come: "To be sure [Jarreau] is an inventive singer of protean ability, but an unremarkable songwriter and an indulgent improviser. As good as he is, and we have reason to believe that his talents will ripen sharply, he doesn't yet possess the acumen to sustain a two-record set. More disciplined arrangements and a more demanding producer are in order."

Interestingly, Al would soon get a more demanding producer, but not until after a short period of transition. And the product that resulted from the demands of that producer (Jay Graydon) probably did not please Gilmore or many other hard-core "jazzers" any more than *Look to the Rainbow* had. But whatever reviewers might have thought about Al's third album, it was a big commercial success. The Jarreau team does not seem to have been overly concerned about the reservations of this small segment of the listening public as Al took this big step forward in his singing career.

WE GOT BY
Warner/Reprise, 1975

Al Jarreau's debut album was produced by Al Schmitt. By this point in his career, Schmitt had already engineered or produced sessions by Elvis Presley, Sam Cooke, Henry Mancini, Jefferson Airplane, Neil Young, and Jackson Browne. He was to go on to even greater fame in the future.

The basic band sound on the album is piano (Tom Canning), bass (Paul Stallworth), and drums (Joe Correro). In the credits, Al is listed for voice, vocal percussion, flute, and miscellaneous effects—a brief summary of the sounds he was known for at the time. David Grusin, who already had a stellar career in the studios and would go on to become a top composer and producer (cofounding GRP Records in the late 1970s), arranged the somewhat minimal string and horn parts for the record.[23] Al's background vocals appear on several tracks. Tonal color was added by Larry Bunker on vibraphone—a timbre that would also enrich the sound of Al's 1977 album, *Look to the Rainbow*. The songs were arranged by Al and Tom Canning.

This recording, which introduced Al to the wider musical community, remains unique in his discography, as it is the only album to feature Al's compositions exclusively. It certainly opened eyes and ears to Al's singular mixture of R&B and pop, delivered with a jazz sensibility. "You Don't See Me" is a brilliantly funky exposition of Al's vocal gifts. The deeply soulful ballads, passionately delivered, comprise another essential element of the album. Even if it did not sell in large numbers, *We Got By* was an important first statement from Al to the world.

New to the recording business at the time, Tom Canning would later express his regret that he played so conservatively and carefully on the record.[24] Yet he admitted that the "core" trio tracks were solid and that the "bass and drum groove on all those things [was] just great." Canning was not present as Grusin made his additions, but expressed appreciation for them, saying that "he made it sound like a real album."

"We Got By" remained in Al's repertory until the very end of his career. Along with "Letter Perfect" and "You Don't See Me," it was reprised on 1977's breakthrough *Look to the Rainbow*.

More than thirty-five years after the album was recorded, Al related an interesting story about the sessions:

> I went to the studio on any number of occasions . . . and Al [Schmitt] produced that record and brought Tommy LiPuma in, who did several records with me later on. But the first record was Al Schmitt with me, and a staff of Warner Brothers people were saying, "Go for it, guys." And I remember the two of us sitting in that studio looking at each other and going, "We built a chapel, Schmitt."
>
> That [line] comes from *Lilies of the Field* with Sidney Poitier, where he is this carpenter, and his name is Smith. A group of nuns from Germany in a small town somewhere are trying to build a chapel in which to worship, and they come across Homer Smith. And they build a chapel, and the sister would say, every morning, "We built a chapel, Smith." And there we were, Al Schmitt and I, building a chapel. If we said it twice, we said it a hundred times. That's it, we built a chapel.[25]

GLOW
Warner/Reprise, 1976

Glow was recorded in February and May of 1976, both before and after Al Jarreau's successful first European tour. Tommy LiPuma joined Al Schmitt as coproducer. The album was a mix of Jarreau originals and songs—some of them already well known—written by other artists.

The band was still, at its core, a trio. Tom Canning and Joe Correro held down the piano and drum chairs, respectively, as they had on *We Got By*. Paul Stallworth, who played bass on the first album, plays on just one track here; the rest of the bass work is handled by Crusaders bassist and studio regular Wilton Felder and the lesser-known Willie Weeks. Felder's Crusaders bandmate Joe Sample adds some keyboard colors. Larry Carlton—who would later join the Crusaders and was, like Felder, a studio regular—adds tasty touches of guitar to a number of tracks. The added synthesizer tracks and the sweetening of the late-1970s-style string section were arranged by Al's old Iowa acquaintance Dale Oehler.

None of Al's compositions on this album have had the longevity of "We Got By" from the first album, but they are still noteworthy. "Milwaukee," his paean to his home city, repeats the line "I find myself two thousand miles from my sweet home, Milwaukee," while referring to Los Angeles as "a city of broken dreams." "Hold On Me" is a short, virtuoso, multitracked a cappella track of Al sounding like a very large and hip doo-wop group. "Glow" is a sweet bossa-ballad that does indeed seem to have a sort of glowing quality to its sound.

Elton John's "Your Song" and another virtuoso showpiece, Antônio Carlos Jobim's "Agua de Beber" (a leftover from Al's "Brazilian period") remained in Al's repertoire for years. Tom Canning called Al's performance of James Taylor's "Fire and Rain" an "absolutely all-time personal favorite" track from his ten-year history as Al's pianist. He described how it was recorded:

> I [was] sitting there and playing some little pattern or something, and Al comes over, and he said, "Hey, man, what are you doing there?" And I said, "I don't know, I'm just wondering if

something like this might be cool for the intro." He said, "Play me what you're doing again." So I played it, and he went, "Oh, that's great. Let's start the song that way." So, we hadn't done it that way until right then. . . . So you know that kind of chord progression at the beginning of "Fire and Rain," before it kicks into the melody? That happened right there on the session, without any plan.

And the song, as recorded by James Taylor, is kind of just . . . a folk James Taylor thing. You know; it's got a great lyric, but it's not a funky arrangement at all. It's kind of Southern California pop, [a] white bread arrangement. And Al turns it into a workout. I mean it's as funky as it gets, man. You know, the whole groove on it and everything. And the stuff at the end, all of that improvising about "driving six white horses." . . . He vamps on that chord progression, which we'd never done before. . . . [I asked him], "What are you talking about there at the end?" And he goes, "Man, I don't know what I'm talking about. I just [sang] whatever came into my head. . . . I don't know what it means, it just sounds good, man." But that tune to me, that performance, *that* is the definitive "Fire and Rain."[26]

LOOK TO THE RAINBOW
Warner Bros., 1977

This album was recorded on Al's early 1977 European tour. Exact locations where each track was recorded are not listed, but according to tour director Jerry Levin, Warner Bros. recorded every date on the tour, including rehearsals in Delft in the Netherlands and performances in Brussels, Amsterdam, Munich, Hamburg, Berlin, Paris, Oslo, and other cities over the period of a month. Producers Tommy LiPuma and Al Schmitt were along for the entire tour. Reflecting Al's popularity in Europe, the credits were listed on the album jacket in English, French, and German.

The band was partly a carryover from the previous two albums, with Tom Canning on keyboards and Joe Correro on drums. New to the band was Abraham "Abe" Laboriel on bass. This highly skilled and funky bassist ended up as a fixture on the Jarreau albums of the early 1980s, but this was the only time he toured with the band. Lynn Blessing on vibes was another new addition to the band. According to Jerry Levin, adding Blessing was something Al "had in his head," perhaps recalling the contribution of Larry Bunker to We Got By. Levin recalled auditioning many vibes players in Los Angeles before deciding on Blessing. Canning, though, remembered that adding vibes was the suggestion of manager Pat Rains, who wanted a certain look and class added to the band and its sound—and was firm about not adding guitar. Blessing was a known quantity on the West Coast at that time, and however he came to join the group, he enriched the color of the live band.[27]

Al and the band revived several tunes from We Got By (the originals "Letter Perfect," "You Don't See Me," and "We Got By") and Glow (Leon Russell's "Rainbow in Your Eyes"), but the live versions are clearly different from the studio versions. Al is freer in his interpretations of the tunes and does more improvising, and the increased length of some of the tunes allows him to build to more dramatic climaxes. A new original that makes a real impression on this record is the gospel-influenced (and, eventually, almost trancelike) "One Good Turn." "Could You Believe," "Burst In with the Dawn," and "Loving You" are other originals. Besides the title tune and "Take Five," the other nonoriginal that first appeared here was David Wheat and William Loughborough's "Better Than Anything." Al sang the latter tune on and off during the rest of his career.

Important to this album was the inclusion of the 1959 Brubeck/ Desmond jazz hit "Take Five." This showcase for Al's outstanding rhythmic vocal improvisation remained an audience favorite for years.

It's a surprise that after two albums of contemporary material, the title track on this album is the 1940s Broadway song "Look to the Rainbow." Al obviously wanted to do the tune, and while few in the buying public likely recognized the title, those who did must have liked the image it conjured up. Regardless, the album sold very well, outselling the first two albums by an order of magnitude.

10

Transition

By the spring of 1978, Al Jarreau had gone from a supremely gifted but virtually unknown regional singer to an up-and-coming global star in only a few years. He had multiple European tours under his belt, in addition to three records on a major label—the last of which earned a coveted Grammy Award. His life had changed greatly, and while the professional side of his life seemed to be a classic rags-to-riches narrative, these big changes in his career meant changes in the rest of his life as well.

Al's marriage to Phyllis Hall had ended in 1968, as he was just beginning to experience some success not only in the San Francisco Bay Area, but in Southern California as well. Years later, Al talked about how he had not been ready to be married at that time, although the marriage lasted for four years. In fact, he had opened up about that relationship publicly as early as a 1982 article in *People* magazine: "'For a long time I wasn't nearly as thoughtful about people and their needs as I should have been,' says Jarreau, whose first marriage failed, he says, 'because of my stupidity—I had illusions about the whole institution.'"[1]

Al and Susan Elaine Player met at the Bla Bla Café during his long residence there, in 1971 or 1972. She first went there with a date and heard a singer whose name she thought was "Alchero." Al met her that night and, shortly thereafter, ran into her at a nearby restaurant and invited her to another show. Soon, Susan took a job bussing tables at the Bla Bla, and the relationship between her and Al developed. Susan, who had "divorced her family" and was living in a foster home, was in her late teens at the time, fourteen years younger than Al, who was in his early thirties.[2]

During the 1970s, Susan was cast in several movies, including *Invasion of the Bee Girls* (1973), *High School Girl* (1974), and *The Pom Pom Girls* (1976).[3] Two were bit parts, but Susan had the lead in *High School Girl*, which was filmed in Italy, produced by Carlo Ponti (a well-known movie producer and the husband of Sophia Loren), and in Italy was known by a somewhat more interesting title, *Cugini Carnali* (First Cousins).

In Al's early days at the Bla Bla Café, Susan became friends with Al's musician friends Rich Dworsky, Julio Martinez, and Tom Canning. The couple married in 1977. Photos from the wedding show the beautiful bride with flowers in her hair and the handsome groom in a wide-lapel jacket. They are basking in the Southern California sunshine among their friends and family, seemingly without a care, with the prospect of a promising life ahead of them.

In the 1982 article in *People*, which was sometimes almost a gossip tabloid, it was reported that "[Al] and his second wife, Susan[,] have had troubles too; they separated briefly two years ago." However, by 1982, she was accompanying him "for part of his six months a year on the road."[4]

Susan Player at her wedding to Al in 1977. COURTESY OF ROSE MARIE FREEMAN

Perhaps these details of their personal relationship were made public because Al was a new celebrity and, therefore, more candid with a reporter than he would be later in his life.

Al had been similarly candid in his first feature article in *Down Beat*—a short spotlight written by Lee Underwood in 1976. After Underwood's written introduction to Al's career and a brief but reasonably thorough look back at Al's early life and youth, Underwood let Al carry the rest of the interview, with the columnist supplying only some connective material. The first part of that exposition is one of the first times Al publicly described his philosophy in his own words:

> After 15 years as a performer, Al Jarreau has finally emerged as a recording artist. "I just kept on doing what I do," he said, "never getting overly discouraged. I was aware that when the time was right, I would know it. Now the time is right, so right, in fact, that it's scarey [*sic*]. It's a total affirmation of the positive flow of my life."
>
> In his music and conversation, Al Jarreau brims over with that spirit of affirmation. "Every thought, whether positive or negative, is creative thought," he said. "So it is important to think positively and constructively about the things you want to unfold in your life.
>
> "Proper thought is prayer. Prayer is proper thought. Thought and prayer are *casual* things. All the Source, God, wants from me is the highest good—peace, love, joy, actualizing my highest potential.
>
> "I believe we are all rooted in that central core, that creative source of the universe—which is good, and which creates beautiful things. Like the lily, the mountain and the tree, we are all part of it. There are certain natural events that occur that we interpret negatively—floods, earthquakes, droughts, etc.—but these things don't have any positive or negative value in themselves. It is for us to understand the positive *flow* from which they come.
>
> "I think the Source wants to recreate itself. It wants to recreate beauty. If it didn't, it would be at cross-purposes with itself. It would tend to destroy itself.
>
> "Mankind, because he has thought and can remember and project and think, can think in a negative manner if he so chooses, but he can

also turn it around and put it in a positive direction and make himself more beautiful and much, much stronger."[5]

This was the first public statement of Al's philosophy, which clearly reflected the religious aspect of his upbringing, as well as an optimism that he seems to have maintained through thick and thin. And it was by no means the last time he would go public with his outlook. Al's positivity was something he came back to in interviews until his death, and it appeared in his song lyrics throughout most of his career as well.

Yet, in this 1976 interview with Underwood, Al opened himself up in a way that he never really did again in a national publication. For all the positivity that Al projected in public, he had also experienced fear and anxiety in his life.

"True," he said, "there have been times when I have not dealt with certain truths the way I should have, and I have had to learn to cope with certain moments of neurotic negativity in my life.

"I remember one time, for example, when I was scared, rolling on the floor in fear . . . rolling on the floor. I was so scared, I couldn't look at the moon. I was *afraid of the moon*. It was the first time I had ever confronted the profound realization of the inevitability of death.

"You see, I don't think any of the things we experience come to us by mistake or happenstance. They come to us in order to get us a little bit higher. God forbid that I should have to experience that ever again, but it did help me look at something I perhaps should have been looking at all along. That awareness of mortality helped me learn that although I will give up my body someday, my spirit is immortal.

"In the grand scheme of it all, there is *only* life. Alive . . . alive . . . *living*. Once I began to see that, it opened up another way of thinking for me."

Even in the 1970s, when many public figures talked with considerable freedom about their feelings and attitudes about life, this was a somewhat stunning personal revelation in a jazz publication.

When Underwood spoke with Al again in 1978, Al addressed the philosophy he had discussed in their first interview, revealing a few more insights after likely confronting more questions from journalists in the intervening period. His response to Underwood's question about the "message" of his songs was this:

> I see every day as being a song. The greatest art, and probably the hardest one, is to learn how to live, so most of my songs have to do with living, with little encouragements that I say to myself and want to say to others. "Spirit" on *We Got By*, for example, says, "There is a way to make sweet feelin' last, to the sheltered when the wind is free and cold and chilly." It has to do with finding that center of who we are, of finding the spirit. There is comfort in there for us . . . for me. [6]

Also in this article, Al drew parallels between his singing and his father's preaching: "I'm doing the same thing," he said, "taking up the ministry, only my pulpit is the barroom and the stage. My church is the world." And, using some of the same language he employed in the 1976 *Down Beat* article, he told Underwood in 1978 that he wanted to use his music to "build a chapel."

> I want this experience to be a classroom, a church in which I can learn and teach those lessons that will bring me and us closer to what we all can be. I don't mean an organized church or religious group. I just have a religious feeling about life. It has to do with the fact that I am beautiful . . . you are beautiful . . . we all are beautiful!
>   That spirit, that power, that source, that creative principle which caused you and me, the lily, the rose, and the tree is always good. It is always a positive force. It is for us to learn the mystery of its ways. I cling to that. I know in my soul that that's the way it is.

While Al had been performing in public since he was just four years old, he was not used to performing in front of crowds as large as the ones that appeared with regularity as his European tours picked up steam. Both Pat Rains and Tom Canning, who were very close to Al during this period, recalled the adjustment Al had to make to his new performance reality. Rains related a story of one of the first times Al performed in a bigger venue:

We did a show in Santa Monica at the Santa Monica Civic Auditorium, which back in those days was a very popular concert hall. But it was a concert hall, it wasn't a club. And Al was scared to death by it. And it took me forever to convince him that he was absolutely capable of going out on stage and controlling the situation and making it feel like a club. And that was on him. And you know, the good news is that he bought it [laughs]. He bought into it hook, line, and sinker and realized, *Wow, I can do this. I can touch people, I can go out in a three-thousand-seat auditorium and I can touch people.* And I think that stayed with him.[7]

No matter the size of a venue, or how many people were in it, Al just needed to think as if he were in a club in order to feel comfortable. He often singled out individuals in the crowd and spoke to them as if he were carrying on a one-on-one conversation. Canning remembered,

[Al] had that very rare ability to engage the audience. . . . It became a very personal experience for people. And I've always just admired it, because, I mean, I couldn't even conceive of doing a thing like that. Especially when you're talking about thousands of people out there. But it just came naturally to him. . . . Once in a while when we were out on the tours, the big outdoor venues or whatever, and I'd see him doing just that, and I would immediately think back to the days at the Bla Bla. And I'd go, *He's doing the same thing* [laughs]. . . . He's just talking to the crowd. He's engaging people. And somehow he's able to do that in front of this colossal crowd, and you feel like you're in a club.[8]

Evidently, though, Al continued to feel some performance anxiety well into his career. In his notes, written in 2010, to a deluxe edition of his 1984 *In London* album, Al discussed the experience of playing the huge Wembley Arena where the album was recorded. "I try not to think about [it]," he admitted, laughing. "If I think about it . . . I get scared." Again, comparing a large venue to the smaller, more intimate club setting, Al expounds on how he had to approach it:

As his career continued to trend upward, Al clearly enjoyed performing at the Greek Theatre in Los Angeles in 1979. PHOTO BY SUSAN JARREAU, COURTESY OF JERRY LEVIN

If you had that experience of relating and doing the music to a small audience, there is something in a club, and making that reach for the audience, and getting comfortable with that audience[,] knowing what intimacy with the performance is all about and know[ing] what the fire should feel like in the performance. You learn that craft early on in your career. Then it's just a question of kind of expanding that into a bigger venue, conceptually in the same kind of way. It's a small audience, how do I bring them in, and how do I get this across to this small audience, most of which I am looking at in the front row. I don't kind of see all of those people all the way in the back, but you try to bring them the same intimacy. You have lighting directors and sound engineers that make it [an] intimate, edge-of-the-seat kind of listening experience. Knowing how to make the music explode and be powerful, in the back of the cushions in the seats. And you use that experience to make it feel [like] a room of 40 or 50 people when you are playing to an audience like Wembley.[9]

In 1978, Al was at something of a musical crossroads. The first three albums (with Warner Bros.) were quite different from one another: *We Got By* was all Jarreau compositions; *Glow* mixed in the songs of other well-known contemporary artists with Al's originals; and *Look to the Rainbow* presented Al doing familiar material (including selections from the two earlier albums) in live performance—arguably, his greatest strength.[10] The three albums had the same basic sound, however, as the core group for each was Al accompanied by piano or electric keyboards, bass, and drums. On each album, additional instruments had been added for color—vibes, guitar, extra keyboards, and percussion—but did not detract from the overall sound created by the basic group.

Warner Bros. clearly believed in Al by this time. The company extended his contract beyond the three albums promised in the original agreement. The next album, *All Fly Home*, turned out to be a little different from the three that had come before. The core band was still essentially a trio plus Al, although Lynn Blessing, the vibraphonist who had been added for the European tour that resulted in *Look to the Rainbow*, supplied a more prominent role for vibes than had been the case on earlier albums. The bassist on the album was Reggie McBride, a Detroit native and veteran of the Motown scene. McBride immediately formed a rock-solid musical connection with keyboardist Tom Canning and drummer Joe Correro. Once again, guitar and percussion can be heard on the album, but the most noteworthy addition was virtuoso jazz trumpeter Freddie Hubbard, contributing as a guest artist. In retrospect, based on the lineup of musicians on Al's subsequent albums, Hubbard seems like a curious addition. Although Hubbard's albums at the time were selling reasonably well on the CTI and Columbia labels, he was definitely a jazz artist, and his contributions to *All Fly Home* were most definitely jazz solos.

Was Warner Bros. trying to pitch Al as a jazz artist? Perhaps the label had mixed feelings about Al straying too far from his categorization as a jazz singer, which had earned him a Grammy and a rapidly growing fan base. But the company certainly knew that a jazz album would not sell

The transitional album *All Fly Home* (1978) earned Al his second Grammy Award.

nearly as much as one in the pop or R&B genres, and it must have been looking for bigger sales from this promising artist. Jerry Levin, Al's tour manager at the time, remembered Warner Bros.' interest in widening Al's reach. "I think that Al had gotten a reputation, deservedly or not, as a jazz singer," Levin said. "And I think the record company was looking for a larger audience. They were looking for . . . songs that might be played on more types of radio stations."[11]

According to Tom Canning, who cocomposed three of the songs on *All Fly Home*, Al and the rest of the Jarreau team were also interested in making music that couldn't be strictly categorized as jazz on the album. Canning remembered his part in the making of this "transitional" record:

> The first thing we wrote was "Thinkin' About It Too." It charted immediately. At that point, before then, [Al had] been mostly on the jazz charts, and way down in the 90s on the R&B charts. And "Thinkin' About It Too" came in at 50 on the R&B charts, it was on the radio, and we wrote it in twenty minutes. You know, it just was one of those things, you go "Pow!" He had the hook, he had the lyrics, he had everything done. I gave him the groove, and I had the title and went, "Hey, that wasn't that hard. We should do more of that" [*laughs*]. So we cowrote three songs on that record. And you know, it was the beginning of our writing relationship. So that's why I would call [*All Fly*

Home] transitional, in a way, because it was sort of all over the map, you know, I mean stylistically here and there. But if you just listen to the three things that Al and I wrote . . . I'm not singling it out just because I'm involved, but that was the beginning of [the] next three albums. . . . [We thought], "Well, okay, this will work. We should keep doing this, man. . . . We've got a chemistry and the vibe, and you know, we should do this." And besides, it got on the charts. So that's what we want[ed] to do. We [didn't] want to be on the jazz charts forever, we want[ed] to get on the R&B charts and we want[ed] to get on the pop charts.[12]

Of course, jazz fans and critics had their own reaction to this transitional album. *Down Beat* reviewer Douglas Clark had a conflicted response to *All Fly Home*. His three-and-a-half-star review began with a bit of a backhanded compliment: "This album has grown on me. The more I listen to it, the more I enjoy it, especially side one. It's pop-jazz that works—most of the time."[13] Clark especially liked the album's opener, "Thinkin' About It Too," calling it "a perfect pop tune, with its catchy hook and disco-boogie beat." But he took issue with Al's singing on other tracks. "Jarreau seems to sing words more for their sound than their meaning," he reflected. "They *sound* good. . . . But since Jarreau plays with word sounds so well, why doesn't he scat more?" Clark seems to be implying that scat singing is what defines a jazz singer. He went on to acknowledge that the album had some good lyrics scattered among its songs, but none as good as the lyrics of Joni Mitchell or Bruce Springsteen.

In addition to "Thinkin' About It Too," Clark also praised another new Jarreau-Canning collaboration on the album, writing: "A way with words is not Jarreau's only asset. He also has range, control and an excellent feeling for nuance, most obviously on 'I Do.' After a gentle first half, the song begins to build. Jarreau climbs slowly through three octaves, about one octave every eight bars, and then parachutes down, skillfully."

Clark did not care for Al's handling of the well-known covers on side two, the Beatles' "She's Leaving Home" and Otis Redding's "(Sittin' On) The Dock of the Bay," claiming that Al missed the irony of the Beatles' lyrics. That Clark was apparently unmoved by Al's deeply expressive rendering of the song might suggest that the critic did not understand Al's interpretation of those lyrics. In the closing paragraph of his review, Clark thanks both Al Jarreau and producer Al Schmitt "for not adding strings" to the album, suggesting that the reviewer wanted Al to maintain his more traditional jazz sound.

For his part, Al's manager, Pat Rains, felt that Al, his musicians, and his management were all "treading water" on *All Fly Home* and that it was not much of a step forward from the previous albums. But he agreed that Al and the rest of the team were trying to branch out with the album, whether or not they were successful. He reflected, "The only way to go bigger and broader than [being a jazz singer] is to come up with material that's more accessible."[14]

Transitional or not, accessible or not, jazz or not, *All Fly Home* won Al his second Grammy Award for Best Jazz Vocal Album in two consecutive years.

ALL FLY HOME
Warner Bros., 1978

All Fly Home, the last Al Jarreau album produced by Al Schmitt, won a Grammy in 1979 for Best Jazz Vocal Album.

The core band on this album was the same group that played on *Look to the Rainbow*—Tom Canning on keyboards, Joe Correro on drums, and Lynn Blessing on vibes—with the exception of Reggie McBride replacing Abe Laboriel on bass. In a March 1978 article in *Down Beat*, Al told Lee Underwood that bassist Simeon Pillich was going to be working with him, Canning, and Correro for six weeks, and that Al looked forward to recording with that group.[15] For unknown reasons, Pillich did not appear on *All Fly Home*, but McBride was a great find for the bass chair. As on Al's previous studio albums, guitar and percussion were added on some tracks, in this case by two of the up-and-coming stars of the period, Lee Ritenour on guitar and Paulinho Da Costa on percussion. Larry Williams, who would become another important member of Al's circle for years, added some keyboard parts. The biggest addition was that of jazz trumpet star Freddie Hubbard on several tracks.

An important development in the making of this record was that Al and Tom Canning recorded their first three cocomposed songs. It was the start of what would be a flurry of collaborations between the two on the next three albums. Al was the sole composer of two other songs on *All Fly Home*.

The originals on this album did not end up having the staying power of other Jarreau compositions. However, "Brite 'N' Sunny Babe" and "Fly" include early examples of lyrics that are clearly aimed at inspiring listeners to do and feel better. Freddie Hubbard contributes mightily to the tracks he plays on: "I'm Home," a beautiful ballad that displays Al at his romantic best, and Al's "Fly," the one really rhythmically exciting track on the album, where Freddie is just burning. Al also shines on his achingly slow rendition of the Beatles' "She's Leaving Home," an interpretation he would re-create on record some years later. The group's reimagining of Otis Redding's ten-year-old "(Sittin' On) The Dock of the Bay" is also notable.

Larry Williams, who contributed some keyboards to this record, later made a vital statement on Al's 1980 album *This Time*, and he became one of Al's most valuable and trusted associates on the road and in the studio. About *All Fly Away*, his first Jarreau record, Larry had the following recollections, revealing much about Al the musician:

In the studio, Al is just a fountain of ideas. And most of them were incredible. I mean they were parts [he] would sing. It's not like most singers can do that. As you know, Al can't read or write music, but he sure could hear the fuck out of it. He could sing up all the bass notes if he needed to. Which would blow my mind. He would give me the notes of the chord. If I was looking for a chord that he wanted to hear, he would just sing it straight up [*laughs*]. So that was a mind-blowing experience as well, being in the studio with Al. I went just like, "Wow, this is cool."[16]

11

———— ▓–▓–▓ ————

BREAKIN' THROUGH

While *Look to the Rainbow* sold very well and *All Fly Home* had some success as well, they gave only a hint as to the kind of sales that Al's next albums would have. The first step toward gaining a much bigger audience was the hiring of a new producer for the next album.

Al Schmitt had produced *We Got By* and *All Fly Home*, and he coproduced *Glow* and *Look to the Rainbow* with Tommy LiPuma. Both Schmitt and LiPuma ended up having "hall of fame" careers in the music business. By 1979, LiPuma had risen to a top executive position with Warner Bros., and he would remain a bona fide force in the business until his death in 2017. LiPuma would also play a part in Al's career in the early 2000s. But neither of these heavy hitters was right for Al's career as the 1980s dawned.

According to Tom Canning—who was by this point a vital member of Al's team, not just as Al's keyboard player but also as his cocomposer—the hunt for the next album's producer took on a particular significance. "After *All Fly Home*," Canning said, "the conversation was: we need somebody who's a musician who would be able to get Al—really, literally—onto the pop charts, without spoiling what he actually [does], without damaging the core of who Al Jarreau is, but just enhancing it, and widening the audience. But it has to be the real Al Jarreau."[1]

Pat Rains, who was always searching for a way to move Al to the next level, originally had his sights set on producer David Foster. After seeing one of Al's shows, Foster had contacted Rains to see if Al was interested in being the singer in Foster's band. But that, Rains remembered, "didn't make any kind of sense, because at that point Al was developing enough of

a profile as his own person that to have gone and been this singer in somebody else's band . . . would not have been the right move by any means."²
Rains spent hours trying to convince Foster to produce Al's next album,
but he was too busy. Rains suspected that "maybe, at the end of the day,
[Foster] may not have been convinced that Al had the commercial potential
that he wanted." Canning remembered Foster responding to their requests
by saying something like, "You need a producer that knows something
about jazz—and that's not me. You should call Jay Graydon."

Foster introduced the Jarreau team to Graydon, his partner, and they
ended up moving forward with him as the producer of the album. "David
committed that he would be part of the production," said Rains, "and that
he and Al and Jay would cowrite some number of songs." Graydon was at
the beginning of his career as a producer, having produced a few albums
by Richard Page (before Page became a member of the chart-topping band
Mr. Mister) and the Manhattan Transfer's recent album *Extensions*. As
Canning put it, Graydon "hadn't really had a big hit." But the business end
of things was not Canning's bailiwick; the music was his concern. So, while
Rains worked out the details with Warner Bros. and Graydon, Al and Tom
continued to work on songs. Tom recalled,

> We had "Never Givin' Up," "Gimme What You Got," and maybe a
> couple others that we had just recorded, a couple on a cassette some-
> where. And after Jay was officially going to produce, then we had a
> couple of meetings and we brought in the tapes . . . and as soon as we
> played him "Never Givin' Up" first, he said, "Wow, that's fantastic,
> absolutely. That's going right on the record. I'd like to start the record
> with that song. That's fantastic, men." So he heard the other one,
> "Gimme What You Got," and there was one other one we had already,
> I think. He went, "Oh, this is great. I'm hearing the whole record right
> now. Keep writing. We're gonna have a hit record, we're gonna have a
> gold record."

Once the recording process had started, Al had to think and operate
in the studio differently than he had grown accustomed to. Graydon did
things in a very controlled way, creating a precise product as an end result.
According to Canning,

Al was used to recording like a jazz musician. He didn't really spend any time redoing his vocals, or fixing anything up, or maybe singing the melody a little more specifically. There was not a lot of fixing or overdubbing or long rigorous discussions about arrangements. . . . It just hadn't happened before. . . . And [Al's previous mode] wasn't necessarily a bad thing, because it captured all that spontaneity, what he was all about anyway, whether he was in a three-minute song or an eight-minute jam. But it's a whole different thing when you get in the studio, as opposed to being out in front of an audience. You're making an album. So Jay brought that.

Canning also recalled that Graydon didn't "waste a lot of time with diplomacy"—he would give his unvarnished opinion if he didn't like something or if he felt that a musician wasn't playing his part well enough. His philosophy, according to Canning, was: "Don't settle for something; you can't change it once you release an album. If there's something that's kind of lame in an arrangement, or a bad note in a vocal performance or something, if we don't fix it now, before we mix it, it's always gonna sound bad. So let's get it as good as we can possibly get it even if it takes a little longer."

As a result, Canning remembered Al feeling a bit constrained and initially resisting some of Graydon's suggestions. After a track was cut, the three of them—Al, Graydon, and Canning working as an unofficial assistant producer—would spend time in the studio, discussing the music and fixing things up. "At first, [Al] did not like the idea of cleaning things up and maybe resinging a chorus," said Canning. "But I began to see the method to the madness very quickly. And actually Al eventually began to embrace it."

Driving this new method was Graydon's goal of producing Al's first gold record. "He wanted a hit," Canning said.

He was pretty outspoken. For example, Jay would say, "Al, you've got to sing the melody. You can't sing a jazz version of the melody. If you're gonna go, 'Never givin' up' or 'Gimme what you got,' you have to sing it the same way every time you get to the chorus, because the audience is not made up of professional musicians. The audience we want to reach are people that maybe play a little piano or maybe

The creative team of (left to right) Tom Canning, Al Jarreau, and Jay Graydon takes a break in the studio in the early 1980s. COURTESY OF TOM CANNING

play a little guitar for fun. They just like music. They're not trained; they're not in the business. That's how you get a hit. That's how you get on the pop charts." Of course Jay was right. But it led to some . . . extended conversations, let's just put it that way [*laughs*]. . . . For me, the more I heard where Jay was coming from, the more I liked it. . . . So I went, "I'd rather trust this guy than stick to what happened before, because we haven't had a gold record yet."

As Rains remembered, "We had learned some things from the fourth album [*All Fly Home*] that didn't work. The radio marketplace had changed again, so we were kind of set up for [*This Time*] to have more success than we'd had. And it became [Al's] first gold record."

From the album's opening notes, *This Time* marked the beginning of a new era for Al Jarreau. In fact, Al and Canning's "Never Givin' Up" did end up being the first track on the album, and its bright but rich synthesizer sounds, like those that defined much of the pop music of the era, were different from anything that had appeared on a Jarreau album previously. While many of the catchy melodies and rhythmic grooves were not entirely different from some of those on *All Fly Home*, the music sounded different—slick and highly produced. But by most measures, it did just what Canning was hoping for: it maintained the essence of Al Jarreau. It was Al Jarreau with "the A-team."

This polished, catchy vibe continued with the other Jarreau/Canning song, "Gimme What You Got," and two more songs the duo cowrote with Tom Kellock, "Love Is Real" and "Your Sweet Love."[3] Bluesier numbers included Canning's collaboration with Allee Willis, "(If Only I Could) Change Your Mind," and Al's "Distracted."

In the mid-1960s, Allee Willis had attended the University of Wisconsin–Madison, where, like so many of her generation in Madison, she became a social activist. After being introduced to Earth, Wind & Fire's bassist, Verdine White, Willis had written the lyrics for two of the band's huge hits in the late 1970s: "September" and "Boogie Wonderland." She would go on to write for a who's who of pop artists in the last decades of the twentieth century. She also got into the movie soundtrack business, writing for Eddie Murphy's star vehicle *Beverly Hills Cop* and, in 2005, the major motion picture milestone *The Color Purple*. She also cowrote the theme song for the long-running television series *Friends*.

Tom Canning recalled that he had come up with a kernel of the song "Change Your Mind," as well as the title.[4] He brought this to Al, and as was often the case in their working arrangement, Al took the song and wrote lyrics. However, in this one case, what Al came up with was not good, according to both Canning and Jay Graydon. Al didn't want to change what he had written, so Graydon suggested that Canning take the song to Willis to see what she might devise. Her version ended up being much preferable to Graydon and Canning, but Al did not happily accept the idea of singing someone else's lyrics for a song he had worked on. Eventually, he said he would use Willis's lyrics if she would change some of them. Canning learned a lot about diplomacy as he had to go back to Willis and ask her if she would be willing to make a few changes. In the end, everyone came to an agreement, and another successful song resulted.

The other songs on the album supplied the variety that made the total package so successful musically. Of most interest to Al's jazz fans was the jaw-dropping version of Chick Corea's "Spain," a tune that was only a few years old but had already attained classic status in the jazz repertory. Al amended the title to "Spain (I Can Recall)." His romantic lyrics were effective, but it was his remarkable singing of the very instrumentally conceived song—as well as an excellent "scat" solo—that attracted so much attention. His scatting was similar to what he had done with "Take Five" on *Look to the Rainbow*, but on a much more contemporary-sounding tune. (The importance of keyboardist Larry Williams's contribution to this arrangement and performance cannot be overstated.[5]) Al closed the album with the gentle "(A Rhyme) This Time," a composition by the acoustic guitarist Earl Klugh, another young Warner Bros. artist who was also a featured instrumentalist on the tune, with lyrics by Al.

Finally, the album included another Jarreau original that is something of an anomaly in his entire recorded output. "Alonzo," with its reference to a character who was "king around the Bay," might well have been a reference to Al himself, who some years earlier had musically conquered the Bay Area at Gatsby's. The biblical image of a "scene where the lamb and lion play" is pure Jarreau. And when Al dramatically declaims that "Alonzo declared he must 'Reach to heaven—for heaven,'" listeners are transported right into Al's sacred quest. In the next section of the song, Al writes, "Don't you know Alonzo put out his hand one day / Don't you know Alonzo lifted up his head to pray?"[6] The words are a powerful expression of Al's journey. But when coupled with some of the most dramatically effective music he ever wrote, and an impassioned and flawless performance, the end result is electric.[7]

The song's closing minutes consist of an instrumental coda (with some vocal effects from Al) that, with its gnarly, shockingly dissonant chord progression, can be interpreted as representing the constant challenge of a spiritual pilgrimage. It is a stunningly conceived and executed piece. For whatever reasons, the song never became a standard part of Al's repertoire. Many fans were happy to see it revisited years later at Al's 1993 performance at the Montreux Jazz Festival (which was released on CD in 2016) and as a part of Al's "symphony concerts" later on.

This Time didn't just sound different, it looked different, too. On the front and back covers, Al appeared in stark, beautiful black-and-white photographs taken by the highly in-demand and esteemed fashion and portrait photographer Richard Avedon. Like the music, the cover exuded a certain cachet and class that Al's previous albums had not.

Although *Look to the Rainbow* eventually became a gold record (in 2001), *This Time* was an even bigger hit, going gold in 1982 by selling more than five hundred thousand copies. It reached number one on the jazz charts, number six on the R&B charts, and peaked at number twenty-

This Time (1980), Al's first album produced by Jay Graydon, featured a stylish cover photograph by famed fashion photographer Richard Avedon. PHOTOGRAPH BY RICHARD AVEDON, © THE RICHARD AVEDON FOUNDATION

seven on *Billboard*'s Top 200 listing. But despite the incredible success of *This Time*, it would be eclipsed by Al's next album.

As Al set out to record a new album after *This Time*, the now-familiar issue was once again raised: what kind of singing would he do at this stage of his career? Many years later, in 2010, Al reflected on Graydon's influence on this point: "The most important thing that Jay did, besides getting some of the best work out of me as a singer in the studio, technically and all, is he said, 'Al, you're a wonderful jazz singer, and you're a great R&B singer, and a great pop singer, but you turn everything you do into a jazz performance. Would you just try to not scat on this song?'"[8] Graydon described his intentions similarly in the 2020 documentary *Unsung: Al Jarreau*, saying *This Time* "brought [Al] more into the R&B style, right? The album went gold; did well. It was time to do the next one, which was the *Breakin' Away* album. Now the hardest thing with Al is, well, how do I get a jazzer into R&B and pop radio? We found 'We're in This Love Together.' And I said, 'That tune's a hit.'"

"We're in This Love Together" materialized as Al's production team was planning the next album and thinking about where Al's career might go after the success of *This Time*.[9] Jerry Levin, who was Al's tour manager at the time and also worked for Patrick Rains, explained, "When we weren't planning tours, we were always looking for new songs. Dozens of publishing companies were continually sending songs." Levin's assistant, Leslie

Lee, would take every tape they received, log it, and record who sent it, the date it was received, and other details, for legal purposes. Levin told her, "Play each one of these things first to make sure that the recording is of quality enough to listen to. Just listen to the first chorus." If Lee found anything she really liked, she was to keep the tape out to pass along to Levin. By that time, Al's prominence and promising trajectory meant that they were receiving a huge number of tapes. "We had all the cassettes in garbage bags," said Levin. "That's how many there were in a month's time or so." Lee put the ones she liked in a brown paper grocery bag, and Levin would go through at least one of these bags every week or two.

Very shortly before *Breakin' Away* went into production, Lee set aside the cassette featuring "We're in This Love Together" for Jerry. It was written by Roger Murrah and Keith Stegall—two songwriters from Nashville— and, Jerry admitted, "It was stupid; it was a country song." But he loved it right away and played it over and over again after his first listen. He immediately took the song to "a full-time promotion guy who was working with all of our artists, James Lewis." Lewis told Levin, "I'm not hearing

Jerry Levin and Al at Aunt Fanny's Cabin outside Atlanta in 1980. This was one of many soul food restaurants that Al frequented as he toured around the country. COURTESY OF JERRY LEVIN

it." Next, Levin took it to Pat Rains, who said the same thing. But, Levin remembered, "Pat said, 'Look, if you love it, then take it to Al and let him hear it.'"

At this time, Al and Jerry Levin were sharing a house. It was the first day that the team was going to lay down preliminary tracks for the new album. Al was just getting ready to leave to go to a meeting with Graydon and Canning when Jerry called him and said, "Just wait for me, wait till I get there. I have something to play for you. I think I really found something." When Levin got to the house, Al was in his bedroom; he kept a cassette player next to his bed, just in case he woke up in the night and needed to record a musical idea. He popped the cassette of the new song into the machine and barely got through the first chorus of the tune when he apparently called Jay Graydon. He said, "Jay, I have something that I want you guys to hear, and I think we're going to want to record it tonight."

Canning remembered the rest of the story from that evening:

[We] were sitting around trying to write something and working on the preproduction. In comes the cassette. Jay puts it on; and we listen to it, and he goes, "Wow, it's a hit. It's a number one." I think we were getting ready to go in the studio in a couple of days to start the album. . . . He said, "We're cutting this. This is going to be a hit. It's going to be the hit off the album." . . . And I didn't hear it—at all. My immediate reaction was: *That is such a piece of shit. . . . Why is he so sure this thing is a hit?* Now, the demo, to be fair, came in from a couple of Nashville songwriters, so it was not written as an R&B song. . . . It didn't have a jazz flavor whatsoever. . . . It had a really dorky, like, a bad drum machine kinda goin' on. But that's the difference between a guy like me and a guy like Jay Graydon. Jay heard it right away. He said, "It's a hit, it's going to be a hit for Al Jarreau, no question about it."

Canning, Rains, and Lewis weren't the only ones with doubts about the song. Even Murrah, the song's cocomposer, was self-deprecating about it. "It's pretty simplistic, in the lyric," he admitted in the *Unsung* documentary. "I would say it's so meaningful because of [Al's] phrasing. He's a master phraser." For his part, Graydon plainly stated, "'We're in This

Love Together' is the most milquetoast of them all. But, [Al] sang it great, and it was a big hit, so that was the bait for the album. . . . This album was so loaded with jazz, but still enough pop and funk to catch both those markets."[10]

"We're in This Love Together" went on to become Al's first top twenty pop single, and it expanded his reach into new genres like none of his previous songs had done. "It broke open a lot of barriers for Al," said Steven Ivory, veteran music and cultural journalist. "He got airplay in places that he never thought he'd be played." "He pulled it off, man," said Marcus Miller, one of the most influential producers and bass players in the business (who both produced and played on Al's 1994 *Tenderness* album). "And that's the song that really kinda changed his career."

"Roof Garden," one of the funkier songs on the album, was at least partly responsible for pushing *Breakin' Away* to the top of the R&B charts and to number nine on the pop charts. Tom Canning related how "Roof Garden" came to be:

Al had his writing habits, . . . and he'd be boppin' around and coming up with ideas, and he'd just sing them into the cassette player. . . . So he was still doing that, and he gave me a cassette [and] he said, "I've got a lot of stuff on here. And just tell me if you find anything you think's good [that] we could bring in to work on with Jay." So, as had been my habit in the past, I listened to the entire cassette. . . . I'm listening along, and I just didn't hear anything that I thought was cool. . . . And then all of a sudden there was one thing that came out. And all he had was *[Canning sings the opening riff to "Roof Garden"]*, and he just kept singing that. . . . So I called him and told him, and he said, "Oh, yeah, cool. Let's take that in and see what happens." . . . Jay really got involved in the writing, but it started from the humblest of beginnings, with just some little fifteen-second thing on a thirty-minute tape that just had the little germ of the idea there.[11]

"We went funk central on 'Roof Garden,'" Jay Graydon said. "We wanted a party song. And you know, by the end of the tune it's in party land and groovin'. It's funk." A great deal of the funkiness was contributed by George Duke, Al's former collaborator at the Half Note in San Francisco,

Breakin' Away (1981) won Grammy Awards in both pop and jazz. The cover photograph was taken by Al's wife, Susan.

who played Fender Rhodes piano on the track. *Breakin' Away* definitively contained songs that could be variously defined as pop, jazz, and R&B. "Why not sing pop, jazz, and R&B?" Chris Walker, Al's longtime bassist, asked in the *Unsung* documentary. "I mean he's one of the few people on the planet that could do it—and do it convincingly."

Though Al never spoke of it publicly, the lyrics and the title of "Roof Garden" may have been inspired by a famous ballroom in downtown Milwaukee. Known as the Wisconsin Roof Ballroom or the Wisconsin Roof Garden, the room was on the top floor of the prominent Carpenter Building, which later housed the Wisconsin Theatre. In the 1920s and 1930s, the Wisconsin Roof hosted many of the great swing bands of the era, and some of the most important of these were Black bands. The clientele in those decades, however, was white, whether by policy or simply by unspoken rule. The ballroom survived the swing era, finally closing in 1958, the year Al graduated from high school. Although Al probably never went to the Wisconsin Roof due to his age, his strict upbringing, and his race, he must certainly have been aware of it.

The rest of *Breakin' Away*, like *This Time*, presented some variety, but held together as a showcase of Al Jarreau in 1981. With Graydon now playing an integral part in the album's production, *Breakin' Away* included five Jarreau/Canning/Graydon originals: "Roof Garden" and "Easy," which has a nice, slightly funky samba feel, both give Al some room to improvise and display his jazz chops; "Our Love" is a ballad that allows Al to flaunt his romantic side; the album opener, "Closer to Your Love," is a catchy funk-disco groove; and the title cut, "Breakin' Away," perhaps surprisingly, charted in the top 100 as a single, even though it doesn't immediately seem like the type of song that would stick in listeners' ears. Richard Page contributed a very nice song, "My Old Friend," which Al reprised on his 2014 tribute album to George Duke.

The big jazz tune on *Breakin' Away* was another Dave Brubeck piece, "Blue Rondo à la Turk." Like Al's earlier jazz hits "Take Five" and "Spain," Al's version of the Brubeck, which he titled "(Round, Round, Round) Blue Rondo à la Turk," was a virtuosic display of Al's abilities on a complex mixed-meter exercise that Brubeck must have delighted in back in 1959. Al solos imaginatively on this one and wows listeners with his delivery of the lyric. Milcho Leviev, a recent immigrant from Bulgaria, supplied the arrangement and brilliant playing, as Larry Williams had done for "Spain."[12] The album closes with a pop song from the 1950s, "Teach Me Tonight." The most famous previous versions of this song were probably those by Dinah Washington and Joe Williams, who was accompanied by Count Basie's band, but over the years, the tune was recorded by everyone from Nat King Cole, Peggy Lee, and Frank Sinatra to Marvin Gaye, Phoebe Snow, and, in 2020, James Taylor. Al's version was popular—he recorded it again a couple of years later, in 1984 (on *In London*), and performed it for many years of his career.

One aspect of the music business came into play with *Breakin' Away* that had not been crucial earlier, despite Patrick Rains's foresight back in 1977: video. Music Television, or MTV, debuted in the summer of 1981, just a month after the release of *Breakin' Away*. It would still be a couple of years before Michael Jackson would dominate MTV, radio, and the broader pop culture with his *Thriller* album and its attendant videos. But MTV immediately became a venue for any artist wanting to push new "product." And Warner Bros. was willing to jump in with videos for Al. Although Al was already forty years old, he still looked youthful, handsome, and athletic on the screen.

The "Roof Garden" video opens with an empty dance studio; Al fades into the picture, along with Tom Canning, who plays the opening musical lick on a Fender Rhodes piano. (Although Canning appears in the video,

George Duke played on the album track.) Soon, a racially mixed group of professional dancers enters the room, and they energetically dance their way through the whole film. Al gets plenty of screen time, lip-synching the vocals; Canning is the only instrumentalist to appear on screen. Al gets in a few modest but agile dance steps during the video. And at the very end, other "amateur" dancers show up, presumably just young people wanting to dance and have a good time.

The video for "We're in This Love Together" was recorded on the same day and in the same space as "Roof Garden." This one, though, features only a band (Fender Rhodes piano, electric bass, guitar, alto saxophone, and drums) and Al. The "band members," who were Tom Canning's friends (and possibly musicians in their own right), try mightily to look as if they are actually playing in the background. Al is dressed in an outfit quite similar to the one he is wearing on the album cover of *Breakin' Away* (in a photograph taken by his wife, Susan): a pink shirt, white trousers, and jacket.

Canning has pleasant memories of that day spent in a warehouse. He recalled the dancers had already worked out much of their routine beforehand. Al enjoyed jamming with them, improvising his part in the dancing as he would in his music onstage. The quick day of filming was a far cry from what the production of music videos would soon become, when huge amounts of money were spent on snazzy locations, exotic settings, and all sorts of extravagances. Surely, though, this straightforward presentation of a relatively simple song, delivered by a master singer who also happened to be attractive and engaged in his craft, was effective in helping to sell records.

Breakin' Away was a huge commercial success for Al. It reached the number one spot on both the jazz and R&B charts, and it stayed on the Billboard top 200 chart for two years (a very impressive run), peaking at number nine. The single "We're in This Love Together" made it to number fifteen on the pop charts, and up to number six on both the R&B and adult contemporary charts. In 1982, the singles "Breakin' Away" and "Teach Me Tonight" also charted in all three categories. The album became certified platinum, selling more than one million copies. And the success was not strictly commercial. At the 1982 Grammy Awards, the album won Best Pop Vocal Performance, Male, while "Blue Rondo" won Best Jazz Vocal

Al holds the two awards he won for *Breakin' Away* at the 1982 Grammy Awards show.
AP PHOTO/REED SAXON

Performance, Male. As Patrick Rains said, the success of *Breakin' Away* "changed Al's life."

Predictably, *Breakin' Away*'s big success was greeted with mixed reactions in the jazz press. Al was treated to his second big feature in *Down Beat* in the February 1982 issue—and this was even before the Grammys had been announced. Not surprisingly, Steve Bloom's article was titled "Breaking Away." It's prefaced by a literary bit of description that almost sounds like poetry, "The sound is metallic and airy and generally reminiscent of a flute, but there is no flute. The next sound thumps and bomps like a conga drum, but there is no drum. Finally, we are treated to a Brazilian orchestra of snaps, crackles, and pops, but again, there is no orchestra. Ladies and gentlemen, jazz-pop singer Al Jarreau, a human synthesizer of sorts, is simply strutting his stuff."[13]

The article proper begins with a description of a Jarreau performance that Bloom had attended at the Uris Theatre on Broadway in New York City. Although it "happened not to be one of Jarreau's better performances," Bloom recounts a moment in the middle of the show when Al "climbed aboard a stool for a stellar recital of Jerome Kern's *All The Things You Are*."

"As he sustained the song's last note," Bloom writes, "choruses of 'bravos' began cascading throughout the theater. For those who must question, Jarreau had proven that he is more than just a vocal chameleon—he is a consummate jazz singer."

While extoling Al's jazz singing on the one hand, Bloom also mentions his pop influences. He adds, "Jarreau is certainly neither Joe Williams nor Mel Tormé, and few would argue that he has the scatting ability of the late Eddie Jefferson. He's more of a '70s creation; schooled in jazz but weaned on pop, Jarreau's your basic Top-40 radio baby." Interestingly, rather than referring to Breakin' Away as a pop or R&B album, Bloom calls it "the hands-down commercial jazz success story of 1981."

Bloom also mentions Al's appearance on several late-night television shows and describes at some length a skit that Al did on one of the newer entries in late-night television: "His visit to NBC's SCTV Network 90 was especially hilarious. In one skit Jarreau starred as The Jazz Singer, a black orphan boy who was adopted by a Lower East Side tailor and decides (against his father's wishes) to become a cantor instead of a pop singer. 'So, vat about da rhythm and bluce?' his dad cries out at one point, 'I should've adopted Barry White.' Disowned, Izell (Jarreau) heads out for a life devoted to the Talmud."

This skit was obviously a spoof of the classic 1927 movie The Jazz Singer starring Al Jolson, the son of Jewish immigrants who had come to fame performing in vaudeville theaters in blackface. The SCTV writers inverted the plot from a story about a youth trying to break out of his family's conservatism to a story about a traditionalist youth (Al) whose family wanted him to strive for popular (and commercial) success. Considering Al's strict upbringing as the son of a Seventh-day Adventist minister, he must have found this skit particularly entertaining. It should be noted that at the time when the SCTV show aired, The Jazz Singer had been recently remade with Neil Diamond in the starring role, probably inspiring this spoof.

Much of Bloom's article is a recap of Al's life and career, with a few insights that had not appeared in print before. But at the end of the article, Bloom addresses the issue of Al's commitment, or lack thereof, to jazz: "At the time when I started recording," Al is quoted as saying, "I was probably much closer to that hard-core jazzer kind of guy. I'm loosening up now. I don't have any axes to grind anymore. The jazz character is always going to be in my music, but I'm kind of curious about how things are going and how my music is developing. It's definitely going in different ways than it was going then."

Bloom includes a quote from an unnamed review of *This Time* that describes Al as "an exceptional vocal artist whose mind seems to be turning to cotton candy." Bloom then does his best to interpret the quote: "The suggestion is that his lyrics are increasingly lacking depth. It could also be submitted that his songs carry less emotional punch than before and that they sound more and more like stylishly imitable pop-funk. Finally, it seems that his usually unusual vocal fun & games are somehow getting lost in the shuffle."

Bloom then transcribes Al's response to this critique:

"I think those are all valid comments," Jarreau rather calmly responds. "At times I feel I want to be a little lighter than, say, being heartrending. I also honestly think I can reach more people that way. But, then again, I like to do a lot of music, so I don't intend to be confined by my critics or anybody else. I might want to do some punk rock & roll someday. And I like to sing rhythm & blues, too. I may funk for an album and then do some jazz. Or my next thing might be inspired by some classical pieces of music 'cause that's in me too. But you can be sure of one thing—whatever it is I do, it'll always be fine music."

The issue of Al's weak songwriting also surfaced in an article that appeared in *The Black Collegian*. Reviewer James Borders begins with a critique of both Jarreau and the music business of the time:

This latest release by the singer's singer, Al Jarreau, is another example of the state of the art in musical vocalization with a conscious eye toward commercial appeal. As he has in every album save his first [*We Got By*], Jarreau outclasses his material. The difference in *Breakin' Away* is that he does it with a lighter touch this time around.

The album is an exercise in upbeat production, but try as it might, it cannot conceal the facts that: 1. Jarreau's songwriting skills are definitely not being heavily taxed, and 2. There is a general crisis in good, contemporary lyrics.

The economics of the music business are, in many cases, [forcing] singers to write their own songs. They can make more money that way. But does that mean they have to write banal material just to save a buck, especially when, in Jarreau's case, they have demonstrated highly developed song-writing skills?[14]

This subject was addressed by two of Al's musical colleagues in the *Unsung* documentary, as well. Larry Williams admitted that Al "got a lot of criticism from jazz purists for not being a jazz purist." And Marcus Miller added, "There's no support for jazz musicians. So, Al was like, 'Am I gonna go back to just going straight jazz, or should I ride this train for a little bit and see where this takes me?'"[15]

Patrick Rains put a slightly different spin on the same idea years later when he said, "The jazz community doesn't want you to be successful, because they take the position that you've sold out."[16] And although Al gave the impression of being unfazed by critics who called him a jazz sellout, Rains conceded that it may have wounded Al more than most people knew: "I think that for Al, he wanted the commercial success; he wanted, [or] at least he grew into wanting, it. And grew comfortable having it. But he always . . . when something would happen, and there would be a jazz guy or a critic who would pan something, you know, he was able to let it just slide off his shoulders. At the same time, that doesn't necessarily [reflect] what's going on inside of his belly, right?"

Al had made a conscious decision not to limit himself—musically or commercially. Similar decisions made throughout the rest of his career would continue to position him in an uneasy place between convenient categories.

THIS TIME
Warner Bros., 1980

This Time, the first of Al's albums produced by Jay Graydon, represented a departure from Al's earlier albums, from the look of the record jacket to the first notes of the first track.

A large, impressive group of musicians worked on the album—and they were definitely the "A-listers" of the time. An important addition was the horn section, which would become increasingly prominent on Al's next two albums. Trumpeter Jerry Hey was on his way to becoming one of the very top sidemen in the Los Angeles studios, and his arrangements and lead trumpet playing on *This Time* and upcoming albums were a vital part of Al's sound during this period. Guitarist/producer Graydon was relatively inconspicuous as a player here. Especially important in the rhythm section on this album, besides Al's constant sidekick Tom Canning, were Abe Laboriel on bass and drummers Steve Gadd, Carlos Vega, and Ralph Humphrey. Larry Williams contributed both the Fender Rhodes comping and a superb synthesizer solo to "Spain." Additional keyboard layers were added to the album by other crack studio musicians Greg Mathieson, Michael Omartian, and David Foster (who had been Pat Rains's first choice to produce the album). Al's former collaborator George Duke supplied the funky Fender Rhodes comping for "Distracted." According to Canning, Duke was also crucial to the production of "Alonzo."[17] In his special thanks and acknowledgments for the album, Al wrote: "George Duke, your early work on 'Alonzo' and 'Distracted' turned out to be major and invaluable to the final concept. Thank you."

Outside of his reworking of Chick Corea's "Spain," Al does not improvise much on this album, but he does scat briefly on the fadeout of "Distracted." His vocal percussion is briefly highlighted on "Love Is Real," on which he also sings a complicated jazzy solo line in octaves with Jerry Hey's harmon-muted trumpet. Al's vocal flute imitation shows up—in harmony, no less—on "Alonzo."

After the high energy of most of the album, Earl Klugh's lovely "This Time," featuring his tasty solo, makes for some welcome musical and sonic relief as the closing track on the record. It is a rare moment of gentleness among the higher-energy songs on the four records discussed in this chapter and chapter 13.

At the sessions for *This Time*, Al did attempt to record "Spain" with its composer, pianist Chick Corea, and his longtime bassist, Stanley Clarke—both of whom played on the fabulous original recording of the piece on Chick's 1973 Return to Forever album, *Light as a Feather*. Things didn't work out with Corea and Clarke, but Al thanks them in the album's acknowledgments, writing, "You guys really helped us to make the classic 'Spain' a classic again. All my love."

BREAKIN' AWAY
Warner Bros., 1981

Breakin' Away was Al's first album to go platinum. It earned him two Grammys in 1982 and marked a significant milestone on his path to stardom. The record has tended to be overwhelmed by its one huge hit, "We're in This Love Together." But, as producer Jay Graydon suggested, there is a lot of jazz-influenced material on this album. "(Round, Round, Round) Blue Rondo à la Turk" is obviously a jazz tune, and Al improvises on several other songs, even if the improvisational sections are short. He is at his creative best, however, on his more extended improv on "Roof Garden," fueled by George Duke's seriously funky comping.

According to Tom Canning, "Breakin' Away" was conceived on the streets of New York, where he and Al each came up with one of the riffs that define the first section of the song. Sometime later, when Graydon heard that combination, he quickly wrote the chorus. The soulful "Teach Me Tonight" was not the first pop cover Al had done, but it became one of his most popular remakes.

Many of the musicians on the album overlap with those who played on *This Time*, including the critical rhythm section trio of Tom Canning,

Abe Laboriel, and Steve Gadd. Other important rhythm players included keyboardists Michael Omartian, David Foster, Larry Williams, and Michael Boddicker, as well as drummer Jeff Porcaro. Williams, a vital contributor to *This Time*, supplies the fine synthesizer solo on "Easy." The horn section, once again arranged and led by trumpeter Jerry Hey, is a significant aspect of this album; Hey has a lovely flugelhorn solo on "My Old Friend."

Canning, who had learned a great deal about record production from Jay Graydon while working on *This Time*, is listed as associate producer on *Breakin' Away* (although he doesn't play quite as much here as on the earlier albums). And as he did on *This Time*, David Foster makes his presence known on *Breakin' Away*, playing beautifully on three tracks and arranging the strings on "Our Love." Hollywood studio veteran Billy Byers arranged the strings on "Teach Me Tonight."

The cover of this album isn't as stylish as the Richard Avedon photos that adorned *This Time*, but the cover photos taken by Al's wife, Susan, present him as the handsome, welcoming figure that he was.

"Girls Know How," written for the film *Night Shift* by Burt Bacharach and Carole Bayer Sager (evidently with some help from Foster, who produced the track with Graydon), appears on at least one of the expanded CD versions of *Breakin' Away*, suggesting that this track was recorded during the same period as the rest of the album. This song is discussed in more detail in chapter 16.

12

TOURING AND HOMECOMINGS

As important as Al's albums were, touring and live performances were his lifeblood in the 1970s and 1980s and, in fact, until the end of his career. In the 1982 *Down Beat* profile written by Steve Bloom, Al discussed that side of his career that was *not* about making records—a side that was ultimately more important to him. He told Bloom, "And there's one thing more that you can be sure of[:] . . . in the concert situation you'll always get every bit of Al Jarreau you've ever wanted. It's always in that situation; it's saturated with all the inventiveness and all the tripping the light fantastic."[1]

Al's tours did not remain static throughout his career, either in their length, frequency, locations, or general practice.[2] By the late 1970s, Al's concerts were being booked through the William Morris Agency, one of the largest and most prestigious agencies in the business. The "personal" agent assigned to Al at William Morris, Jay Jacobs, would line up the dates and routing on the tour and present it all to Al's manager, Patrick Rains, for his approval. Rains concentrated on the promotion of each event, working with the individual promoters' dates, and he also coordinated with Warner Bros. for its tour support, financial backing, and publicity.

Tours generally happened after the release of an album, to encourage the album's sales. But most years, Al went on at least two tours per year, so a tour might also foreshadow an as-yet-unreleased album. And while the European tour of early 1977 was a follow-up to the release of 1976's *Glow*, its primary purpose was to record the tracks for the forthcoming *Look to*

Al works his magic onstage at the Internationales Congress Centrum in Berlin, Germany, in the mid-1980s. © NOOP1958 / WIKIMEDIA COMMONS / CC-BY-SA-3.0

the Rainbow at major venues around Europe. A key reason for every tour, of course, was to keep Al in front of his audience, regardless of the status of his recordings. From 1976 to 1988, the time when Jerry Levin worked as Al's tour manager, Al toured about five to six months a year, usually in two distinct segments. And during the early years of Levin's time as manager, Al probably toured more in Europe than in the United States.

A portion of a national tour might have Al traveling throughout the Midwest, mid-Atlantic, and up and down the East Coast in just one month, playing in more than a dozen cities in venues that ranged from major concert halls and historic theaters to outdoor amphitheaters and festival stages.[3]

Throughout this period, Al had the luxury of being on double bills with other top artists. On the West Coast, he would frequently be paired with George Benson; on the East Coast, a frequent billing partner was Grover Washington Jr. The saxophonist David Sanborn (who was also managed by Patrick Rains) shared tours with Al as well. Angela Bofill, a singer-songwriter who had a hot career for a couple of years, served as opening act on the first tour that Al headlined. These artists, with Al, drew many, many fans in the late 1970s and 1980s.

Once a tour was set, Levin would deal with, as he said, "everything from A to Z." Before the tour began, he was in charge of auditioning musicians for the touring band, renting rehearsal space for the musicians to prepare, and lining up instruments and gear for the rehearsals. On the road, Levin was responsible for arranging transportation—air and ground (Al preferred to travel by train in Europe)—and all hotel bookings. For the gigs themselves, he hired all of the trucks, buses, audio gear, and lighting—everything that had to do with the production of the stage show. Most important, he settled the box office receipts with the local promoters at every performance. Levin was well qualified for all of these duties, having been a tour manager for Fleetwood Mac as well as Kenny Loggins and Jim Messina before he worked with Al. Later, while touring with Al, Jerry also served as tour director for Bette Midler. And he was not just a tour manager, but a lighting director for these artists as well. The contacts he made while working for Loggins and Midler served him well with the Jarreau organization.

Once the band got on tour, Levin explained,

My role as tour manager was more like a movie director. . . . The
thing about touring that makes it most difficult is moving around
from city to city. And I learned early on . . . that the secret to making it all work is finding the simplest amount of travel in the least
amount of time. And paying a little bit more money to stay in better
hotels. The difference that it makes is night and day, for a lot of reasons, the most important being that the amenities are a lot better,
making people feel more comfortable on the road. Usually the dining
facilities are better; there's usually a bar that stays open late—that's
really important for traveling bands. Even if guys don't drink, it's a
place to hang out—and especially on nights off. You know, it was a
way to build camaraderie. Al used to always make a point of, when
we'd go out to dinner with a record company guy or promoter, he'd
always tell me, "Make sure we get to bring the guys in the band." So
that was one of the things that made all of his bands a lot closer and
made them feel more involved and part of the project.

Another of Levin's duties as tour manager was definitely not "in the
contract." He explained, "Al never bought any clothes in his life." Perhaps,
occasionally, Al might "go in a vintage store to buy a five-dollar flannel
shirt or something." But while Jerry was manager, he said, "I bought every
bit of stage clothes that [Al] ever wore." Every time Levin saw something
that he knew Al would look great in, he'd buy it. And then, he recalled, "[Al]
was like a kid opening up Christmas presents. He'd love to get new things
to wear onstage, but he would never even go in a store."

Levin also introduced Al to the audience every night. Running the
lights, as he did, he would be stationed right next to the sound engineer.
The sound guy would hand Jerry a mike at the beginning of the show, and
he'd announce the entrance of the star. One of his introductions is saved
for posterity at the beginning of the *Look to the Rainbow* album.

Levin even participated in Al's exercise regimen while on tour. Both
men enjoyed running, and shortly after arrival in a new city, at hotel
check-in, Al would say to Jerry, "Okay, I'll see you downstairs in twenty

minutes." Then, according to Levin, "we'd go put on our jogging shoes and shorts, and we'd hit the streets. And we'd be out there for about an hour or so. Stop someplace, have an espresso, and continue on. It was really a bonding thing for us. We saw so much more of these cities that most people never see, because we'd go places where only locals would be."

This practice could lead to complications, however. On the *Rainbow* tour, the two runners took off through the streets of Oslo, Norway, in a bit of a snowstorm. They got lost, and as it approached time for the sound check at the venue, they figured they would never get there on time, especially since they didn't know where they were. They eventually flagged down a friendly Norwegian motorist who got them where they needed to go on time. One of the many photographs inside the gatefold of the double album *Look to the Rainbow* shows Al in his running gear—shorts, shoes, sweatshirt, and stocking cap—smiling and heading down the streets of some European city.

A quite different touring story sheds light on Al's interest in history and his empathic nature. On the second of two European tours that Al did in 1977, he performed in Bremen, Germany. Al, the son of a Seventh-day Adventist minister, got it in his mind that he wanted to go to the nearby site of the notorious Nazi concentration camp Bergen-Belsen. Jerry, who is Jewish, felt the experience would be traumatizing and had no interest in going. But, according to Levin, Al talked him into it, convincing him that it was part of his heritage, even though no one in his family had been at any of the camps. "It was everything I thought it would be and more," Levin said. But what he remembered most was watching Al as they went through the camp and registering how traumatized Al was. The experience was much more profound than Al had anticipated. As they drove back to Bremen, Al didn't say a word, yet Levin noticed tears streaming down his face. "Al was well versed in just about any religion you could imagine," Levin said. "He could have a conversation with just about anybody about their own religion. And I think this was just part of his education . . . and his life experience. And I'll never forget that he talked me into going. Despite the trauma, in the end, it probably was worth it, having that for my own experience."[4]

While Al enjoyed the adventure of touring in Europe, appearances in his hometown were special. In September 1980, Al sang in Uihlein Hall, the home of the Milwaukee Symphony Orchestra in the Performing Arts Center downtown. It must have been a source of considerable local pride that Al performed at this venue, a symbol of "high culture" in Milwaukee and a giant step from Al's humble professional start at the Driftwood on the north side.

Bill Milkowski reviewed the concert for the *Milwaukee Journal*, reporting: "A return visit from singer Al Jarreau is usually hailed as an event, a happening, a triumph. And Jarreau always seems to rise to this special occasion by giving a little bit more of himself before his hometown fans. . . . From entrance to exit, he wooed and won the people with his own inimitable presence—the incessant glow, the cool, down-home banter, the graceful, sensual movements about the stage. And that voice!"[5] Milkowski also did his best to describe Al's vocal feats, a task that challenged writers throughout Al's career:

It's a wonder how this impassioned vocalist keeps from straining that wonderful instrument and blowing it out every night. He uses every little sigh and corner of sound that the larynx can possibly produce. Grunts, hisses, ahhhhhs. Outrageous, uninhibited scat-singing and heavy vocal coloring that goes well beyond the realm of conventional bebop.

He imitates conga drums, flutes, cellos, trumpets, mandolins, electric guitars hooked up to wah-wah pedals. There is an endless supply of sounds in his throat, and each one comes forth as spontaneously as the next.

Al knew members of the hometown crowd personally, and Milkowski described the "shouts of encouragement [that] rang throughout the room" when Al became playful and interacted with the audience. At one point, Al put on a "funky hat" to perform a bluesy number and some women in the crowd yelled, "'Go on, honey, put it to the side.' He obliged by tilting the headpiece to a jaunty angle, then proceeded to strut about the stage like a soulful peacock on the prowl. That good-natured bit of theater harkened back to his funkier days at Lincoln High School, apparently an inside joke for the hometown friends who knew him well." After going through some of his more recent songs, he gave in to shouts for "We Got By," the auto-biographical song that was "a sentimental favorite with this audience."

A little over a year after this gig, Al was back in the Performing Arts Center. This time, Kevin Lynch reported for the *Milwaukee Journal* with the headline "Al Jarreau's Inner Electricity Charges Crowd," writing that "organic electricity engulfed Uihlein Hall" that night. He waxed poetic about this energy, revealing just how starry-eyed Al's Milwaukee fans and critics could be: "It pours straight from the vortex of the man, a force seemingly larger than one human being in its projection and multiple manifestations. But it's undeniably the solitary soul of Al Jarreau. And it is truth—the truth of honest expression, a soul releasing its essential concerns to the listener."[6]

Lynch described the capacity audience as witnessing the "extraordinary powers of a hometown singer who now belongs to the world." Milwaukee had given Al to the world, and Lynch can be forgiven for crowing about it. After talking about Al's roots and providing commentary about the band, just like Milkowski and countless other writers, Lynch could not resist trying to describe Al's unique gifts. He was about as successful as most writers, using colorful language to describe talents that are impossible to put into words. Lynch wrote, "Jarreau himself is a remarkable vocal improviser who jumps off on a rhythmic prod as easily as a Mexican jumping bean, his tongue remarkably creating quicksilver noises and peppery snatches of mimicked drums, flutes and guitars."

The review mentions a number of the tunes performed that evening, only one of which, "Easy," was on the brand-new album, *Breakin' Away*. Perhaps "We're in This Love Together" was not performed, so wasn't noted. Preventing the review from becoming completely fawning, Lynch did suggest that Al was "merely above-average as a songwriter." But his closing comment is glowing: "Whether purely creating or wisely borrowing, Jarreau makes for a show that would be electrifying even if the band unplugged to simply listen and marvel."

Only seven months later, Al was back in town, performing at what is still, at the time of this publication, advertised as the "World's Largest Music Fest," Milwaukee's Summerfest. For years, Summerfest was held over eleven consecutive days at what is now called Henry Maier Festival Park, right on the Lake Michigan shoreline. Divina Infusino wrote "Jarreau

Thrills Hometown Crowd" for the *Journal*, opening with the lines: "Milwaukee gave Al Jarreau the laurel-wreath treatment Friday night [July 2]. He had come home."[7]

Infusino traced Jarreau's career as he climbed the venue ladder of Milwaukee, from 1962 to the 1982 concert. It is notable that even the sold-out Uihlein Hall crowd of seven months earlier would have been about 2,300 fans; at Summerfest, the "conquering hero" sang for approximately 17,900. Infusino reminded readers that Al had, during his interview with Steve Bloom for the February 1982 *Down Beat* article, described his hometown as "a workaday town, you know. Lots of industry and manual labor. That's what the people do. The mentality kind of matches that thing." And at Summerfest, Al apparently "told the members of his Milwaukee audience to stand up and take a look at themselves. 'You're beautiful,' he exclaimed." While Jarreau was known throughout his career for being able to connect to just about any audience at any location, he always held a special place in his heart for Milwaukee and Milwaukeeans. "If his hometown's Cream City bricks don't look quite as glamorous to him as the adobe of Los Angeles, his present home," Infusino wrote, "the warmth that Milwaukee showed him helped him remember the virtues of his roots." The journalist also noted the racial diversity of Al's audience in Milwaukee: "Of all the Summerfest Main Stage acts so far, Jarreau drew perhaps the most racially mixed audience. With his soul in jazz and his feet in pop, Jarreau reached out to both white and black festivalgoers, or anyone else who could appreciate a remarkable voice set to pop classics and modern-day rhythms."

By this point, just a year after the release of *Breakin' Away*, the album and the hit single were definitely in the consciousness of the Milwaukee audience. According to Infusino, "They screeched after 'We're in This Love Together,'" and at one point, he bragged, "I've got a platinum record, y'all. I'm getting played on radio in the daytime now." The article concluded, "It all added up to a nearly two-hour performance by a vocal wonder who had his audience beaming with pride at a native son's international recognition."

Of course, it wasn't just Milwaukeeans who were drawn to Al's magnetic performance persona. Jerry Levin remembered the way Al could work a crowd in the late 1970s and early 1980s, especially in locations where concertgoers were not predisposed to be impressed:

He was awesome in that he never, [or] hardly ever, did anything the
same way twice. . . . And there are so many times that I remember
watching an entire audience grow from passive people . . . or [from]
not knowing who he was, especially the crowds in the larger cities
all over the world—Paris, London, New York, Los Angeles—people
would sit with their arms crossed, and their attitude would be like,
"Okay, show me. What have you got?" And to watch the crowd's
transformation from the time that he would walk onstage until
when he left was unbelievable.[8]

Al would, in fact, as Steve Bloom had predicted in his 1982 *Down Beat*
profile, deliver "every bit of Al Jarreau that you've ever wanted," night after
night, year after year. And even after seeing hundreds of Al's live shows
over more than a decade, Levin admitted, "I'm serious, I cried almost every
night. There was something about almost every show that was emotional."

At another concert in the Midwest a few weeks after the Summerfest
date, Al gave one fan the experience of a lifetime. The *Indianapolis Star*
related: "After seeking an explanation of the word 'Hoosier' from the crowd
[Al] was given the following definition by a pretty lady who edge[d] up to
the stage to whisper to him: 'A Hoosier is someone who loves you very
much.' Jarreau got down on his hands and knees, took her hand in his and
sang the next song, 'Teach Me Tonight,' right to her. Needless to say, the
poor woman had to be led away by a security guard as she was too dazed
to move by herself."[9]

This "poor woman" was one of a legion of Al's huge following of female
fans, some of whom had been following him since his early days with Julio
Martinez. It didn't matter whether he was in Milwaukee or Indianapolis,
Hamburg or Paris. Many women were drawn to this tall, athletic, handsome
man who sang beautifully about love. And, as mentioned by almost everyone who knew him or attended his concerts, he had the ability to make every
member of the audience feel that he was singing directly to them.

Some of these female fans were not shy about showing their affection.
Al's older sister Rose Marie remembered a number of occasions when she
would be hanging out backstage after one of Al's concerts and see women
practically flinging themselves at Al.[10] She saw the very same thing happen when Susan was right alongside Al. He surely received even more

attention when his wife and sister were not around. Al was never without female attention and companionship.

A sort of after-show routine was established during Jerry Levin's years on the road with Al. Once everyone had been greeted backstage, and business and niceties had been taken care of, Al would go somewhere, often back to the hotel bar, and hold court—or, as Levin put it, "preach." The group that followed—one could even call it an entourage—might be large or small, made up of fans, friends, or members of the band and crew. But Al would be in the middle of it all, thoroughly enjoying the socializing—and his red wine—after a hard night's work. The gatherings would extend into the wee hours, and chances were good that Al would be the last to leave.

Another Wisconsin appearance, in 1982, merits mention. Probably influenced by the explosion of good fortune in Al's career, his alma mater Ripon College contacted him early that spring about receiving a "distinguished alumni citation" in May.[11] Although that date didn't work for the Jarreau team, arrangements were made for Al to receive the citation in October, on homecoming weekend. Al's class of 1962 would be celebrating its twentieth reunion. Though strings likely had to be pulled in Al's schedule to get him to Ripon the weekend of October 15–17, he said yes to the engagement.

Al arrived at the nearby Oshkosh airport around 9 p.m. on a private plane on Friday, October 15. After dropping his things at the campus's faculty club, where he would spend the next two nights, he arrived in the Rodman Center for the Fine Arts around 10:15. He was led to the choir room, where an eager crowd of close to a hundred met him, despite the fact that the room was certainly not approved by the local fire marshal to hold more than seventy-five.[12] Al held a lively conversation with the starstruck audience of students, faculty, alumni, and community members until after midnight. The discussion was wide-ranging, with Al's charisma and laid-back charm on display throughout. According to the *Oshkosh Daily Northwestern*, "Jarreau's answers [to the audience's questions ranged] just as widely as his voice—from humorous to philosophical, poetic, but above all, sincere."[13] Prompted by a member of the college's admissions office, Al talked about how he ended up at Ripon from his high school in Milwaukee, and he went on to relate stories from his time as a student, including some of his embarrassing academic moments. He spoke at some

Al holds court with Ripon College friends, fans, former schoolmates, and students in the choir room at the Rodman Center for the Arts in October 1982. COURTESY OF RIPON COLLEGE

length about the early days of his career, from Milwaukee to Iowa to San Francisco, and then about the second phase of his career in which he began to achieve a considerable amount of fame; in 1982, he was still in the relatively early stages of this phase.

He also made a couple of personal disclosures. Al confessed that he still got nervous before some shows, even as an experienced performer. Of all his shows, he claimed he had been the most nervous at one in Lake Tahoe with Sammy Davis Jr. in the audience.[14] An article in the Ripon student newspaper later reported: "Jarreau admits that his career has been a detriment to other important things in his life. 'Family life is hard,' he said, 'because I'm gone a lot, and when I am home I'm gone a lot in the recording studio.' He makes his home in Los Angeles now, 'once in a while.'" At the end of the session, Al happily signed albums and other memorabilia.[15] Surprisingly, a photograph taken at this event appeared in the December 11 issue of *Billboard*, on the news page.

On Saturday, Al was presented with the alumni citation at halftime of the homecoming football game by college president Bernard Adams and the president-elect of the alumni association. A group photo was taken of the returning members of the class of 1962. In the evening, Al relaxed with old friends at a reception and dinner. His companion for much of the weekend was Peter Bock, his old buddy from their college vocal quartet, the Indigos.

After brunch on Sunday morning, Ripon's usually calm day of rest was interrupted by the sounds of a helicopter lifting off from one of the school's athletic fields as Al left for Milwaukee. He arrived in the city just in time to sing a rousing version of the national anthem at County Stadium prior to Game 5 of the 1982 World Series. Months later, in a 1983 *USA Today* article, Al said that singing the anthem during the World Series "was the nicest dream [he'd] ever had come true."[16] A photo of the anthem's presentation by an intense-looking Jarreau appeared prominently in the next day's *Milwaukee Journal*.[17]

Wisconsin, however, was not the only place that wanted to lay claim to Al Jarreau. On the eve of a concert appearance in the Minneapolis–St. Paul area in 1977 (which would kick off the tour to promote *Look to the Rainbow*), the *Minneapolis Star* published an article by Jon Bream titled "Jarreau's Parading Home with Breakthrough Punch."[18] Bream reported on Jarreau's progress since he had been "the leader of a popular Twin Cities bar band" seven years earlier. Bream quoted Al discussing how important live performance was to him. "Generally, my thing works better live," he said. "The magic, the magnetism, the energy flow is so much more prevalent than it is in the studio." Bream agreed, writing, "Jarreau is a physical, dynamic singer whose stage improvising was missing on his first two studio albums. Onstage, he becomes a boxer with his voice being his instrument to kayo [KO, or knock out] the crowd. He bobs, weaves, jabs and punches with scat singing that puts him as far above the competition as Muhammad Ali was in his prime."

Seven years later, when Al returned to the Twin Cities and performed in Northrop Auditorium in Minneapolis in the summer of 1984, Bream reviewed the concert in the *Minneapolis Star and Tribune*. Noting again that Jarreau had been a local star, Bream gave this perceptive assessment of just where Al was in his career at that moment: "In the 13 years since he left Minneapolis to find stardom in Los Angeles, [Al Jarreau] has been swept up in vocal gymnastics, mired in scat jazz, enamored with easy-listening

Al sings the National Anthem at Game 5 of the 1982 World Series between the Milwaukee Brewers and the St. Louis Cardinals at Milwaukee's County Stadium in October 1982. *MILWAUKEE JOURNAL*, OCTOBER 18, 1982

pop music and attracted to disco boogie. Now he has finally put all the elements together in a well-defined, sophisticated pop-soul style that is immediately recognizable as Al Jarreau music. And that helped make his concert Friday night . . . the most focused and satisfying performance he has given here."[19]

While writing a serious critical piece, Bream gave a glowing review of Al's stage persona and didn't ignore the local connection: "The warmth of and generosity of Jarreau's personality matched the warmth and generosity of his music. He told spontaneous and canned jokes with equal finesse, he made a few of the right local references (e.g., the Depot, his old stomping ground . . .), he danced like a graceful mime[,] . . . he answered a request for the jazz standard 'Take Five,' and he tossed in a couple of dramatic scenarios to let his faithful know that he has been preparing for his foray into acting." Bream ended by acknowledging the sense of ownership felt by the Minneapolis crowd. Just as Milwaukee and Ripon rightfully touted Al as their own, the Twin Cities wanted to claim a piece of him, as did Iowa City, southern California, San Francisco, Hamburg, and probably many other towns and cities around the world.

13

CHANGING COURSE

The 1983 album *Jarreau* was a continuation of the process and the sounds that had made *This Time* and *Breakin' Away* such big successes. Jay Graydon's production work (with Tom Canning again as associate producer) led to Al's third straight hit album, with *Jarreau* peaking at number six on the traditional jazz chart in *Billboard*. It stayed on that chart for an amazing eighty weeks. The album's opener, "Mornin'," rose as high as twenty-one on the pop singles chart, six on R&B, and all the way up to two on the adult contemporary list. The album's second cut, "Boogie Down," got as high as nine in R&B and in the seventies on the pop charts. Both singles were also very popular internationally, especially in Europe. A third single from the album, "Trouble in Paradise," had its own healthy life on the charts.

The success of the first two hits was due, as is almost always the case, to the skillful combination of music and lyrics. Both songs reflected the positive philosophy that came to be associated with Al—that the world is basically a good place and that, if people work at it, everyone can get along and succeed.

Jay Graydon, who cowrote "Mornin'" with Al and David Foster, reflected, "It's almost a perfect song. I can't find any fault in it. . . . We changed everything. We broke the rules." Bassist Nathan East described it as a song that "seems like it was written a thousand years ago." "For me," he said, "it's almost like a spiritual awakening."[1] "Mornin'" is a love song, with the focus on the narrator's upbeat state of mind. The climactic verse reinforces the positive message: "I know I can / Like any man /

Acting out the words of his hit single "Mornin'," Al reaches out to "touch the face of God" at the Palais des Sports in Paris, France, in 1983. © NICOLAS PERRIER / DALLE

Reach out my hand / And touch the face of God."[2] Marcus Miller addressed the musical highlight—and high point—of this infectious song, where Al builds through an ascending line that climaxes on his high A: "It just goes into echo. And it's beautiful, but that really gives you the sense that he's touching the face of God. . . . And Al was pretty proud of that [high] note."

The official video for the song is truly remarkable. Only someone as sunny as Al Jarreau could pull off an animated feature talking to a radio ("Mr. Radio"), a bowl of breakfast cereal ("little Cheerios"), a bird ("sister Oriole"), a diminutive "Mr. Shoe Shine Man," and a bridge ("Mr. Golden Gate"). He strolls, dancelike, through what is almost a fairyland, eventually grabbing a large bunch of balloons and floating off into the sky. By the time he is ready to approach the face of God, and his climactic high A, he is suspended in the sky without the support of the balloons. Throughout, he has a beatific look on his face and a smile so big, it's a wonder he can even sing. Of course, he was actually lip syncing, not singing, in the video. "Some guys would do a Disney cartoon video like that, and it would be really cheesy," Larry Williams reflected years after the song's release. "It really fit Al. I mean Al has so much lightness of spirit. I think that all came through."[3]

Although some might dismiss the album's second song, "Boogie Down" (written by Al and keyboardist Michael Omartian), as just a straightforward dance tune, Al regularly pointed out that there's a message in this song.[4] In the 2020 *Unsung* documentary, Al's nephew Kenton Clayton translated the song's lyrics "I can be what I want to / and all I need is to / get my boogie down" as being "about having hard work and focusing [on] your craft." According to Clayton, "It's an inspiration to anybody who wants to dream big."[5] Al's longtime bassist Chris Walker had a similar understanding of the song's meaning: "With inspiring lyrics like that, it's like, how can you just slouch? No, you owe it to yourself to be the best you can be." When Al spoke about the song, he said, "It feels great. Maybe that's the most important thing I do, is to say something to somebody that gives them the inspiration to 'be all that you can be' [*laughs*]. Yeah, that's great stuff."

Interestingly, the official video for "Boogie Down" reverts back to the low-tech, low-budget look of the videos for "We're in This Love Together" and "Roof Garden," with an even smaller cast. Al is the focus of the film, lip-synching to the album's track, dancing in place, and doing some "air" bass, drum, and saxophone playing as a photographer snaps shots of him in several different outfits (one of which appears on the cover of the *Jarreau* album). It's somewhat surprising that a flashier video wasn't produced for this riotously funky tune.

Of the *Jarreau* singles that charted, "Trouble in Paradise," by the songwriting team of Graydon, Greg Mathieson, and Trevor Veitch, is probably the least distinguished. Decades later, it doesn't grab a listener like "Mornin'" or "Boogie Down." But it works, and by the end of the track, Al is definitely selling it.

After the release of *Jarreau*, Al was interviewed by Craig Modderno in the summer of 1983 for a feature in *USA Today*.[6] In the article, Al still seemed to be searching for a straightforward way to describe his musical style—not just to readers, but also to those in the music industry. "I'm a fusion singer," he said. "I take different styles of music and blend them together." Yet, Modderno acknowledged that Al's most recent albums had produced "some carping from jazz purists that Jarreau [had] sold out for pop success." Al responded to this by bringing up the issue of accessibility. "At times I think I've given people too many types of music at once, more than they can deal with," he reflected. "With my album *Breakin' Away*, I started to make my music more accessible to a mass audience. Now I'm writing or co-authoring many of my tunes. That's opened me up emotionally to my fans."

Also in this feature, Al made an interesting statement about race, an issue he very rarely discussed publicly. He said, "I've always wanted to help break down the racial and musical barriers of contemporary radio," suggesting that his attempts to appeal to larger audiences may have been motivated by the racial inequities he recognized in the music industry. By this time, as radio stations had begun to focus on particular genres, like pop, R&B, and adult contemporary, they targeted audiences that were often split down racial lines. Not only did that fracturing of the market go against Al's values, but it was also bad for his album sales.

Whatever his motivation, Al's efforts to create accessible, appealing pop music were successful. Propelled by its two hit singles, *Jarreau* was another big hit, staying on the charts for a year and a half. This third huge record in a row for Al solidified his position as a major artist in the worlds

Jarreau (1983) was the third
consecutive hit album for the
team of Al Jarreau, Jay Graydon,
and Tom Canning.

of pop, jazz, and R&B. And those three hit records—*This Time, Breakin'*
Away, and *Jarreau*—were all tied together by Graydon's production; the
songwriting trio of Graydon, Canning, and Al; the key rhythm players on
the records (such as Steve Gadd and Abe Laboriel); and the horn arrangements of Jerry Hey.

Tom Canning considered the late 1970s and early 1980s to be a magical
period in American popular music, pointing out that music could thrive
commercially, even if it wasn't in the pop category.[7] Al Jarreau and George
Benson had broken down barriers between jazz, pop, and R&B; Steely Dan
was making great "pop" records featuring top studio musicians (including, prominently, Steve Gadd) and even jazz greats like Wayne Shorter;
and Earth, Wind & Fire had concocted a mix of R&B, funk, and soul that
crossed boundaries. Weather Report—an ensemble revered by Al that
was generally classified as a jazz group and featured jazz greats Shorter,
Josef Zawinul, Peter Erskine, and Jaco Pastorius—was creating records,
especially 1977's *Heavy Weather*, that sold almost like pop hits.[8] Wayne,
Jaco, and Erskine even performed and recorded with another genre buster,
singer-songwriter Joni Mitchell.

For Al, that magical period included a record label that stayed with
him, a talented and savvy producer, and the ability to hire the right players.
These elements made it possible for Al's very personal music to attract an
audience larger than anyone could have dreamed ten years earlier. Years

later, Al talked about this era in his career with great fondness: "I think that period with Jay Graydon was a very creative period, during a time [when] the attitude of the music community allowed for that kind of creativity and they gave me a kind of license to go for it in that way."⁹

But by 1984, this golden age was beginning to come to an end. Radio shows, and even radio stations, that featured a wide variety of music started to disappear. This fragmentation of the market was not good news for those artists in the middle. Within Al's camp, there was a sense that it was time for Al to move on, musically.

Canning described his sense of stagnation and attempts to find a new path forward:

We were continuing, planning on going ahead with another album after *Jarreau*. And . . . the touring leading up to that, in support of *Breakin' Away*, was getting a bit taxing. Even though we had great cats who had been playing in the band—I mean, the drummers Carlos Vega, Ralph Humphrey, and Alex Acuna [were] major dudes. And Larry [Williams] went out sometimes, and we did double keys [two keyboardists]. So, it wasn't like there was a lack of musicianship. But to me, something was missing. There was nothing wrong with the big audiences and the increase in the receipt at the box office, the hotels, and all of that. And we were all trying to do our very best. But . . . for me personally . . . it really needed something, some new blood. Something. I was not initially thinking, "Well—maybe it's time for a new musical director" [someone who would replace Canning]. But more like, thinking ahead, we really don't want to do another record just like [*This Time, Breakin' Away*, and *Jarreau*]. . . . There's a language and a vocabulary that had started, and then reached a kind of high-water mark.

Jay [Graydon] and I had actually been talking about the same thing, and he said, "Man, we gotta get a little more modern with what's going on." Drum machines [and] the synth world were starting up. . . . So, he and I wrote two or three grooves, which he seemed to really like, and we thought they were pretty cool. However, when we got together with Al and played them for him, he hated them. Not just "I don't know about that." He really didn't like them at all. And I

· was going, "Whoa. That's the first time that's happened." I didn't take it like, "Well, he doesn't know what he's talking about." I was just very surprised. So, we tried some other things and . . . just didn't get anything. It was very unexpected—and unsettling.

After some serious deliberation, Canning decided it was time for him to leave Al's team. As he put it,

> We had ten amazing years together. Starting from absolutely nothing in 1974, we gradually stepped into uncharted territory and eventually reached that very rare intersection of creativity and commercial success. There was an audience of millions in that era that loved and appreciated Alwin for just that. It was so incredibly beautiful and wonderful, especially in light of what's happened to the music business since then. It really was a magic time. Looking back on it now, I feel incredibly lucky to have been a part of it.

Al's next album, *High Crime*, would sound markedly different from those that had come before as the team dove head-first into what Canning referred to as "the synth world"—drum machines and the electronic sounds that were in the vanguard of pop music in 1984. Synthesizers had been a part of the Jarreau sound since at least 1977, when Canning began playing unobtrusive string lines on a "string machine" on tour. On the first two Graydon-produced albums, *This Time* and *Breakin' Away*, synthesizers became increasingly conspicuous and important. (On tour, however, they did not seem quite as integral to the band's sound as they were on record, even when two keyboardists played on the tours.)

The team went all in with synths on *High Crime*. Just one song on the album features acoustic piano and a live drummer—the most traditional track on the record, "After All"—and a live bass player, the excellent Nathan East, appears on just two tunes, including "Fallin'," which East cocomposed. Someone had fun in the credits of the album's liner notes naming fictitious drummers for almost every track, with such monikers as Skinsoh Umor, Chip McSticks, Tyrone B. Feedback, and Tubs Margranate. On "Let's Pretend," a fictitious Pat Mostelotto is listed as playing "Your

Fill of Electronic Drums," and O. Rapage—a thin disguise of cocomposer Richard Page's name—is also listed on drums.

The album's opening cut, "Raging Waters," blasts in with a very funky, fast synth bass line and a driving electronic drum beat. The music was contemporary, edgy, and compelling; but it was not the Al Jarreau that audiences were accustomed to. Written by Al, Graydon, and keyboardist Robbie Buchanan, "Raging Waters" also prominently features Graydon's guitar work. Al sings with a palpable intensity. It's not surprising that Al performed this song as the opener at concerts during the follow-up tour to this album, which resulted in the *In London* album. "It was a great opportunity to see if those aggressive songs fit Al," Graydon said. "Of course I think it worked out, but I said we shouldn't make ["Raging Waters"] the first song of the album so we don't surprise Al's fans who are not familiar with this type of song. In the end, Al's manager [Pat Rains] insisted we make it the first song, so that's what happened."[10] "Raging Waters" was the second single to be released from the album. It did not make the pop charts, but it reached number forty-two on the R&B list.

Side one of the original LP features a number of different electronically established grooves, yet the only song that really caught on commercially was "After All," the one song on the album that sounded like "traditional" Al Jarreau. It is a richly romantic ballad, composed by Graydon and David Foster, with lyrics written by Al. Foster supplies lush keyboard sounds to the arrangement, and Graydon contributes effective 1980s power guitar. In fact, "After All" had been recorded for the previous album, *Jarreau*, but according to Graydon, they had not ended up with a version they liked at that time. Since the remake was satisfactory, the decision was made to release it as the first single from the album.[11] Perhaps ironic is the fact that this more traditional song was the album's only single that made multiple charts, though probably not quite the way that the Jarreau team had hoped. It reached only sixty-nine on the pop charts and twenty-six on R&B. But it rose to number six on the adult contemporary chart. Hitting the top ten on the adult contemporary list, already broached by "Mornin'," could indicate a lucrative market for an album, but it probably wasn't the goal for Al in 1984.

"High Crime," written by Al, Graydon, and Al's new music director,

Bobby Lyle, opens side two of the album, and it has a funky groove that would have been at home on one of the previous albums. Soulful background vocals and Jerry Hey's patented horn licks contribute to the good feelings, even as the lyrics tell the unhappy story of a lover who is leaving and thus is guilty of a crime against the song's narrator. Al directly tells the object of the song that she "better get a lawyer" and that he is "claiming non-support." Treating one's lover poorly, in this song, amounts to a high crime, or even a "high high crime (in the first degree)." Al gets a sixteen-measure break to show off his percussion sounds.

Tour manager Jerry Levin reported that the album closer, "Fallin'," a song by Al, Graydon, and Nathan and Marcel East, was frequently a concert selection for Al in the mid- to late 1980s. Though filled with some of Al's typically evocative lyrical images, it never became one of his hits. Washed in keyboards, the romantic descending progression that defines the chorus is classic Al. The sound of Nathan East's bass guitar on this track is a welcome change from the synth bass on the rest of the album.

Not only was the music for *High Crime* different from what had come before, but the look was different, too. Unlike the beautiful Richard Avedon portraits on *This Time*, Susan Jarreau's inviting shots on *Breakin' Away*, and Al's big friendly face on *Jarreau*, the two cover photos of Al on the *High Crime* record jacket are tinted a cool blue, and his face is contemplative—almost expressionless. Although the cover photos are not particularly inviting, the inside sleeve features a smiling photo of Al that seems to ask "Wouldn't you like to get to know this person?" Taken together, the different images seem to reveal an attempt to market Al in two ways simultaneously: the old upbeat, friendly Al and the new moodier, cooler Al.

The music videos for the first two singles from this album were also a study in contrasts. The video for "After All" appears to be fairly low budget. Set outdoors in the evening, next to a newsstand in a large city (the backdrop is a painted set of skyscrapers), the film features Al only from time to time. He sings but does not dance or play a part in the video's plot. A beautiful mixed-race woman (Galyn Görg, who would go on to a successful television and movie career after this) and a handsome white man dance together, their modern movements mirroring the romanticism of the song. This video might be seen as reflecting the more traditional side of Al's musical personality.[12]

The cover of *High Crime* (1984) reflected a change in Al's music, as well as his public image.

The "Raging Waters" video—representing the edgier side of Al—was a completely different animal and, without doubt, a very expensive proposition. One could hardly conjure up the plot of the film just from listening to the song. As the opening riff plays, a World War II–era newsreel is re-created, with the headline "Navy Repels Attack on Convoy." Vintage black-and-white stock footage of warplanes and a large naval vessel morph into a color film. A group of sailors debarks from a large naval vessel to be greeted by young women awaiting their returning heroes, but Al, in full uniform, has no one waiting for him. A little later, he encounters quiet hostility from white passengers on a train, at a small-town depot, and in a tavern before finally encountering a welcoming face: an attractive, young white woman working behind the bar. They enter into a friendly conversation, and Al touches her face, but when the bar quickly empties due to some unseen emergency, the woman dons a uniform and rushes off. A group of sailors who have taken umbrage with Al's behavior toward the woman grab Al and beat him, leaving him lying on the sidewalk. An ambulance driven by the woman flies by as pieces of burning buildings rain down.

Next, after striding purposefully through a hospital looking for the woman, Al bursts through a set of doors and sees her after a flash of light. She is in her ambulance driver's outfit, but Al and most of the rest of the crowd are dressed in 1980s clothing. They are on the deck of a ship where a line of chorus girls, a baton twirler, jivesters, the ambulance driver with a saxophone, dancing girls in skimpy nurses' uniforms, and others are partying. The music fades out as Al and the woman walk down a street, and a sign on the sidewalk announces Al Jarreau and "Raging Waters."

With all of this action in a video just over four minutes long, it must have cost a small fortune to produce. The storyline is difficult to sort out, but certainly racism is a significant part of the narrative. It's possible that the message, embodied in the closing celebration, is about the power of song and dance to bring people together. The song's lyrics are largely about the power of love: "Lovers stop the time in order / To take the moment in their hands."

An interesting anecdote about this video is that the saxophonist from Al's touring band, Michael Paulo, is the only member of the film's cast besides Al who was not a British actor. In the film, Paulo is Al's aide, jeep driver, and one of the celebrants at the party. Paulo, who was born and grew up in Hawaii, first gained notoriety playing with the band Kalapana.[13] He also became friends with members of a Hawaiian band called Ox, which later became Seawind. The members of Seawind moved to Southern California in 1976, where two of its members—Larry Williams and Jerry Hey—became important contributors to Al Jarreau's music. Eventually Paulo, too, decided to prove himself in what he called the "big pond" of the Southern California music scene. Al first heard Paulo play in a club with bassist Bobby Watson's band, a group made up of members of the original Rufus band that played with Chaka Khan.

When the decision was made in 1983 to expand Al's touring band to include two horn players, Paulo remembered, there was quite a buzz around the music community and "everyone was vying for the gig." Paulo's name came up for the saxophone chair, and Al remembered him. With the Seawind guys putting in a good word for him, Paulo was hired without an audition and ended up playing on Al's tours for the better part of a decade.

Paulo believed Al welcomed him into the band for reasons other than just his connections or his playing ability; he called Al an equal-opportunity employer. "When Al saw me," Paulo said, "saw what I was about—a kid from Hawaii—you know, [being] the man that he was . . . [he thought,] 'Let me give this kid a break.' I would like to think this is part of the reason I got the gig. Of course I could play saxophone, but because he had that kind of heart, I got the opportunity, and it basically changed my life."

In December 1984, Paulo had just arrived home from a long Jarreau tour when he got a call from Al's manager, Pat Rains, asking if he wanted to be in a music video. Paulo replied that he would love to, and he was flown to London for two weeks. He said the whole experience was a blast, and he appreciated that he was able to spend time with Al for much of the two weeks of filming—a luxury that was hard to experience on tour when there was a much bigger Jarreau entourage. Paulo believed Al liked having an Asian American both in his band and in the "Raging Waters" video. As the video was one of the few times Al made a public statement about race relations, Paulo believed he deepened the message by featuring an Asian American.

When *High Crime* was reviewed in Al's hometown *Milwaukee Journal*, staff writer Roberta J. Wahlers was relatively immune to the newness of the sound.[14] She never mentioned the band's sound transformation, focusing instead on the eternal verities of Al's singing. "Jarreau uses his marvelous voice as effectively as always," she wrote. "He has the ability to work each note as though he were an instrument, and performs the same magic on lyrics: Every syllable is thought out from the standpoint of both musical quality and meaning." Wahlers admitted to favoring Al's ballad singing and names "After All" as her favorite on the album. She also offers an opinion that many fans probably shared: "This album isn't one of his best. For my taste, there are too few of the slower-paced songs that let his marvelous voice shine." But, she concludes, "even lesser Al Jarreau . . . is far superior to much of what's being sent across the airwaves."

According to those close to Al at the time, he was quite disappointed with the sales of *High Crime*, which he and his team thought was musically outstanding. It was hardly a flop, making it to number forty-nine on the *Billboard* 200, twelve in R&B, and two in jazz. But this performance didn't match the commercial success of the preceding three albums.

Perhaps the two musical poles on this album—"Raging Waters" and "After All"—with their diametrically opposed musical styles and starkly contrasting videos, were a problem for Al in the market. He was one of the few artists who could convincingly pull off two songs as stylistically different as these, but maybe this versatility ultimately had the effect of watering down who he was to his audience. Al Jarreau was never going to be an artist who did just one thing.

With *In London*, the follow-up to *High Crime*, the Jarreau team took another shot at catching Al's magic in live performance. Could lightning possibly strike twice? Back when Al's recording career began, the studio releases *We Got By* in 1975 and *Glow* in 1976, although largely praised, were thought in many quarters to be pale imitations of Al's performances at his live shows. While this could be argued of many, if not most, artists, it may be an especially apt critique of Al Jarreau. Although a record or video can never completely capture the excitement of live performance, 1977's *Look to the Rainbow* gave record buyers an experience that was much more representative of Al's musical breadth and depth than earlier records had provided.

Since then, of course, Al had become a star. Records still couldn't fully convey the magic of his live performances, but Al's fans had more opportunities by the early 1980s to see him on television and in videos than they had previously, and they were at least getting a broader view of his talent as a result. In fact, a few might argue that by the mid-1980s, hearing Al's records was a more satisfying experience than seeing him live, given the level of the studio production that marked his three recent hit albums. On a good budget, the team was able to do things in the studio—like including extra horns and percussion, adding more keyboard layers and layers of background vocals, and balancing the instruments perfectly—that just could not be done live with only a six- or eight-piece band. Nonetheless, while most music fans are aware of the limitations of live performance, they still prefer the authenticity, immediacy, and spontaneity that come with a live show.

The shows that contributed to *In London* were recorded over a series of nights in November 1984 at London's huge Wembley Arena. In the notes to the release of the deluxe edition of the album in 2010, Al responds to the question, "Could *In London* have been a sequel, a thank you if you will, to the *Look to the Rainbow* fans?" by stating:

> I like that as a notion, more than anything, my feelings and sentiments about Wembley and the U.K. audience were just a joyous celebration. . . . Here's an audience that found me early on, and now they invited me to come to one of their celebrated palaces/venues for doing music. . . . [*In London*] arrived more out of the circumstances

In London, recorded live in 1985, may have been an attempt to re-create the magic of Al's 1978 live album, Look to the Rainbow.

around me [than] out of my planning. It happened because it was a good place for me to go, and the local promoter wanted to bring me there. I think there were over 12–15 thousand people there, and we were just thrilled to be in that classic venue and have a great audience.[15]

While performing one of the songs that made it onto the deluxe edition of the album, Al draws a distinction between his live performances and his studio albums. At the end of "Our Love," during an extended solo cadenza, Al sings that his improvising is "what I love about jazz." "I know it wasn't like that on the album," he tells the audience at the song's end. "The album's the album, and this is live." Al's live performance of that song is about twice as long as the original version on Breakin' Away. His live versions of other songs are performed slightly faster than the originals, and Al frequently sings with more edge and excitement in the live versions, especially near the ends of songs, as musical momentum builds.

In London was something of a mixed musical bag, but given the stage of Al's career, that is not surprising. His biggest hit, "We're in This Love Together," was included, of course; it closes the album (as well as the later, expanded deluxe edition CD). Other favorites from Breakin' Away also appear: "Roof Garden" and "Teach Me Tonight." Warner Bros. had only released Jarreau two years earlier, but this reprisal of several songs from

that album, along with the *Breakin' Away* selections, give *In London* the feel
of a greatest hits package. The 2010 deluxe edition CD even includes extra
tracks not on the original LP: "Take Five" from *Look to the Rainbow* and
"Boogie Down" and "Trouble in Paradise" from *Jarreau*. The biggest *Jarreau*
single, "Mornin'," is not on *In London*; perhaps its wholesome innocence
just didn't fit the theme of these concerts—or the touring band, which was
a very funky outfit. The other remakes on the *London* album are "Our Love"
(on the deluxe edition), a ballad from *Breakin' Away*, and "Black and Blues"
from *Jarreau*. From *High Crime* came "High Crime," "Let's Pretend," and
the electrifying album and concert opener, "Raging Waters."

The *London* album differs greatly from *Look to the Rainbow* in a couple
of interrelated ways. *Look to the Rainbow* featured Al's band of the time:
keyboards (largely Fender Rhodes piano, some acoustic piano, and a tiny
bit of string machine), bass, and drums, with the subtle added color of
Lynn Blessing's vibraphone. The band on *In London* included James Studer
and music director Bobby Lyle playing a veritable battery of keyboards,
the outstanding Nathan East on bass, funky Ricky Lawson on drums, the
scorching electric guitar of Charles "Icarus" Johnson, percussionist
Malando Gassama, background vocals from four of the band members,
Michael "Patches" Stewart on trumpet and flugelhorn, and Michael Paulo
on saxophones and flute. The band was bigger and louder than Al probably
could have imagined one of his bands would be in 1977; yet, a band that
big was necessary to play the music of *High Crime* and other recent Jarreau
tunes. And while Jerry Levin had done creative lighting on the 1977 tour,
the light show of the London concerts was above and beyond the one from
just seven and a half years earlier. Al's entrance at the beginning of the
London shows was preceded by a clip from the highly produced "Raging
Waters" video. What a difference nearly eight years had made!

Al Jarreau in London, a video from the Wembley concerts, was recorded
and released by WEA, the Warner Bros. parent company, on videotape and
laser disc in 1985. It captures not only the aural excitement but also the
visual excitement of Al's shows of that period. The band looks and sounds
supercharged, but so does the headliner. At age forty-five, Al was still
a very physical performer, with slick stage moves, including a brief but
skilled moonwalk, which had only recently been popularized by Michael
Jackson. And late in the video, when Al sheds his shirt and continues to

perform in a sleeveless undershirt, it elicits a tangible reaction from the audience.

Although Al had been an electrifying performer for some years already and would continue to enthrall audiences for several more decades, always with great bands, these performances by a singer at the top of his game with an excellent band stand out as a high point in Al's distinguished career.

JARREAU
Warner Bros., 1983

This classic album—which peaked at number six on the traditional jazz chart, stayed on that chart for an impressive eighty weeks, and included two very popular singles—is possibly Al's finest ever, beginning to end.

The horn section, fueled by great arrangements by trumpeter Jerry Hey, makes a bigger contribution to this album than it had to the previous two Graydon productions. These horn arrangements and their flawless execution have achieved legendary status forty years after they were recorded. Hey established a sound that became inseparable from a certain kind of music in this era—not just on Al's albums, but also on records by his own band, Seawind; Earth, Wind & Fire; and the Jackson Five; as well as on Michael Jackson's megahit, *Thriller*. The horn arrangements on Al's albums are different from most, in that there are no saxophones. According to Larry Williams, who would have played saxophone parts if they existed, Jay Graydon didn't want a saxophone in the mix. He reportedly told Hey, "I don't want that buzz, man," to which Hey replied, "That's going to make our job a lot harder." It was harder for the rest of the horn section, but these extraordinarily skilled players—including Hey, his fellow trumpeters Gary Grant and Chuck Findley, and trombonists Bill Reichenbach and Lew McCreary—made it all work.[16]

David Foster, whom Pat Rains once courted to be Al's producer, is a more significant presence on this record than he was on *This Time* and *Breakin' Away*. He played on only one track, but he cocomposed three of the songs, including the huge single, "Mornin'."

While *Jarreau* was most assuredly a pop album, Al gets a couple of chances to improvise, at least for a few measures. Interestingly, his improvising happens on the two songs that became hit singles, "Mornin'" and "Boogie Down." He makes the most of these brief opportunities, especially on "Boogie Down," where he sounds like the jazz vocalist he was on his early albums.

"I Will Be Here for You (Nitakungodea Milele)," by the songwriting team of Richard Page, Steve George, and John Lang, is another strong song with a lovely, catchy melody, especially the hook at the end of each verse.[17] At the time of the *Jarreau* album, Page and George were just about to form the highly successful band Mr. Mister. Jerry Hey makes a very subtle contribution on this song, with some beautifully sculpted flugelhorn lines. This song delivers a message of support, with the repeating lyric: "I will be here for you when you're falling." It also appears on the 1985 album *In London*.

"Save Me," with its outstanding horn work, is the second Jarreau/Graydon/Foster collaboration on side one of the original record ("Mornin'" is the other). Side two features three songs by the successful songwriting trio of Jarreau, Graydon, and Tom Canning, who made such a mark on *This Time* and *Breakin' Away*. Drummer Jeff Porcaro's extraordinary groove on "Step by Step" is a crucial piece of the song's success, along with its catchy chorus and stellar horn work. Canning expressed pride over the arrangement (the combination of the songwriters' rhythm arrangement and Hey's horn arrangement), which was nominated for a Grammy Award. "When those horn charts came in," he recalled, "we were just literally laughing at how good it was."[18]

"Black and Blues" is another Jarreau/Canning/Graydon song; this one is, as the title suggests, a sad song, summed up perhaps in the line "solo dancin' ain't no fun." Al may have been familiar with the 1929 Fats Waller song "Black and Blue," with lyrics by Andy Razaf and Harry Brooks, in which the "Black" of the title is a clear reference to race. (Canning did not recall the Waller song coming up at this time.) On Jarreau's song, Canning makes a convincing contribution of what the album credits refer to as a "blue synth[esizer] harmonica solo." Jay Graydon makes a rare appearance on a Jarreau record, too, with a strong bluesy guitar solo. On an album filled with tremendous horn section work, this tune may have the most impressive examples of all.

Jeremy Lubbock wrote "Not Like This" and does all the accompanying in effect—the lush keyboard playing that morphs into a rich string section that Lubbock scored. It is a beautiful song, one of the little gems that is almost hidden away (in plain view) in Al's work from this period. Al absolutely nails the performance. The British-born Lubbock also arranged the strings on "Mornin'." He went on to have a brilliant career, arranging for artists ranging from Patti Austin and Diane Schuur to Barbra Streisand, Whitney Houston, and the band Chicago.

The third entry by the Jarreau/Graydon/Canning trio is "Love Is Waiting," the album closer. Again, this one doesn't really stand out because of the strength of so many other songs on the record, but it's another solid song with a grabby chorus.

A fourth tune by this same trio of composers, "I Keep Callin'," was not on the original LP, but appeared on later CD versions of the album. It seems to have been on at least most cassette versions of the album as well. In addition, it ended up being the B-side for single releases of "Boogie Down," "Let's Pretend," and "After All." The song is a twelve-bar blues with a bridge. Canning said they were trying to create another song like "Roof Garden," one of the popular dance songs on *Breakin' Away*. "Callin'" features more big, fat-sounding horn work and an excellent improvised scat chorus by Al. It was obviously good enough to release, and it was probably a difficult decision to leave it off the LP. But, according to Canning, the team thought: "It's really good, but in view of all the other material that we've got here . . . it isn't quite up to it."[19] The song also appears on the 2021 Japanese release of Jarreau rarities.

HIGH CRIME
Warner Bros., 1984

Some argue that the shift to a heavily electronic sound on this album took away much of Al Jarreau's hallmark romanticism. And the one tune that had staying power from this album, "After All," is the one song on the record most like Al's previous work. Perhaps Al and his team can be pardoned, however, for trying to stay current. Since his recording career was only a decade old, Al wasn't ready to start re-creating what he had already done. On *High Crime*, he was more interested in trying something new—and he maintained this interest throughout the production of his next few records.

Besides the tracks mentioned in the chapter, some other observations about this album are worthy of note. While the electronic grooves, created with drum machines and synthesizer bass, have similar sound colors throughout, the rhythmic feels vary from track to track. No other song has the driving feel of "Raging Waters." No other track includes the sparse but subtly complex rhythmic pattern that characterizes "High Crime." "Imagination," the second track on the album, has a happy and funky vibe like some other tunes Al had done before; it also has some white-hot horn licks scored by Jerry Hey and the very funky bass playing of Nathan East. But the drumming on this track comes from a machine. Although some nice drum breaks on "Imagination" are exchanged with Al's patented percussion sounds, they are drum set sounds and not real drums. The lyrics, too, convey a typical Jarreau message in lines like "take this dream to heart" and "believe and it shall be."

"Tell Me," one of two songs on the album written by Al, Graydon, and studio keyboard whiz Greg Phillinganes, has an almost robotic, rhythmically square feel, relieved briefly by the chorus. For much of the song, the bass sounds like a jug in a jug band, and the synthesized bass playing is credited to "Jake Jugs," though it must have been one of the keyboard players. Al improvises with some of his personal sounds during the fadeout.

The catchy "Let's Pretend" establishes a bouncy reggae-like feel (as occurs, to a lesser extent, on "Murphy's Law"), but the heaviness of the keyboards weighs it down. ("Let's Pretend" feels better in the live version on *In London*.)

"Fallin'," especially the bridge of the song, hearkens back to earlier Jarreau, but the rest of the tune is a tug-of-war between the lush Fender Rhodes and synthesizer sounds of that style on one side and the impersonal inevitability of an electronic groove on the other.

Al ventures in some new directions on this album with his lyrics. Besides "High Crime," which is addressed in the chapter, there is the lesser-known "Sticky Wicket," which features an edgy message to a bad lover. Al's reference to a "17-year-old who wiggles and walks like she's 24," which leads to "grown men weepin'" and "a ten point temperature rise everywhere you go," is not what his listeners had come to expect from his lyrics.

According to Joe Turano, who was Al's longtime sideman starting in 2000 and later music director, Al performed with the great service jazz band Airmen Of Note in the early 2010s and "one of the arrangements was a faithful version of 'Sticky Wicket,' which was great."[20] Turano also noted that Al's road bands during the 2000s often "did a burnin' 'High Crime.'"

"After All," the first and top single from the album, remained in Al's repertoire for the rest of his career. Joe Turano said it was "a staple throughout" the last two decades of Al's life. It also appeared on several Jarreau compilation albums: *Best of Al Jarreau* (1996), *Love Songs* (2008), and *The Very Best Of: An Excellent Adventure* (2009). Finally, "After All" was also remade on the *Metropole Orkest* album recorded in 2011.

IN LONDON
Warner Bros., 1985

In Al Jarreau's catalog, this album can be distinguished by the very high level of performance, both by Al and by the band. Although the members of Al's touring bands were not the same A-list studio musicians that he used on his albums starting with 1980's *This Time*, the touring musicians were still top shelf. The members of the band on *In London* prove that point.

Keyboardist Bobby Lyle, who served as Al's music director on tour for a couple of years, was already a distinguished performer before he took on the music director job. After he moved from the Midwest to the West Coast, Lyle worked with George Benson and Sly and the Family Stone, and he became Bette Midler's musical director. Nathan East, who played bass on *In London*, had already played with Patrice Rushen, Hubert Laws, and Lee Ritenour before contributing to 1984's *High Crime* and joining Al's touring band. In later years, he and drummer Ricky Lawson would go on to record hundreds of sessions with a who's who of jazz, funk, and popular music stars. East eventually became a founding member of the band Fourplay; Lawson was a founding member of the Yellowjackets.

By the time *In London* was recorded, guitarist Charles "Icarus" Johnson had already recorded with Stanley Clarke, Airto Moriera, Al's friend George Duke, and even jazz legend Sonny Rollins. Johnson toured with Al for years. In the late 1990s, he left the music world, founded a software company, and became an influential political blogger.

Michael Paulo's story is told in the chapter. His mate in the horn section, trumpeter Michael "Patches" Stewart, was born and raised in New Orleans. He eschewed college, went to the West Coast, and, after struggling for a while, was discovered by Quincy Jones. Like Paulo, Stewart became a charter member of the Jarreau touring horn section in 1983. He went on to a distinguished career, often working with bassist Marcus Miller, who also became an important musical figure in Al's career.

Both horn players display outstanding skills on *In London*, often playing Jerry Hey's demanding parts even faster than in the original recordings (check out "Boogie Down" as an example). Paulo also brings his improvisational skills to the fore on a number of occasions, notably on "Trouble in Paradise," "Black and Blues," and "Teach Me Tonight." At the end of "Teach Me," Al says to the audience, "Michael Paulo! He can play a little bit, can't he?"

Notable, too, are the excellent background vocals throughout. The credits suggest that the singers were East, Johnson, Lyle, and keyboardist James Studer. However, on the video, Michael Paulo and Patches Stewart can also be seen singing at various points during the show.

This album is "hot" from beginning to end, thanks in large part to the great, exciting playing by the core of the rhythm section: Lyle, East, and Lawson. Many of the performances on the album are more engaging and convincing than the originals. Although it tends to get overlooked by many Jarreau fans, this is one of Al's recorded highlights.

As noted in the chapter, the November 26, 1985, concert at Wembley was also recorded and released on videotape and laser disc as *Al Jarreau in London*. Watching it adds another dimension to the music. Viewers will immediately notice the physical involvement of the band. While Lyle, Studer, Lawson, and even percussionist Malando Gassama are more or less limited by their ties to their instruments and specific places on-stage, East, Johnson, and the hyperactive young horn players—Paulo and Stewart—are not. Paulo and Stewart had worked out some energetic choreography that must have drawn the eyes of many in the audience. East, who was just establishing a stellar reputation as one of the finest bass players in the business, also moves more than he ever could have in the studio. Like the others, he seems to be thoroughly enjoying himself—there is a huge smile on his face virtually every time the cameras pan to him. Al has the moves, too, and the audience reacts audibly when he does the moonwalk in the opener, "Raging Waters."

The order of songs at the November 26 Wembley concert is similar to that on the deluxe edition of the album. A couple of differences are worth mentioning, however. On both the LP and the expanded CD of *In London*, Al's big hit "We're in This Love Together" is the closing selection;

yet, at the concert it was performed early in the show, right after the first two numbers, "Raging Waters" and "Trouble in Paradise." At the concert, Al ends the evening by wishing the audience a good night after a superheated version of "Boogie Down," during which he left the stage and mingled with the front row of fans on the floor. Not surprisingly, after bows and bouquets, the band comes back for an encore: an extended version of another grooving dance tune, "Roof Garden." Toward the end, the audience is invited to join in the fun, singing a simple chorus focused on the word *party*. The crowd will not let the band off easily after all that, and the musicians follow "Roof Garden" with a version of Sly and the Family Stone's "Thank You (Falettinme Be Mice Elf Agin)." That segues into some more of the "party" chorus and a very happy ending for all. It is also worth noting that the deluxe edition of the CD, released in 2010 on Friday Music, is titled *Live in London*.

One last aspect of the album should be noted. Listed on the album cover, in addition to the members of the touring band from the show, are credits for vocals by Richard Page and Steve George, bass by Robbie Buchanan, trumpet by Jerry Hey, and synthesizer by Larry Williams and Buchanan. All of these musicians had contributed to several of Al's previous albums, and Larry Williams recalls doing considerable overdubbing in the studio after the fact.[21] That being the case, perhaps some of that material was used in the video as well, since the live set on the video sounds almost identical to some of the album's tracks. Producer Tommy LiPuma, and perhaps others on the Jarreau team, must have thought the overdubbing was needed, though some fans might disagree.

14

WORKING IT OUT

A l's career, so long in its incubation, had more or less moved slowly but surely forward and upward since his signing with Warner Bros. in 1975, with just the smallest of setbacks along the way. He had gone from being a niche jazz (or something like jazz) singer to a major pop star. *Look to the Rainbow*, an excellent accomplishment artistically and commercially, eventually led to the crossover explosion of *This Time*, *Breakin' Away*, and *Jarreau*. When the winds of American pop shifted, Al moved in a slightly different direction and created *High Crime*, a fine album of newly directed material. *In London*, and the tour that surrounded it, seemed like a project that might mirror his earlier *Rainbow* triumph.

But Al's career did not continue along that trajectory. The sales of *High Crime* were disappointing. Whether this was due to the musical direction Al and Jay Graydon had chosen to pursue or to factors in the market, the album simply did not sell the way Al's team had hoped.

In a September 1985 article in the *Orlando Sentinel*, journalist Gary Graff wrote that *High Crime* had not been as successful as Al's previous albums, even though it was "musically far better than his other pop-oriented efforts."[1] Graff laid out two reasons for the album's underwhelming performance: it was missing the hit single that would have attracted a mainstream audience, and its "high-tech trimmings" turned off his jazz fans.

While there are legions of fans, and musicians, who would argue that *High Crime* was not "musically far better than his other pop-oriented efforts," Al believed that it was. At the time of its release, he said, "I've really thought it was the right and best merger statement I've made to date."

Clearly, Al felt the tension that existed between trying to keep up with current pop by using the latest sounds and pleasing his jazz fans by retaining his earlier style. Graff wrote, "Jarreau is working on mending the conflict, and he confessed he has no idea how it will be resolved." It was reported that Al was "talk[ing] with Jay Graydon," the producer of the "hit" albums, but he was also "considering other producers and songwriters with more expertise in the styles he wants to try"—a hint of the changes that would, in fact, come to pass.

Al's concluding statements in the *Orlando Sentinel* article were those of someone who was thinking carefully about his career and the direction he felt his music should go: " 'I'm taking it all in and trying to figure out how best to do this the next time out,' he explained. 'I think you have to be conscious of where you've been, who you've touched and how they feel about you, but you still have to follow your heart, too. That's a big job.' "

In the opinion of Al's friend and road manager Jerry Levin, *High Crime*'s relatively poor showing was temporarily offset by Al's appearance in Brazil at the Rock in Rio Festival in January 1985.[2] Jerry remembered the huge festival drawing more than one hundred thousand people each night. Al appeared on two programs, separated by several days. First, he and the band played between sets by James Taylor and George Benson. On the second night, they preceded the hit progressive rock band Yes, which was the night program's closer. Jerry said, "The response we got was just awesome."

And another occurrence boosted morale that week: Levin recalled that, while in Rio, Al received a cassette tape in the mail with the demo of "Moonlighting." Al, Levin, and Patrick Rains listened to it in the hotel and all agreed that it was going to be a hit.[3] They were right, it was a hit, but not until the song's delayed release in 1987.

At some point in 1985, it was announced that Al was going to star in a feature film, likely to be called *The Nat King Cole Story*. The idea had originated with Rains, who believed Al could pull it off and who made the initial connection with Cole's son, Kelly.[4] Eventually, the project came to mean a great deal to Al. Not only did he believe it would be a major step in his career, but he also thought it would allow him to pay tribute to a jazz singer he greatly admired.

Cole, who had died twenty years earlier of lung cancer at the age of forty-five, was not just a famous musician—he was an icon.[5] Cole's early life was one that Al could certainly relate to: he was born the son of a minister, his parents grew up in the South, and he came up in a northern city (Chicago). Relatively few of the millions of Cole fans from the 1950s and 1960s knew that he had been one of the most respected pianists in jazz earlier in his career. His trio had been lauded and imitated by many in the jazz community before anyone even knew he could sing. Once Cole started singing, the King Cole Trio had numerous hits: from hip jive like "Straighten Up and Fly Right" to the lovely standard "Sweet Lorraine."

In the 1950s, Cole had more hits and sold more records than any other artist, including his friendly rival Frank Sinatra—and this success occurred both before and after the appearance of Elvis Presley. From the release of early hits like "Nature Boy" and "Mona Lisa" right up until months before his death when he recorded "L-O-V-E," Cole produced one big record after another. He successfully moved from making hits of the Great American Songbook to bestselling records in Spanish, semicountry songs such as "Ramblin' Rose," and even lighthearted fluff for the younger market, epitomized by "Those Lazy Hazy Crazy Days of Summer." Cole could make weak material sound good (and sell records), and his interpretations of great songs remain untouchable classics.

While accomplishing all that, Cole broke down racial barriers. He was the first Black headliner at clubs all over the United States and the world. He was the first African American to host his own television show, which ran for two seasons on NBC. (The show was dropped—despite very good ratings—because no one in corporate America was willing to step up to sponsor a show with a Black host.) Cole also appeared in feature films, though without great success. He and his family suffered personal indignities, large and small. Cole was denied entrance to many restaurants and hotels due to his race, and when his family purchased two homes (ten years apart) in Los Angeles, they were confronted by racist neighbors and neighborhood associations attempting to keep them out. In one horrifying instance in 1956, Cole was attacked onstage by a white supremacist at a concert in Alabama. At the same time, Cole became one of the first Black entertainers to be widely accepted by white American audiences.

While many musicians would surely have liked to star in a film about Cole's inspirational life and career, Al Jarreau particularly wanted the role—not solely due to his great love and respect for Cole's music but also because there were so many parallels between their lives.

In April 1985, a teaser for the film appeared in *Jet* under the title "Al Jarreau to Star in Nat 'King' Cole Movie": "Al Jarreau, Grammy Award-winning artist hailed for his contemporary scat and bebop style, has been chosen to play the title role in the feature length film, *Nat 'King' Cole's Story*. Jarreau, a native of Milwaukee, Wis., will make his film debut in the flick portraying the legendary pianist-vocalist."[6]

Word that Al would play the role had been circulating around the music and entertainment business for quite some time before the *Jet* publication, and rumors continued to spread for many months leading up to a slightly more substantial article appearing in the *Chicago Tribune* in December 1985:

Four-time Grammy winner Al Jarreau is gearing up to make his acting debut in "The Nat King Cole Story." He's been committed to the big-screen project for several years and reports it's now reached the stage of development that he expects to be spending next summer on the soundstage—instead of on the concert stage as scheduled.

At one time, the "Nat King Cole" story was to have been made by CBS Theatrical and Cannon Films. Now it's Cole's son, Kelly, and Jarreau's manager, Patrick Rains, who are producing the drama about the singing star who died of lung cancer 20 years ago at age 45.

It will detail Cole's rise, his years in the limelight and his breakthrough as the first black [person] to have his own network series (which no company would sponsor). And it will feature the singing of—Al Jarreau.

"There are any number of really fine actors who could do the role and lip sync. If I'm going to do it, I ought to do my own vocals," he says.

Jarreau hasn't done any acting and candidly admits, "I don't know what I have to offer as an actor." He does feel "some things will be transferable," but does not intend to rely on that. He starts studies with a drama coach soon.[7]

The screenplay was initially slated to be written by Ernest Tidyman, well known for writing the famed *Shaft* novels and the screenplays for

Shaft, *The French Connection*, and other hit movies.[8] Jerry Levin remembered, "Al was really looking forward to the Cole project, moving into a different kind of entertainment. He was terrified of doing that, but it was such a real challenge and something that he felt that he would really be able to do well. He had learned all the Nat King Cole songs and everything."[9] But as deadlines approached, Tidyman passed away in July of 1984, setting the stage for the project to fall through.

For a brief moment, it seemed that Tidyman's wife, Motown soul singer Chris Clark, would finish the project.[10] But then funding also fell through. Rains explored the possibility of turning the project into a Cole stage show, but that idea did not pan out either.

Al, who was already upset with the record sales of *High Crime*, was as close to being depressed as Jerry had ever seen him.[11] As Levin said, Al "was never a guy who had an extended time of being down." But ten years of growing success and professional fulfillment had stalled, and it was a challenging time for Al. In September of 1985, journalist Gary Graff directly addressed Al's malaise:

> Right now, Al Jarreau is just "sitting back and reassessing" his career, an uncharacteristic move for a singer who's been working non-stop in both jazz and pop for the last 10 years.
>
> But this hasn't been the finest of years for Jarreau. His planned starring role in a movie about Nat King Cole was set back when scriptwriter Ernest Tidyman died. Then his latest album, *High Crime*, was received with considerably less enthusiasm than his previous efforts.
>
> To make matters worse, a European tour was cut short when several concert promoters worried that Jarreau wouldn't be a big enough draw.
>
> "I shouldn't say that it doesn't bring you down a bit," Jarreau, 45, said. "It does bring you down, but, hey, I'm familiar with that. I walked that road for a long time. You just press on."[12]

According to this article, the movie wasn't completely doomed at this point. Though Clark had not finished Tidyman's screenplay, Jarreau apparently told Graff that Cannon Pictures had since recommitted to the project and that they were looking for a new script.

Al was clearly uneasy about his career circumstances, but things weren't all bad. Even though the Cole movie did not come to fruition, other things turned up. Of note was Al's appearance on the star-studded gigantic hit "We Are the World," described in chapter 16, and Al was still experiencing the glow that accompanied the arrival of his son, Ryan. Ryan's birth, after Al and Susan had been married for seven years, was a life-changing event. "When Ryan was born, it was such a joy," Al's sister Rose Marie reflected years later.[13] It added a huge dose of positivity to Al and Susan's somewhat nontraditional marriage.

Another interesting opportunity presented itself at the end of 1985: hosting CBS's live New Year's Eve show in Times Square. As reported in a feature article by Susan Stevens in the *Fort Lauderdale News/Sun-Sentinel*, "When jazz singer Al Jarreau was invited to host CBS's Happy New Year America, he replied, 'Let's do it! We'll work out the details later.'"[14] Interestingly, the host of the show for the previous two years had been a much more musically conservative figure, Andy Williams. The base of operations for the show remained New York's Plaza Hotel, but in 1985–1986, NBC was hoping to reach a wider and more diverse audience with the music for the show. Al was joined by the jazz vocal quartet Manhattan Transfer, R&B/soul/funk band Kool & the Gang, Latin/jazz percussionist and singer Sheila E., country singer Louise Mandrell, and rock/country band Exile, with live remote broadcasts by satellite from around the country. Al's partner for the big event of the evening—Kermit the Frog, one of Jim Henson's Muppets—would join him for the show's highlight: the dropping of the ball in New York City's Times Square. If there was a celebrity who could effectively partner with Kermit the Frog, certainly it was Al, who had already proven himself able to interact with animated creatures in his famous "Mornin'" video.

The *Sun-Sentinel* article noted Al's slight apprehension about the show: "The usually cool Jarreau is more than a little excited about the ambitious project. But he admits, 'I'm a little nervous. To actually host . . . and talk . . . and come off with interesting, clever patter is a different kind of approach for me.'"

Also notable in this article was a brief aside about one of Al's habits that was rarely discussed in public: his smoking. "Sitting in the living room of his Studio City home," Stevens wrote, "the 45-year-old 'vocal musician' . . . puffs on his third cigarette. The effect of nicotine on his vocal chords doesn't seem to bother him, 'it keeps them liquid and golden,' he says, joking. 'Actually, smoking is one of the stupidest things I do.'"[15]

Stevens ended her article by recapping Al's busy year, most of it "spent on the road promoting his ninth LP, the popular High Crime, and the less successful Live in London album." She mentioned that Al was working on his tenth LP—due out in early summer of 1986—and had recently finished recording the vocals for "Since I Fell for You," a song that would appear on the David Sanborn/Bob James LP, *Double Vision*. "I think it's going to be one of the tunes that pops off the album," Al predicted. (And he was right—not only did the album later win a Grammy, but Al's track was specifically nominated for a Grammy, as well.)

While noting his recent slump, Stevens seemed to think things were ultimately looking up for Al's career. She wrote,

It's been three years since Jarreau made a broad impact with *We're in This Love Together* and *Morning* [sic]. But his mass appeal has since increased. There was an Emmy nomination this year for his Moonlighting theme, the guest vocal on We Are The World, as well as an appearance on Night of 100 Stars, in which Jarreau, along with Mel Torme, Sarah Vaughan and Wynton Marsalis, brought the audience to its feet with a lively 15-minute tribute to jazz.

And now the big screen beckons. He expects to start shooting his long-planned Nat King Cole Story next summer. Another movie project—about a powerful political figure—is also in the works, but he wants to keep that under wraps for the moment.

Either Al had not yet come to grips with the fact that the Cole film was going nowhere, or perhaps no one had given up on it yet. Nothing more about the other project seems to have been mentioned publicly. No matter what else was going on in his life, though, music remained Al's primary focus. He and his team had come to a decision about how to proceed in the turbulent musical world of the mid-1980s.

15

SEARCHING

A fter the relative failures of *High Crime* and *In London*, it was time for Al and his team to determine a next step. Al would continue to tour for the rest of his career, usually with great success, and everyone involved in his career probably assumed that would be the case, even in the mid-1980s. The bigger question at this time seemed to be: what kind of music would come next? Jay Graydon's production style, which had brought such success to Al's early-1980s albums seemed to have played out by the second half of the decade.

Al and his team turned to a quite different and somewhat unlikely source for the next Jarreau album, 1986's *L Is for Lover*: Nile Rodgers. To say that Rodgers was in the midst of a hot streak in the music business at the time would be an understatement. He had first become well known in the business for the group he cofounded and co-led with Bernard Edwards, Chic. In the late 1970s, Chic had fabulous success in the marketplace, particularly with the band's singular hit "Le Freak," one of the giant successes of the disco era. It went triple platinum, selling more than three million copies.

But Chic was more than a band; it was a brand and an organization essentially run by Rodgers and Edwards. By 1986, they were among the most in-demand producers in popular music. Rodgers was the primary producer in the duo, and his first huge producing success was with Sister Sledge, for whom he and Edwards wrote the hit "We Are Family." That was followed up by their coproduction of albums for Diana Ross and Debbie Harry. On his own, Rodgers also produced an album for Duran Duran and a hit single for Peter Gabriel. It seemed like practically everything Rodgers touched turned to gold (to money *and* gold records); in 1983 and 1984, he produced smash albums for two contrasting superstars, David Bowie (*Let's Dance*) and Madonna (*Like a Virgin*). Both were huge, over-the-top bestselling records.

Yet in his almost phantasmagorical autobiography, *Le Freak*, Rodgers emphasizes the jazz elements of his musical development and personality.[1] As a teenager, he was strongly influenced by the great jazz pianist Billy Taylor, who was running the Jazzmobile in New York City at that time; Rodgers studied guitar through that organization with the excellent guitarist Ted Dunbar. However, there are only the slightest traces of jazz on *L Is for Lover*. And just two songs on the album were cowritten by Al, which was also unusual. Although *High Crime* had been something of a musical break from what had preceded it, Al had still cocomposed seven of its songs.

The Rodgers-produced sound was considerably different from any Jarreau music that had come before. Rodgers himself played guitar on the album, sometimes multitracking. The record doesn't have the thick synthesizer texture that characterized the Graydon albums, and the sound of the band seems more transparent as a result. The singles—"L Is for Lover" (a "list song" and a "spelling song") and the funky "Tell Me What I Gotta Do"—had some commercial success and were performed on tours promoting the album.

The cover of *L Is for Lover* (1986) presented an arresting image of Al, and the album represented yet another evolution in his music.

On the record's striking front cover, Al is pictured looking serious, sitting backward in the passenger seat of a vehicle with a young woman behind the steering wheel. On the back cover, the woman sits on the ground leaning against a stone wall in a beautiful wooded area as Al stands in a driveway with a quizzical look on his face. As Al explained in Warner's promotional magazine, the woman is Robbie Chong, the daughter of the popular actress of the moment Rae Dawn Chong, who had just appeared in *Quest for Fire, Commando,* and *The Color Purple.* "[Robbie] lives in Paris," Al said. "I'm not sure how it happened that the photographer knew that she was in town for the short period of time that she was, but he thought, well, let's get her over here and do something. We did."[2] On an album filled with love songs of various sorts, these photos of a man and a woman in an ambiguous relationship add to the allure of the whole package.

While Rodgers may have had the magic touch with many artists of this era, his magic did not carry over to *L Is for Lover.*[3] Perhaps he simply didn't have time to figure out how to produce a hit album for Al. Al was just one artist out of a remarkably long list of clients whose albums Rodgers produced during this period.[4]

There was one song that didn't make it onto the album but ended up becoming far more popular than the album in the end: "Moonlighting." "Al and I thought it wasn't cool enough," Rodgers said. "So we took it off the album. That becomes a hit, and the album sank. Shows what I know."[5]

Cowritten by Al and Lee Holdridge, "Moonlighting" gained its popularity as the theme for the wildly popular television show by the same name, a romantic private-eye vehicle for Cybill Shepherd and a young Bruce Willis that debuted in 1985. The sheet music lists Holdridge as the writer of the music and Al as the writer of the lyrics—and the music seems to have existed prior to Al supplying the words.[6] Holdridge went on to have a long and successful career as a film score composer, but he is perhaps best known for his long musical partnership with singer Neil Diamond. Al's recording of "Moonlighting" was a one-off, predetermined by the show's schedule, with Rodgers producing. "I guess you could say the 'Moonlighting' recording was Nile's audition [for Al's next album]," Jerry Levin reflected years later.[7] *Moonlighting* ran for five seasons on ABC, and the short version of the theme (about one minute long) was heard at the beginning and end of practically every episode of the show's five seasons.[8]

On the *L Is for Lover* sessions, the song is three minutes long. It is unclear as to whether the long version was edited to the shorter length or if they cut two versions—one for possible album inclusion, and the other for the show's credits. In the longer version of the song, there is a Milwaukee reference in the lyrics, as Al sings that "he loves the blues and the Braves"; the Milwaukee Braves were his hometown baseball team and he'd even had a tryout with the team.

"Moonlighting" was released as a single in 1987, a year after *L Is for Lover* was released.[9] It reached number twenty-three on the *Billboard* Hot 100 and spent one week at number one on the adult contemporary chart. In the end, *L Is for Lover* had no hit singles. And for all of Rodgers's success with other artists, the crucial issue with this album may have been that it didn't have the feel and sound of what people had come to expect from Al Jarreau.

Was the decision to hire Rodgers strictly a business decision? Should the Jarreau team have gone with the big hitmaker of the moment? Pat Rains suggested that the decision was made for a variety of reasons. "Everyone wanted commercial success," he said. "No one any more than Al himself. . . . [And] Al very much bought into the notion of not repeating himself, although sometimes he did need some coaxing. . . . We were trying to find the right groove between what was happening in the US and, by contrast, the UK and Europe where Al's audience was substantial."[10]

While Warner Bros. and others associated with Al were surely disappointed with sales of *L Is for Lover*, the album—like the similarly disappointing *High Crime*—was hardly a bust. *Lover* made it up to number seventeen on *Billboard*'s contemporary jazz chart, nine on the traditional jazz chart, and thirty on the R&B chart (called the soul chart at the time), and it spent a respectable twenty-eight weeks on the Top 200 list, peaking at eighty-one. The singles "L Is for Lover" and "Tell Me What I Gotta Do" rose to forty-two and thirty-seven on the R&B chart. ("Moonlighting," the cut left off the album, had greater success on the R&B chart, adult contemporary, and Hot 100 charts.) But after the huge success of *Breakin' Away* especially, the level of success of *L Is for Lover* was not good enough.

In 2011, when *L Is for Lover* was rereleased in its deluxe edition, Al clearly still felt a fondness for the album, telling reissue producer Joe Reagoso:

This is one of those albums that my international audience knows
every song, the track order, who wrote the songs, who played on it.
I mean it's really great that it has resonated so highly with the fans so
much over the years. I live for this from the audience. It just lets me
know that they get what we did. They understand and feel what we
were going for. It was really great working with Nile—a really consummate producer, writer, musician who added more of a pop and
soul edge for this particular album.[11]

Al's friend and tour manager Jerry Levin saw some positive effects
of Al working with new people.[12] Noting that this was the first Jarreau
album Al had made with anyone but West Coast musicians, Levin said
it was valuable for Al to move out of his comfort zone and work with
such outstanding musicians as bassist Anthony Jackson, drummer Steve
Ferrone, Nile Rodgers himself, and keyboardist Philippe Saisse, with
whom he established an important musical relationship. In Levin's opinion, Al's getting into a "New York sound" was important for broadening
his experience and moving forward. But in the end, L Is for Lover was a
one-off album. Al never did another album that sounded like it or had the
same mix of material.

When Al returned to his hometown in the fall of 1986, he created a positive stir, as he had in previous years. In her review of the show, Milwaukee
Journal critic Tina Maples did some civic cheerleading for the returning
hero: "The city that didn't always support Al Jarreau when he was struggling in the jazz clubs turned out only 3,834 of its residents Wednesday
night for the singer's latest homecoming at the Arena. But those who came
found out that few know better than Jarreau how to warm a stage on a
cold night."[13]

She wrote about the continuing excellence of Al's live shows. With the
animated "eight-piece band fueling [Al's] vocal fire," Maples reported that
Al "gleefully roughed up the soaring voice that brought him mainstream
acclaim on such romantic oozers as 'We're In This Love Together.'" She described how his rendition of the song "High Crime" "made divorce sound
like a party." While he "shied away from material from his current album,
'L Is for Lover,'" he "invigorate[d] such oldies as 'Imagination' [and] 'Since
I Fell for You,'" his collaboration with David Sanborn and Bob James that

was about to become a radio hit. When he did sing the title track of *Lover* (described by Maples as "a bland, musically unchallenging recitation of cities"), it "came alive in concert."

Two other aspects of the show drew Maples's special attention. One was Al's physical appearance: "With his long, sinewy body tucked into an outfit that included a high-collared silver shirt and black cummerbund, Jarreau was the physical epitome of cool jazz gone pop. Once set loose onstage, however, the 46-year-old singer took on the loose-limbed mannerisms of a little boy." The other notable aspect of the night was the special attention Al paid to his home city: "Jarreau took his life in his hands—or, at least, gave the bouncers conniptions—by uttering crowd-rousing words such as 'Milwaukee' and 'the Bucks' while standing smack in the middle of the floor seating, then climbing on a chair to sing 'I Need Someone' while the band wailed away on stage."

There was more appeal to local pride two nights later when Al performed at the Dane County Coliseum in nearby Madison. "A Wisconsin Badger pep rally it wasn't," wrote Kris Kodrich in the *Wisconsin State Journal,* "but when Al Jarreau sang a scat version of 'On Wisconsin,' nobody complained."[14] Al also brought up the University of Wisconsin football team, "gave a few cheers," and "during the encore, wore a red Badgers sweatshirt."

As journalists had been doing since the earliest stages of Al's career, Kodrich used colorful language in an attempt to describe Al's vocal abilities: "Jarreau's voice can do wonders—twang like a guitar, boom like a bass, thump like a drum, wail like a saxophone." Kodrich also stressed the ease with which Al engaged his audience. "A highlight of the evening was the rapport Jarreau had with his audience. Several women gave him flowers and he shook hands with many in the front row." Finally, the article noted that the crowd of "2,700 was up on its feet for nearly all of the second half of the 100-minute show" and that the audience sang along to the older hits. Al's live performances continued to thrill and delight.

After the musical "experiment" of *L Is for Lover* in 1986, Al's next album— *Heart's Horizon*—was not released until 1988. "It became apparent kind of early on that the album wanted to set its own pace, so we just let it go that way," Al told Martha Southgate of *Essence* magazine in 1989.[15]

Heart's Horizon was a return to a comfort zone for Al in a number of ways. First, and perhaps foremost, the majority of the album was either produced or coproduced by his old San Francisco friend, George Duke. Duke could have been a contender to produce for Al in the early 1980s, when Jay Graydon, who had more experience, was hired instead.[16] But by the late 1980s, Duke was a veteran of the craft, having produced hit albums for soul vocalist Jeffrey Osborne, as well as for many of his own solo and band projects. Notably, Duke also produced a track on Miles Davis's heralded 1986 Warner Bros. release, *Tutu*.[17]

From the very first track, *Heart's Horizon* sounds more like a quintessential Al Jarreau album than *Lover* did. The pace is more relaxed—and more in Al's musical wheelhouse. Going by music industry categories, *Heart's Horizon* is more soul- or R&B-oriented than *Lover*, which has more of a pop-rock bent.

"All or Nothing at All," the opening track, begins with a funky bass vamp underneath keyboard sounds that would not have been out of place on Al's hit albums of the earlier 1980s. The song boasts soulful saxophone interludes and faux-horn licks (played on synthesizers) that also would have been at home on those albums. The second track, "So Good," extends the soulful mood, with Al's friend David Sanborn contributing his signature "crying" saxophone style to great effect.

After being left behind on *L Is for Lover*, Jay Graydon reappears on *Heart's Horizon* as coproducer of three of the songs, including two that he cowrote. One of his songs, "Pleasure Over Pain," is rather adventurous—in the unusual direction in which the track develops, as well as the overall sound of the instruments (largely synthesizers). Al has a short but welcome improvised phrase in the tune, searching out the real "color notes" of the harmony.

The one track for which Al is listed as sole composer, "Yo' Jeans," was surely of interest to Al's jazz fans. It is an unaccompanied duet featuring Al and fellow vocalist Bobby McFerrin. Many believe McFerrin owed a great debt to Al for paving the way for innovative jazz-oriented vocalists in pop music and even for inspiring some of McFerrin's stylistic idiosyncrasies. He was just about to catapult himself to stardom with his huge hit "Don't

Al returned to his musical comfort zone with *Heart's Horizon* (1988), which won a Grammy for Best R&B Vocal Performance.

Worry, Be Happy," from the album *Simple Pleasures*, also released in 1988. Many years later, McFerrin said, "I learned a lot of things from Al about the flexibility of the voice, the color palette of the voice, the emotional content of the voice, the immediacy of the voice, the spirituality of the voice, the soulfulness of the voice."[18]

On "Yo' Jeans," Al sings the jivey melody and lyric while McFerrin supplies the busy arpeggiated bass line in his signature style, also supplying body percussion to further energize the short performance. Al's lyrics slyly reference the perennial chestnut "Carolina in the Morning," a song written way back in 1922.[19]

Al and Graydon were cocomposers of "Way to Your Heart" (along with the relatively unknown Gardner Cole). It is almost a throwback to the hard-driving mechanical sound of "Raging Waters" and other tunes from *High Crime*. It includes horn licks from Jerry Hey and his cohorts in their patented style. Acoustic guitarist Earl Klugh, a welcome instrumental voice on the title track of *This Time*, makes another nice contribution to the lightly Latin "One Way." And in a first, at least on record, Al sings the last chorus in Italian.

Philippe Saisse, a notable presence on *L Is for Lover*, cocomposed (with Al) and produced the track "10K Hi," featuring Al on lead vocals, background vocals, drums, and miscellaneous percussion "as sampled through the Akai MPC 60 and the Emulator III," according to the credits. Saisse supplies the remaining colors on keyboards. The track features fascinating modern sounds and a short "jazz" vocal interlude.

The lush ballad "More Love" was written by songwriting veteran Jack Segal, who had previously written the lyrics to such standards as "When Sunny Gets Blue" and "Scarlet Ribbons." "Killer Love" came from the legendary film composer Henry Mancini for the Blake Edwards film *Skin Deep*; Al evidently wrote the lyrics. "Heart's Horizon" reunites Al and Jay Graydon again as composers, along with Randy Goodrum.

The album is a real potpourri, with a variety of styles and sounds. As Al put it to Martha Southgate for her *Essence* magazine audience: "[Using multiple producers on the album] gave me a breadth of material as interesting and excellent as any I've ever had. I love that kind of breadth. It just turns my crank, you know!"[20] While the mixture doesn't make for a beautifully integrated collection, it is a reminder of Al's great versatility as a singer and his continuing wide-ranging interests as a musician.

Several articles published around this time period included commentary on Al's success at this stage in his career. *Jazziz*, a relative newcomer to the jazz journalism scene (it launched in 1984), featured Al on the cover of its March 1989 issue. Written by Wayne Lee, "Al Jarreau: The Fate of a Natural Winner" presents Al as an incredibly lucky man: on the cover, he is photographed holding playing cards and wearing a sly, slightly sinister closed-mouth grin.[21] A woman's hand, holding two large dice, sensually holds a finger to the side of his face. The article begins: "Some people are born lucky. Some good. Others, like Al Jarreau, seem to be both lucky and good. We know he's good because he's had a string of hits, awards and accolades longer than a waiting line at a Soviet potato sale. His eleventh album, *Heart's Horizon*, is just the latest in his series of recordings that somehow, against all odds, have continued to earn the respect of both jazz and pop audiences."

Of course, while Al's albums did still earn respect from many in both audiences, some of that respect continued to fray in the jazz world. However, at this time, the *Jazziz* reading audience was not as hard core about jazz as the audience of *Down Beat*, and it probably included many jazz listeners who respected, or even loved, Al's music.

After relating a brief history of Al's life and career, Wayne Lee writes, "When he finally did get around to making music his day job, he became almost an overnight sensation. . . . Whatever he tried his hand at, Al Jarreau was good." But when considering whether or not Al is lucky, Lee let Al do the talking: "Yes, I'm *immensely* lucky. . . . It didn't *have* to happen for me, but it did. I don't know why, but I do know I did a lot to make it happen through right thinking and hard work."

And, Lee pointed out, "even though Jarreau doesn't like to hit people on the head with any kind of dogma, he believes his 'right thinking' is there to hear in his music." Al particularly mentioned that listeners should pay attention to "10K Hi" as an example of this. "That's what I want to be remembered for," he told Lee. "It's all right there in that song."

When encouraged to talk about jazz, Al expressed his flexible definition of the style: "For me, jazz is a dynamic changing force of music that has at its roots the desire to create beyond the melody, to improvise. Bach was doing it. Miles does it. It constantly changes." But Lee didn't want Al to evade the issue of his own music by simply defining jazz. So, he asked, "Why are you considered a jazz singer, when so much of what you do is pop?" Al replied,

It's because there are so few singers who venture any kind of toe in the jazz pool that way back when (I first started), I got claimed by jazzers and sort of assigned to that category, to the denial of all that other stuff I do. My [tack] was largely determined by the influence of Jay Graydon, who said, "You're a great R&B singer, so don't turn every tune into jazz. If you're gonna do R&B, do it straight. And do pop like a good pop singer would do it. Reach that audience you want to reach."

Lee asked Jarreau to place himself on a jazz-pop scale that ranged from Mel Tormé on one end to an artist like George Michael on the other. Al sensibly, and somewhat vaguely and safely, said that he fit somewhere in the middle. At this point in his career, he seemed quite comfortable with the music he was doing and not worried about being one thing or another, musically. "It's a biological need in me to do the other stuff I do," he said. "I love both. It's not a shirt that I put on. It's all me. It's been there since the beginning. It's an incomplete definition to call me a jazz singer, even though I'm flattered to be called that."

Lee wrote that "jazzers may still get their way," mentioning projects that Al talked about for years, both before and after 1989: a big-band album, an all-Brazilian album, a "straight-ahead" recording. Al said that he would like to work more with a number of his collaborators on *Heart's Horizon*: Earl Klugh, Bobby McFerrin, David Sanborn, George Duke, and Philippe Saisse. Al concluded by saying, "There's a lot to do, but I'm doing the things I want to do. I owe it to myself."

Veering away from Al's professional life, the article also reveals some notable details about Al's personal life during one of the rare times when he was actually home. Lee sets the scene with Al making potato soup in his kitchen, a place Al describes as "therapeutic." "A few feet away," Lee continues, "is his favorite vacation spot: his living room. Outside sits his fully-restored orange '68 Camaro and his '64 Chevy Nova wagon. The '49 Cadillac is in the shop. His wife, Susan, and their five-year old son, Ryan, are living up in San Francisco, where Susan is going to school." It is notable that Al and Susan were living apart at this time; a similar situation was brought up when *People* magazine did its feature article on Al in 1982. "The commuter marriage is tough on all of them," Lee wrote, "but Jarreau says, they make it work. 'You have to be committed to the project,' he says emphatically. 'You have to believe that this is it, forever.'"

Three years later, Al would speak about the very same issue with Elizabeth Chur of the *Chicago Tribune*. Discussing an upcoming European tour, Chur wrote, "Because he's gone so often from his Los Angeles home, [Jarreau] said he has 'a dog who doesn't recognize me and a son who doesn't cry when I leave.'" But, she reported, "his wife of 20 years, Susan, has adapted to his absences as well." And Al echoed his comments from 1989: "Marriage is tough stuff to make work, under the best of circumstances. . . . Then add to it a person who's always staring out the window, thinking of something else . . . but she knows this is what I do—no surprises."[22]

Lee also recorded that, in order to relax, Al "likes to read 'trashy adventure novels' and go to 'escapist' movies where he dines on hot dogs and popcorn." Al was quoted as saying, "I'm pretty serious most of the time, so when I go to a movie, it's like 'Let's get unreal for awhile.'" The last movie he had seen, however, was *Mississippi Burning*.

The mention of *Mississippi Burning*, a story loosely based on the 1964 murder of three civil rights workers—James Chaney, Andrew Goodman,

Al, Susan, and their son, Ryan, in a family portrait from 1987. COURTESY OF ROSE MARIE
FREEMAN

and Michael Schwerner (Chaney was Black, Goodman and Schwerner
white)—led to a noteworthy if brief detour in the article. The movie starred
two prominent white actors, Gene Hackman and Willem Dafoe, and after
its release, there was some controversy about the handling of the fictionalized plot.

Lee wrote, "Despite that unusually serious selection [*Mississippi Burning*], race hasn't really been an issue in Jarreau's life." For one of the few
times in his career, though, Al publicly addressed, at least to some degree,
the issue of race. He revealingly referred back to the importance of his
family and the bedrock grounding of his upbringing:

"My parents did such a good job on my ass making me comfortable
with who I am that I still have trouble seeing the things around me
that everyone else sees," [Jarreau] says, without a trace of cooler-than-
thou. "But there are racial problems in the world; I'm not blind." He
gets around those problems by putting things in perspective. "I am
OK being who I am, and I am responsible for who I am at any given

moment. It's about you and your relationship with God, and when
you know that, ain't nobody can touch you with no earthly bullshit."

Al was the subject of a feature in *Down Beat* shortly thereafter, in April
1989. Manager Patrick Rains and perhaps the publicity folks at Warner
Bros. must have been working hard to land this article and the one in *Jazziz*
soon after the release of *Horizon*, even if the jazz press wasn't necessarily
their primary target. Robin Tolleson's article in *Down Beat* was colorfully
titled "Al Jarreau: A Troubadour's New Tones."[23] Tolleson crafted an interesting introduction to his story that spoke to Al's place in his career
and the labels used to pigeonhole artists: "It's not the typical story of the
jazz singer who goes Pop and loses his Soul. Even though the songs on Al
Jarreau's *Heart's Horizon* are contained to a very un-jazz-like four minutes
or so, they're still alive with emotion. What Jarreau has learned so well,
at the age of 48, is the art of fashioning a song, of putting his own Glad
Rap [*sic*] on it."

In this interview, Al anticipates that *Down Beat* readers will expect—or
hope for—a certain kind of material to appear on his next album. "We
don't have a 'Spain' on this album," he says. "Some tastes will want that
kind of song." But he goes on to defend the rhythm and blues tunes on
Heart's Horizon, saying he's beginning to be noticed by hard-core R&B
fans: "I haven't been nearly as close to them as I think I should be, and as
the music I've been doing historically deserves to be," he said. "But I think
it's going to come."

Tolleson admitted that "So Good," the album's first single, should make
a positive impression on just about any listener. Al agreed, saying, "It just
sits people down. . . . As soon as you hear that huge downbeat, with David
[Sanborn] blowing that thing, man, you just say, 'Wait a minute, shit, hold
the phone. I gotta sit down and find out who and what this is. Go ahead,
I'm listening.'" Finally, Tolleson returned to the issue of how Al's music
had changed since his earlier albums. Al's response closely resembled the
one he gave to Wayne Lee in the *Jazziz* article.

After talking at length with producer Jay Graydon several years ago,
Jarreau made some decisions about the direction of his music, about

staying truer to form on the pop, rock and r&b material. "I have a tendency to turn every song into a jazz piece, you know," he laughs. "And in doing that I miss that r&b listener whose eyes just roll back in his head when a good old r&b groove suddenly becomes a jazz song. What I needed to do was just discipline that thing a bit. Sing the pop song like a good pop singer, and the r&b song like a good r&b singer. So I think that is a recognizable difference in my work."

Heart's Horizon did slightly better on the charts than *Lover*, peaking at seventy-five on the *Billboard* chart, although remaining on the Top 200 chart for twenty-three weeks, slightly fewer than its predecessor. It made it all the way to number one on the contemporary jazz chart and remained on that list for thirty-three weeks. "So Good" rose to number two on the R&B singles chart.[24] Finally, "All of My Love" and "All or Nothing at All" made a dent in the lower end of the R&B charts. Mary Kane reported in the *Milwaukee Journal Magazine* in July that "by the end of May, the album, released in mid-November, had had 460,000 unit sales"—not quite enough to reach "gold" status (500,000 units), but still a considerable number for an artist who didn't fit comfortably into any single category.[25] But evidently, even that was not considered enough by those who were trying to manage the trajectory of Al's career.

*** *** ***

L IS FOR LOVER
Warner Bros., 1986

The deluxe edition of this album—which includes the single "Moonlighting," the 45 rpm remix version of "L is for Lover," and an extended mix of "Tell Me What I Gotta Do"—was released in 2011 on Friday Music.

This album sounds and feels quite different from Al's preceding records, and two of the most interesting songs are Al's originals, "Says" (cowritten with Philippe Saisse) and "Across the Midnight Sky."

"Says" is cleverly constructed musically, and the melody of the chorus seems to have been conceived instrumentally, rather than vocally. It moves quickly from note to note, outlining chords, and it is difficult to sing accurately, rhythmically, and in tune. Al, however, makes it sound easy. Twice he sings the chorus in French, possibly as a bow to the great Nat King Cole, who performed songs in French and Spanish as well as English; or perhaps it was a bow to Philippe Saisse's native language.

"Midnight Sky" is a creation of Al, Jay Graydon, and Richard Page, a cocomposer of the songs "Let's Pretend" (*High Crime*), "My Old Friend" (*Breakin' Away*), and "I Will Be Here for You" (*Jarreau*). After the romantic, swirling introduction, the song develops a seductive Latin feel.

"L is for Lover," the title song, hearkens back to Nat King Cole's hit "L-O-V-E" in some ways. Al puts a twist on the standard spelling song structure with the lyrics "L is for Lover, O is for an offer, V you got to venture, E maybe forever." He also lists places where the song's lover may be "looking for you": London, Boston, Houston, and Kingston in the first chorus, then Moscow, Glasgow, Rio, and Tokyo, followed by Sydney, Philly, Lisbon, and Brooklyn in the later choruses.

The extended version of "Tell Me What I Gotta Do" on the deluxe edition gives Al a chance to stretch out with some scatting/improvising.

Nile Rodgers, in what might be seen as a "producer's privilege," takes a lengthy guitar solo on "Golden Girl." Rodgers's jazz chops are not obvious here, but the solo does get more interesting, in a jazzy way, as it goes along.

Nothing on this record would end up on the list of Al's greatest hits, songs known by all real Al Jarreau fans. However, according to Joe Turano, Al's longtime sideman and eventual music director, "By the first year I was with the band (2000) we performed 'Across the Midnight Sky' as part of a medley with 'Golden Girl.' . . . We also did 'Says,' which was fun musically and vocally with the French lyrics. 'Tell Me What I Gotta Do' was a regular as well and was also fun live. But we never played these like the recorded versions. [The live versions were] much more organic, not synthy, and with some very interesting intros and extended solo sections."[26]

Finally, in the credits, Al dedicates the album to his son, Ryan Adam Jarreau.

HEART'S HORIZON

Reprise, 1988

The deluxe edition of *Heart's Horizon*, which includes the Club 7" mix of "All of My Love" and the long versions of "So Good" and "One Shot," was released in 2012 on Friday Music. In 1990, after its initial release, the album won a Grammy for Best R&B Vocal Performance.

George Duke's touch can be found throughout this album, both in the overall sound of the production and in his contributions as a keyboardist.

Jay Graydon is listed as producer along with Duke on "Pleasure Over Pain," "Yo' Jeans," and "Way to Your Heart." It may be significant that Duke's name is listed first on "Pleasure" and "Way to Your Heart," while Graydon's is listed first on "Jeans."

"All My Love," "Pleasure Over Pain," "One Way," and "Heart's Horizon" all begin with what might be described as "misterioso" introductions. When one hears these somewhat murky, unsettled intros, it's impossible to guess how the songs will eventually lock in, and in fact, all four end up sounding different from one another.

"All My Love" made it to number sixty-nine on the R&B singles chart in 1989. The more substantial "All or Nothing at All" did slightly better, reaching fifty-nine.

The sinuous "One Way," in addition to benefiting from the lovely, understated presence of guitarist Earl Klugh, also profits from the unmistakable sound of bassist Abe Laboriel, who plays on a few other tracks. Percussionist Paulinho Da Costa, a ubiquitous presence on 1980s West Coast albums, is a subtle but key contributor to the colors of this beautiful little gem.

It would have been fascinating to have witnessed the process by which Al's voice was transformed into the many sounds on "10K Hi." This track could only have been created in the studio. In the April 1989 *Down Beat* feature, Robin Tolleson reported that the track featured "live and sampled Al Jarreau," and that "[Philippe] Saisse sampled the singer on an Akai S900," which produced nearly all the backing music and vocals. Al said that 97 or 98 percent of the sounds on the song were made by him: "The rhythm section stuff, even the drum sounds, it's all me. And the thing about it is that it doesn't come off like a super circus, like a carnival act. It's a genuine piece of material which is quite a nice song."[27] It would have been virtually impossible to re-create this song in live performance in the 1980s.

It's a pleasure to hear the little guitar contribution of studio legend Michael Landau on Bill Champlin's "I Must Have Been a Fool."

Jack Segal's romantic "More Love" is yet another showcase for Al's ability to sing classic ballads as convincingly as any singer around.

"Killer Love" will never be considered one of Henry Mancini's great compositions. And hearing Al sing it in this funky arrangement—with lots of George Duke keyboards, heavy background vocals (both male and female), a touch of Jerry Hey, and saxophone licks from the up-and-coming Kirk Whalum—certainly does not immediately make one think of Henry Mancini. But it is good fun.

"Heart's Horizon" sounds unlike any other Jarreau-Graydon collaboration. Its opening chord and melodic progression have a touch of the "Spanish tinge" of the Joaquin Rodrigo guitar concerto movement that was the centerpiece of Miles Davis's classic *Sketches of Spain* and that served as the introduction to Chick Corea's "Spain," which was so notably covered by Al on *This Time*.

"One Shot," an up-tempo groover by songwriters Clif Magness and Glen Ballard that features some seriously funky bass playing, originally appeared as the B-side on some single releases of both "I Must Have Been a Fool" and "All or Nothing at All."

16

GUEST APPEARANCES

A ll through the 1970s and 1980s, Al was invited to appear on other artists' records. And the invitations became more frequent as he became more visible in the music industry. He also was tapped to contribute
music to television and movie soundtracks. Some of these musical encounters were quite successful; others less so.

For one of his earliest guest appearances, Al supplied "vocal effects" on
Quincy Jones's 1974 hit album *Body Heat*.[1] Although the album was a big
seller, Al's performance on it is rather obscure. He appears on two tracks.
On "Soul Saga (Song of the Buffalo Soldier)," Al quietly contributes some
of his vocal percussive sounds in the introduction. He is definitely way back
in the mix, where he can barely be heard. His voice is more audible on "If
Ever I Lose This Heaven," which features the lead vocals of Leon Ware and
Minnie Riperton. His rhythmic inhalation and exhalation of breath, as well
as some consonant sounds ("chu"), can be heard behind the instrumental solos of Hubert Laws on flute, Frank Rosolino on trombone, and Pete
Christlieb on saxophone. He can also be heard in the introduction, under
Laws's flute solo, and even more prominently during the saxophone solo
(presumably by Christlieb) later on. Some of the sounds behind the last
chorus might be Al's conga sounds.

Body Heat was released a year before *We Got By*, Al's debut album.
Someone who knew Al and his capabilities must have brought them to
the attention of Quincy Jones, a longtime jazz musician, then artists and
repertoire (A&R) man, composer, and arranger who was about to rise to

superstardom in the music business as a producer, most prominently for
Michael Jackson.

Four years later, in 1978, Al had the opportunity to work with star jazz
pianist Chick Corea. At a commercial high point in his career, Corea was
recording one of his themed albums, *Secret Agent*. He is pictured on the
album's front cover wearing a trench coat and fedora, in a noirish light.
However, the tunes on the album don't suggest any espionage; rather, a
poem in the typewriter pictured on the back cover hints at a new world
order in which "We're really secret agents of / This new life."

Whatever somewhat muddled theme was intended for the album, Al
is featured on the Corea composition "Hot News Blues." Like many blues
tunes from the early days of blues and jazz in the 1910s and 1920s, this song
is not a classic twelve-bar blues; it doesn't even revolve around the traditional I and IV chords of most blues. It has some bluesy feeling, but in a very
1970s way. Al sings the melody of the opening section, having to stretch all
the way down to a low E-flat, a note that he rarely sang. The somewhat free
verse is backed at times by a sort of faux-gospel female chorus, with Corea's
wife, Gayle Moran, supplying all of the parts. Eventually, the song shifts
into a driving up-tempo 3/4 or 6/8 feel, with drummer Tom Brechtlein
and electric bassist Bunny Brunel fueling the energy. During this chorus,
Al is rhythmically loose and relaxed. Between repetitions of the chorus, he
improvises freely. Again, Chick pushes Al to extend vocally, as he ascends
all the way up to a high B-flat, which he sings in falsetto. After a Corea
Fender Rhodes piano and synthesizer solo, Al modestly improvises during
the fadeout at the end of the track. As is the case for a number of Al's guest
appearances on record, his voice sounds slightly different here than on his
own records; in this case, it sounds somewhat huskier. He was the perfect
choice to deliver this rather jivey song—one that required a very skilled
singer with a great sense of style.

Al cowrote the lyrics for "Hot News Blues," in conjunction with Corea
and Moran. The individual words are difficult to decipher, due to Al's elastic delivery of the melody line and the lyrics. The basic message is about
how the news media focuses on bad news, but there is "good news" as
well. Al sings that "lots of good things go on every day," and he sees that
"most people worked hard." Finally, there is a plea to "please print some
good news."[2] Corea was well known for the positive messages in his songs,

perhaps reflecting his strong affiliation with Scientology; Al had at least a
flirtation with Scientology around this time as well.[3] Perhaps, by the time
of this session, Al was already thinking about recording Corea's classic
"Spain," which would become a celebrated showcase two years later on
Al's 1980 *This Time*.

Keyboard player and singer Gayle Moran first came to the attention
of most music fans with her appearance on John McLaughlin's Mahavishnu Orchestra's 1974 album with the London Symphony, *Apocalypse*. She
played keyboards but made a bigger impression with her ethereal vocals.
She had quietly married Chick Corea a couple of years earlier. She began
appearing with him on Return to Forever's 1977 album, *Musicmagic*, and
made contributions to a number of Chick's subsequent albums.

Moran made one album as leader—the 1979 Warner Bros. release *I
Loved You Then . . . I Love You Now*—and Al was guest vocalist on one song,
"Do What You Do." This track features a few musical echoes of Corea's
Secret Agent—Al being accompanied by a women's chorus and his inter-
play with the Bunny Brunel-Tom Brechtlein rhythm section. After a short
introduction, Moran sings a verse, accompanied by a cappella voices, that
has a faintly Baroque flavor. The band enters, playing funk (and featuring
Corea's rhythm section bandmates Brunel and Brechtlein again, as on
Secret Agent). Moran and Al trade phrases during the opening section,
before ending together. Al then takes over, backed by a large ensemble
of horns and a vocal chorus. Another vocal duet follows, spilling into a
chorus blasting with horns and multiple backup voices. Al solos for much
of the rest of the cut. Al did all of the male voice parts in the richly scored
"choral" sections. It was a unique setting to highlight Al's gifts.

Also in 1979, Al was a guest on a much different singer's record, Brazilian vocalist Flora Purim's *Carry On*. While Al very possibly was friends
with Flora, who was then living in California, it seems most likely that
he came to this project through his old friend George Duke, the record's
producer. The fact that Flora, like Al, had been a Warner Bros. artist for a
couple of years at the time was likely another factor in the collaboration.

Al shares lead vocals with Flora on the title track. Given that "Carry
On" was written by Duke, he may have had Al in mind all along for this
exciting Brazilian-influenced cut. While both Al's and Flora's voices are
quite processed electronically, their signature sounds are unmistakable.

The two of them trade off phrases during most of the opening section of the song, with Al first making sounds (clearly pitched), then singing the lead. In the middle and closing sections of the piece, he does some of his vocal percussion. It's difficult to tell whether some of the sounds are coming from Al's voice or from a cuica, or "talking drum," played by virtuoso percussionist Airto Moriera, who was Flora's husband at the time. That says something about Al's ability to vocalize percussion sounds. When the track goes into a funk jam at the end, Al improvises with repeated lines about caring for one's sisters and brothers—one of his signature themes.

On yet one more 1979 release, Al appears on jazz trumpet great Freddie Hubbard's album *The Love Connection*, singing his own lyric to Hubbard's jazz standard, "Little Sunflower." After moving to New York from his native Indianapolis in the late 1950s, Hubbard had developed a sterling reputation as one of the most accomplished, respected, and influential modern trumpeters through his tenure in Art Blakey's Jazz Messengers; albums with great jazz artists John Coltrane, Ornette Coleman, Eric Dolphy, Herbie Hancock, and Wayne Shorter; and his own highly praised records for Blue Note and Atlantic. The popular—and artistically successful—albums Hubbard had cut for CTI Records in the earlier 1970s had led to a contract with the industry giant Columbia. The CTI records were more targeted to a mass market, and once Hubbard signed on with Columbia, the commercialism accelerated. Hubbard was at the height of his commercial success in the late 1970s.

The Love Connection, as was typical for Hubbard's Columbia albums, features excellent trumpet playing and some fine jazz; it also includes some beautiful arrangements by ace arranger Claus Ogerman. But Hubbard had pretty much already been written off by purist members of the jazz community, as would also happen to Al.[4] In notes for the rerelease of *The Love Connection* in 2013, Ogerman, who also coproduced the record, said, "Al came to the studio and that lyric was written by him in the studio while he was there. Freddie did 'Little Sunflower' twice before—on Atlantic and with Milt Jackson for CTI—but maybe he was thinking to make a little more royalties as a writer or something."[5] Though it seems somewhat unlikely that Al would have shown up at the studio without writing the lyric ahead of time, this was not the first time he had done lyrics for jazz standards. He'd already had the great success of "Take Five," and his vocal versions of "Spain" and "Blue Rondo à la Turk" were not far off. With their focus on flowers, these were not Al's most distinguished lyrics, but they work. Al's singing on this track is definitely not his best. Scored along with flutes, he sings the song very straight, with little rhythmic displacement, which is appropriate for this piece. His voice sounds a little strained, however, and his usually spot-on tuning is just slightly off at times. The track features excellent solos by Hubbard and Corea, with some flute commentary by Joe Farrell. Despite the shortcomings of Al's vocal performance, his appearance on the formidable Hubbard's major label release was another feather in Al's cap. Given that Hubbard had played on Al's *All Fly Home* just the previous year, this could have been a "payback" appearance, possibly even arranged by the respective record labels.

A few years later, at the 1981 Montreux Jazz Festival, Al was recorded for what would become *Casino Lights*, an album featuring a number of Warner Bros.' up-and-coming artists that was released in 1982. No artist is listed as headliner, but the group includes singer Randy Crawford, Al's friend David Sanborn, the instrumental group the Yellowjackets, the duo Neil Larsen and Buzz Feiten, and vibraphonist Mike Mainieri.[6] Al sings on three songs that made the album, all in duet with Crawford. Besides the fact that Crawford, Sanborn, and Larsen and Feiten were, like Al, managed by Pat Rains, Al was also connected to *Casino Lights*'s producer Tommy LiPuma, and to Al Schmitt, who recorded this album.

Al's vocals here are really in service to Crawford and do not sound like the vocals in his other recorded material. Although the songs could have been tailored to feature Jarreau, they were not; this is definitely duo material, with a lot of give and take between the principals. Al sings almost exclusively in his higher register; sometimes he's in unison with Crawford, and the two frequently sing their phrases in the same register. While Al sounds simply like a background or harmony singer for Crawford at times, it's a pleasant outing for both. And Sanborn solos on two of the tracks.

In 1982, Al was one of a number of stars to contribute to the soundtrack of the film *Night Shift*, one of director Ron Howard's earliest films. Although the plot revolves around a morgue and a prostitution ring, the movie is basically a screwball romantic comedy starring three bankable Hollywood personalities: Michael Keaton, Henry Winkler, and Shelley Long. Songwriting giant Burt Bacharach wrote original songs for the film with his lyricist wife, Carole Bayer Sager. These songs featured stars, too: the Pointer Sisters, Al Jarreau, and Rod Stewart (and the little-known band Quarterflash, which had recently had a hit album). A few other songs not originally intended for the movie, nor written by Bacharach, appeared on the soundtrack. The one hit song from the movie was "That's What Friends Are For," sung by Stewart and reprised instrumentally on the album as the "*Night Shift* Love Theme."[7] (Bits of the melody were woven throughout the movie.)

Although Bacharach wrote Al's feature, the pop confection "Girls Know How," the track was produced by two members of Al's team at Warner Bros.: Jay Graydon and David Foster; Foster was listed as cocomposer with Bacharach and Sager. Musically, "Girls" wouldn't have been totally out of place on one of Al's early 1980s albums, but despite synthesizer sounds and horn parts similar to those on so many of Al's songs of the period and a strong driving bass, there is really no jazz aspect to this song.[8] And nothing in the song says "this is Al Jarreau," except for his inimitable voice.

In 1983, Al got the opportunity to contribute to the highly successful group Sister Sledge on their album *Bet Cha Say That to All the Girls*. Their breakthrough 1979 album, *We Are Family*—spurred by the two hit singles "He's the Greatest Dancer" and the title track—had gone platinum, rising to number two on the pop charts and number one on R&B.[9]

Bet Cha was produced by Al's old friend George Duke, who likely suggested bringing Al in on the project. This is one of the few times that Al's speaking voice, rather than his singing voice, was front and center. The sassy title track tells the story of a slick operator who uses smooth lines on unsuspecting young women. The sisters sing the setup, then Al enters with the main character's sales pitch. He delivers his lines at a fast clip, almost like a rapper. Rap, at this time, was about to descend upon the pop music scene with great force. Despite the women's resentment of Al's character, this song is all good fun; it lacks the frequent dark edge of rap or hip-hop. Al gets to join the other vocalists for one fast and intricate melodic line that was probably written by Duke, who arranged the song with the sisters.

Al contributed to another film soundtrack in 1984. *City Heat* was originally supposed to be directed by Blake Edwards, responsible for classics such as *Breakfast at Tiffany's*, *The Days of Wine and Roses*, and the *Pink Panther* films beginning in 1963 and continuing until 1993. Later his films

featured his wife, Julie Andrews—most notably *Darling Lili* and *Victor/
Victoria*. Though Edwards had initially planned for the film to be titled
Kansas City Jazz, it was first changed to *Kansas City Blues* and then finally
to *City Heat*.[10] The vicissitudes of Hollywood politics led to the two big
stars of the film, Clint Eastwood and Burt Reynolds, choosing Richard
Benjamin to replace Edwards as producer. The stars were cops in what was
essentially a buddy movie.

Eastwood brought with him to the production his favored film
composer/scorer, Lennie Niehaus, who after a stint as a successful saxophonist with Stan Kenton, had moved into film scoring.[11] Niehaus orches-
trated and/or composed for all of Eastwood's films spanning from 1984's
Tightrope and *City Heat* through 2008's *Gran Torino*. Especially notable in
the jazz community was his score for the Eastwood-produced biography
of Charlie Parker, *Bird*, in 1988.

Niehaus wrote swinging music for *City Heat*, some of it sounding like
the 1930s, some of it sounding more contemporary. Songs from the 1930s
were used in the film, in new recordings by contemporary singers. Al's
song, "Million Dollar Baby," had been written by Harry Warren, Billy Rose,
and Mort Dixon for the 1931 show *Billy Rose's Crazy Quilt*, where it was
first performed by Fanny Brice. The instrumental arrangement written to
back up Al doesn't sound like authentic 1930s jazz or pop, but it includes
enough elements of the era's sound and style to suggest that period to
1980s filmgoers. Many listeners do not immediately register the fact that
it is Al Jarreau singing the song, as he is (as the album's annotator says)
"channel[ing] his inner Rudy Vallee." Indeed, Al's voice is processed so
that he sounds as if he could be singing through a megaphone, as Vallee
did way back in the 1930s. Al's buoyant, upbeat delivery assures a winning
performance.

With his career going very well indeed, and just recently back in the
United States from the concerts that became the *In London* album, Al was
one of an outsized group of pop music stars who appeared on the legendary
song "We Are the World."[12] Recorded in late January 1985, this anthem
was written by superstars Michael Jackson and Lionel Richie. Al's friends
in the business Quincy Jones and Michael Omartian produced the record,
which must have been a mind-boggling feat given all of the singers involved in the group dubbed USA for Africa. Eventually sales of the record

At the 1985 recording session for the superhit "We Are the World," Al stands in the middle row at the far left among many of America's most prominent pop stars. AP PHOTO

(over twenty million copies of the single) and its associated products raised $63 million for a variety of humanitarian aid projects in seven countries, with much of the aid going to Ethiopia and Sudan—countries in the midst of terrible droughts and famines. This marked one of the all too few times that the music business overcame commercial and legal barriers to put together some of the biggest names in the industry for the greater good.

Musically, the record was successful despite having to accommodate more than twenty star soloists and more than twenty other stars in the chorus. Featured most prominently are Stevie Wonder, Bruce Springsteen, and Ray Charles. Like most of the soloists, Al gets only two measures to make his solo contribution, sliding in between short bits by Willie Nelson and Springsteen. The record won three Grammy Awards, as well as other honors.

In the documentary *We Are the World: The Story Behind the Song*, a short diversion brings Al to the forefront.[13] After four long hours of rehearsal during the recording session, a spontaneous tribute to Harry Belafonte occurred. "We Are the World" was only the latest of Belafonte's forays into social activism; he had been known as an advocate for a variety of causes, but especially civil rights, since he exploded onto the music scene in the mid-1950s. Belafonte was not a soloist on the record—rather, just a chorus member, standing unobtrusively in the back row. But in the video, when the group finishes rehearsing around two in the morning, someone belts out an apt few lines from Belafonte's earliest signature hit, "The Banana Boat Song": "Daylight come and we want go home." A few singers, and then the rest of the group, continue to sing more lyrics amidst growing laughter. After several minutes, the camera pans to Al during this joyful interlude, and it seems as though he is the lead singer of this improvisatory treat. Al had been listening to Belafonte since he was a teenager, and he had the utmost respect for his predecessor in the business.[14]

While this session didn't add anything to Al's musical development, it was surely an honor for him to be in the company of so many other contemporary hitmakers on such a worthwhile project.

Another superstar in the mid-1980s and one of jazz's all-time greats, Miles Davis, honored Al during this time. Miles and his band began regularly performing a piece in their concerts called "Al Jarreau." It was not recorded and released commercially at that time, though performances of it can be seen and heard on various live dates from this era; one was included on the 1991 documentary *Miles Ahead*.[15] In fact, the track was recorded in the studio in 1985 or 1986. It was remixed, reworked, and finally released with other tracks from the period in 2019 on Miles Davis's *Rubberband*. An article in *Down Beat* at that time revealed that "Davis had intended to recruit guest vocalists for the project, including Al Jarreau."[16] The track is titled "I Love What We Make Together" on the 2019 release, but its original title is acknowledged in the notes.[17] In the mid-1980s, Al must have been proud to have been recognized in this way by one of jazz's iconic performers—and, interestingly, another jazz figure who, like Al, had been abandoned by much of the hard-core jazz community.

The mid-1980s were, indeed, a busy time for Al. In 1985, he recorded with the British pop group Shakatak. The band has been variously identified as "post-disco," jazz-funk, R&B, smooth jazz, and jazz fusion. But in the United States, it would almost certainly be described as pop (their instrumentals excepted), despite their sound containing elements of all the styles listed above. By the time of their 1985 album *City Rhythm*, the band's prominent features were catchy melodies sung by skilled lead singer Jill Saward and solid dance grooves anchored by the funky bass playing of George Anderson. (The band was remarkably long-lived, recording albums into the late 2010s.) "Day by Day," written by Saward and Anderson, features the alternating and simultaneous vocals of Saward and Al, on a typically attractive little song. The voices easily mesh, and Al, as usual, sounds as if he's enjoying himself.

Another movie session in 1985 once again brought Al into the limelight. *Out of Africa*, starring Meryl Streep and Robert Redford, was one of the hit movies of the year, receiving both popular and critical acclaim. "The Music of Goodbye," with lyrics by the ace team of Alan and Marilyn Bergman, is also known as "The Love Theme from *Out of Africa*." According to notes that accompanied a later rerelease of the song, the Bergmans turned "venerable composer John Barry's sweeping main theme to the 1985 multiple Academy Award–winning epic (for which he picked up a Best Original Score trophy) into a radio-friendly pop mode."[18] The single did well, rising to number sixteen on the adult contemporary chart in April 1986.

Vocalist Melissa Manchester was listed as the lead artist for the song, which did not appear on the original soundtrack recording. However, Manchester and Al are equals on the track, trading lines at times, but singing in duo for most of the song. Decades later (not long after Al's death), when the song resurfaced on a collection of Manchester albums from the 1980s, Melissa had loving words for Al:

> My precious Al Jarreau! Al and I had toured together for a while, and he was the dearest. I always refer to him as the world's largest elf! He had gone through a lot, but in the end, he was just a dear, optimistic soul. When we made the video for the song, VH1 was a very new channel, and the concept of videos was still relatively new. I was not in the studio with him; he was in an entirely different location than I, but they edited it together beautifully.[19]

The next year, in 1986, Al joined saxophonist David Sanborn on an album he was cutting with pianist Bob James, another artist who was having considerable commercial success in the subgenre of jazz that was being referred to as fusion (some of which would later be called smooth jazz). While Al and Sanborn had just missed each other in Iowa in the early 1960s, by the mid-1980s they had interacted on numerous occasions, as they were both in Patrick Rains's stable of artists and on the same record label. In fact, they frequently toured together.[20]

The album that Sanborn and James were recording, *Double Vision*, turned out to be a rousing commercial success. It stayed on the *Billboard* charts for more than a year, getting up to number ten on the R&B list and even reaching fifty on the pop list. At the 1987 awards show, it won a Grammy for Best Jazz Fusion Performance, Vocal or Instrumental.[21] The track Al sang on, "Since I Fell for You," was nominated in the Grammys' R&B category.[22] Al and Sanborn had been playing this classic Buddy Johnson song together since at least the previous year, when they were touring together.[23] James first plays the melody, followed by Al singing a segment that is not on Johnson's version, though it may be a verse that Johnson wrote. Going into the chorus, Al gently croons the familiar melody. He builds through the bridge and the last phrase, with Sanborn soulfully adding commentary behind the vocal. Then, there's a return to the bridge with Sanborn in the lead. Al reenters for the last section, singing at his bluesiest, all the way through an extended coda, where he improvises and holds a long high note for maximum effect before going into some of his classic percussion sounds.[24] Years later, reflecting on his time playing with Al, Sanborn said, "You look for material you can kind of inhabit. It's like clothes that fit. And I think Al has a really unique quality of whatever he sings, he makes it his own. You know even if he sings songs you've heard people [sing] a hundred times before. When you hear him do it, it's like he owns that song."[25]

Around this time, Al was featured on an album by Hiram Bullock, a skilled guitarist who contributed a solo to "Give a Little More Lovin'" on Al's *L Is for Lover*. By the time Bullock released his second album as leader, 1987's *Give It What U Got*, he had already recorded with such other well-known acts as Billy Joel, Steely Dan, Paul Simon, and Jarreau associates David Sanborn and Bob James. In 1982 and 1983, Bullock had been visible to much of America as a member of The World's Most Dangerous Band led by Paul Shaffer for David Letterman's late-night television show.

The song on *Give It What U Got* featuring Al, "You Send Me," had been the first and most popular single ever released by singer Sam Cooke, the

"King of Soul." Cooke's place in the civil rights movement has recently come to the consciousness of many Americans who were not aware of it (or had forgotten), as he was one of the principal characters, along with Malcom X, Muhammad Ali, and Jim Brown, in the 2020 film *One Night in Miami*.[26] The 1957 release of "You Send Me" became a number one hit on both *Billboard*'s R&B chart and the *Billboard* Hot 100.[27] Bullock and Jarreau's remake of this classic differs from the original, but it is an obvious tribute to that version and has the same essential feeling, musically and emotionally. The newer version is slightly slower than the original, has a rhythm section with different instruments and sounds, and includes new harmonic variety in the introduction and interludes. It is also longer than the 1957 single, and the second verse and concluding section feature Al and Bullock exchanging improvised bluesy phrases. Al sings the lead and is also overdubbed for the background chorus near the end. Al's voice quality and delivery are remarkably similar to Cooke's: silky smooth and soulful.

Toward the end of the 1980s, Al had the opportunity to work with another skilled musician of the era: pianist Joe Sample, who is best known for being one of the founding members of the Jazz Crusaders (later, simply the Crusaders)—one of jazz's most popular groups from the late 1960s into the 1980s. The Jazz Crusaders were generally considered to play "hard bop," but they were increasingly influenced by rock and funk. By the late 1960s, Sample and his fellow cofounders Stix Hooper (drums) and Wilton Felder (bass and saxophone) had become active in the L.A. studios.

By 1989, Sample had already made a contribution to Al's 1976 album *Glow* (acoustic piano on two tracks and organ on another); in a few years, he would be a major player on Al's 1994 *Tenderness*. Sample had cut a number of albums as leader, but 1989's *Spellbound* was his first on Warner Bros. On the album, Al sings "Somehow Our Love Survives," a song cowritten by Sample and jazz vocalist Michael Franks.[28] Heavily produced, this funky midtempo groover puts Al right in his comfort zone on a song that musically reflects the era—its style was moving in the direction of what would later be known as smooth jazz. Sample, not surprisingly, has a tasty acoustic piano solo in the middle of the track, and Al improvises over the fade at the end.

In yet another 1989-released guest appearance, Al supplied music used in Spike Lee's highly acclaimed film *Do the Right Thing*. Appearing on a number of lists of the greatest films of all time, *Do the Right Thing* is considered by many to be Lee's finest work. The plot involves tense race relations in New York's Bedford–Stuyvesant neighborhood on a sweltering summer day, and its tragic climactic incident is the killing of a Black man by a white police officer. This fictional event still resonates deeply in the 2020s, as it so remarkably foreshadowed the killing of George Floyd nearly thirty years after the film's release.

As was the case with a number of Lee's other films, the original music for *Do the Right Thing* was written by his father, jazz musician Bill Lee.[29] That music largely features jazz musicians, including Branford Marsalis, Terence Blanchard, James Williams, Robert Hurst, and Jeff "Tain" Watts. Music of other genres was also used in the film, with the hip-hop group Public Enemy's "Fight the Power" attracting the most attention, acclaim, and controversy.[30] That song's use of quotes from a variety of civil rights activists and bits of music by iconic artists like James Brown captures the spirit and thrust of the film's message.

The film also includes music by artists ranging from British reggae band Steel Pulse to Panamanian politician and salsa artist Rubén Blades to the star a cappella group Take 6. Al's feature, "Never Explain Love," plays over the end credits of the movie. Written by Cathy Block and Raymond Jones, the song's lyrics explore just what love is, or if it can in fact be explained.[31] The romantic music is in stark contrast to much of what precedes it in the film, both in plot and soundtrack. Al is completely in his element with this song, however, which also features a string arrangement and an extensive (almost two-minute-long) coda for strings alone—almost a whole separate piece—written by the highly respected West Coast writer and keyboard artist Clare Fischer. Al's name is also intoned by a deejay played by Samuel L. Jackson in the film, along with other names in a roll call of great Black musicians.[32]

As the 1990s dawned, Al appeared on one more soundtrack: that of the big-budget *Dick Tracy*. This major film starred Warren Beatty in the title role of the comic strip hero, Glenne Headley as his significant other, Tess Trueheart, and Madonna—one of the very biggest pop musicians of the 1980s, known as the "Queen of Pop"—as the enticing bad girl Breathless Mahoney.

Danny Elfman wrote the movie's score shortly after his breakthrough

the year before with the big hit *Batman*; he was on his way to becoming one
of the most in-demand film composers of his era. The film also featured
nonoriginal music, ranging from selections by 1950s icons Jerry Lee Lewis
and Brenda Lee to R&B/pop specialists Darlene Love and Patti Austin to
Tommy Page of the boy band New Kids on the Block to a rap by Ice-T. As
he had done on 1984's *City Heat*, Al re-created a facsimile of 1930s pop
vocals, once again with a sort of Rudy Vallee-esque megaphone sound
on "Rompin' and Stompin,'" accompanied by a band of skilled (and jazzy)
studio players from London. (Stephen Sondheim's contribution to the
score, "Sooner or Later (I Always Get My Man)," won an Academy Award
for best original song but did not appear on either the album of original
music by Elfman or the one with new songs that Al was on, but rather on
Madonna's album associated with the movie, *I'm Breathless*.)

In contrast to all of the pop and R&B appearances that Al made during
the 1970s and 1980s, in 1990 he had a guest spot on a real jazz record by
his one-time inspiration, Jon Hendricks. Al's featured track on *Freddie
Freeloader* was a vocal rendition of the title track; it featured an all-star cast
re-creating the instrumental solos that had appeared on the classic recording of the song on Miles Davis's all-time most loved album, *Kind of Blue*.

Hendricks was one of the few people in the business who could have
recruited this vocal cast to re-create the solos for which he had crafted his
typically clever lyrics. Bobby McFerrin sings Wynton Kelly's piano solo; Al
does Miles's trumpet solo; Hendricks navigates John Coltrane's intricate
tenor saxophone choruses; and George Benson stands in for Cannonball
Adderley's alto solo. In the album's liner notes, Hendricks wrote, "When
invited guests such as George Benson, Al Jarreau and Bobby McFerrin,
masters all, accept your invitation to come and sing with you, the first
thing you must do is give them a masterpiece to sing. This I believe I have
done."[33] The result is wonderful fun. A film was made of the session and
can easily be found online.

With the star-studded Miles re-creation, another track from the album
tends to get overlooked: a jam on Hendricks's take on a Thelonious Monk
tune, "Rhythm-a-ning." Hendricks described how it came to be:

> This particular track is not a "take" at all. I simply left the mikes run-
> ning during a lull in the recording of "Freddie Freeloader," suggested

to George (Benson) and Al (Jarreau) that we "have some fun," gave Tommy Flanagan the instructions you can hear that launched us into orbit in what is one of the most fantastic scat singing performances in history, especially since nobody was aware that they were being recorded for public consumption.

George (Benson) goes first and sets a brilliant pace that never lets up. Another hard act to follow. Then Al (Jarreau), one of three Pisces on this album (Tommy Flanagan and Bobby McFerrin being the other two) exhibits fantastically the artistry that is the keynote of this sign of the poet by giving us all a lesson in impeccable time in the midst of burning creativity. All I could do after that was try to justify my being on the date at all, while it was left to [pianist] Tommy Flanagan to show us all how it 'posed t'go, after which George, Al and I trade fours with the undoubtedly redoubtable [drummer] Jimmy Cobb, as [bassist] George Mraz plucks us all into good health. Actually, a personal treat for me, and, really, the reason I did the album.

Al's performance as a guest at "Absolut Vocalese: An Evening with Jon Hendricks" at Carnegie Hall in March of 1990 was a fitting way to round out these two decades of impressively wide-ranging and entertaining guest appearances.[34]

SIDEMAN

Here is the list of sideman appearances discussed in this chapter, in chronological order by song, along with each album's primary artist, album title, record label, and date. An asterisk (*) indicates selections that appear on the Japanese set *Works*, by Al Jarreau, WEA Japan, 2021.

- "Soul Saga (Song of the Buffalo Soldier)" and "If Ever I Lose This Heaven." Quincy Jones. *Body Heat*. A&M, 1974.

- "Hot News Blues." Chick Corea. *Secret Agent*. Polydor, 1978.

- *"Do What You Do." Gayle Moran. *I Loved You Then . . . I Love You Now*. Warner Bros., 1979.

- *"Carry On." Flora Purim. *Carry On*. Warner Bros., 1979.

- "Little Sunflower." Freddie Hubbard. *The Love Connection*. Columbia, 1979. Recently available on BGO Records (UK) (along with Hubbard's *Bundle of Joy* and *Super Blue*).

- *"Your Precious Love," "Who's Right, Who's Wrong," and "Sure Enough." Various artists. *Casino Lights*. Warner Bros., 1982.

- *"Girls Know How." Various artists. *Original Soundtrack, Night Shift*. Warner Bros., 1982.

- "Bet Cha Say That to All the Girls." Sister Sledge. *Bet Cha Say That to All the Girls*. Cotillion, 1983.

- "Million Dollar Baby." Various artists. *City Heat, Original Motion Picture Soundtrack*. Warner Bros., 1984. More recently released on Varèse Sarabande, 2016.

- "We Are the World." Various artists. *We Are the World*. Released on various Columbia, CBS, and Polygram imprints, in several countries, on both vinyl and CD, 1985.

- "Al Jarreau." Miles Davis. *Rubberband*. Rhino Records and Warner Records, 2019.

- "Day by Day." Shakatak. *City Rhythm*. Polydor, 1985.

- "The Music of Goodbye (Love Theme from *Out of Africa*)." Melissa Manchester and Al Jarreau. *Out of Africa: Music from the Motion Picture Soundtrack*. MCA Records, 1986. Originally released as an MCA single, 1986. Currently can be found on *Melissa Manchester: Ma+hema+ics (or Mathematics): The MCA Years*. Real Gone Music, 2018.

- "Since I Fell for You." Bob James and David Sanborn. *Double Vision*. Warner Bros., 1986.

- "Moonlighting." Various artists. *Moonlighting: The Television Soundtrack Album*. MCA Records, 1987. The "single" version of this song is also on the Friday Music deluxe edition of *L Is for Lover*, 2011. (See chapter 15 for more on this song.)

- *"You Send Me." Hiram Bullock. *Give It What U Got*. Atlantic Jazz, 1987.

- *"Somehow Our Love Survives." Joe Sample. *Spellbound*. Warner Bros., 1989.

- "Never Explain Love." Various artists. *Music from Do the Right Thing*. Motown, 1989.

- "Rompin' and Stompin'." Various artists. *Dick Tracy*. (Note: This is not the soundtrack album.) Sire/Warner Bros., 1990.

- "Freddie Freeloader." Jon Hendricks and Friends. *Freddie Freeloader*. Denon, 1990.

17

MORE TOURING

After the release of *Heart's Horizon* in 1988, it must have seemed to Al and his fans like a very long time before his next album, *Heaven and Earth*, was finally released in 1992. Since the excitement of Al's debut album, *We Got By*, in 1975, either Warner Bros. or its sister label Reprise had put out a new Al Jarreau album every year except for three: 1979, the year between *Glow* and the milestone *This Time*; 1982, when Al was so busy touring to support the 1981 blockbuster *Breakin' Away* that he couldn't finish *Jarreau* until 1983; and 1987, between *L Is for Lover* and *Heart's Horizon*, when Al and his team were searching for their direction.

During these four years without any new records, however, Al continued to tour with excellent bands, as he always did. 1989 was a particularly heavy year of touring, both in the United States and Europe. Looking into several dates from that year—in different places, with different audiences, with different critics weighing in—offers a diverse slice of Al's touring at this time, focusing on the music he was performing and on his band members. The personnel of the touring band, one that saxophonist Michael Paulo described as "stellar," indicates the kind of talent that Al could attract.[1]

The musical director for these tours was keyboardist Neil Larsen, who had been playing and directing with Al for some years by this point. Larsen had his own career as a solo artist, but he also had a long partnership with guitarist Buzz Feiten in the bands Full Moon and the Larsen-Feiten Band (managed by Patrick Rains). Larsen (who was still active in Los Angeles at the time of this book's publication), had a long successful career in the studios and television. Tris Imboden, the drummer in Al's touring band, also had an eminent career in popular music; he is best known for drumming for the band Chicago for almost three decades, beginning in 1990. Ricky Lawson, who was Al's drummer for the California concerts in 1989, had toured with Al before, including on the 1984 tour that produced *In London*. He was well known as a founding member of the jazz group the Yellowjackets and for his long stints working with superstars Michael Jackson and Whitney Houston. In the late 1980s and early 1990s, bassist Rickey Minor was already known for his work as musical director for Houston, and after working with Al, he would go on to a distinguished career in television as music director for a legion of specials and awards shows, as well as for *American Idol* and (for four years) *The Tonight Show with Jay Leno*. Like Minor, guitarist Felicia Collins was in her midtwenties at the time of these tours. In 1993, she joined the CBS Orchestra with Paul Shaffer, and she remained in that house band on *The Late Show with David Letterman* until its end in 2015. Background vocalist N'dea Davenport, in her early twenties on the 1989 summer tour, would move the next year to London and become lead singer in the Brand New Heavies, an important group in acid jazz. Al's personal valet, Gene Reed, also sang background vocals and took part in the band's active stage choreography.[2] Percussionist Leonard "Doc" Gibbs worked with Al for years, as well as with such artists as Grover Washington, Anita Baker, Bob James, and (like Lawson and Minor) Whitney Houston. He later led the house band for the Food Network's *Emeril Live* with Emeril Lagasse. Horn players Michael Paulo and Michael "Patches" Stewart joined Al's band together in 1984 and stayed with him for years. Paulo became known for his appearance in the 1984 video for "Raging Waters." Stewart would be a key contributor to Al's 1993 *Tenderness* album.

Vonda Shepard, who played in Al's band as second keyboardist from 1986 to 1990, was on the brink of a significant career. While covering the keyboard parts, Shepard became known as an exceptional singer. In 1989, her self-titled debut album was released on Reprise, the Warner imprint of many of Al's records. She had been working in artist development with Warner Bros. for four years prior to that, and she eventually toured with Al from 1986 to 1990. In the late 1990s, TV writer and producer David E. Kelley heard Shepard singing in a nightclub and promptly put her on his new hit show *Ally McBeal*, where Shepard appeared in 108 episodes as a nightclub singer.[3] On the California shows mentioned later in this chapter, Kiki Ebsen, who had some notoriety as the daughter of actor Buddy Ebsen, took over the second keyboard position from Shepard. Ebsen went on to a successful, if somewhat low-key, career as a singer-songwriter.

A late-winter European tour began on January 28, 1989, in Offenburg, Germany. On February 3, Al and the band played the Wiener Stadthalle in Vienna, Austria. The next concert of the tour was February 6, in Rome, Italy, at the Palazzo dello Sport. It was filmed for Italian television.[4] Herbie Hancock and his band were also part of this concert, which purportedly raised a substantial amount of money for a relief fund for those affected by two recent devastating earthquakes in Armenia.[5]

The music performed in Rome is a good representation of what Al was programming at this time. After a grand, Hollywood-sounding musical "greeting," the band segued into the opener, "Way to Your Heart," from the latest album, *Heart's Horizon*. Next up was "Says," from *L Is for Lover*. (Saxophonist Michael Paulo played a particularly hot saxophone solo on this song.) Then Al worked in his greatest hit, "We're in This Love Together." With that out of the way, after a lengthy free-form introduction, Vonda Shepard and Al sang the soul classic "Since I Fell for You" from the hit record Al had made with David Sanborn. This was followed by "I Must Have Been a Fool," from *Horizon*, "Pleasure," from *Lover*, and "All of My Love," also from *Horizon*. Even though these two most recent albums had not been as popular as earlier ones, Al clearly wanted to highlight his newer material.

From his spoken introduction, Al made it sound like the next song may have been a request, but request or not, it was a staple of his concerts for decades. Al's virtuosic, unpredictable introduction led into an epic version of the Dave Brubeck and Paul Desmond jazz hit "Take Five." In addition to extensive improvisation by Al, mostly imitating congas and shakers (shekere), Doc Gibbs has two solo spots on either side of a long drum solo by Imboden. Then, switching gears after all this rhythmic energy, Al sings the exquisite "Alonzo," one of his compositional gems, which features him imitating flute and whistling, along with an actual flute solo by Paulo.

Al goes into another "drum thing" while sitting on the edge of the stage with Rickey Minor, and eventually they perform "Yo' Jeans" from *Horizon*.

On the album, the song was a vocal duet with Bobby McFerrin on the bass line; here Minor takes McFerrin's place on bass guitar. From this pared-down duo, the full band moves into a long and excitingly funky version of "Sticky Wicket" from 1984's *High Crime*. Larsen and Shepard join the "front line" onstage with portable keyboards, and dancing and high-stepping abound throughout this long extravaganza of musical fun, highlighted by a slapping and popping bass solo by Minor.

The concert closer was Chick Corea's "Spain," another of Al's "jazz" hits like "Take Five," as opposed to his "popular" hits. This extended performance featured Neil Larsen's keyboard work and some welcome soloing from the talented Patches Stewart on flugelhorn. There was a long encore, "Roof Garden," which was also from 1980's *This Time*. A good time seems to have been had by all on this grooving song as well.

This concert, while featuring plenty of Al's more recent material, also presented a more jazz-focused version of Al in the late 1980s, not just on the jazz tunes "Spain" and "Take Five," but also with Al improvising during and between tunes throughout the concert. Perhaps he felt that his jazz side was more respected, or more expected, in Europe, where he had his first great musical triumphs, than in the more pop-oriented United States.

Watching and listening to this concert confirms the truism that live performances are usually, if not inevitably, more exciting than studio recordings of the same material. And Al Jarreau was an artist for whom this was especially true. Al in live performance, with this band in particular, was electric. Just weeks before his forty-ninth birthday, the star looked sleek and slick dressed in all black. He still moved freely and smoothly around the stage, but he left the extraordinarily energetic dance moves to his twentysomething band members. Most importantly, Al's voice sounded as good as ever; he was still at a vocal peak in his career.

As usual, it was a busy tour of Europe. After Rome, the band stopped in cities throughout France, Italy, Germany, the Netherlands, Switzerland, Austria, Norway, Denmark, and Scotland, finally concluding with dates at Birmingham and the Wembley Arena in London (where *In London* had been recorded in 1984). It was an exhausting tour, and it included at least eight pairs of back-to-back nights, with travel in between.[6]

A week after the London concert, the band played a weekend of three concerts at Radio City Music Hall in New York City—a bit of a tack-on to the European tour, though at a revered venue. Stephen Holden reviewed one of the Radio City shows for the *New York Times*, and he voiced some of the same perceptions and reservations that other critics had expressed over the years. He summed up his sense of Al in his opening paragraphs:

> Al Jarreau, who appeared at Radio City Music Hall for three nights beginning Friday with an eight-member band and two backup singers, is half crooner and half improviser. As a ballad singer, he carries forward the tradition of Johnny Mathis by way of George Benson. As an improviser, he is an arsenal of sound effects who especially enjoys imitating funk bass lines and the clicks and snaps of Brazilian percussion instruments.
>
> If the 49-year-old singer is neither one thing or another, his upbeat stage demeanor helps him to homogenize the different facets of his music in shows whose liveliest moments have the free-for-all exuberance of a Brazilian carnival. On Friday night a mood of celebration prevailed on the stage, as the singer moved between traditional pop ballads, sleek pop-funk songs and vocal showpieces.[7]

The Johnny Mathis comparison had been appearing in critiques of Al's work ever since the beginning of his career in Milwaukee. But "Johnny Mathis by way of George Benson" is a description on somewhat shaky ground, given that Al and George were contemporaries and it could be just as likely that Benson was influenced by Al as vice versa.

Holden comments on several of the show's selections, including the "billowing duet between Mr. Jarreau and the soul singer Vonda Sheppard [*sic*] on 'Since I Fell for You,'" "a cheerfully chirpy rendition of his biggest hit, 'We're in This Love Together,'" and "the evening's most elaborate song, 'Spain,' which found Mr. Jarreau putting all his resources into a single piece of musical pageantry."

Though Holden mentions the poor sound reproduction, he concludes the review with some faint praise: "The uniform sunniness of Mr. Jarreau's personality offered little in the way of expressive contrast. Yet the evening still provided enough opulence and communal high spirits to prove uplifting."

Diane Patrick's review in *JazzTimes*, from that same weekend at Radio

City, had a different spin. Patrick began by relating a comment Al made to the audience that possibly revealed his frustration with the smaller crowds appearing at his shows on recent tours. She reported, "He was glad we came, acknowledging that we could have stayed home and watched MTV . . . 'with them no playin', no singin' people.'" But, she said, "We'd come to see him. [And] he gave the audience a show that contained the bonus of leaving you eager to hear more." She especially sang the praises of the band and its members, calling out Vonda Shepard, "with the Teena-Marie-ish pipes," and Rickey Minor and the "frisky, funky Felicia [Collins]."[8]

Patrick was clearly a critic who was also a fan, and she spoke to Al's tremendous ability to connect with an audience: "Jarreau's superior vocalizing, on its own, could sustain a concert. He just loves to sing! Yet his performance is staged to provide maximum visual enjoyment, too: lots of dancing and audience communication." She also noted that he "invites ladies to come up and kiss him," echoing the *Indianapolis Star* review from 1982.

The repertoire in the show Patrick attended included "Moonlighting," "We're in This Love Together," "Since I Fell for You," "Spain," and "Roof Garden." Al sang the old standard "You Are So Beautiful," and on "Yo' Jeans," he "acted as a drum kit, scatting and Bobby McFerrin-ing all the way through." Patrick concludes her somewhat gushy review with an interesting observation: "'He's so *regular*,' my companion exclaimed appreciatively. Indeed!"

These two reviews of similar concerts at the same venue reflected the differing views of two contrasting critics from widely different publications. In some ways, they represented two poles of opinion about Al's music and persona at this point in his career.

While Al frequently toured Europe during the summer, he spent other summers barnstorming the United States, which had many summer festivals. In 1989, from mid-June until early September, the Jarreau band played several major cities: Orlando, Houston, Dallas, Charlotte, Milwaukee, Cincinnati, and Los Angeles. Lesser-known towns on the itinerary included Antioch, Tennessee (near Nashville); Columbia, Maryland (outside Baltimore); Holmdel, New Jersey; Westbury, New York (on Long Island); Noblesville, Indiana (north of Indianapolis); Bonner Springs, Kansas (west of Kansas City); and Greenwood Village, Colorado (a suburb of Denver).

Other major venues outside large cities included the Great Woods Center for the Performing Arts between Boston and Providence, Rhode Island; the Pine Knob Music Center outside Detroit; the Blossom Music Festival outside Cleveland; and the JVC Jazz Festival at the Concord Pavilion, not far from San Francisco.

Years later, referring to one of the hazards of live performance that nonmusicians rarely think about, Al joked about getting his "yearly quota of Memphis mosquitoes at Mud Island [Amphitheater]," on a peninsula that juts into the Mississippi River. He said, "You never stood on that stage and had moths and mosquitoes fly in your mouth when you're inhaling. Unbelievable! But still one of the greatest venues there are [sic]."⁹

A set list from the June 30 concert at the Santa Barbara Bowl in California near the beginning of the tour (and one night after Al had appeared on *The Tonight Show*) reflects a similar lineup to what the band had played at the Rome concert. The openers, "Way to Your Heart" and "Says," remained from the earlier show, followed by three more tunes from *Heart's Horizon*: "I Must Have Been a Fool," "So Good," and "All My Love." These led into the obligatory "We're in This Love Together." Two more tunes performed in Rome were repeated here: "Yo' Jeans" and "Sticky Wicket." A new entry from *Lover*, "Across the Midnight Sky," appeared in this set. Ricky Lawson was featured on a drum solo on this tune, probably in conjunction with percussionist Doc Gibbs, somewhat in the same manner that Tris Imboden and Gibbs had been featured in Rome. The percussion extravaganza led into the groove tunes, with "Roof Garden" as the concert closer and "Boogie Down" as the encore.

Veteran *Los Angeles Times* critic Don Heckman reviewed the concert that took place only three days later in Costa Mesa, on the coast south of Los Angeles. Heckman was one of the few "mainstream" jazz critics who steadfastly kept a positive opinion of Al throughout his career, unlike others who held Al in disdain for straying from what they considered to be America's finest art form. Heckman eventually wrote the notes for Al's 2009 retrospective collection *Al Jarreau: The Very Best Of: An Excellent Adventure*. In his review of the Costa Mesa show, he wrote that "the mood of the evening had been established early on as the singer (who insisted that no 'fun-busters' would be allowed to participate) seemed determined to sustain the proceedings at a virtual fever pitch." He described the instant when the show went from good to great: "There was a magical moment about two-thirds of the way through Al Jarreau's concert . . . when the audience finally surrendered to his unique brand of musical wizardry. The flash point came during 'Does Anyone Want to Go Dancing?' [That is, 'Roof Garden.'] An otherwise-enthusiastic but relatively staid audience jumped to its feet and began to boogie in time with the hip-notic rhythms."[10]

Heckman's one mildly critical remark was leavened with a positive twist. "Despite the apparent lack of musical variety, Jarreau was never boring—and never predictable. He worked with his eight-piece band as virtually equal partners. His between-songs raps worked the audience with the skill and humor of a professional stand-up comedian." Heckman also singled out band members Rickey Minor and Michael Paulo (unfortunately referred to with the misspelled name Powell).

Much of the review was directly focused on the headliner: "Almost constantly in motion, [Jarreau] produced a startling array of vocalized drum sounds in combination with his two percussionists; he sang convincing bass lines and somehow mimed the sound of a feedback electric guitar. He danced and strutted like a peacock, then sat on the apron of the stage and transformed the vast arena into the intimacy of his living room."

Arguing that "the material was secondary to the performer: Jarreau has become such a masterful stage presence that it almost does not matter what he is singing," Heckman concluded his glowing review saying, "By the time he was finished, Jarreau had made good on his threat: There had been no 'fun-busting' in an evening of extraordinary entertainment from a performer at the very peak of his powers."

Regardless of what was going on in his life, whether he was making records, or how well those records sold, Al remained a dynamic performer, seemingly able to win over any crowd, in Europe or the United States.

18

—⫘—

PLUGGING AWAY

While his next album would not be released until 1992, Al continued to tour in the first two years of the decade, though with a
somewhat slimmed-down schedule as compared to that of 1989. In July
of 1990, he made yet another appearance at the Montreux Jazz Festival in
Switzerland. But besides that, apparently the only gig he and the band had
in Europe that summer was at the massive North Sea Jazz Festival in The
Hague, Netherlands. One of the only other performances he was advertised as playing that summer was a single night at the Mountain Winery in
Saratoga, California. Very possibly the touring band did not accompany
Al for this gig, although he probably played with one of the scaled-back
"local" bands that he would pick up for special (and limited) occasions.

In April, Al appeared at the Dorothy Chandler Pavilion in Los Angeles
for an event called "Singers' Salute to the Songwriter." This was the sixth
annual edition of this event, a fundraiser for the Betty Clooney Foundation
for Persons with Brain Injury, founded by Betty's sister, the distinguished
jazz and pop singer Rosemary Clooney. The songwriter honorees for that
year's gala event represented a wide range of music: Matt Dennis, composer of such classic songs as "Angel Eyes" and "Everything Happens to
Me"; Jerry Herman, composer of *Hello, Dolly!*, *Mame*, and other musicals;
and the songwriting team of Jerry Leiber and Mike Stoller, who wrote hits
ranging from "Kansas City" and "Hound Dog" to "Love Potion No. 9" and
"Is That All There Is?" In addition, Cole Porter was given a posthumous
American Legend Award, and Marty Paich received an award for outstanding arrangements.

12

The performers reflected the musical diversity of the honorees. As *Los Angeles Times* critic Kevin Allman noted in the opening to his review of the concert, "It was probably the first time Carol Channing and the rock band Toto have played the same bill."[1] The star-studded event featured singers ranging from R&B legend Ruth Brown to actress Suzanne Somers and from Vikki Carr to Barry Manilow; many other singers from practically every genre of American pop were listed in the article, although it's unclear who actually sang on the show. After Rosemary Clooney opened the show, it carried on for more than three hours and was closed by Little Richard. As Allman reported, Al performed with the evening's orchestra, conducted by Peter Matz.

In May, Al received an honorary doctoral degree in music from the Berklee College of Music in Boston, one of the most respected jazz and popular music institutions of higher learning in the country. The three honorees that spring were a diverse group: Al, rock star Phil Collins, and Atlantic Records founder Ahmet Ertegun.[2]

Al also performed close to home at The Strand in Redondo Beach in July, then at a three-night engagement at the Circle Star Theatre in San Carlos, California, at the beginning of August, followed by a night in Gresham, Oregon. A week later, the band went cross-country to play in Baltimore and Cohasset, Massachusetts.

In October, there were three nights at Caesars Palace in Las Vegas. Prior to this appearance, Al had been interviewed by Michael Paskevich of the *Las Vegas Review-Journal*. Al spoke to the current state of the music business, and particularly to how rap music was taking over a significant part of the market.[3]

Hip-hop was still a small part of the overall music market in 1991, but for much of the year, *Billboard*'s R&B chart was dominated by the soundtrack albums from *New Jack City* and *Boyz n the Hood*, which both featured various hip-hop artists. Albums by Public Enemy and rapper Ice Cube—who, with his group N.W.A., first popularized gangsta rap—also topped the R&B chart in 1991. Since Al's albums of this period were mostly associated with R&B, he may have been particularly sensitive to the power of hip-hop in that segment of the business.

Al found a sympathetic ear in Paskevich, who wrote: "They're not making singers like Al Jarreau these days. In fact, some might ask how many of today's young artists are even singing." "It's a strange time right now," Al said, "because the record companies are so caught up in rap (music) that the typical singers have been forgotten," yet Paskevich notes the lack of bitterness in Al's voice. It seems that Al mostly regretted the dwindling opportunities for young singers to turn their talent into a career. "As a musical veteran," Paskevich wrote, "[Jarreau is] aware that the industry moves in cycles, yet the influx of rappers does have him concerned about artists who have yet to achieve even a small part of his stature in the industry. . . . [He] believes it will get even harder for musical neophytes to follow a timeworn if rugged path toward success." After describing the way Al established himself in small clubs before having a record contract, Paskevich quotes him as saying that "the small club is a dinosaur [in 1991]. . . . There's no place where a guy can just do what he does with four or five players. . . . That kind of place has been disappearing since the '70s." But Al had not forgotten where he—and so many other great singers—*originally* came from: "About the only place left is the church," he said, "and thank God for that. The church will continue to produce the singers."

This appearance was Al's first at Caesars Palace, the very symbol of Las Vegas nightlife, and as Paskevich pointed out, it "mark[ed] one of Jarreau's rare forays into a showroom environment." Al, who did notice a difference playing to casino crowds, looked at this opportunity through his usual rose-colored glasses, saying, "It's very valuable, though, because it gives you the opportunity to introduce yourself to people who don't necessarily know who you are. You have to reach deeper inside to describe who you really are."

At long last, four years after *Heart's Horizon*, *Heaven and Earth* was finally released in June of 1992. For this album, Al's team had chosen the spectacularly successful producer Narada Michael Walden. Walden had first received wide recognition in the mid-1970s as a drummer in the Mahavishnu Orchestra. He added the name Narada to his birth name, Michael Walden, after it was chosen for him by the Indian spiritual leader Sri Chinmoy, who was also influential to the Mahavishnu leader, guitarist John McLaughlin. Walden's brief spot on Weather Report's *Black Market* in 1976 further cemented his reputation in the "fusion" world. He began recording as a leader for Atlantic Records, enjoying modest success in the late 1970s. But he saw more success as a producer. By the time he and Al

In 1992, after four years without a new album, Al released the heavily R&B-influenced *Heaven and Earth*, which went on to win a Grammy Award for Best R&B Vocal Performance.

put together *Heaven and Earth*, Walden had produced successful records for George Benson, Whitney Houston, Aretha Franklin (five records by 1991), Gladys Knight, Natalie Cole, and others. He was a hot commodity in the business.

Heaven and Earth reflects the times. It sounds like many records from this era—not just R&B, but pop and rock albums as well—in its incorporation of some hip-hop sounds, particularly in the sound of the drum set. It is not a studio sound that had a long successful life, at least in the music of Al Jarreau. Some of the album's tunes are catchy in their own way, but none of them became Jarreau standards. Walden's name appears as a cocomposer of every tune on the album (Louis Biancaniello's name also appears frequently) except for the title track and the closing Miles Davis/ Bill Evans jazz classic. In contrast, Al is listed as cocomposer on just "Love of My Life" and "If I Break," and he wrote the lyrics for "Blue in Green."

The album seems to have been an experiment in trying to keep up with the market of the times, and also in pushing Al out of his comfort zone with a new, white-hot producer—very much like the experiment of 1986's *L Is for Lover*.

In a high-visibility article that appeared in the *Chicago Tribune* in late July, Al told Elizabeth Chur about working with Narada Michael Walden. At a certain point during the recording process, Al recalled, Walden said, "'Come on, buddy, give it to me.' He coaxed me to do things I don't typically

do. It was a nice pairing—he's a high energy guy, a catalytic converter."
Al also put a positive spin on the fact that he had no original tunes on the
album, saying, "If I don't limit myself to only the stuff I write, then I get
to do the best of what there is. Is that socialism at work in the arts? [laughs]
It's collaboration, anyway."[4]

After the album's release, Al appeared on Donnie Simpson's *Video
Soul* show on BET (Black Entertainment Television), clearly having been
booked to plug the new record. Al also told Simpson about working with
Walden. He comically but good-naturedly (and knowing Al's uncanny
skills of mimicry, probably very accurately) imitated Walden's manner of
speaking, fast and furious. The value of working with Walden, Al said, was
that "he is so aware of what's happening today, and with that sensitivity
and that kind of awareness, and knowing his artist, he's able to find ways to
bring things out of you that were little corners that you hadn't 'lit' before."[5]

Al described the aura in Walden's studio, which was outfitted with in-
cense, mood lighting, candles, and fresh-cut flowers.[6] "I walked in the first
day," Al said, "and the music stand where I was going to put my music and
lyrics and stuff had a drape over it. The pope would have been proud."

Al related that Walden and "his gang," with help from Al on a couple
of tunes, wrote all the music except for the Miles Davis/Bill Evans classic
"Blue in Green," the one song on the album that connected to the jazz tradition. Walden had asked Al if there were any tunes that he wanted to do
on the album, "fantasy things," and this one came up. They recorded the
song and left it for possible use; then, with jazz giant Davis's death in late
September 1991, the deal was sealed and "Blue in Green" became part of
the album. Al revealed that he first began working on his lyrics to this song
in 1964: "And I was such a young, dumb lyricist at the time; it's probably
best that I didn't finish a lyric, because I surely would have recorded it. I
love the song, but it would have been some goofy lyric, you know? But we
did a new lyric, Frank Martin [who arranged it and played piano] and I, . . .
which is kind of a tribute to Miles and Bill Evans . . . and I'm really proud
of that; I feel like we really pulled a coup d'état there."

Al also stated that Davis was one of his biggest influences: "I think . . .
every musician, contemporary musician, was touched by Miles. And if you
listen carefully to me, you can hear Miles in how I sing."[7]

Continuing to talk about the inclusion of "Blue in Green" (in its two versions) on the album, Al first spoke to what might remain of his "jazz audience," although one wonders how many of them would even be listening to this album. "I hope that I don't offend too many purists by, you know, doing a lyric for such a classic piece," he said. Simpson asked if he worried about that, and Al replied, "Oh, I think about it. . . . Some purists are really pure about things as they were and [think they] should be untouched. But I did it with the greatest respect." Then, Al spoke about the audience that would be more likely to listen to this album, believing that "finally it will turn a lot of young listeners on to some things Miles did, and they may go looking for that stuff, and be re-introduced, or be introduced for the first time, to Miles. Which would be wonderful."

The album found some commercial success. The singles "Blue Angel" and "It's Not Hard to Love You" rose to number seventy-four and number thirty-nine, respectively, on the US R&B chart; and the album peaked at number two on *Billboard*'s contemporary jazz chart, remaining on the list for twenty-nine weeks. More important, and perhaps even surprisingly, the album scored another Grammy win for Al in 1993, as Best R&B Vocal Performance, Male, his first win since his dual 1981 awards in pop and jazz (for "Breakin' Away" and "(Round, Round, Round) Blue Rondo à la Turk"). In an interesting footnote, the late Miles Davis also won a Grammy, not for jazz but for R&B Instrumental Performance.[8]

The interview with Simpson also revealed Al's thinking about his career in 1992. Noting that *Heaven and Earth* was Al's twelfth album, Simpson asked if Al had pictured himself having this kind of longevity when he started in the business. Al responded, "Well, that's what I was hoping for, that's the dream; that's the picture I put up before my face every day and walked towards that picture. . . . Yeah, I'd really hoped for this, and worked at it, and envisioned it. Although I *should* say it's a surprise . . . but . . . it's what I've been working for."

Yet, when asked if he ever worried about this path not leading to a "dream ending," Al thoughtfully replied, "Oh, yeah, I think we all have that kind of concern." Dropping into a stylized voice, he added, "It just *behooves* one to work a little harder." Simpson referred back to Al's classic first album, *We Got By*, and asked about Al's needing to adjust and change, despite the fact that he was a unique figure and had his own niche. Al responded, "Well, I'm affected by the times, like everybody, you know. And

Al (far left) with his brothers (left to right) Emile, Alphaeus, and Marshall at a 1992 reunion in Milwaukee. COURTESY OF ROSE MARIE FREEMAN

I hope in my music that there is some sense of . . . the times. I don't want to keep sounding like 1975."[9] Al also acknowledged, "I probably leaned in the R&B direction harder than I really have ever. [*Heaven and Earth* is] really a solid R&B album that I wanted for this first step into the '90s." Al made a similar comment in his interview with Chur: "I see that the R&B scene is changing. . . . It's a revolution. . . . The music is live and angry."[10] So, his message to record buyers was, "While you listen to rap and scratch, take this album along with you as an alternative."

Stressing that he was not about to leave the music business, and responding to Simpson's question about touring to back up the album, Al said, "I'll be singing in your shower. You'll be sick of me."

As a short summer tour to support the new album kicked off, interviews appeared in newspapers around the country. At the beginning of the tour, Al played New Orleans and Memphis on consecutive nights in June, and features about him appeared in both cities' major papers on the same day, June 26, 1992.[11]

Keith Spera of the New Orleans *Times-Picayune* titled his article "A Renaissance for Al Jarreau," responding to Al's relative inactivity during the previous couple of years. The interview was conducted by phone while Al was in Rome, and Al joked that he was enjoying "'pasta and vino' with the Pope." But, Spera reported, "when the conversation shifted to the new record, he spoke in careful, measured tones, explaining why he made an album that may bewilder longtime fans." Al answered this question at length in his interview with Larry Nager of the Memphis *Commercial Appeal*: "I really wanted to just make my first statement of the '90s to that core of people who have always been there for me, the R&B lover and listener who digs Stevie (Wonder) and Aretha and the traditional sound of R&B. Maybe he's been in a kind of whirlwind of new urban music. And I just wanted to tap him on the shoulder and say, 'here is what I want to do as an R&B guy in the '90s."

In a big reveal, Al also talked to these reviewers about two additional albums that he had recorded between *Heart's Horizon* and *Heaven and Earth* but ultimately decided not to release. "The first consisted of original jazz, the result of a collaboration with noted musicians Steve Gadd, Marcus Miller and Joe Sample," he explained. Al told Nager, "That album was not trash. . . . It'll surface again." (Unfortunately, as of 2023, it has not.) Al then explained to Spera that he created "another album's worth of material with producer and longtime friend Greg Mathieson."[12]

With its R&B sound and style, *Heaven and Earth* was not reviewed in any jazz-centric magazines like *Down Beat*. Yet, the *BRE Music Report*, published by Black Radio Exclusive (which touted itself as "Black Entertainment's Premiere Magazine for 16 Years") chose *Heaven and Earth* as its album of the week.[13] "The soulful vocal styling of Al Jarreau shines throughout this album," the *Report* gushed. "There are great vocal arrangements and even better musical arrangements which bring out his unique voice."

In contrast, Gordon Chambers—writing for the relatively new, popular, and widely circulated *Entertainment Weekly*—was not enamored of the album. *EW* was known for short, to-the-point record reviews for the general reader. Chambers wrote: "Except for the fusionish 'Whenever I Hear Your Name' and the two-part rendition of Miles Davis' lyrical 'Blue in Green' (one slow and sparse, the other in Brazilian-inflected up-tempo), Al Jarreau's new album, *Heaven and Earth*, his first studio effort in three years, finds the ingenious singer haphazardly jumping into the fountain of youth. Next time around, instead of scatting and crooning beautifully over saccharine slow jams and new-jack grooves unworthy of his expansive talent, perhaps he should stay closer to his pop-jazz roots."[14]

Reviews from fall shows in Chicago and New York ran the gamut of reactions associated with Al's work of this era. Achy Obejas reviewed a September concert at the Chicago Theatre in the *Tribune*. He reported on Al's joy in performance, undiminished vocal abilities, and the makeup of his audience:

> Al Jarreau had a very good time Sunday night. He smiled that big smile of his, tossed his head back and, for all the world, looked as though he'd just heard a delightful secret, or taken a big bite of heaven.
>
> Scatting, improvising highs and lows, Jarreau used his voice as an unearthly, angelic instrument that played with, against, and on top of his band. . . .
>
> And what a fine time he had up there, swinging his arms in the air, caressing the microphone, dropping down as if he were going to kneel, then popping back up and taking the notes somewhere else, new and unexpected.
>
> . . . During each solo, the racially mixed audience would whoop and holler, and Jarreau would grin back, nod, and reach again.[15]

Stephen Holden, whose review of Al's 1989 concert at Carnegie Hall was examined in the previous chapter, caught Al in the Big Apple again in November 1992, at Madison Square Garden.[16] Some of his observations, made in what is arguably the entertainment capital of the world, are worth citing. He found more to praise in this concert than he had three years earlier and also felt that the demographics of the audience would be of interest to his readers: "'Look at you! It kind of resembles the United Nations!' Al Jarreau exclaimed to the upscale, interracial audience near the start of his concert at the Paramount at Madison Square Garden on Friday evening. The popular jazz singer went on to point out that he was 'an equal-opportunity employer with women in key places.' He was alluding to the fact that in addition to two female backup singers, his ensemble included Ter[r]i Lyne Carrington on drums."

Holden referred to Al's "upbeat cultural ecumenism" that extended to his "pop-funk style with Brazilian and Afro-Cuban inflections," and noted that "throughout the concert . . . he kept the mood almost giddily upbeat." Echoing some of what he experienced in 1989, Holden writes, "Joy has always been the stock in trade of the singer, who at 52 years old remains a phenomenal vocal technician." Holden mentions the Johnny Mathis influence, as he did three years earlier. But he also points out Al's "supple voice [that] dips into a booming bass-baritone, then soars into a piercing, percussive top register."

But as before, Holden has his reservations, expressing his opinion of Al's shortcomings: "What limits Mr. Jarreau's artistry is his very sunniness. Instead of getting inside song lyrics, he treats everything as a showcase for his formidable technique. He also has a weakness for run-of-the-mill pop-soul songs, which even when tricked up with sound effects and improvisation are hardly worth the bother." Whether Holden was using *sunniness* to indicate a lack of depth is open to interpretation, but many listeners would probably agree that the songs Al was performing during this point in his career were not the highest quality.

Interestingly, neither Obejas nor Holden mentioned the performance of any songs from the new album (at least by name), except for a rendition of Miles's "Blue in Green" in New York.

With *Heaven and Earth*, Al once again showed that he didn't want to repeat himself, that he wanted to keep current, and that he was always trying to reach new audiences. The fact that *Heaven and Earth* has not worn as well as much of his other recorded work does not lessen the validity of those ambitions in the moment. Al's next project, the live album *Tenderness*, would be another of his attempts to try something different.

HEAVEN AND EARTH
Reprise, 1992

Al always wanted to keep moving forward—he did not want to be old-fashioned, musically—and this album is a clear product of its times.

The drums on the opening track, "What You Do to Me," and on "Blue Angel" and "Love of My Life," among other songs, give a hint of what was then a contemporary hip-hop feel. But the drums sound quite different on the second track, "It's Not Hard to Love You," and others. These tracks feature a huge 1980s "arena-style" drum sound: the snare drum that sounds like a rifle shot, and bass drum and tom-toms that sound like some other kind of military ordnance. Although "It's Not Hard to Love You" made inroads on the charts, its lyrics—including the phrase "Girl you're lookin' good, I knew you would / And I love that dress you're wearin'"—and a moaning female voice at the end do not exactly fit a distinguished fifty-something-year-old singer like Al Jarreau. Eight measures of vocal improvisation on each of those first two tunes are about the only thing that suggests they were crafted for Al Jarreau.

"Blue Angel," the other tune that made the charts, has a little doo-wop section at the beginning and in the middle, but otherwise it is similarly generic, except for a mysterious repeated vamp. Its horn parts hearken back to Al's earlier work, but they are without the spark of the great Jerry Hey arrangements of the past. Hey, incidentally, plays on "What You Do to Me," but he did not do the arrangement.

The title track is a dramatic ballad (perhaps overly dramatic, as some of the music of this era tended to be), with huge drum sounds, as well as massive echoey keyboards, including the bass sound.

"Superfine Love" features some nice harmon-muted trumpet commentary in the background and another few bars of good Jarreau improvisation. But for most of the song, Al sings with the clichéd phrasing of the soul music of the time. There is also whistling on the track, which could be Al.

The spoken introduction to "Whenever I Hear Your Name" (following a thunderclap and the sound of rain) will either invite listeners in or turn listeners off, depending on how they feel about that particular device.

The up-tempo "Love of My Life," for which Al is listed as cocomposer, has more rhythmic life than most of the album's other songs, as well as some more complex vocal lines, both in the lead and the backups. And Al improvises with energy over the fade at the end. The lyrics, presumably by Al, are far from his best, including the uncharacteristic line "Can I believe it's me you're pimpin' for?"

"If I Break," another tune for which Al is listed as cocomposer, sounds like a Jarreau statement, both musically and lyrically, including the lines "Makin' mistakes is all so very human / Have to press on is what to do." A brief statement by oboist Paul McCandless over the fade adds a nice touch to this piece.

Al's lyrics to "Blue in Green" showcase the impressionistic images that he often included in his adaptations of preexisting jazz songs.[17] The lines "Poured honey from a horn so sweet / So bitter sweet—each, each melody" are obviously a reference to Miles Davis, whose name is always listed as composer for "Blue in Green" and who first performed the composition. (Jazz insiders almost unanimously credit pianist Bill Evans, who also played on the original track, as at least cocomposer, although he never received legal credit.) Bassist Jeff Chambers, who grew up in Milwaukee but lived and worked in the Bay Area for many years, plays on the slow "acoustic" section of this performance. The second section—the up-tempo Latin-based "(Blue in Green) Tapestry; The Dance"—features some fine jazz scatting from Al, a keyboard solo (presumably by Frank Martin), and some of Al's patented vocal percussion.

With the exception of "Blue in Green," much of *Heaven and Earth* sounds as if it could have been written for any other singer of the era. Though Al brought his special skills to the production, the album has never been considered one of Al's best or most personal efforts.

19

LOOKING BACK

Following the Grammy Award ceremony of February 1993, at which Al won his award for *Heaven and Earth*, the *Milwaukee Journal*'s music critic Thor Christensen saw an opportunity for an interesting cross-generational feature about Milwaukee vocalists. In addition to Al, Milwaukee native Todd "Speech" Thomas of Arrested Development won Grammys with his group for Best Rap Performance by a Duo or Group and for Best New Artist. As Christensen pointed out, "Both [Al and Speech] grew up in Milwaukee's black community, graduated from Milwaukee public high schools and found their fame and fortune only after moving away from their hometown. . . . Yet when Jarreau was asked what advice he would give his fast-rising colleague, the singer struggled with the question."[1]

Al's hesitancy is not surprising, especially in light of his 1992 interview with Donnie Simpson on *Video Soul* when he described *Heaven and Earth* as an alternative for urban listeners who might prefer some music other than "rappin' and scratchin' and samplin' and techno and all [that] stuff."[2] Also, in his 1991 interview with Michael Paskevich in the *Las Vegas Review-Journal*, Al had expressed his concern about the popularity of rap music and decried the opportunities available for up-and-coming singers. But, putting his feelings about rap aside, Al's response to Christensen's question displays his characteristic generosity:

What do you say to a 23-year-old guy whose career explodes like that, where the sky opens suddenly and pours out a blessing? . . .
We're talking about two totally different careers. I started singing

224

in Milwaukee when I was 4 and didn't get a record deal until I was 35. Mine has been a slow, plodding career . . . without smashing record sales. What can I say to a guy who walks onstage at the Grammys with an album that's just sold two or three million copies? I feel like I should touch him so it rubs off on me.

Al didn't know prior to the Grammy ceremony that Speech was from Milwaukee, although his father grew up, according to Christensen, less than a block from the Jarreau family's home on West Reservoir. Al also admitted that he was not familiar with Arrested Development's music. Yet, after what Christensen described as "several long pauses," Al weighed in on Speech's situation by saying:

The short path that [Arrested Development] traveled to success is strewn with the broken hearts of people who try to succeed forever and ever, but never even get their foot in the door of a record company.
    Success like they've received doesn't happen very often. But God smiles on you for a reason. It's important you keep trying to be worthy of the blessing and to turn it into as much as you can . . . because just as success can come in a flash, it can disappear in a flash, too.

Christensen concluded the article with a comment about how "record buyers have largely ignored many of [Al's] records, including his latest." While Al's Milwaukee audiences were always enthusiastic, at this point in his career in early 1993, he may not have been happy with their size. Furthermore, it seems that he hoped the local press would seize on positive role models like Speech and himself to inspire the local community:

"The Grammy comes at a time when I really needed it," [Al] said. "It's a great shot in the arm for me, because this record has gotten very little attention from radio, and even less attention at the cash register." Jarreau said he's also learned you can't count on getting attention from your hometown, either. The singer who wrote and recorded "Milwaukee" [on 1976's *Glow*] and who often does charity work when he's in town has expressed disappointment over the years with the reception given to him by Milwaukee audiences and the Milwaukee media.

"Stories are written about me far and wide, from Paris to Tokyo, so another blurb in the *Milwaukee Journal* is not necessarily what I'm after. But there's so much negative stuff that happens in the city and in the community you'd think the media would jump at any opportunity to say 'Ladies and gentlemen, here's a kid who came right out of the heart of Milwaukee who is doing things that are recognized around the globe.'

"I don't know if [Speech] will experience that same thing with the Milwaukee media as I have as he continues his career. But I do know that the kids in Milwaukee need to hear about other people from Milwaukee who do important things with their lives."

As Al and his team prepared themselves for the next project, which would end up being 1994's *Tenderness*, the idea of performing a live album took hold. "The first record I heard of Al was a live record," said bassist Marcus Miller, referring to *Look to the Rainbow*, "and all that emotion, and all that stuff that he sings with comes right through his feet. We were talking about what to do on this album, and what I wanted to do was see if we could get that again. 'Cause it'd been a long time. See if we could get what Al Jarreau is when he's just performing in front of people, without having to worry about being perfect, you know?"[3]

By this time, Miller was not just an extraordinary bassist; he was also greatly respected in the business as a producer—particularly for Miles Davis's recent albums *Tutu*, *Music from Siesta*, and *Amandla*, which all contained music by Miller. When it came to *Tenderness*, Miller believed that setting a clear goal for the album was critical to its success: "Al and Pat Rains, our manager, and myself, we all talked about it together, what we wanted to accomplish. And that's the important thing, to know what you want to get. I think also we got the band to know what it was that we were trying to get to. . . . We wanted to draw people into the Al Jarreau experience. And everybody got into it."

Al, too, mentioned the importance of setting specific goals for the project. In the video that was made during the production of *Tenderness*, and later used as publicity for the album, Al said: "Typically, a project that has the notion of being a live project is a project that is music that the artist has recorded at an earlier time. And that's pretty much it. But we set out this, this mountain of a goal for ourselves of trying to not only do that, but to look for some standards that have been performed by other people, and do some things that are kind of classic Jarreau pieces."[4]

The album was recorded in front of a live audience, but not in a traditional performance setting. Audiences of roughly two hundred were invited to attend several nights of recording, between May 13 and 20, 1993, at SIR Film Stage in Los Angeles. The venue allowed the band the space it needed for an optimum recording setup, while also providing Al the sort of kick he always got when interacting with an audience—and in this case, a select audience. Over multiple nights, he could record as many songs as he wished in the hopes that he'd capture a magical performance of each one by the end of the week.

Al felt a deep level of trust and comfort with the band, all of whom had worked with him before. The group consisted of Joe Sample on piano, Neil Larsen and Philippe Saisse on keyboards, Steve Gadd on drums, Paulinho Da Costa on percussion, Eric Gale on guitar, Michael "Patches" Stewart on trumpet, and Marcus Miller on bass. Miller was also music director and arranger—in effect, the mastermind for the venture. Stacy Campbell, Sharon Young, and Jeffery Ramsey sang backup vocals. The featured guests included Al's old friend David Sanborn on saxophone and, a surprise to many listeners, noted opera star Kathleen Battle as vocal soloist. Jazz saxophone titan Michael Brecker was listed as a member of the band, not as a featured guest, in the album's credits, but he contributed a memorable solo to "My Favorite Things."

According to Miller, Al's ability to respond to the unexpected was what made his live performances so special: "The great thing about Al is, and the thing that makes him different from all the singers, is that he's reacting, you know? If you're playing the piano, you're accompanying Al, and you play a different chord, instead of the one it was supposed to be, Al sings something different. Because he's always listening to what's going on." And, he added, "what we wanted to do was get a band of musicians who were the same way."

This dynamic between Al and his band is demonstrated by the fact that the performances on the *Tenderness* video are not all the same

Recorded live in the studio in 1993, *Tenderness* became one of Al's fans' most loved albums.

performances that ended up on the *Tenderness* audio recording. Possibly the audio takes chosen for the album were not as arresting visually as those that ended up on the video, although plenty of performances from the sessions probably would have been perfectly acceptable for the album.

Although Al didn't want the album to be completely made up of songs he had recorded before, he did include a core sampling of familiar material. Two of Al's personal "golden oldies" (both his original compositions) made it onto the album: "We Got By" and "You Don't See Me." In the film, Miller explains that "We Got By" meant a lot to him. He says, "Al wasn't sure if he wanted to record that again, just because, you know, guys like Al, they write a song in a period of time and that song is connected to the time, you know? So for him, performing the song was kind of like going back in a time machine. . . . But the song, to me, is timeless. I mean it's real touching and real descriptive." Al stunningly performs that beautiful ballad—the very personal, largely autobiographical title tune from his first Warner Bros. album—and David Sanborn makes a major contribution.

"You Don't See Me," in contrast, is Al at his funkiest. The song had already appeared on both *We Got By* and *Look to the Rainbow*. As convincing as those versions are, this one—particularly the version on the video—is possibly the best yet, highlighted by the interaction between Al and Miller on the opening bass line, and the deep locked-in groove established between Miller and Steve Gadd.

Other previously recorded songs were the longtime Jarreau favorite Elton John's "Your Song," and the Beatles' "She's Leaving Home." For many fans, the versions on *Tenderness* became Al's definitive readings of each (at least, with the exception of concert performances). "Your Song" was a favorite of Al's, and of his audiences, from its appearance on *Glow* in 1976 until the end of his career. His somewhat radical remake of "She's Leaving Home," however, had its fans and detractors when first released on *All Fly Home* in 1978. Speaking on the *Tenderness* video, Al gave some history about doing the song back then and again on the *Tenderness* album:

There are times . . . you find a piece of music written by somebody else, and . . . man, oh, man, you just get swept away by what they were saying in the song. And, very often . . . what they said in the song inspires you to want to say it in just a little bit different kind of way. And so you find that essence . . . and you look for those corners in you that it's speaking to, and . . . there's a kind of marriage of that thing, and what they said, and then this maybe new approach to it, that allows you to say it in your way . . . hopefully with as much meaning as the original artist.

"She's Leaving Home" was in fact on an album of mine in [1978], and that song of the Beatles did have a really kind of special meaning for me, as it has for, I think, any music lover and listener who's heard it. And particularly those who went through that period of time— kids were leavin' home. And the reasons why they left, and went to, lots of them, to the Haight-Ashbury. I was right around the corner from the Haight-Ashbury during those days, so it really had a kind of special meaning for me since a long time ago.

Al also talked about rediscovering the early 1960s hit "Go Away, Little Girl," written by the Hall of Fame songwriting team of Carole King and Gerry Goffin: "It's one of the essential joys for me, . . . to find a piece of music that someone wrote in a meaningful way [*laughs*]—rarer and rarer these days. But one song in particular, after looking at hundreds, maybe a thousand songs, here comes 'Go Away, Little Girl.' And I'm going, oh, man, what a great song."[5]

Tenderness's opener, the Brazilian standard "Mas Que Nada," first popularized in the United States by Sergio Mendes and Brasil '66, had not previously appeared in Al's recorded output. However, Al's great affinity for this style—going back to his duo days in the late 1960s and early 1970s with Julio Martinez, what he often referred to as his "Brazilian period"—is immediately evident.

"Try a Little Tenderness" was first recorded by the Ray Noble Orchestra, with vocals by Val Rosing, in 1932. Pop music giants Bing Crosby and Frank Sinatra had recorded well-known versions, but Al was surely inspired by Otis Redding's popular R&B-infused 1966 rendition. This song seemed to strike an especially sympathetic and enthusiastic reaction from the women in the audience.

"Summertime," from George and Ira Gershwin's and DuBose Howard's 1935 "folk opera" *Porgy and Bess*, is one of the most beloved songs in the Great American Songbook. It has been performed and recorded innumerable times, by great singers and instrumentalists alike.[6] Al and Marcus Miller turned it into another seriously funky affair, with soloing by Eric Gale and Al, and with Paulinho Da Costa featured on a section of percussion breaks.

"My Favorite Things," even with the jazz saxophone solo, is quite different from the other selections on this album. Unlike the other songs recorded in L.A. in May, this track was recorded in December of that year, in New York. The song had made the transformation from the Broadway (and Hollywood) musical hit *The Sound of Music* to iconic status in the jazz scene through John Coltrane's indelible modal outing from 1961. The version on *Tenderness* features Kathleen Battle and is graced by a typically outstanding tenor saxophone solo by Michael Brecker. Al described the origin of the song's surprising inclusion on *Tenderness* to James T. Jones IV of *USA Today*. Jones wrote that Al was

> especially proud of his collaboration with opera diva Kathleen Battle on *My Favorite Things*. The duet came about accidentally.
>
> "We wanted to do a duet with a female singer," says Jarreau. "The obvious ones were not available. By the second or third night (of the recording) in walks Kathleen Battle just to hear what we were doing."

He sent her a demo of an arrangement that combined his pop-jazz vocalese with her operatic singing, and, he says, "she started skipping, and hopping up and down."

Battle had established a reputation in the opera world as a true diva—temperamental, demanding and one of the most challenging stars of that stage to deal with. But, "She's not difficult to work with as has been reported," Jarreau says. "She was no diva around me. She was a sweetheart, a delight, with childlike innocence."[7]

A final song that Al and Miller pulled from the great R&B tradition was Buddy Johnson's "Save Your Love for Me." Al had already struck gold with Johnson's "Since I Fell for You," on David Sanborn and Bob James's 1986 *Double Vision* album. First popularized in the jazz world in 1962 by Nancy Wilson and Cannonball Adderley, "Save Your Love for Me" had been done by a legion of jazz artists since; this cut featured the distinguished alto saxophonist Kenny Garrett.

The two new songs on the album clearly held a lot of meaning for Al. In the video, before launching into "Wait for the Magic," an original by the virtually unknown singer-songwriter Todd Urbanos, Al mentioned that the song had become a favorite of his friend who had died the previous year.[8] Al dedicated the song to this friend on the recording, saying, "This one's for you, Andy."

The lyrics of the other new song, "Dinosaur," included many lines and images that reflected Al's thinking in 1993 about his career, his life, the music scene, and more broadly, life in the United States. On the video, Al says, "It's a special song for me, maybe one of the better things that I've ever had a part in writing. I really do think it'll end up being a favorite, for lots of people, because it's something that speaks to people. D is for darling values that we've kind of, in these days, sort of allowed to become extinct." Al apparently felt that a collective belief in long-held values—both musical and societal—had gone the way of the dinosaurs, expressing in the lyrics that it "made me mad when melodic music died" and that "there is nothing wrong with a love of god traditional."

In a September 1994 *JazzTimes* article, veteran music journalist Don Heckman wrote at length about *Tenderness* and Al's reaction to making it.

He led off his article with a quote from Al: "Just call me a troubadour. . . . A guy who goes out, travels from town to town, does a little dance, makes a little love, sings a little song and says 'Get down, tonight!'"[9]

Heckman continues: "At 54, Jarreau has done a lot more in his multi-faceted career than simply play the role of troubadour. But there's a nice kind of lyrical imagery to the label—an imagery that is perfectly captured in Jarreau's newest album, *Tenderness*." Pointing out that the new album was Al's first live album since 1985's *In London* set, the article, largely through Al's own statements, delineates the difference between the live concert experience—arguably the lifeblood of Jarreau's career—and the studio experience.

Al raved about the "band of super-duper, who's who, billion dollar players" on the album. The combination of the brilliant band and the live audience in the studio created an unbeatable musical product. Al told Heckman, "Fact is, I'm just a different performer in a live situation, where there aren't the strictures and restraints and the sterility of the studio. . . . My forte is standing out there in front of an audience, feeling the emotion and the sentiments that they are feeling, interacting, talking, having fun with them. It's what I do best."

Later in the article, Al expanded on the idea: "When you're working live, you play your horn a certain way because someone screamed something from the audience, or someone sighed in the audience or someone cried in the audience. And it made you play the next line differently than you otherwise would have. That kind of thing doesn't happen in the studio." He made it clear that he was a performer who loved being in front of an audience, relating immediately to people, and working hard. He described the "kind of artist who shines in a live performing milieu. And that's me. I'm a concert artist. I don't just record an album and then stay home. I'm out there singing—whether it's in the living room, in the shower, or in front of an audience. And for me, the audience is the other instrument that's playing along."

Al also eloquently expressed his view of performing and art-making as religious experiences: "The thing that never ceases to amaze me about this wonderful process of performing . . . is the way in which it is at once a chapel and a classroom. A chapel because if we are in the image of God, at all, one of the ways, certainly, is that we are allowed to create something where there was nothing a moment ago. A painting: pick up the brush. A piece of music: open up your voice or pick up an instrument. Something where there was nothing a moment ago, something that has emerged, creatively, out of someone's mind. That is a gloriously satisfying thing to be doing."

In the closing section of the article, Heckman asks if Al, as he approaches his midfifties, is a happy man. "Oh yes," Al responds, adding:

> Now, remember, I'm still working on me. Al isn't complete yet. I have a potential that I don't think I've quite reached yet. And there are some things that I need to fix about me. But, on the other hand, there's no doubt that I have realized some real wonderful dreams. . . . You know, when I was a kid, . . . I had a very specific dream. It went something like this: Wouldn't it be wonderful to be a recording artist, and to make a living as a singer. And until then, it would be wonderful to go to school, and maybe the dream will come true. That was the dream. And that's kind of basically what I did. I went to school, singing at the same time, always knowing that I'd sing somewhere—at a Holiday Inn, or with a Top 40 band, or with just a piano player—and I wound up where I am right now.
>
> So, yes, I'd say it's accurate to say I'm a happy man. . . . Truth is, I wake up every morning happy.

This response marks a decided shift away from the darker place where Al had found himself after the tepid sales of *High Crime* and the disappointment of the Nat King Cole film in 1985. In the intervening years— with the output of *L is for Lover*, *Heart's Horizon*, and *Heaven and Earth*, as well as many tours—Al and his team had continued to push his music in new directions. Some projects were more successful than others, but by the time of *Tenderness*'s production in 1993 and its warm reception in 1994, Al was feeling as good about himself and his music as he had in quite some time. In the accompanying video to *Tenderness*, he said, "The project itself is a kind of highlight for me. . . . But I think in years to come, in retrospect, it will be a highlight album as well." His concluding remark was prescient, as *Tenderness* has remained a Jarreau fan favorite ever since its release. As a bonus, although it did not make the pop charts, *Tenderness* had some commercial success. It peaked at number two on the *Billboard* contemporary jazz chart on June 11, 1994, and remained on the chart for an outstanding forty-two weeks.

Just a couple of months after the bulk of *Tenderness* was recorded in May 1993, Al made his fifth appearance at Switzerland's Montreux Jazz Festival. Not surprisingly, he chose to feature selections that he had just recorded for the album. He enlisted the band that played on the album— Paulinho Da Costa, Steve Gadd, Eric Gale, Marcus Miller, Philippe Saisse, Joe Sample, and Patches Stewart—along with singers Stacy Campbell, Sharon Young, and Jeff Ramsey.[10] David Sanborn made a noteworthy guest appearance at the Montreux show, although his name is not listed on the recording of the concert, which was released in 2016.[11]

The album does not include the band's full set, but all of the songs on *Tenderness* were performed except "My Favorite Things" and "Wait for the Magic." Al began the program with his biggest hit, "We're in This Love Together." Other tunes in the set that were not on *Tenderness* and did not end up on *Live at Montreux* were Al's hit version of "Take Five," and in a preview of a cut that would appear on a future album, "Tutu," which Marcus Miller wrote for Miles Davis's 1986 album of the same name.[12] The encore for the program and the album was new to him, or at least it had not been recorded previously. Al supplied lyrics for Joe Sample's song "Put It Where You Want It" (giving it the new title "Puddit"), a funky jam that concluded the performance. Like most recordings of live performances, especially by Al, this one was loose, with longer versions of the songs; it was even longer and looser than the more controlled "live" recordings of the *Tenderness* sessions. Al stretched out on more of his improvisations than he ever did on a studio recording.

Both *Tenderness* and *Live at Montreux* reveal Al as the playful, improvisational, and versatile musician that critics had described in the days of his earliest albums. But with thirteen albums under his belt showcasing such a wide variety of sounds and styles, critics continued to speculate about whether Al should be considered a jazz, pop, or R&B artist. A widely distributed *USA Today* article published in June of 1994 addressed this issue. James T. Jones IV had written a brief review of *Tenderness* for the paper.[13] In his follow-up feature, "Al Jarreau's 'Tenderness' Brings Back His Jazz Feeling," Jones wrote: "Al Jarreau has hung up his dancing shoes, at least for now. With songs such as *Summertime, My Favorite Things* and *We Got By*, his new album, *Tenderness*, returns the versatile vocalist—who's been known recently for R&B dance hits like *Boogie Down*—to his early days when he wowed the jazz world with his free-wheeling vocalese and scat singing."[14]

Jones noted how appropriate it was that Al would be headlining the first annual road tour of the Playboy Jazz Festival that summer, which would take him to Detroit, Denver, Chicago, Washington, DC, and Atlanta in late August and early September. Jones dubbed *Tenderness* Al's "most vocally spontaneous project in years" and quoted Al as saying, "We came up with an album that really does have a kind of jazz feel about it . . . because we have musicians who've kept feet in both pop and jazz worlds."

Arguing that Al had "straddled both worlds himself [pop and jazz] since splashing on the scene in 1975," Jones related a very short history of Al's career, focusing on 1977's *Look to the Rainbow*, a work that he said was "heralded for combining contemporary rhythms with ear-boggling jazz vocals." But lately, Jones went on, "Jarreau's work has been more pop than anything else," and he particularly noted the lack of jazz on Al's most recent studio album, *Heaven and Earth*. In conversation with Jones, Al recycled his frequently stated desire to find a particular kind of R&B listener, one who had not been converted to rap; but, Jones reported, despite the Grammy Award, *Heaven and Earth*'s "sales were lackluster. [Al] was ready for a change."

When Jones asked Al what his next project might be—jazz? pop? both?—Al responded: "I'll let the reaction to this one let me make the decision to what to do next." Jones reported that "eventually [Al] wants to make a traditional jazz album." Nevertheless, Al didn't regret his more commercial ventures. "That's part of me. I feel *Boogie Down*," he said. "I'm gonna boogie down when I want to. I perform that kind of R&B very well."

Little did anyone know that it would be six years before Al's next completely new album would appear. And by then, the music business—in typical fashion—would have changed yet again.

TENDERNESS
Reprise, 1994

Although this album in many ways reflects the looseness of an Al Jarreau concert, the songs are nonetheless rendered in tighter versions than one might expect to hear at an actual live performance; that is, at a concert venue, not in a studio. What would be more prominent in a concert setting would be more extended improvisation, both from Al and from band members, as on *Live at Montreux*. However, Al improvises more on *Tenderness* than he had on his more recent albums. His patented "vocal percussion," a signature of his style and a vehicle for much improvisation, appears on this album on "Mas Que Nada" and "You Don't See Me."

Al's version of what is generally considered scat singing is heard on "Mas Que Nada," "My Favorite Things," "Summertime," "We Got By," and "Go Away, Little Girl." On the latter, he freely interprets the melody on the verses, especially the first—perhaps even beyond the recognition of some listeners who thought they knew the tune. He improvises a bass line at the beginning of "Your Song," and there is an extended vocal cadenza right before the end of "Your Song," which includes a segment from Johann Sebastian Bach's "Jesu, Joy of Man's Desiring."

Besides the instrumental solos mentioned in the chapter, attention should be directed to Joe Sample's stellar piano solos on "Mas Que Nada" and "She's Leaving Home," and Patches Stewart's understated solo statement on harmon-muted trumpet in "Save Your Love for Me."

Overall, this album is one of the extraordinary achievements of Al's career.

LIVE AT MONTREUX 1993
Eagle Records, 2016

If one compares the performances on this live recording to those that appeared on *Tenderness*, a theme could be "It's not quite like on the record," an expression Al sometimes uttered during concerts. The ways in which they differed would be expected when comparing an album created from a series of live-in-the-studio performances (*Tenderness*) with an album of one live concert (*Live at Montreux*). At Montreux, Al interprets the songs more freely (for a notable example, listen to "Summertime," on which he improvises a whole chorus), and both he and the band members get a little more solo space. One could argue that those characteristics make the Montreux performances of the songs "jazzier" than the performances of the songs on *Tenderness*. However, Al and the band play almost the same set of songs in each instance; and the Montreux concert was much more R&B than jazz.

Lending even more of a pop sensibility to the concert was that Al began the show with his biggest pop hit, "We're in This Love Together." Surely he knew the audience would expect this hit, and perhaps he just wanted to get it over with at the beginning, even though he could have started the program with something fresher and jazzier. That being said, this rendition of "We're in This Love Together" is not like any other on record, largely because of the rhythm feel set up by Marcus Miller and Steve Gadd. Al also inserts a brief vocal flourish at the end.

The two band members who especially profited from the opportunity to stretch out at Montreux were guitarist Eric Gale and trumpeter Patches Stewart. Gale trades bluesy guitar licks with Al (using his voice, of course) on "Try a Little Tenderness," and Gale is also prominent on "Your Song" and "Puddit (Put It Where You Want It)," on which he has a lengthy solo. Patches has a much more extended spot on "She's Leaving Home" than he had on *Tenderness*, and he makes a busier statement here than he did on his other recorded solos with Al. He also took the spot held on *Tenderness* by saxophonist Kenny Garrett on "Save Your Love for Me."

Philippe Saisse is not officially featured until "Puddit," the last number on the program, but throughout the show, he makes ample use of the Hammond B-3 organ sound on whatever keyboard he was playing, a sound closely associated with soul and R&B.

Joe Sample gets plenty of chances to shine, with one of his longer electric piano solos coming on "Puddit." Sample's composition "Put It Where You Want It"—which was originally released on *Crusaders 1* in 1972, shortly after the Crusaders removed "Jazz" from their band name—was one of a small number of instrumental records of that era to climb as high as number fifty-two on *Billboard*'s Hot 100, as it did in September of that year. Al had written lyrics for the song by 1993, but Al's version, "Puddit," didn't appear on a Jarreau studio album until 2000's *Tomorrow Today*, where Al sang it unaccompanied.

Bassist Marcus Miller, who did not have to worry about being the producer of this album as he had throughout *Tenderness*, is his usual rock-solid musical self throughout; he shows off his formidable "slapping" chops on the closer, "Puddit."

It's good to hear a rare recorded version of "Alonzo," one of Al's most arresting songs.

This album received a mostly descriptive but positive review in *JazzTimes* upon its 2016 release (only a half year before Al's death), stating that it "showcases the soul-jazz master not only at his vocal peak but also among the most exemplary company of his long, distinguished career."[15]

This is not an essential Al Jarreau record, and it could be argued that it is primarily for completists, who want every Al Jarreau recording available. But it's always good to have a well-recorded live performance from Al.

20

TAKING STOCK

The second half of the 1990s marked a period of uncertainty and low studio output for Al—due, in large part, to the fact that his two-decade contract with Warner Bros. expired in the mid-1990s. As a result, Al did not record any albums of completely new material between 1994's *Tenderness* and 2000's *Tomorrow Today*. His absence from that milieu made him a sort of "missing person" in the music business. Likewise, he does not appear much in the media of the time, either.

In 1996, probably a year or two after his contract expired, Warner Bros. released *Best of Al Jarreau*—a compilation featuring two new tracks, as well as thirteen favorites from previous Warner/Reprise albums. Al's old friend George Duke produced the two funky new cuts, "Compared to What" and "Goodhands Tonight." These were quite likely the last recordings Al had done for the label while his contract renewal was being discussed. The album's final track, "Like a Lover," hadn't previously appeared on a Jarreau album, but it had been released on a heavily produced collection of bossa novas featuring various artists.

A 1997 *Los Angeles Times* article by Al's longtime advocate Don Heckman sheds considerable light on Al's recording situation with Warner Bros. during this period—as well as a personal situation. The article begins:

Al Jarreau is feeling betwixt and between.

And with good cause. After living in temporary digs for the last 18 months, he's still waiting for contractors to finish up the work on his earthquake-damaged Encino home.

While Al and Warner Bros. un-
successfully tried to negotiate
an extension to his contract,
the label released the first of his
compilation albums, *Best of Al
Jarreau*, in 1996.

"But it wasn't just the earthquake," he said in a conversation last
week. "We took a pretty good hit, but we also had some basic problems in the house from the very beginning. Practically every major
system—except for the plumbing—had to be replaced. In other
words, we got a lemon."

To compound the problem, Jarreau is also beginning to see some
distinctly lemony qualities in his recording career, which has been in
limbo for virtually the same period of time. And the veteran performer
is no more happy about that than he is about his housing problems.[1]

Al described his situation with the label in colorful language: "'We've
begun to circle each other like jungle lions, and look each other up and
down,' he explained. 'But I don't know if we're going to get together or
not.'" Heckman also interviewed Matt Pierson—Warner's vice president
for jazz, who had produced the *Best of* album—and described him as
"guardedly optimistic" about the situation with Al. Pierson apparently
told Heckman, "We want to do a deal, and we've been in negotiation, . . .
but it's one of those things where—let's say you had a relationship with a
woman, and it breaks up, then you decide to get back together—there's a
lot of baggage to work through. And that's sort of where we are. But we
certainly want to work with Al, who is an incredible artist."

Heckman provides an insightful description of Al's broad-based audience, stating that Al is "admired by jazz fans for the imaginative, improvisational qualities of his singing, [and] cherished by R&B and pop listeners for the entertaining, rhythmically explosive qualities of his live performances." And, considering Al's large fan base and the gold albums he had accrued for Warner Bros. over decades, Heckman wrote that Al "continues to be bothered by what he sees as a lack of record company support and interest." Heckman continued:

> Like many mature pop artists, Jarreau sees the record business no longer willing to make long-term commitments to support performers' careers.
>
> "They sit there and throw handfuls of artist mud against the wall. And what sticks they go and build a frame around for a few minutes. And I can tell you it's not a gilded frame in which they've invested a whole lot. What they really want is these still wet-behind-the-ears people who will color their hair a strange color, turn their lives over to some hot producer, be there for five minutes of airplay in a year, get their pictures in a magazine and then be gone. They don't want to deal with someone who understands the mechanism of this madness."

Pierson, according to Heckman, noted "that artists are frequently unhappy with their record companies." And Pierson is allowed the last words in the article's back-and-forth between artist and label representative, saying:

> Al, and nearly every artist I've ever worked with, has been critical of the record business in general, . . . and critical of us specifically, from time to time, because that's the nature of the business. You can always look back on any record and say, "I could have done it differently." And that's probably true here. But there also are times when you can say, "I really blew that one." And I don't think that's the situation with Al Jarreau. I think that Warner Bros. Records feels that it did a very good job with Al when he was on the label.

Despite his complaints about Warner Bros., Al seemed determined not to panic about his uncertain recording situation. He was well aware of the fact that his arresting live performances were at least as important as records to the success of his career. As he said to Heckman:

> Everything that's happened for me up to now . . . has worked because I go out there and I do a good show. I've been doing that for more than 20 years, and that's got nothing to do with the record company. I've stayed alive in the record business because I've been out there being a salesman, telling people, "Listen to this." They listen and bring a friend back, and that friend goes and buys a record and that's my new customer.
>
> I'll keep pounding on people's doors, and just keep on doing what I've been doing, asking them to listen to the songs I have to sing.

In addition, Al was taking other measures to keep his career afloat without a label. He reduced the size of his team and band, and he began traveling with a smaller group of musicians and singers than he had when he was under contract with Warner Bros. "His backup vocals now come from the musicians in his group rather than a separate group of singers," Heckman reported. "And his booking and management have been combined into one operation."

In fact, a couple of years after the Warner Bros. contract expired, a major change in Al's business operations occurred: he parted ways with Patrick Rains, who had been his manager since before his breakout in 1975. "We'd had a long and mutually successful career together," Rains reflected many years later. "And for a long time we were . . . able to stay in solidarity in terms of goals and ambitions and all the rest of that. But eventually things run their course. Not everything lasts forever. And I think we both had gotten to the place where we felt like it was time to shake hands and say goodbye on an up note [rather] than . . . maybe not such an up note. So . . . it was a mutual decision that it was time to move on, for both of us."[2]

Al and Rains had worked together for what amounted to a very long time in the music business. Rains's skill and efficiency were coupled with a vision for growth and exploration that served Al extremely well and had been crucial to his career success. In the wake of their breakup, Al chose to replace him with a familiar face, and Bill Darlington made the transition from tour manager, a position he'd held for ten years, to manager. As Rains described it: "It was easier for [Al] to stay with somebody that he knew, who also knew Al's routine, and Al didn't have to go through that whole, you know, reeducation process of how to do things. Because every artist has their likes and their dislikes, and the way they like to travel, and how they want things to happen on a gig day. Or how they want things to happen backstage. And it takes time to learn all that, and I think . . . Al was much more comfortable sticking with somebody he already knew."[3] By almost all accounts, Darlington was a dedicated, sympathetic, resourceful, and problem-solving manager, and he and Al went on to work together for ten more years.

Not coincidentally, Susan became more active in the business side of things during this time of transition. Years later, Theresa Robinson, Susan's good friend and sometime assistant, reflected that "[Susan] put all of her energy, a lot of her time and energy, [in]to mak[ing] sure that her husband's career, from the time that she met him going forth, was where he wanted it to be—[that] his ideas, his focus, his dreams were met."[4] On the other hand, some members of Al's circle viewed Susan's increased involvement as an intrusion into Al's business, and possibly even musical, affairs.

With the loss of his longtime manager, the expired contract, and a significant gap between albums of new material, Al's career was in flux. Some critics and fans may have wondered if this was the beginning of the end. But in fact, Al was in no way ready to wind down his career. As critic Alan Sculley noted, an album like 1996's *Best of Al Jarreau* "very well could have signaled a move to a more relaxed recording and performing schedule. Instead, Jarreau, still looking youthful at age 57, saw the record as a launching pad for an ambitious slate of new projects."[5] "If I were of a different mind, I might be thinking about finding a little hut on the beach and going and retiring," Al joked in response. But that particular fantasy is not at all the one Al chose to pursue.

In more than one interview in the summer of 1997, Al used a sports metaphor—perhaps a holdover from his youthful days as a competitive athlete—to describe how, at age fifty-seven, he saw himself as being at "halftime in the locker room, putting together some new plans, getting ready to come out smoking for the second half."[6] In one article, he went into a bit more detail: "It's halftime for me. I'm in the locker room drawing circles and arrows and dotted lines on the blackboard . . . putting together a lineup for this second half of the ball game. I'm coming out smoking for the second half and I've got some plays that you haven't seen before."[7] Related to the idea of an athletic comeback, Al began taking better care of himself during this period, curbing some destructive behavior such as drinking and smoking that had been getting out of hand.

One of Al's "new plays" was a collaboration with the iconoclastic composer Lou Harrison. Harrison was born in Portland, Oregon, in 1917, and after studies with the important twentieth-century composers Henry Cowell and Arnold Schoenberg, he formed professional alliances and collaborations with fellow composer John Cage and a number of professional dancers and troupes. He became best known for his many works inspired by non-Western music, most particularly Javanese gamelan music.

Harrison's Symphony No. 4 (which the composer jokingly referred to as his "Last Symphony") was recorded in 1997 by the California Symphony (directed by Barry Jekowsky), along with a number of Harrison's other works, for the album *Lou Harrison: A Portrait*. The symphony's last movement, titled "Three Coyote Stories," features Al's vocals. The stories come from the Navajo tradition, in which Coyote is a mythological character central to many ancient stories (in some First Nations cultures, Coyote is a divinity). In the symphony, the vocalist is required to both recite and sing parts of these stories, and Al excels at both. His voice is clear and expressive, both while reading and while singing the extended pentatonic melodic sections that appear over a washlike drone of percussion instruments. "They wanted a different kind of voice to do it rather than a straight-ahead classically trained kind of singer," Jarreau explained to Alan Sculley at the time. "You'll catch a little different edge in my performance." Al's controlled interpretation and clean diction and delivery fit the piece beautifully.

Another classical project that Al hinted at in the Sculley article was a series of performances with symphonies around the country. In the article, which was published in the Allentown, Pennsylvania, *Morning Call* shortly before the performances began, Al stated: "I'm trying to find some things from different areas that I've looked forward to performing for a long, long time. . . . I'm thinking some music from Broadway. I'm even looking at some classical things that might work for me." And, indeed, while much of Al's contributions to the concerts featured predictable selections such as

"We're in This Love Together," "Spain (I Can Recall)" and "Take Five," there was one musical surprise: a Leonard Bernstein tribute with "a spirited condensation of tunes from *West Side Story*." Al's fondness for this musical can be traced all the way back to his days as a teenager in Milwaukee at the Driftwood Inn and the Holiday House, where he sang the arrangement of "Something's Coming" crafted for him by Lincoln High School band director Ron DeVillers. To kick off this symphony project, Al played with seven different orchestras during October and November 1997.

A review in the *Washington Post* of a November 1998 concert gives some insight into the progress of this project in its early days, performed with an outstanding orchestra in the nation's capital, at a symbol of American "high culture," the Kennedy Center. Mike Joyce reported:

"We're in Washington, D.C., we got a symphony," scatted Al Jarreau as he strutted across the Concert Hall stage at the Kennedy Center Friday night, kicking off what turned out to be not your average symphonic pops concert.

Assembled behind the singer, who is capable of producing an orchestral palette of sounds by himself, was the National Symphony Orchestra, conducted by Jarreau's longtime collaborator Gil Goldstein. The unusual setting clearly inspired the singer, who wore a beret and nurtured a mood that was "loose, very loose." He spent much of the evening demonstrating the full range of his voice, singing and improvising with remarkable tonal agility and accuracy. At various times, in fact, the orchestra's reed, string and percussion sections could each count the singer as one of its own.[8]

Joyce felt the need to express one reservation about the collaboration: "Given Jarreau's penchant for unpredictable flights and flourishes, it was perhaps inevitable that the blend of vocal and orchestral dynamics wasn't always perfect. Yet those moments were fleeting."[9] His review, as many others would be over the course of the project, was overwhelmingly positive.

Yet another project Al discussed in the Sculley article from 1997 was a collaboration with the German classical singer Gregor Prächt. The two recorded a single of the Charlie Chaplin song "Smile" backed by a full orchestra conducted by David Benoit, who also arranged the piece.[10] In December 1997, Robert Koch, the A&R manager for the pop/rock division of Koch Records, was quoted as saying, "This cooperation with such high-quality, internationally renowned artists as Al Jarreau and Gregor Prächt is an honor for us. We believe in this powerful team as well as in the high-quality artistic production."[11] An album and tour were purportedly on the docket for the following year. But, despite the obvious high hopes for this project, there is no evidence that anything was ever recorded or released besides the single.

In addition to the classical collaborations, Al also told Sculley that he was pursuing the idea of a big-band album. Apparently, someone had approached Al with a specific big-band project in mind, including an interested record label, but the project had since stalled. Still, Al loved the idea and had become convinced that such a project—along with several others—would be right for him. "I need to do a big-band album," he said. "I don't know how soon. I just really need to find about 36 hours in a day and I could get to that Brazilian album that needs to happen and a simple little trio album with acoustic bass and acoustic piano and drums."[12]

On top of all of the varied musical projects Al was contemplating in 1997, he was also beginning to dip his toe into the world of acting. In the spring of 1996, he had done a three-month stint on Broadway, playing Teen Angel in a revival of Grease at the Eugene O'Neill Theatre. He took over the Teen Angel role from another iconic African American musician of a considerably different ilk: Chubby Checker.[13] Checker (born Ernest Evans, in 1941) was Al's contemporary; however, Checker's heyday began when he was a teenager in 1960 with "The Twist," a hit that preceded Al's first major record release by fifteen years. Evidently, there was a push to integrate the cast of the Broadway production of Grease in the mid-1990s, in contrast to the virtually lily-white cast of the hit 1978 film based on the show. At the same time Checker, and later Al, played Teen Angel, another Black music star, Jody Whatley, played the role of Rizzo. Teen Angel, an imaginary guardian angel, is a relatively small part in the show and primarily requires strong singing from its actor. (In the movie version of Grease, the 1950s teen idol Frankie Avalon played the part.) This role occupied only a few months of Al's life, but by all accounts, it was an enjoyable interlude.

By the time of his interview with Sculley in 1997, Al was turning his interest away from Broadway and toward acting for television and film. "I really would like to get a little foot in the door . . . to do some acting roles," he said. "I'm talking about screen acting, not real stage acting. I think there's a difference, and I think there may be something for me in screen acting. . . . Nobody's beating down my door and asking me to come to Hollywood, but eventually I think there will be some things that will come from it from time to time, which is just the way I should be approaching it. I don't want to stop doing music, but from time to time there may be things (acting roles) for me to do."[14]

At this point, Al's other acting credits included guest appearances on Fox's *New York Undercover* in 1995 and NBC's *Touched by an Angel* in 1997. He also performed a very hip scatted duet with R&B sensation Vesta Williams for a McDonald's commercial advertising its Big Mac for the 1996 Olympics. The appearances on *Touched by an Angel* are particularly noteworthy. The series ran from 1994 to 2003. One of its stars was Della Reese, who, after being discovered by the great gospel singer Mahalia Jackson, had a significant career as a singer before moving to television and movies. Reese played an angel in this religious-themed series. In the two episodes in which Al appeared, "Amazing Grace" Parts 1 and 2, most of the action takes place at a strip mall in "the hood," as it is described in the show. In addition to Reese, these episodes feature a cross-section of some of the finest African American acting talent of the period: Esther Rolle, Lynn Whitfield, Loretta Devine, and Louis Gossett Jr., who ends up pretty much stealing the show. Al is cast as a minister, a role in which he probably felt quite comfortable, given his upbringing in a minister's churchgoing family. His brief appearances also allowed him to sing a little, although his voice does not stand out as he sings along with the congregational chorus and Devine.

Even without a record, Al made some notable live appearances in the United States during this time of transition. He performed two concerts at Carnegie Hall in the summer of 1995 as a headliner of the JVC Jazz Festival; the eclectic all-female vocal group from Belgium (with African roots), Zap Mama, shared the program. Stephen Holden's review in the *New York Times* mixed praise and criticism; overall, he was lukewarm about Al's show. Similarly, *The Christian Science Monitor*'s Frank Scheck, in his review titled "Jarreau Borders on Excess," praised Al's considerable skills and enumerated the various vocal sounds Al could produce, but also expressed his reservations about how those sounds were put to use, writing that Al's "seemingly inexhaustible supply of tics and mannerisms" trivialized Elton John's "Your Song" by "stripp[ing] it of feeling." Still, Scheck admitted that "there were many fans who had acquired a taste for Jarreau's peculiarities, and who cheered vociferously."[15]

Al also had a signature appearance in August 1996. He and his band were the closing act at the storied Newport Jazz Festival, America's oldest jazz festival. The band was smaller than it had been just a few years earlier. There were no backup singers—instrumentalists supplied the extra vocals—and the only horn player was Scott Mayo, who played soprano and alto saxophones, as well as keyboards, and contributed vocals.[16] As usual, the band was very skilled, including three veterans of earlier tours: Neil Larsen on keyboards, Rickey Minor on bass, and Charles "Icarus" Johnson on guitar. Besides Mayo, drums were played by another first-timer, Michael Baker, who, like Minor, later came to fame with Whitney Houston's band. Al was not in his best voice, but it was, as always, an entertaining show, and the crowd certainly seemed to have a good time.[17] Shortly after this, the touring band became a quartet—an even more stripped-down group that included some new faces. This smaller ensemble reflected the "unplugged" phenomenon in the music industry at this time, when acoustic performances were popular in many areas of the business. This smaller group allowed Al to perform more jazz, since the lineup more closely resembled a jazz combo.

Pianist Freddie Ravel became Al's music director in 1998, taking over for Neil Larsen. Born to a father of Eastern European heritage and a Colombian mother, Ravel grew up in Los Angeles. He first came to fame while working as a band member for Earth, Wind & Fire and on the soundtrack of the movie *Evita* with Madonna. He would make a major contribution to Al's 2000 album, *Tomorrow Today*.[18] Guitarist Ross Bolton ended up playing in Al's band for about ten years.[19] Argentinian drummer Jota Morelli first came to the United States in 1985. He worked mostly with other Latin American artists prior to joining Al's band.[20]

Bassist Chris Walker grew up in Houston and attended the highly regarded High School for the Performing and Visual Arts, which has trained many notable jazz musicians.[21] After graduation, he went to New York, attending the New School. While interacting with many mainstream musicians, his most important early association in the city was with the avant-garde pioneer and icon Ornette Coleman. Walker ended up living with Coleman, and he toured with Coleman's band for several years. His next career move was a complete turnaround, as after alternating tours with Coleman and R&B singer Regina Belle, Walker became a soul singer. He made two highly successful records as a solo artist. But a call from a mentor from the New School, Gil Goldstein, who was conducting and arranging for Al's orchestra project, turned Walker's career around. Walker joined one of the orchestra tours in 1996, and at the end of that tour, Al asked him to join the regular touring band. He became Al's music director in 2000 after Ravel, and while both playing and singing, Walker remained in that position until 2008, when he took a two-year hiatus to be with his family. He then returned to Al's band and remained until the end. His outstanding bass playing and superb vocal skills made him an extraordinarily valuable member of the group.

Ravel, Bolton, Morelli, and Walker remained the heart of Al's touring group for some years. However, the response of Al's core audience, and concert promoters, to this band transformation was not particularly positive. Many people still wanted to hear Al's hits, in renditions that sounded at least somewhat close to the original versions. This was not possible with the smaller band, no matter how skilled the players were.[22]

Al also had a few guest appearances during this unsettled part of his career. On guitarist Lee Ritenour's tribute to the great Brazilian composer Antônio Carlos Jobim, A Twist of Jobim, Al comfortably sang duets with Oleta Adams on two of Jobim's well-known songs. He also guested on the Danish-born Doky Brothers' second Blue Note album, Doky Brothers 2 (1999), singing on the opening track, "How Can I Help You Say Goodbye."

Additionally, Al guested on a track on smooth jazz saxophonist Boney James's 1997 album Sweet Thing. James was a skilled player, like most smooth jazz artists who gained any measure of fame. Yet fans of "real" jazz, and many other audiences, are turned off by the atmospheric soft sounds and the lack of excitement and drama that are associated with the genre. Despite what some critics may have thought, Al was probably happy to take this recording opportunity at this point in his career. James asked him to supply a smooth vocal to the track "I Still Dream." While this title might have indicated some sort of inspirational message had it been a Jarreau song, this "Dream" is simply a love song. The deeper importance of this appearance, though, relates to the fact that James's coproducer on the album was Paul Brown. Brown would play an important role in the next phase of Al's recording career.

Though many people must have speculated about the state of Al's career in the late 1990s, he had several acts ahead of him. In fact, his new manager, Bill Darlington, was in the process of successfully buying the rights to Al's Warner Bros. recordings from the company, which would turn out to be a very valuable career move. "It's been a good career," Al said in his 1997 interview with Don Heckman. "Am I concerned about where things now stand with my recordings? Sure. I'm as nervous as a frog on a freeway. I keep waiting for one of the shoes to fall. But I have high hopes, high apple pie in the sky hopes, and I'm still thinking that there's some serious success ahead of me."[23]

BEST OF AL JARREAU
Warner Bros., 1996

Besides its two new George Duke–produced tracks—"Compared to What" and "Goodhands Tonight"—two other tracks on this album were well-known hits that had not appeared on previous Al Jarreau albums: "Moonlighting" from the *Moonlighting Soundtrack* (1987) and "Since I Fell for You" from the Bob James and David Sanborn album *Double Vision* (1986).

The compilation's last track, "Like a Lover," was from *Symphonic Bossa Nova* (1994), an album featuring Italian conductor Ettore Stratta leading the Royal Philharmonic Orchestra. Al's performance of "Like a Lover" (titled "O Cantador" in Portuguese) is not one of his very best, as his tuning is not as precise as usual and his tone quality varies. But he contributes his signature style to the interpretation, including some risky changes of register. This sits on top of a lush full orchestra and rhythm section arrangement that is quite lovely. And Al Jarreau, even at less than his best, still produces far better vocal performances than most singers.

The other cuts on *Best of Al Jarreau* are "Agua De Beber" from *Glow*; "Take Five" from *Look to the Rainbow*; "Spain (I Can Recall)" and "Never Givin' Up" from *This Time*; "Roof Garden" and Al's big hit "We're in This Love Together" from *Breakin' Away*; "Mornin'" and "Boogie Down" from *Jarreau*; "After All" from *High Crime*; "So Good" from *Heart's Horizon*; and "Heaven and Earth" from *Heaven and Earth*.

While it seems that Warner Bros. may have given up on Al by this time, this compilation did relatively well on the market. It peaked at number eight on the *Billboard* contemporary jazz chart on November 29, 1996, and remained on the chart for a highly respectable seventy-two weeks.

LATE 1990S RECORDINGS

California Symphony conducted by Barry Jekowsky. *Lou Harrison: A Portrait.* **Argo, 1997.**
Al recites and sings on movement IV of Harrison's Symphony No. 4, "Three Coyote Stories."

Lee Ritenour. *A Twist of Jobim.* **i.e. music, 1997.**
Guitarist Ritenour, a longtime studio and fusion stalwart, made a number of albums devoted to Brazilian music. Al was a logical choice to interpret a couple of Jobim's standards: "Waters of March" and "Girl from Ipanema." Oleta Adams, whose greatest fame came from her collaboration with the British band Tears for Fears in the 1980s, was a less obvious choice. But she and Al seamlessly make these great songs work.

Boney James. *Sweet Thing.* **Warner Bros., 1997.**
"Sweet Thing," the title track that features Al, is a very sweet tune—that
is to say, smooth jazz at its smoothest. It may take some listeners a while
to realize that it is Al singing. His personality is most certainly minimal-
ized in this type of setting. But this proves his versatility as a singer. If Al
had never had a solo career, he probably could have been quite successful
as a studio singer, singing "for hire" in whatever style was needed for any
particular session.

Doky Brothers. *Doky Brothers 2.* **Blue Note, 1999.**
Pianist Niels Lan Doky and bassist Chris Minh Doky grew up in Copenhagen; their mother was Danish, their father Vietnamese. Both brothers
attended the Berklee School of Music in Boston, then embarked upon
successful careers in mainstream jazz. *Doky Brothers 2*, like their Blue
Note debut, featured many well-known guest artists. "How Can I Help
You Say Goodbye" is a simple yet interesting song, delivered in a straightforward but soulful manner by Al.

21

BACK TO THE STUDIO

At the turn of the century—and the millennium—on January 1, 2000, the widespread fears that the "Millennium Bug" would shut down the proper functioning of financial institutions, power plants, and other essential services were allayed. The vast segment of the world that depended on modern technology heaved a collective sigh of relief.

Al Jarreau was likely doing some reflecting of his own around this auspicious marker on the calendar, given the hitch in the latest phase of his career, as well as the fact that he was approaching his sixtieth birthday. But after his long recording drought, Al finally returned to the studio to make his next album, *Tomorrow Today*, which was ultimately released in March 2000, just days before his milestone birthday.

The project resulted from a couple of reunions for Al—most significantly, with Tommy LiPuma. LiPuma was the first Warner Bros. executive who had heard Al at the Troubadour in 1975—a connection that led to Al's signing with the label. LiPuma subsequently coproduced Al's early albums *Glow*, the Grammy-winning *Look to the Rainbow*, and 1985's *In London*. LiPuma was also a longtime friend of Al's manager at the time, Bill Darlington, and the two worked out a contract for *Tomorrow Today* that was to everyone's liking.

In the 1970s, Larry Rosen and pianist-composer Dave Grusin had begun producing records by artists such as Earl Klugh, Angela Bofill, Patti Austin, and Lee Ritenour, for a variety of labels; by the end of the decade, they had established their own label, GRP/Arista. Eventually, GRP became the home of some of these artists, in addition to more mainstream jazz figures like

Chick Corea, Dizzy Gillespie, and Gerry Mulligan. LiPuma took over the label from its founders in the mid-1990s. He signed singer-pianist Diana Krall to the label, and her records almost immediately became bestsellers in this specialized corner of the music market. In 2000, Al was a perfect match for the label, which was then called GRP/Verve.

Al had worked with Paul Brown—the ultimate producer of *Tomorrow Today*—when Al recorded as a guest on Boney James's *Sweet Thing*, which Brown coproduced. According to stalwart studio veteran and Al's close associate Larry Williams, Brown was known as "the go-to guy" in smooth jazz by 2000.[1] He had worked with Boney James, smooth artists Kirk Whalum and Rick Braun, and even more established veterans and "pre-smooth" figures such as Bob James and George Benson. Al was searching for a way to get back, not just into the studio, but also into rotation on the radio. While Al may have bristled a bit at being associated with the "smooth" label, he wanted his records to sell, and he wanted people to hear his music.

Tomorrow Today, by Al's standards, was definitely on the smooth side. Over twenty years after its release, many of today's listeners might hear the music as undistinguished and formulaic. A musical change of pace on the album doesn't really show up until the fifth track—the joyful-sounding title track, cowritten by Al and his music director Freddie Ravel. In an early 2001 interview with Jim Abbott of the *Orlando Sentinel*, Al described how the tune originated: "I had it in my mind that I wanted to do a salsa tune and I wanted it to be called 'Tomorrow Today.' . . . That would be the title of the next album that I thought would hit around the turn of the century. I don't often begin with that clear a notion in my head."[2]

"Tomorrow Today" is the first of two cuts on the album that sound like real fun ("Puddit" being the other). But it is also a song with a message, addressing some of Al's social concerns by speaking to joblessness, homelessness, and other issues that Al worried about passing along to the next generation. These lyrics suggest the gist of the song: "Will we ignore, or save some for / Tomorrow's child today?"

"Tomorrow" is followed on the album by two other distinguished musical efforts. "Flame," often referred to by Al's musical colleagues as "Larry's Tune," was written by Larry Williams, Al, and bassist Andrew Ford. It sounds and feels similar to much of the rest of the album, but it is a much more sophisticated and interesting song than most of the other tracks. It remained in Al's repertoire for years.

Another song on the album, "Something That You Said," allowed Al to write lyrics to music he loved, as he had done for other jazz pieces such as "Take Five," "Spain," and "Blue Rondo à la Turk." Al's close friend from the 1970s and 1980s Jerry Levin has spoken of their shared love for the great jazz fusion band Weather Report, particularly during the band's heyday in the late 1970s. Josef Zawinul's beautiful "A Remark You Made," from the band's 1977 album *Heavy Weather*, made a lasting impression on Al, and he decided to write a lyric for the tune. According to Levin, "[Al] was writing lyrics for that song, seriously, over a four-year period, and there was always something that just wasn't right for him . . . until finally he got it right, and it became 'Something That You Said.'"[3]

Al's ability to vocally re-create the complex lines originally recorded by Wayne Shorter on saxophone, Jaco Pastorius on bass, and even Zawinul on keyboards is most impressive. This cut stands as a testament to Al's unique skills, and it's an example of Al's continuation of and modernization of the jazz vocalese tradition epitomized by his early influence Jon Hendricks, whose vocal arrangements and words (for Lambert, Hendricks & Ross) Al had sung way back in his student days at Ripon College.

In a short feature in the August 2000 issue of *Down Beat*, Paul MacArthur asked Al what drew him to craft the lyrics for this composition. Al replied, "The same thing that drew you to it. You knew the song before you heard me do it, and I would daresay it did the same thing to you that it did to millions. And working on it was a real journey for me, a high water mark for my lyric writing."[4]

When MacArthur asked about Al's process in creating the arrangement and lyrics, Al supplied interesting background:

That was quite a process. What was Jaco's statement? What does Wayne say? What little comments does Joe begin with? (*scats Zawinul's part*) What do these voices individually say about a remark? That's where you begin. I had an image to set the scene: Paris, it's raining and we are talking and walking and having an in-depth conversation.

I apologized to Joe and said, "I want to talk to you about what I'm writing." I gave him a preview, and his comment was, "Al, go ahead

and do what you want. I forget how good a singer you are. For me
the song is complete as it is, but go ahead and do a lyric." I still don't
know what he thinks. I suppose he thinks the song was complete.

But I'm real happy with what I wrote. I don't think it's ordinary,
and it may draw people to the original version like I was drawn to it,
and give them yet another experience with music and the Weather
Report experience.

Al's lyrics represent an approach he sometimes took in songs that were
neither funky dance tunes nor love songs. In these instances, he often
wrote colorful and romantic impressions, which do not clearly tell a story
or make strictly linear sense. For "Something That You Said," he establishes
a setting in the first lines of the song, then continues with a series of images
including "Ice cream and thunder . . . night beasts and butterflies." Also,
some interesting, rather obscure rhymes reveal his interest in wordplay:
"Froze in the attitudes / Toasting the latitudes / Old empty platitudes."
These lyrics do not express a simple narrative, nor are they the stereo-
typical lyrics of a standard love song, but, with their variety of images and
concepts, they evoke scenes—and a sensibility—unique to Al Jarreau.

Another track on *Tomorrow Today* that meant a lot to Al was "God's Gift
to the World." He told MacArthur that he had been hoping to record it for
twelve years with no success: "Ever since I first heard it, my wife's been
fighting a running battle for me to include it on a record, . . . but every
time I presented it to one of the guys producing my records, their feelings
were a little bit lukewarm about it." When Al pitched the song for inclusion on *Tomorrow Today*, Al's manager Bill Darlington suggested a duet.
Al told Abbott in the *Orlando Sentinel*, "The light bulb was so bright and
clear that I was astonished it had never occurred to me before. It was obvious to me the moment it was mentioned. Even with Pee-wee Herman, it
would have greater strength as a duet." So, Al contacted Vanessa Williams,
who "agreed immediately, and the ballad about racial unity finally was
recorded—though not the way Jarreau had originally envisioned it."[5]

While there is no direct reference to race in the lyrics, the message is,
essentially, that every person, no matter where he or she is from, is equally
important as a gift of God. Al acknowledges both "the remembered . . .
[and] the forgotten / From every single nation."

The album's closer, "Puddit (Put It Where You Want It)," written by Al's longtime friend and collaborator Joe Sample of the Crusaders, has an interesting backstory. As Abbott reported, it was originally created to be a demo track that would later become a full-band arrangement. "I didn't know that it was going to turn out to be an a cappella piece because I had been doing it in concerts with my band off and on for 10 years," Al explained.[6] After recording a basic guide vocal, Al's producer Paul Brown started chuckling. As Al recalled, "[Paul] said, 'You know that's it, don't you?' And I'm resistant. I'm saying 'No, no, no,' and Paul is laughing to himself."[7]

The public's reaction to *Tomorrow Today* was decidedly mixed. Comparing two viewpoints on popular websites displays the great divide on what Al was doing in this new phase of his career. The review on the wide-ranging music database AllMusic.com was positive. Jonathan Widran was enthusiastic about the reunion of Al and LiPuma, saying that the "combination sounds as fresh now as it always has." He also felt that Al's collaboration with Paul Brown was a good thing, saying Brown "helps the singer bring out his adult contemporary best." Widran especially appreciated Al's versatility, which was always a key to what he wanted to do in the music world and was probably also a good part of his appeal to his loyal fans. "The best part of Jarreau is his unpredictability," he stated. Widran talked about each of the album's tracks, all of which he liked. The review concluded, "Whether it's yesterday, today or tomorrow, Al Jarreau never fails to keep listeners on their toes."[8]

Coming from the jazz world, John Sharpe, at AllAboutJazz.com, had little good to say about the album. Sharpe remarked that Al's "voice remains as strong, quirky and flexible as ever, even if he long ago abandoned his jazz beginnings." "Unfortunately," Sharpe continued, reflecting his jazz bias, "Jarreau's song choices now lean towards slick R&B, soft and airy ballads and contemporary pop." The review calls out "Al's rather unconvincing attempt at sounding funky on 'In My Music,'" adding that he "then looks to cash in on the current Latin craze with the title track." Yet, Sharpe saves his sharpest barb for the duet: "'God's Gift to the World,' a duet with Vanessa Williams, will appeal only to all those Celine Dion fans out there who can't get their fill of vacuous 'power ballads.'"[9] Years later, in 2008, another disappointed critic penning a retrospective of Al's albums wrote, "[*Tomorrow Today* is the] type of thing that's fine, I guess, if you're into white wine and Brian McKnight, but as an Al Jarreau record, it really stinks."[10]

The album was not a huge commercial success, but it could not be called a failure. While it rose to only number 137 on the *Billboard* top 200, it hit number one on the contemporary jazz album list and remained on the list for over a year. The single "It's How You Say It," a track that doesn't impress twenty years later, made it to number fourteen on the *Billboard* adult R&B songs chart.

When faced with questions about his career during the promotion for this album, Al presented himself as over the slump of the past several years. Attempting to explain why there had been such a significant break between albums of new material between 1994 and 2000, Al said, "I left my recording company of 20-plus years and figured out who my new family was going to be. . . . I found myself with my first producer, Tommy LiPuma. Finding a new home was really like returning to old family, folks who know me, what I'm about, what my dreams and ambitions are as far as the music I want to do and who share my vision that we can put more of my music in people's living rooms than I have ever done before."[11] He talked about wanting to make more recordings over the next several decades and mentioned other projects that excited him, like the symphony program and the big-band project.

In the summer of 2000, shortly after *Tomorrow Today*'s release, Al headed to Europe for one of his frequent tours of the continent. But a week before that tour began, he played the Festival International de Jazz de Montréal (known colloquially as the Montréal Jazz Fest). The band who played with Al in Montréal included musicians who would be important to his touring bands for some time. The core quartet of Freddie Ravel, Chris Walker, Ross Bolton, and Jota Morelli remained the same. But that band, while it worked very well for some of Al's more intimate music, proved unsatisfactory for much of Al's most popular, and funky, repertoire.[12] Three more key musicians were added to fill out the band's sound and allow it more versatility and power.

Percussionist Arno Lucas's family had moved from California to Omaha, Nebraska, when he was ten, and he graduated from high school there. He had gone on to play with a laundry list of great name artists, from Harry Belafonte to Michael Jackson to James Taylor to Gladys Knight. Singer Debbie Davis, who was born in El Paso, Texas, jump-started her career in Europe, recording for numerous soundtracks and commercials in Paris in the 1980s and 1990s. She returned to the United States in 1999 and shortly thereafter joined Al's band, where she remained through the late 2000s. Vocally, she served as a replacement for Vonda Shepard (although Davis did not play keyboards), including taking over Shepard's duo-vocal feature with Al, "Since I Fell for You."

Joe Turano, like Chris Walker, stayed with Al until the end.[13] Born and raised in West Allis, Wisconsin, a suburb of Milwaukee, Turano began singing and playing at a young age; by high school he was playing in local bands. After graduation, a chance meeting with a couple of "California girls" on a sidewalk in Milwaukee led him to head to the West Coast for a 1970s kind of adventure.[14] He stayed for decades. After hearing Al early on at the Bla Bla Café, Joe got a job as a singing waiter at the Great American Food and Beverage Company in Santa Monica. Soon, he was working with singer Rickie Lee Jones in the lead-up to her hit album *Rickie Lee Jones*. Turano became an in-demand background singer, recording on albums for such stars as Rod Stewart, Cher, Tina Turner, and Joe Cocker. Prior to joining Al's band, he got back into playing piano; picked up the saxophone, which he had never played before; and toured with Michael Bolton in the 1990s.

Joe remembered the embrace and the warm welcome he received when meeting his new leader: "Al comes waltzing into rehearsal. . . . I walk up and Al puts his arms around me and says, 'I heard about you; you're from Milwaukee. I've never had anybody from Milwaukee in my band.'" When Chris Walker took a leave of absence from the band in 2008, Joe took over as musical director, staying in that role even after Walker returned. He remained Al's sidekick and confidant until Al's death in 2017.

The program at Montréal opened with "Puddit."[15] While Al had sung this solo on the album, during this performance it was an a cappella feature for not just Al but also the whole vocal section of the band—Ravel, Davis, Bolton, Turano, and Walker. The 1983 hit "Mornin'" (from *Jarreau*) came next, followed by another track from the new album, "Just to Be Loved." "I Will Be Here for You," also from *Jarreau*, then led to the aforementioned "Since I Fell for You," during which Al and Debbie Davis made a strong connection with the audience. The title cut from 1984's *High Crime* made a slightly surprising appearance. After an energetic and exciting percussion interlude, a vamp led into a lengthy version of two of Al's favorite Brazilian songs, "Agua de Beber" and "Mas Que Nada," with sly references to "The Girl from Ipanema" and the old hit "Brazil" ("Aquarela do Brasil"). That led into another riff over the introduction to "Take Five," during which Al spoke about recently singing the song with jazz icon Dave Brubeck, whose quartet made it famous. The band's vocal group then made another appearance, which moved into another percussion extravaganza and eventually morphed into a joyous version of "Tomorrow Today." As was common with Al's performances, even a happy album cut like this one became much more fun in its live rendition.

Highlights of Al's European tour included repeat appearances at the Montreux Jazz Festival and the North Sea Festival at The Hague, Netherlands. The Montreux program, which was probably representative of other shows on the tour, was similar to what had been played at Montréal, with a couple of additional selections from the new album.[16] Besides "Puddit," "Just to Be Loved," and "Tomorrow Today," Al sang "In My Music" and the sublime "Something That You Said." Montreux being a jazz festival, Al and the band also did the jazzier selections "My Favorite Things" (from *Tenderness*), Miles Davis's "All Blues," and the standby "Take Five."

The early 2000s also brought some accolades for Al. On March 6, 2001, he was presented with a star on the celebrated Hollywood Walk of Fame, where big stars of motion pictures, television, audio recording, radio, and live theater are recognized for their contributions to the entertainment industry. Also in 2001, Al served as a judge for a jazz vocalist competition in Budapest. While there, he performed a selection with the competition's winners and his old friend from Milwaukee, Budapest native Les Czimber.[17]

In 2002, another significant change to the band took place when drummer Mark Simmons joined the group. He had recently played with Dianne Reeves and George Duke, and he was friends with another member of the Jarreau team—his hometown Houston buddy Chris Walker. "There was no auditioning required," said Simmons years later. "I simply went to their rehearsal and nailed it. Al was so impressed that, towards the end of the rehearsal, all he could say to me was, 'Welcome aboard!' Initially,

I did not realize it at the time, but I was joining more than just a band. I was joining a familyhood, and we had a special kind of bond. . . . We were like family."[18]

Tomorrow Today was successful enough that GRP was willing to do another record, and 2002's *All I Got* was the result. It was similar to *Tomorrow Today* in that Paul Brown remained as producer and the album had a "smooth" vibe. But the sound was different, as the rhythm tracks reflected the hip-hop drum and drum machine sounds that were spreading from hip-hop into more mainstream pop and R&B.

A couple of things are immediately obvious on *All I Got*: the tempo of most of the songs ranges narrowly from medium to slow.[19] Also, Al's voice is not as front and center as on most of his previous recordings—it's often overwhelmed by background vocal tracks that are almost foreground. These vocals are particularly prominent on "Random Act of Love," "Feels Like Heaven," "Life Is," and the lush "Until You Love Me," as well as the two "band tunes" (discussed later in this chapter). On "Random," the vocals are arranged and performed by Siedah Garrett, who had become famous for her musical association with Michael Jackson. "Life Is" features a men's chorus consisting of cowriter David "Khalid" Woods and Kurt Lyke. Sheree Ford arranged and sang the vocals on "Heaven." Al's voice does not really come to the fore as "the voice of Al Jarreau" until the record's fifth track, "Lost and Found." And it seemingly takes the distinctive sound of his duet partner on this song, the singular Joe Cocker, to inspire Al to step up and assert his own unmistakable musical personality. "Lost and Found" also marks Al's musical reunion, after a break of more than fifteen years, with his early pianist and songwriting partner Tom Canning. Generally speaking, Al sounds more like the Al Jarreau that fans knew and loved on the love songs on this record than on the tracks without that romantic element.

Al had not lost his desire to purvey positive messages through his music, and Paul Brown seemed quite willing to indulge that desire. The album's first track, "Random Act of Love," encourages listeners to "Everyday find a cause / And let it flow just like a river / Into a random act of love." The very next track, "Life Is," with lyrics by Al, exhorts one to "Come spark the track with your gift. / God bless your grits bring it on now."

"All I Got" and "Jacaranda Bougainvillea" are, among other things, distinguished by featuring Al's touring band members of the time:

Freddie Ravel, Ross Bolton, Chris Walker, Jota Morelli, Arno Lucas, and Joe Turano, all of whom were listed as cocomposers on both songs. While the title track, a love song with somewhat aggressive lyrics, blends in musically with much of the rest of the album, it is notable for a couple of vocal interludes (or breakdowns) featuring the band's vocalists and for Chris Walker's seriously funky bass playing. In addition to the duet with Cocker, musical relief comes with the album's last three cuts. The dreamy "Oasis," cowritten with Ricky Peterson, musically and lyrically suggests a peaceful place away from life's trials and tribulations.

Al spoke at length about the catchy selection "Jacaranda" not long after the album's release.[20] In an interview with Ron Miller in *Jazz Review*, Al said,

> I think a song for South Africa is going to be so well received. It's well written and a band song[—it's] called "Jacaranda Bougainvillea." Jacaranda is a tree and bougainvillea is a vine. I have one in my front and back yard. It is a tree and vine common to Southern California, as well as Africa, probably because of the warm climates we share. Anyway, I saw a Jacaranda tree (lavender flower) and a bougainvillea vine in South Africa, cuddled up together inside and around each other. I had never seen that before and it struck me as symbolic of what is going on in South Africa today. The symbolism I wanted to use for a metaphor about this new nation. There are all kinds of references in this song to this new nation of South Africa and to [Nelson] Mandela.[21]

Al performed in South Africa during 1995 and was one of the first Black American artists to perform there when the country was transitioning to its post-apartheid status. In one of several appearances, the band performed at Green Point Stadium for a capacity crowd. On a trip to South Africa (where he performed several times in the 1990s and 2000s), Al met Mandela, an international hero, and also performed at a benefit for Operation Hunger.

The album's closer, the classic "Route 66" (popularized by Nat King Cole), features Al by himself—similar to *Tomorrow Today's* closer, "Puddit." He sings both the melody and the bass line, à la Bobby McFerrin,

International hero and president of South Africa Nelson Mandela (far left) poses with (left to right) Al, Nelson's daughter Zindzi Mandela, and concert promoter Glen Broomberg during one of Al's tours in South Africa in the mid-1990s. COURTESY OF GLEN BROOMBERG

but he overdubs the two lines, rather than singing them both at once, as McFerrin probably would have done.

Al's hopes for the album were typically high. He told Ron Miller, an obvious fan and the author of a lengthy and overwhelmingly positive article about the album in the *Jazz Review*:

> I hope it will be played in a lot of living rooms. It's a new album with a lot of variety. I just opened the door up like I typically do and let what comes through the door get my ear and attention for a while. It really made a kind of eclectic . . . approach to an eclectic sounding album, with some things quite funky and urban popish in sound, you know, including some Al Jarreau ballads (none of which I wrote on this record). I didn't write any of the ballads, but other things. Six pieces, or songs, of the eleven are mine. It's very personal in a lot of ways . . . a lot of personal statements I was able to make and some nice surprises for people.[22]

As had become the norm for Al's records, reactions to *All I Got* were patently mixed. On one end of the spectrum, Miller praised the album, espousing the belief that Al's versatility made him appealing to "all music listeners":

> Al Jarreau is synonymous with great vocal acrobatics and a velvety smooth tone that makes people of all listening experiences equally enjoy his music. His latest CD, "All I Got" (Verve 2002) proves Al has a lot to offer any music fan of the contemporary music scene. With Jarreau's acute sense of understanding of what works, and the ability to just have fun with his craft, all music listeners are able to enjoy his vocal jazz exploits. His voice is not only instantly recognizable, but fluid, soulful, funky, romantic, and joyous.

However, Maurice Bottomley, a writer at the British online publication PopMatters.com, delivered a more nuanced review. In his article, Bottomley reframes the argument that Al had changed his sound and bounced between genres over the years, claiming that Al had, in fact, consistently produced his own unique style of music, which simply proved impossible to pigeonhole. He wrote:

> Al Jarreau was going to be as important as Curtis [Mayfield], Marvin [Gaye], or Stevie [Wonder]. At least that was the way he was talked about briefly in 1975 when his debut album *We Got By* was released. It didn't quite turn out like that, and Jarreau, very sensibly, opted instead for a career of slightly less ambition but one of great longevity and industry acceptance. Grammy awards in various categories have come his way and he remains a favourite on adult and smooth radio playlists.
>
> What got journalists and publicists so excited all those years ago was, of course, Jarreau's formidable vocal technique. Here was the man to fuse jazz singing with post-Marvin soul. From this point of view, Jarreau's career has been a disappointment. In this reading, he moved from being an innovator to mainstream pop and then to easy listening schmaltz. The "jazz" label still adheres, although now it is seen as a marker of his failure to live up to those initial promises.

Well, I'm not so sure. The '80s material has dated badly but that's hardly unique to Jarreau. As to the jazz/soul thing, Jarreau was always as much Johnny Mathis as Jon Hendricks and he was never a soul man in any conventional sense. I see Jarreau as a vocal stylist, with specific mannerisms and definite jazz influences, whose interests were always in the shaping and crafting of popular songs so that they became his own. Jarreau is in a tradition that includes Billy [Eckstine], George Benson, and Walter Jackson. Black vocal performers who had an instantly recognisable sound but who were never 100% jazz, soul, R&B, or whatever. They thus get dismissed as "pop." Tony Bennett and Frank Sinatra are not "jazz" either, but they are celebrated for what they actually do; black artists are judged by what they are deemed to have departed from, they are seen as selling out.

What I'm really saying is that this new Li Puma supervised, Paul Brown produced album doesn't seem to me that different to his early '70s work, either in intention or in end results. What has changed is that now we have a pigeonhole (smooth jazz) in which to categorise (and castigate) the singer. Jarreau was smooth jazz before the event. His voice (ageless on this evidence) still does what it always did—he turns and twists around a lyric and melody in a way that captivates many and alienates many more. The tunes themselves are, as ever, well-crafted, contain polite nods to contemporary fashion, and are designed to showcase Jarreau's distinctive brand of interpretative artistry.[23]

All I Got, like *Tomorrow Today*, had some success on the charts. Released in September, it peaked on October 5, 2002, at number four on the jazz albums chart and spent thirty-six weeks on that listing; it peaked at number three on the contemporary jazz chart on the same date, spending a like number of weeks on that chart.

After the release of the album, Verizon Reads (a flagship program of the telecommunications company) selected Al as the first national Verizon Literacy Champion—news that resulted in an extra paper insert in the *All I Got* CD package.[24] Al was "the first celebrity to be accorded this honor." (Prior to this, there had been only local, not national, Literacy Champions.) In an interview with reporter Gail Mitchell, Al spouted statistics about the

Al with his sister Rose Marie Freeman, 1999. COURTESY OF ROSE MARIE FREEMAN

number of Americans who could not read a bedtime story to their kids (nearly 48 percent), and Mitchell drew attention to Al's master's degree in psychology and background as a social worker. "I was a late bloomer who struggled until a teacher in third grade recognized I wasn't getting it," Al told Mitchell. "It was slow going, but I stuck with it. I want to reach those who can't read, letting them know there's help out here and encouraging them to hang in like I did."[25]

A portion of the sales from *All I Got* would be donated to various literacy organizations through Verizon Reads. Al amplified his thoughts about the program in another interview a few months later, saying, "We have a real critical literacy issue in this country. We need to get people back in school and reading. Many of these people are new citizens, immigrants and folks in the center city who need help. They are still having difficulty communicating in English and reading their prescriptions. Forget reading any kind of novel. We're talking about just functioning by reading and communicating better with each other as a country."[26]

As Al tried on this new role as ambassador of a worthy philanthropic cause, he also began experiencing some health problems. Almost hidden away in the *Billboard* story was this ominous bit of news: "The vocal gymnast began visiting and entertaining school children at reading sessions before being sidelined recently by emergency back surgery." It was one of the first indications that Al's remarkable physical constitution, which had sustained several decades of intense touring, was not going to last forever.

TOMORROW TODAY
GRP, 2000

While many think of so-called smooth jazz as being purely instrumental, there is a vocal segment of this genre. And much of the *Tomorrow Today* album is decidedly "smooth." "Let Me Love You" features a solo by saxophonist Boney James, sounding dangerously close to the much reviled (in jazz circles) Kenny G. On the first verse of this tune, Al almost doesn't sound like himself. Although Al always had a tremendous variety of vocal sounds at his disposal, his voice here (and at some other times on the album) sounds either constrained or electronically compressed—and he does not showcase, for example, the rich baritone notes or the nasal guitarlike sounds that were his signatures. Further, he almost "whisper sings" the first verse of "Through It All."

One reviewer spoke of "In My Music" as an unconvincing attempt at funk. Some might argue that it is very controlled and tamped-down funk—but it's nothing like the furious funky grooves that Al routinely got into during parts of the 1980s and 1990s, particularly in his live shows.

"Tomorrow Today," coproduced by composers Freddie Ravel and Al, begins with a brief traditional Latin montuno, a repeated pattern over which improvisation takes place. Al improvises vocally, of course, speaking fast and with jive, in what more than one reviewer referred to as a "Ricky Ricardo" routine.[27] Ravel probably wrote the song's music, with Al supplying the lyrics, but some of the song may have developed spontaneously while the band jammed on the road. Besides Ravel, touring band bassist Chris Walker also plays on this cut. Later on in the track, the horn section kicks and Al's improvised section are a welcome change from the scripted smoothness of the rest of the album.

The arrangement of "Something That You Said" was crafted by Jerry Hey, the outstanding trumpet player who arranged the classic horn parts on Al's hit albums from the early 1980s. It is more or less a copy of the Weather Report version of the tune, with the words substituted for instrumental parts. Larry Williams has talked about how Hey's "big ears" allowed him to do this sort of work, "one of his specialties."[28] Trumpeter Rick Braun supplies some nice little musical commentary. Bassist Jimmy Johnson does a commendable job re-creating Jaco Pastorius's bass sound and lines as necessary.

A review of Kurt Elling's album *Man in the Air* noted three years later, "It's . . . interesting to compare Elling's lyrics to Josef Zawinul's classic Weather Report tune, 'A Remark You Made,' retitled 'Time to Say Goodbye' here, with Al Jarreau's version called 'Something That You Said' on his *Tomorrow Today* album of three years ago. Both contribute to a deeper appreciation of the tune while offering fresh glimpses into the musical psyche of the individual lyricist/vocalists."[29]

"God's Gift to the World" is another song that was possibly more important to Al for its message than for its music. Clearly, it was meaningful to Al's wife, Susan, whom Al described as "fighting a running battle" for him to record it on an album since the first time she heard the song.[30]

On "Puddit," Al takes a page out of the Bobby McFerrin style book, singing the melody and the bass line at the same time—that is, alternating one with the other. For much of his career, Al had sung bass lines, often in tandem with a bass. But unlike McFerrin, who made this a signature of his style, Al used this stylistic device rarely. He seems to be having a good time with it here.

ALL I GOT
GRP/Verve, 2002

All I Got included many notable appearances. In addition to those mentioned in the chapter are a saxophone solo by smooth jazz star Kirk Whalum on "Oasis" and a subtle appearance on oboe by Jon Clarke on "Until You Love Me." Trumpeter and longtime Jarreau associate Jerry Hey reappears here with some of his brass and saxophone compatriots on "Life Is," "Lost and Found," "All I Got," and "Jacaranda Bougainvillea," but the horns are not nearly as prominent as they had been in days gone by. Larry Williams contributes extra keyboards to "Never Too Late" and "Oasis," perhaps foreshadowing his return to Al's touring band right around the time this album was in production. Williams also plays saxophone and flute on the record. Percussionist Paulinho Da Costa—who had appeared on previous Jarreau albums, most notably on *Tenderness*—appears on five of the cuts on this record.

Besides the band vocalists on "All I Got" (Lucas, Turano, and Walker), Al's son, Ryan, and wife, Susan, are listed for background vocals. They happened to be in the studio when the song was being recorded, and they stepped in to join the chorus of voices on the repeated riff in the song's second half.[31] A rhythm section "breakdown" is one of the distinguishing features of this funky grooving tune.

A string section (arranged by Hey) seriously sweetens up "Until You Love Me" and, more subtly, "Jacaranda."

It is good to hear Al improvising, even in a limited way, on "Jacaranda" and, not surprisingly, "Route 66," where his improvised blues chorus recalls his days as a jazz singer and clearly reaffirms his historical debt to Jon Hendricks.

Paula Edelstein's almost fawning review of the album at AllMusic.com praises the diversity of the songs on the record—a trait that some might see as a weakness and that others might not even agree with. She concludes with the following: "Overall, *All I Got* showcases the award-winning Jarreau's unmistakable stylistic diversity in settings that are fluid, soulful, jazzy, and romantic. In some ways, the music even exceeds the versatility heard on the critically acclaimed *Tomorrow Today*."[32]

Like its predecessor, *All I Got* will not be remembered as classic Al Jarreau, but it continues to have fervent fans in the Jarreau community.

22

COMING FULL CIRCLE

A l had been talking about doing a "jazz album" since at least 1989, but
nothing ever seemed to come of it. One likely reason is that the
market at that time was certainly not friendly to jazz. Also, Al may have
been afraid to turn his back on the success he had experienced as a pop
artist from the time that "We're in This Love Together" took off in the early
1980s. Nevertheless, Al and his team recorded *Accentuate the Positive* in the
years after *All I Got*, and this decidedly jazz-oriented album was released
on Verve in 2004.

Larry Williams, who had rejoined Al on the road in the early 2000s and
had worked with him on and off ever since he supplied keyboards on Al's
iconic recording of "Spain" in 1980, described some of the history behind
the album years later. After Al's two early 2000s albums, Larry (and others) had a number of conversations with Al about the kind of music that
he had been recording. At some point, Williams was quite blunt:

> I had a conversation with Al on the bus one night. And spirits might
> have been imbibed by both of us, but that had little to do with this
> conversation. It was after a gig. . . . I said, "Al, lookit, you're making
> records that you don't really like . . . and they're not getting played.
> So why don't you at least make records that you like? Let's go from
> that place. Let's see what that would be like." And that's kind of the
> outgrowth. I'm not saying I turned Al's life around, 'cause I didn't.
> But that was what I thought he needed to get back to what made Al
> special and why people loved Al all over the world.[1]

Around this time, a project began to develop, influenced by Al's manager Bill Darlington. Darlington sold the "brass" at Verve, including Tommy LiPuma, on the idea of making a "jazz album" with Al. It was not a hard sell. Darlington then offered Larry Williams the task of serving as pianist and arranger for the project. LiPuma and Williams had worked together at various times in the past, and all agreed to the partnership. (Although not credited as such, Williams essentially became coproducer of the album.) LiPuma was in the midst of a string of hit albums, at least by jazz standards, with vocalist Diana Krall; it was his idea to use the core of Krall's all-star rhythm section: Christian McBride on bass, Anthony Wilson on guitar, and Peter Erskine on drums. Williams would play keyboards—he certainly wasn't going to complain about working with those A-listers.

Working with Al in this way was a new experience for Larry, who had done overdubs on Al's records but had never done a rhythm arrangement with Al on a record. The budget for the album was tight, but Al and Larry agreed that they'd "spend whatever it [took] to come up with arrangements, demos that [they knew] going in [would be] a great starting point." Williams had been making records like that for a little while. "You're at Capitol Records," he said, "where it's costing . . . $3,500 a day, or whatever, with great musicians that aren't cheap. Engineers, the whole thing." By crafting and developing the arrangements ahead of time, they knew they could enter the studio and feel confident that what they were going to record would sound great.

"That proved to be really perfect for that record," Williams said, "because I think Al and I spent over two months—I know I spent six days a week—on those arrangements. . . . Al was never anybody that would stop me from trying anything. You know, he would edit some stuff that he thought was maybe too much. And we cut a few things that didn't make the record." Williams was also thrilled to work with the team: "For me to work with Christian and Peter and Anthony, in that capacity, and Tommy, at Capitol, on a beautiful Steinway, [a] Hamburg Steinway D, with Al Schmitt engineering, I mean it just doesn't get any better."[2]

A few personnel changes took place on some songs. Larry Goldings played organ and came up with a head arrangement for Duke Ellington's "I'm Beginning to See the Light," and Russell Ferrante played piano on

"Scootcha-Booty," which he wrote with Al. Mark Simmons, from the touring band, played drums on three tracks.

Williams reflected, "I put my all into that record and am really proud of that. And what it did or didn't do? I mean that's about as straight-ahead [an] Al record as you're gonna get. That doesn't mean he's gonna do all swing versions. That's somebody's interpretation of straight-ahead jazz. . . . That's just not who Al is."

Despite the pride that team members like Williams felt about the album, *Accentuate the Positive* did not reestablish Al as a valued member of the jazz community. Instead, the album stirred up the long-running arguments about how to categorize Al's music and how to define him as a musician. This controversy played out in the pages of *Down Beat* magazine, and elsewhere, at the time of the album's release in 2004. Since *Down Beat* is the oldest surviving American publication devoted to jazz, its contribution to the controversy was particularly important.

Since at least the 1970s, most writers at *Down Beat* have taken the stance that "pure" jazz is preferable to jazz hybrids, such as jazz-rock or fusion. Smooth jazz—as Al's *Tomorrow Today* and *All I Got* have been labeled—has not been considered worthy of much of anything to these writers. They prize mainstream jazz, as well as music once considered "avant-garde," "free," or "experimental."[3]

Accentuate the Positive was reviewed in the September 2004 issue of *Down Beat* by John McDonough, perhaps the most mainstream-oriented of the magazine's reviewers at the time. He began by reflecting on Al's jazz roots, though he seems not to have realized just how deep those roots went. "In music terms," McDonough wrote, "two or three generations have passed through the mill since Al Jarreau went AWOL on jazz back in the LP era (*Look to the Rainbow*, 1977). After such an extended sabbatical, Verve positions this CD as Jarreau's 'return to his jazz roots.' The question is, after all these years, will anybody really care, especially since those 'roots' were shallow to say the least in that most vaguely defined of all canons, the one reserved for jazz singers."[4]

McDonough goes on to mostly damn the album with faint praise. He claims that "Jarreau's own credentials as a jazz singer were based largely on his flair with a clever and unexpectedly fresh scat vocabulary." This claim led into a lengthy description of Al's take on Dizzy Gillespie's bebop anthem "Groovin' High." McDonough wrote, "A brief chorus of lyrics (by

Jarreau) feels imposed on the flow of the bop line (a chronic plague of the whole vocalese concept)," showing his bias against putting words to bebop melodies. He also criticizes Al's scat vocabulary, claiming that it "crackles with the jumpy, random energy of popcorn popping" on "Scootcha-Booty" and that "the jerky phrasing and strained dialects sound unnatural and corner Jarreau in an awkward, irreversible self-parody" on the title cut.

In McDonough's opinion, Al had not proven that he could make a convincing "real jazz" statement. "I may be mischaracterizing this CD," he allows, "half of which showcases Jarreau on some fine ballads salted with nice solo work. 'Waltz for Debby' stands out. . . . 'The Nearness of You,' 'My Foolish Heart' and 'Midnight Sun' are sung with earnest tenderness seasoned with a gentle stylization and a touch of scat. It's unlikely this effort will get Jarreau a pass into the next *Encyclopedia of Jazz*, but it remains a nicely crafted pop-jazz effort."

McDonough gave the album three out of five stars on the magazine's rating scale. That seems generous, though, when compared to the unfavorable opinions of his fellow critics. For some years, each issue of *Down Beat* has featured four albums that are reviewed in depth by a single reviewer and also given a star rating by three other critics, along with a short summary of those critics' responses, in a feature called "The Hot Box." For *Accentuate the Positive*, John Corbett, a champion of much progressive jazz, said, "OK, I'll try: The band includes guitarist Anthony Wilson, very nice, and Christian McBride, nearly always a pleasure, and Larry Goldings on one track. That about taps me out on the positive side." Corbett offered two stars. Jim Macnie gave the album two and a half stars, writing, "[Jarreau] goes for it scat-wise, and his lite funk has a certain esprit, but there's little to sink your teeth into here, and the record's resonance is minor because of that. Standards, especially 'Midnight Sun' and 'My Foolish Heart,' are particularly misguided." Finally, Paul de Barros dismissed the album (and Jarreau) with two stars: "The high point is 'Betty,' Freddie Ravel's paean to Betty Carter. The rest, particularly the whispered, conspiratorial ballads, sounds suspiciously like Bob Dorough. But then I never bought into Jarreau's chipper acrobatics anyway." This was almost certainly the first (and last) time that anyone has compared Al's singing to that of Bob Dorough, a true iconoclast and quirky vocalist who, while carving out an interesting niche in jazz history, had a vocal instrument almost nothing like Al's.[5]

Oddly enough, a feature on Al ran in the following month's issue of

Down Beat: "Full Circle: Al Jarreau Attempts to Reinvigorate His Jazz Love Affair."[6] Usual practice would be to run an article about the project in advance of the upcoming review. Nonetheless, Mark Ruffin's article allowed Al to respond to the criticisms and to discuss the change from the pop and R&B albums that he had been making for many years.

Ruffin began by discussing Al's chance meeting with jazz pianist Mulgrew Miller, which led to the composition of "Betty," the tribute to jazz vocalist Betty Carter, Mulgrew's one-time employer. The song, cocomposed by Al's pianist Freddie Ravel, finally appeared on *Accentuate*. In Ruffin's view, Al had continued to keep in touch with jazz even during the development of his pop/R&B career, and as examples, he mentions Al's jazz remakes of Chick Corea's "Spain," Paul Desmond's "Take Five," and Josef Zawinul's "A Remark You Made." "The vocal acrobatics that [Jarreau] distilled from jazz influences Jon Hendricks, the Double Six of Paris and Ella Fitzgerald," Ruffin wrote, "is as much a stamp of who Jarreau, the r&b and pop star is, as the songs that propelled him to the top, including his chart topper from 1981, 'We're in This Love Together.'"

Ruffin makes a similar claim to the one Maurice Bottomley made in his PopMatters.com review: that after the release of his debut album, Al had not become as important as Curtis Mayfield, Marvin Gaye, or Stevie Wonder, as many people had believed he would. Ruffin, however, also addresses the expectations Al faced in the jazz world. "The promise of the future in jazz that many thought came with Jarreau's 1977 Best Jazz Performance Grammy for his breakthrough album, *Look to the Rainbow*, never materialized," Ruffin wrote. But, he continued, "More than 25 years later, with *Accentuate The Positive* (Verve), Jarreau has kept a long-standing commitment to himself and a huge segment of his fan base." Unlike his more dismissive colleagues, Ruffin did, in fact, see the 2004 album as a return to Al's jazz roots.

Al addressed the issue by explaining to Ruffin:

I was claimed by some critics and audiences in jazz, all who turned a blind eye to that other side of me that kept cropping up. . . . There are real jazz lovers who've heard this record inside me. There have always been people with arms across their chests, patting their feet going, "OK, Al, come on, where's the jazz?"

I'm a singer who's jazz-influenced. . . . But when you start looking at the singers who are jazz singers, there is a real difference. They aren't interested in R&B and pop. R&B and pop are as much a part of me as jazz singing, and so with that as my description of what I do, it's always a compliment every time somebody calls me a jazz singer.

While Al had been talking about his career choices in similar terms for quite some time, there lurked in the subtext of his words the sense that he *wanted* to be recognized as a jazz singer—even though he was happy with the fame and fortune that accompanied his career in pop and R&B. But by this point in his life, perhaps he really had come to a sense of peace about his uncategorizable position in American music.

Ruffin credits LiPuma, who had been a major figure in the record business for many years, for his role in *Accentuate the Positive*'s development. Al joked about LiPuma being one of the "sinister forces" that helped the album come together, but LiPuma referred to Al's manager of the time, Bill Darlington, as the instigator. According to LiPuma, Darlington had mentioned that LiPuma and Al would have to do an album together someday, and LiPuma had responded by saying, "I'd love to do an album, but jazz is the album I want to make." LiPuma wasn't crazy about the pop trajectory Al's career had taken since "We're in This Love Together." But once they started working on a jazz project together, the two were all in. Al told Ruffin, "When Tommy and I began to talk about whether this was a good idea, it was quickly obvious that we were amazingly close together on our approach."

Unfortunately, Larry Williams never received the recognition he deserved from critics and reviewers for his herculean effort in creating *Accentuate*. Years after the album's release, Larry was philosophical about the reasons for this, although he may have still harbored a bit of resentment. He said,

Even in record reviews, a lot of reviews would talk about Peter, they'd talk about Christian. Of course, they're jazz magazines. . . . They would often nearly omit me from any of it, because . . . I'm considered a studio musician. . . . I was a "fusion guy" and then made my living in the studio playing [on] any kind of records. . . . I didn't have the same jazz cred, because I hadn't made a name for myself as a "jazz [musician]" on purpose. . . . I didn't want to be a starving jazz artist [*laughs*]. I wanted to bring my jazz sensibilities into the music.

Williams also regretted that Verve Records "put so little promotion into that record."

A good bit of the *Down Beat* feature described the two albums that Al recorded in the mid-1960s: the one in Iowa and the other with George Duke in San Francisco. The legal limbo of the much-bootlegged Iowa recording was a topic of discussion, but both Al and Duke expressed excitement about their collaboration, which Al was hoping would be released soon. This album would ultimately not appear until 2011, but it must have been in the planning stages in 2004, and its jazz bent was definitely on Al's mind. In the sixties, both of the albums would have been considered jazz vocal albums, containing standards and jazz tunes.

Al also talked to Ruffin about where he might go next musically:

I'm not surprised that now I may be beginning all over again to find an audience for the work that's represented on *Accentuate The Positive*. . . . If they come and like it, they or my label shouldn't get too comfortable, because I've got a symphony project in mind that involves a piece by Bach and I've got a Brazilian project.

I have to do things that are a part of me. . . . There are still some things I've got to do and one does smell a lot like this new one. It's a big band album, with me giving Joe Williams and Frank Sinatra a run for their money.

Even if he was being somewhat cynical, it's worth considering the question that John McDonough posed in his review: Would anybody really care that Al saw *Accentuate the Positive* as a "return to his jazz roots"? It's hard to know how the various factions of Al's wide audience base ultimately thought about it, but it was obviously something that Al thought about frequently throughout his career. This album simply brought the question of whether or not he identified as a jazz singer back into the open.

Did the negative criticism of this album affect Al? Friends and colleagues had different perspectives, but his longtime band member and
Milwaukee buddy Joe Turano believed it did. "He was such a sensitive
soul," Turano said. "He really wore his heart on his sleeve and was just such
an unbelievable force of nature, but . . . that stuff [criticism] just hit him
hard."[7] On the other hand, Larry Williams claimed that Al didn't care what
the jazz purists thought, remembering that Al "called them the jazz police
and [said] they were all critics who never created any art, just criticized."[8]

And, of course, the critical reaction to *Accentuate* would have been
different if it had been recorded by a young unknown singer. Perhaps reviewers and the public would have been impressed with the work of a very
talented "jazz" newcomer. But Al had decades of a complicated musical
past behind him, skewing the perceptions of all who attempted to define
him and his music.

As a footnote and counterpoise to the feature article but negative reaction in *Down Beat*, the magazine's rival *JazzTimes* was much kinder to
Al and *Accentuate*. In its September 2004 issue, in the "Opening Chorus"
feature, John Murph described the new album as Al's "first straight-ahead
album since 1977's *Look to the Rainbow*."[9] And Murph reported that Al
"sounds wholly rejuvenated" on the new album. He continued, "Eddie
Harris' soul-jazz nugget 'Cold Duck' and the finger-poppin' original
'Scootcha-Booty' . . . allow Jarreau to channel his R&B roots, [but] it's his
shimmering interpretations of classic material such as 'The Nearness of
You' and 'Midnight Sun' that really lift this date."

When Murph asked Al why it took him so long to record this kind of
album, Al was typically forthcoming, answering with a touch of his inimitable, playful manner. "Well, it's just time," he said. "I'd been promising myself and my audience this kind of CD for close to 20 years now. I
think the stars, my manager and the guys at the record company kind of
conspired against my normal way of doing records, because I talk about
doing things forever, and I seldom get to them. Those guys were probably
chatting about making me do this record while I was in the bathroom or
something."

Murph addressed Al's working on the record with musicians who were
new to him, stating, "That unfamiliarity didn't hinder their interaction."
JazzTimes was also one of the few outlets to give well-deserved credit to

Larry Williams, "who arranged the disc's lion's share of material." "He knows me inside and out," Jarreau said of Williams. "It was just natural for him to do the arrangements, because he knows where I've been, what I like doing and how I am these days onstage."

Al also gave insight into the selection of material: "I picked songs that are good friends—songs that I hung out with for years. . . . These are in-the-shower, driving-the-car, walking-through-the-grocery-aisle songs. Some of these songs I've been singing since I was 10 years old." Murph described the album as "a highlight in Jarreau's nearly four-decade career." When asked about what he had in store for an encore, Al, as always, was happy to look forward: "Well, this is chapter one in this new book. . . . I'll do several other chapters. I don't want to completely forget about doing 'We're in This Love Together' and 'Boogie Down,' but this new book is coming in like a breath of fresh air. I feel a new spring in my step. It's good to have waited until now, if for no other reason than to get that kind of boost."

During other interviews of this time, Al continued to refer to his own tenacity. "I've refused to go away!" he exclaimed in another 2004 profile—this one posted on the All About Jazz website.[10] "I'm an ex-cross country guy, so I know about long-distance running and being lonely. And I wish I had done a little high school wrestling because it gives you grit. I love what I do. I would do it for free. I've done it for free."

Not surprisingly, touring—Al's professional, and in some ways personal, lifeblood—continued unabated throughout this period. Most of his fans probably didn't read the reviews, and even if they did, many surely didn't care what the critics said. They never quit supporting Al's live performances in the United States and, especially, in Europe. Besides the usual places and venues, Al and the band traveled during this time to less expected locales such as Mexico, Australia, Azerbaijan, Tunisia, India, and the Republic of Georgia. And he spoke openly about the fact that his touring abroad made his career in America possible. As he told one reporter, "I've worked hard at developing an international audience. . . . Having that audience abroad has given me power in America, because I don't go away. I have [an] audience over there who supports what I do, so I can survive with a small audience here."[11]

Manager Bill Darlington pushed Al to open up new performance markets around the world, even during the late 1990s when there were no new

Al and his touring band perform in Kiev, Ukraine, in 2008. From left to right: John Calderon, guitar; Larry Williams, keyboards; Mark Simmons, drums; Stan Sargeant, bass; and Joe Turano, keyboards. © SERGUEI TROUCHELLE / WIKIMEDIA COMMONS / CC-BY-SA-3.0

Jarreau records to support, or sell, a tour. But he didn't have to push Al very hard. If he told Al that they were looking at a place where few American artists had been before and that "things might not be easy," Al would reply, "No, let's go!" "He was very adventurous that way," Darlington said.[12]

In the August 2006 issue of *JazzTimes*, a short feature about Al addressed his international travel:

A glance at Al Jarreau's itinerary is to appreciate the global reach of jazz. From Baku, Azerbaijan, to Warsaw, from Lyon to Verona, the legendary jazz vocalist is an international ambassador for America's finest export. "I love taking the music to a worldwide audience," Jarreau says. "I think it's helped me survive. I survived the great disco scare of the late '70s and '80s, and I think I'll survive the hip-hop revolution, too. This is my busiest period, because everyone loves to be outside enjoying music together, and if you think about it, you can trace the start of the summer festival season right back to Newport."[13]

One fall 2004 performance at an all-day jazz festival in Central Park in Huntington Beach, California, close to Al's home, earned a rave review. Jim Santella wrote that Al's forty-minute set, including some of the jazz selections from *Accentuate the Positive*,

> topped everything that had transpired during the day and evening. Filled with unbridled energy and as hip as ever, the 64-year-old jazz singer stormed through "Take Five," "Cold Duck" and other favorites. "Midnight Sun" brought out the singer's vintage romantic spirit and spread his message wide. Jarreau doesn't just sing a melody. He merely hints at it while the band provides a strong foundation. Larry Williams carried the melody of "Midnight Sun," for example, as Jarreau danced around its pattern, popping up with unexpected tones from every direction. It's that quality that makes him unique. He implies a song, and it's up to the band to make it recognizable. In one spiritual piece near the start of the program, singer Debbie Davis carried the melody while Jarreau moved this way and that with vocal spontaneity, thrilling everyone to no end. His encore gave additional proof that this special evening in Central Park would stand out as a memorable occasion.[14]

In 2006, Al's schedule looked different as he both recorded his next album, *Givin' It Up*, and then toured to promote it, in collaboration with fellow great George Benson. In hindsight, this musical partnership may have seemed preordained. Al and George's joint effort made a great deal of sense from a number of standpoints. The two stars were contemporaries (Al was born in 1940, Benson in 1943); both were known as jazz artists in the early days of their careers, and they both went on to have big pop hits. Benson was lauded as one of the most talented jazz guitarists of his generation before his 1976 Tommy LiPuma–produced album, *Breezin'*, yielded the huge single "This Masquerade," revealing Benson's vocal gifts to a wide audience. The instrumental title tune on the album won a Grammy for pop instrumental performance; "This Masquerade" won Record of the Year. Benson, like Al, continued to negotiate the fine line between jazz, pop, and R&B for the next three decades before his album with Al.

In the lead-up to their collaboration, Al was signed to Concord—the

Al and George Benson performing together on tour in 2007, shortly after the release of their collaborative album *Givin' It Up*. © LIONEL FLUSIN

label that had just recently begun representing George. Concord seemed a good fit for both veterans, as the label had just had a significant success with new releases for Ray Charles. In a late 2006 interview in *JazzTimes*, Benson said, "It was time to give [Concord] a shot with where I am in my career now. Then we brought Al Jarreau in. Al came over because I was there, and I convinced him it was going to be an adventure, but a good one because the people loved us so much."[15]

It's hard to know who drove the musical material on this new album, but it ended up being a smorgasbord of styles that both artists felt comfortable playing. In a clever musical twist, the album began with a vocal version of Benson's instrumental hit "Breezin'," with lyrics by Al, followed by an instrumental version of Al's 1983 vocal hit "Mornin'," featuring Benson's guitar. Al also created lyrics for "Tutu," a song written by his old friend Marcus Miller and the title cut of Miles Davis's 1986 record. Al titled his version of the tune "'Long Came Tutu." An old straight-ahead Miles tune, "Four," with lyrics by Al's vocalese hero Jon Hendricks, is given a polite reading, featuring both vocalists, but in large measure Benson's guitar.

The record includes pop and R&B tunes from the 1960s (Sam Cooke's "Bring It On Home to Me"), 1970s (Seals and Crofts's "Summer Breeze"), 1980s (Paul Young's hit version of Darryl Hall's "Every Time You Go Away"), and the 2000s (John Legend and will.i.am's "Ordinary People"). All were in the wheelhouse of the principals, who were aided by distinguished guest stars. On the jazzier side, there were contributions from Herbie Hancock, Patrice Rushen, Stanley Clarke, Vinnie Colaiuta, and Chris Botti, in addition to Miller. Sir Paul McCartney, who just happened to be recording "next door" at the studio, took the lead vocal on Sam Cooke's song. Guest vocalist Patti Austin shared lead with Al on "Let It Rain."

One of the two Grammy-winning cuts on the record was Billie Holiday's classic "God Bless the Child," which earned the award for Best Traditional R&B Vocal Performance. The lead vocal is performed by singer-songwriter and actress Jill Scott, who shared the Grammy with Al and Benson. Al supplies a vocal bass line at the beginning and end of the recording, and Benson sings and provides a guitar solo. Benson won the album's second Grammy, for best pop instrumental, for his interpretation of "Mornin'."

There were considerable machinations between Monster Music and Al and Benson's new label, Concord Records, to make this album's package lavish, with two booklets and a "superdisc" with added features about the recording in addition to the CD.

The album did very well in the marketplace, reaching fifty-eight on the Billboard 200 album chart and peaking at the top of Billboard's jazz album chart in November 2006, remaining at that spot for five weeks. It stayed on the chart for seventy-five weeks.

In typical fashion, Down Beat was relatively dismissive of this release, describing one track as "treacle" and awarding the album a measly two stars on its five-star scale. Reviewer Michael Jackson wrote, "Jarreau is a terrific, risk-taking live performer. But like another vocal genius, Bobby McFerrin, he's bound by his idiosyncrasies."[16] Despite the slam, Jackson understood that Al was a vocal genius and acknowledged the electricity that he brought to live concerts.

And as usual, the JazzTimes review was much friendlier. Calling the Benson-Jarreau collaboration "perhaps inevitable," it refers to the arrangements as "refreshing" and the larger project as a "tremendously personal album by the talented duo, one that benefits from an organic and acoustic approach." The summary paragraph probably reflected the attitude of many of both stars' fans: "This is the right album at the right time. From the new vocal renditions of Miles Davis' 'Four' and ''Long Came Tutu' to unique interpretations of Billie Holiday's 'God Bless the Child' and John Legend's 'Ordinary People,' this album announces: Hey, look at these two legends having fun and making great music."[17]

In a surprising development, while the Benson album was in process, Al let manager Bill Darlington go, evidently at Susan's urging. Several of Al's associates wondered if Susan may have felt that she didn't have enough control over the direction of Al's career or that Darlington had too much. In any case, a ten-year association was ended at a time when a project that Darlington had helped bring to fruition was still short of its completion.

ACCENTUATE THE POSITIVE

Verve, 2004

The mix of songs on *Accentuate* reveals a singer with varied musical interests; but they're all distinctly in the arena of jazz, regardless of some critics' reactions. This is a *jazz* album. It is performed by the jazz/pop/R&B legend Al Jarreau in *his* style, and it is beloved by thousands of his fans. It peaked at number six on the jazz albums chart on August 21, 2004, and spent twenty-nine weeks on the list. It peaked at number two on the *Billboard* traditional jazz chart on the same date and also spent twenty-nine weeks there.

The album includes great standards: Hoagy Carmichael and Ned Washington's "The Nearness of You," Washington and Victor Young's "My Foolish Heart," and Harold Arlen and Johnny Mercer's quirky "Ac-Cent-Tchu-Ate the Positive." (Of "My Foolish Heart," Larry Williams said he knew that Al would want to do "a Brazilian thing; that's why I knew I could take [it] in that direction."[18]) Two songs cowritten by jazz artists that have effectively entered the realm of standards are Duke Ellington's "I'm Beginning to See the Light" and Lionel Hampton's "Midnight Sun"— the latter a devilishly difficult song to sing. (Joe Turano remarked, "[Al's] version of 'Midnight Sun' alone is worth the price of admission to me.... Few people can sing that tune."[19]) Two jazz classics—Dizzy Gillespie's

"Groovin' High" (with lyrics by Al) and Bill Evans's "Waltz for Debby"—are better known as instrumental pieces. Al wrote lyrics for two funky jazz tunes: Eddie Harris's "Cold Duck" and "Scootcha-Booty." On the latter, he shares cocomposer credit with Russell Ferrante (cofounder of the Yellowjackets). Al also wrote the lyrics for his former pianist and music director Freddie Ravel's tribute to Betty Carter, "Betty's Bebop Song." Finally, he wrote lyrics for keyboardist Don Grolnick's beguiling "Lotus."

Besides the core band and drummer Mark Simmons playing on three tracks, Keith Anderson takes a couple of saxophone solos, and Tollak Ollestad has a harmonica solo.

The lyrics of "Ac-Cent-Tchu-Ate" certainly appealed to Al's optimistic life philosophy, and its references to biblical figures Jonah and Noah were assuredly part of that appeal. This version is decidedly funky.

As usual, in Al's notes for the CD, he acknowledged his family: "Tons and tons of thanks to Susan and Ryan, my wife and son, co-captains of the 'A-Team' and both sharing the MVP award. They continue to buoy me up, take up the slack, and watch my back while cheering and bootin' me in the butt. Picturing that is hard to do, but they do it and it's priceless." Al also sent out "a deep bow and many thanks" to the album's two producers: Tommy LiPuma and Al Schmitt, who both produced and engineered Al's first album, We Got By. "Tommy and Al produced my second and third albums . . . literally getting my recording career off and running," Al wrote. "I bow (and curtsy) to them. I'm delighted they came together again with me to make this new CD that I'm sure will be a landmark recording."

Al also made clear the great contribution of Williams, writing, "Larry Williams' arrangements . . . oh my!!! I can't say enough for those long 'midnight candle' hours in coming up with such fresh and inspiring environments for me to sing in." Williams's tasty piano playing is particularly prominent on "Waltz for Debby." Al stated his appreciation for musical director Chris Walker, too, thanking him "for peeking over our shoulders and watching out for the 'truth.'"

GIVIN' IT UP
Monster Music (Concord Music Group), 2006

This collaborative album between Al and one of his longtime musical peers, George Benson, peaked at number fifty-eight on the *Billboard* top 200 album chart in November of 2006; it reached number one on the contemporary jazz list at the same time and spent an impressive seventy-five weeks on that chart.

Keyboardist Larry Williams, who had been so instrumental to the success of *Accentuate the Positive*, was a key contributor to this effort as well. He arranged the new vocal version of George Benson's hit "Breezin'" and the other oldies: Seals and Crofts's "Summer Breeze" and Darryl Hall's "Every Time You Go Away." He also played piano and/or keyboards on those tracks. Joe Turano—who had by this time become a fixture in the road band as saxophonist, vocalist, and second keyboardist—was the cocomposer (with Al) and arranger of "Don't Start No Schtuff." On this funky original, he supplied keyboards—Wurlitzer electric piano and Hammond B-3 organ—while playing with heavyweights Stanley Clarke on bass and Vinnie Colaiuta on drums. Al's former music director Freddie Ravel was no longer on the road with Al, but he was represented on the album by a new piece, "Givin' It Up for Love," from which the title of the album was derived. Ravel plays multiple keyboards on the track, as well as drums and "percussion programming."

A "superdisc" that comes with the CD package mostly includes high-definition files of the album's tracks as well as other audio features. A short, eight-minute video includes commentary from Al and Benson about the making of the record and its sound.

23

⸺⸺▦▦▦⸺⸺

LATE CAREER

I n March 2006, Al played an unusual and unexpected gig. A couple of
years earlier, while touring with Enrique Iglesias, Al's tour manager
from the 1970s and 1980s, Jerry Levin, had met the young Russian singer
Alsou (Alsou Ralifovna Abramova), whom he described as "the Mariah
Carey of Russia." She came from a wealthy family; her father, with considerable interests in oil, was reportedly one of the richest men in Russia. A year after their meeting, Levin was contacted by Alsou's fiancé, Jan
Abramov, also a man of considerable wealth, who was making a fortune
in weapons development. He and Alsou wanted to hire both Al and his
band and George Benson and his band to play at the couple's wedding.
The gala took place in Moscow, and the musicians were afforded first-
class airplane flights; five-star hotel accommodations; assistance from
top audio, lighting, and video companies; rehearsal time; and top dollar
for their performances. As Levin said of the occasion, "Anything's possible
if you pay for everything."[1] This union created something of a stir, even
internationally, as the two celebrities had different religious backgrounds:
Alsou was Muslim and Abramov Jewish. This is one glimpse into what life
could be like for an international star like Al Jarreau.[2]

Although Al was no stranger to luxurious amenities, this was not necessarily what he wanted while on tour—even in the later stages of his career. His green room preferences were very specific. Kaiyoti Pesante, who
worked as Al's personal assistant for almost ten years beginning in the late
1990s, reported that in venues all over the world, they would go into "very
lavish rooms and dumps. Both extremes, [Al] hated."[3] Kaiyoti needed to

convert each dressing room into Al's "work room." Al would say, "I need my table set just like this," which included—in a particular order—hot water, tea, three vials of ginseng, Gatorade, and various other vitamins or supplements at various times. "Al needed his space," Kai said. "He needed things to be how they needed to be."

Over Kai's ten years with Al, the rider for Al's contracts grew longer and longer as Al became more specific about his preconcert demands. When Kai reached the end of his time with Al and was training his replacement, the "new guy" was dumbfounded at the meticulousness of it.

One of Al's specific requests was that he not be transported in a Cadillac Escalade. He didn't like the vehicle itself, but he also resented the assumption that because he was African American he would want to be driven around town in an Escalade, which had become a status symbol for many Black artists and athletes.

On the more modest end of Al's touring schedule, he continued to make appearances in Wisconsin into the mid- and late 2000s, usually in Milwaukee.[4] But a particularly memorable performance occurred in October 2006 at Al's alma mater, Ripon College, where he performed a sold-out benefit to raise money for student scholarships.[5] While in town for only about forty-eight hours, the energetic sixty-six-year-old also read to children at the Ripon Public Library; toured the campus; met with college students and with the alumni board; attended a dedication ceremony for the college's new baseball field; participated in the coin toss at the homecoming football game, where he also sang the national anthem; and filmed a segment of a cooking show for local cable television. After the concert, he spent several hours at a reception for friends and well-wishers, posing for photographs with anyone who wished.

A highlight in 2007 was a short European tour late in the year with the famed NDR (Norddeutscher Rundfunk, or North German Radio) Bigband, a large jazz ensemble known for its premier soloists and its original and striking group sound.[6] The group is based in Hamburg, a city that played a crucial role in Al's triumphant early career in Europe. (He sometimes referred to it as the "musical birthplace of my musical career.") Among the tour dates were engagements in Hamburg, Frankfurt, and Vienna, and at the prestigious Die Philharmonie in Berlin. The program featured reimagined versions of selections from *Porgy and Bess*, arranged by the

Al and his longtime music director Joe Turano entertain Al's home crowd at Ripon College in October of 2006. COURTESY OF RIPON COLLEGE

British pianist-composer-arranger Steve Gray, as interpreted by Al, an inimitable stylist. These jazzy interpretations—some of which are preserved in videos and bootleg recordings from this tour—reflected a side of Al's musical personality that, under different circumstances, could have led to a decidedly different career. A second concert tour with NDR in 2012 featured Al with the band in one set, reviving some of the same material, and Al with his longtime friend and sometime collaborator, keyboardist Joe Sample, in the second set.

Early in 2008, Rhino Records released a "new" Jarreau compilation, *Love Songs*. Al's note in the CD booklet about the inspiration for the album was typically personal and lighthearted:

> Whenever someone asks me if I sing to Susan (they ask her too), I get this faraway, dreamy look on my face and sing a very soft quiet "Oh . . . ," which gradually gets louder until it becomes "OOOOOOOkla-homa, where the wind comes sweeping down the plain . . ." Not very romantic, huh? That's when they shake their heads and mumble something about "crazy" and in a moment they start to snicker. And pretty soon we're both laughing real hard. If it's not romantic, it sure is fun.

Truth is, I'm really making light of how much I love ballads and love songs. As a kid, by the second grade I knew the complete melody and lyrics to more than a dozen very sentimental, heart-tugging love songs that I didn't even know the meaning of. I got hooked early and I still am.

The danger is being too syrupy, sappy, mushy, and boring. At the risk of all of the above, here's a bunch of my favorite love songs.

The album kicked off with "We're in This Love Together" and included selections that spanned Al's career all the way from his second album—"Your Song" from 1976's *Glow*—up to his 2006 collaboration with George Benson—"Let It Rain" from *Givin' It Up*.

From a legal standpoint, the production of this album was relatively simple because Rhino was part of the Warner Music Group. Since Warner already owned most of the tracks, no special permissions were necessary for those. However, the album does include three songs from the early 2000s GRP/Verve albums, as well as the one from the recently released Concord album with Benson.

Whether or not it was Al's idea to issue this set, it proved to be profitable. *Love Songs* ascended to number five on the contemporary jazz chart on February 16, 2008, staying on the chart for nineteen weeks. It also made the "regular" jazz albums list, peaking at number eleven and remaining there for twenty-two weeks.

Love Songs (2008) was a compilation of romantic tunes from throughout Al's career.

In a sign of the times, an insert in the CD package advertises "official Al Jarreau mobile products," with the offer of "We're in This Love Together" for fans to purchase as a ringtone. The ad urges fans to "feel even more together every time your love calls."

The release of *Love Songs* led to the issuing of the *Christmas* album later in the year, also with Rhino. "I should have done a Christmas record a long time ago," Al said in an interview shortly after *Christmas* came out in fall of 2008.[7] In the album notes, Al again suggests that the album was a long time coming: "I've been promising all of you a Christmas album for decades now, but the embarrassing truth is that I've been promising my wife Susan (the most "Christmasy" person I know) for way, way longer. Now Ryan is part of that promise." Al added a bit of a disclaimer about the music on the album by saying, "There are some 'Jarreau-isms' that stretch the boundaries of 'traditional' a little bit, but it's all with the greatest respect and reverence. And it's still real approachable and fun."

The material, both sacred and secular, is mostly old favorites: "Winter Wonderland," "Hark the Herald Angels Sing," "White Christmas," "O Come All Ye Faithful," "The Christmas Song," and others. But there are some lesser-known songs as well, including "Some Children See Him" and "The Little Christmas Tree," in addition to two new original songs, the brief "By My Christmas Tree" and "Gloria in Excelsis," which was cowritten by Larry Williams.

Some fans may have been surprised that Al didn't record a Christmas album until this late stage in his career. The selections on *Christmas* reflected Al's musical personality at the time of its release in 2008.

When Williams talked about the making of *Christmas*, he also mentioned some issues with Al's health at the time: "I did that Christmas record with him, which I thought was faithful to Al. Al was in a bit of [physical] decline, you know, when he did the vocals." Al was having serious trouble with his back, but his drinking, which had been an issue at times during his career, may also have played a part in his diminished vocal capabilities at the time. As Williams said, "We did the best he could. I'm proud of that record, because it was one of the last [of Al's records]."[8]

Getting the record made was a financial challenge. According to Larry, "The record company said, 'Here's an amount of money,'" and Larry figured, "If I do [*laughs*] 75 percent of the engineering and . . . all the vocal production [and] most of the arranging," that they could make it work.[9] He enlisted veteran arrangers Clare Fischer and Jorge Calandrelli, two of the most respected figures in the business, to do a couple of the arrangements. Established Jarreau regulars Joe Turano and Chris Walker contributed arrangements as well, and Al also had a hand in the arrangements, especially the vocals. The rhythm section for much of the album was the touring band's core trio: Williams, drummer Mark Simmons, and bassist Walker. "So we got all hands on deck," Larry continued, "but we did a lot of it in house, meaning, literally my house. . . . I had to be my own arranger, I had to play, I had to do all the paperwork, I had to pay the guys, [and fill out] the union forms." It was a stretch to justify spending the time and money that it takes to create a finely crafted record.

Many of the tracks have a somewhat similar character, displaying gentle rhythmic feels and richly scored backgrounds, with Al's renderings of the tunes being the focus. Of course, certain tracks stand out. Jorge Calandrelli had been a first-choice arranger—for films and television, but especially for singers—for decades, collaborating with Tony Bennett, Barbra Streisand, Diana Krall, Lady Gaga, and many others. His arrangement of "White Christmas" for Al features oboe, and Williams added flute and clarinet tracks. Much of the arrangement sounds as if it was written for a large string section, but Larry effectively creates that string section on synthesizers. Clare Fischer, a favorite among jazz artists, along with his son Brent created a lightly Latin arrangement for "Have Yourself a Merry Little Christmas" that features delightfully intricate woodwind lines rendered by Dan Higgins on clarinets and flutes.

Of special interest is Williams's brilliant, almost orchestral vocal arrangement of "I'll Be Home for Christmas" that the vocal group Take 6 immaculately performs with its distinctive sound. Al just sings the tune over the group's rich tonal carpet. "My God, Larry just deserves a purple heart for that one," Joe Turano said.[10] About his own contributions, Joe expressed pride in his arrangement of "Carol of the Bells," but he was particularly pleased with the very thinly scored "Some Children See Him."[11] The only sounds on that track are Turano's piano and saxophone and Al's vocal. A little-known song by an equally little-known composer, Alfred Burt, the song features a combination of melody, phrasing, emotion, and lyrics (which are about racial equality) that was "made for Al," according to Turano.[12] In Wihla Hutson's lyrics, some children see the baby Jesus as "lily white," others see Him "bronzed and brown" or with "skin of yellow hue" or just "as dark as they."[13] It is a touching performance.

Also in 2008, Al recorded one track with venerated jazz composer and saxophonist Benny Golson. Golson had reformed a "jazztet," modeled on the original Jazztet that he cofounded with trumpeter Art Farmer in the late 1950s. With the new version of the group, Golson recorded *New Time, New 'Tet*; Al sings the Golson classic "Whisper Not." It is good to see and hear Al on an album by a highly respected and thoroughly mainstream jazz artist. Perhaps some critics would never call Al a jazz singer at this stage in his career, but that did not deter Golson. The album was released in 2009, sometime after Al appeared with other guests at a tribute to Golson for his eightieth birthday, held at the Kennedy Center in Washington, DC.

Outside of music, 2008 brought an interesting twist in Al's long career. Because Al inspired the children's author Carmen Rubin, she turned him into a lightly veiled main character in her book *Ashti Meets Birdman Al*. Ashti, a young Black girl, encounters a beguiling old man in a city park who sings, whistles, and scats with the birds. In Robert Muhammad and Simon Stewart's illustrations, Birdman Al closely resembles Al Jarreau. Birdman talks about his love of jazz and encourages Ashti and her mother to advocate for the school's music program through the teaching of jazz.[14] After the book's publication in late 2008, Al occasionally appeared with Rubin at reading and book-signing events. It was, in effect, a continuation of the work Al did with the Verizon literacy program.

The arrangements with Rhino Records continued into 2009 when

The second "best of" collection of Al's hits, released in 2009, has continued to have good sales, even years after his death in 2017.

yet another compilation, *The Very Best Of: An Excellent Adventure*, was released. *Excellent Adventure* is essentially an update of 1996's *Best of Al Jarreau*, and the two sets share nine tracks. While two of the 2009 album's other eight tracks are from albums released after 1996—"Just to Be Loved" from *Tomorrow Today* and "Cold Duck" from *Accentuate the Positive*—the later collection also included many early tunes, including "Rainbow in Your Eyes" from 1976's *Glow* and the title track of *We Got By*, Al's first album from 1975. Perhaps to add jazz content, the Brubeck/Jarreau "(Round, Round, Round) Blue Rondo à la Turk" was selected from *Breakin' Away*. "Moonlighting" had been premiered on the earlier *Best of* collection. And the new track "Excellent Adventure" explained the album's subtitle. This new set was another commercial success, reaching number eighteen on the jazz album chart and peaking at number three on the contemporary jazz list.[15] As of early 2023, it had been on that chart for a total of 140 weeks.

During this period, Al continued to present his symphony concerts. A typical set might include a "Jarreau Overture" that would largely consist of his greatest hits and a variety of selections associated with Al, arranged by Gil Goldstein and Larry Baird: "Alonzo," "We Got By," "Summertime," "Take Five," "My Favorite Things," "Spain," an arrangement of Johann Sebastian Bach's "Air for the G String," "We're in This Love Together," "Mornin'," and, as an encore, "After All." Gil Goldstein had also written arrangements for "Not Like This," "Compared to What," "Something's

Coming" (from *West Side Story*), "Lock All the Gates," "Something That
You Said," and "Mas Que Nada" that were played in some concerts. Goldstein conducted many of the early concerts, but he was later replaced on
the podium by Baird, who had much more pops orchestra conducting
experience, having led orchestras in performances with Michael Bolton,
the band Kansas, the Moody Blues, and other artists.[16]

On July 22, 2010, while Al and the band were on tour in Europe, Al
experienced a major health scare. During a warm-up for a performance at
a jazz festival in the very small mountain town of Barcelonnette, France,
Al suddenly collapsed.[17] His condition was immediately determined to be
grave, and he was transported by helicopter to the somewhat larger town
of Gap, where he stayed in the hospital for one or two days. According
to manager Joe Gordon, who was the only member of the entourage to
accompany Al to Gap, the "doctors gave no promises that he would survive, much less perform again." Gordon feared that Al's death was a real
possibility. Only after doctors stabilized his weak heartbeat and shallow
breathing was it possible for him to be airlifted to Marseille, where a distinguished heart specialist, a jazz fan who had heard Al perform just days
earlier, was able to perform a heart ablation, correcting Al's arrhythmia,
which had led to the collapse.

Prior to this event, neither Chris Walker nor Joe Turano were aware
of Al facing any serious health issues, although his back had been both-
ering him for some years. In fact, Turano had begun to express concern
that Al's back was causing some singing issues—his diaphragmatic problems were affecting his breathing. But this episode revealed a condition—
arrhythmia—that no one in Al's circle had been aware of, including Al
himself. Walker reported that it was only later, when the band reunited
two weeks after the incident, that they found out that this was a heart issue.

The news media reported somewhat conflicting information about the
incident. *Billboard* reported, via the Associated Press, that according to Al's
website, he "had asked to be taken to the hospital . . . after he had trouble
adjusting to the Alpine mountain altitude." Fatigue and the altitude were
cited as the likely reasons for the collapse and Al's need to cancel the concert in the middle of his overseas tour.[18] One headline from July 24 blared,
"Al Jarreau in Critical Condition in France," while yet another section just
two days later said "Al Jarreau Getting Better, Hoping to Resume Touring

Soon."[19] Ultimately, the situation was as serious as some of the more sensational headlines suggested.

While the band idled around Europe for two weeks, there was serious concern about whether or not Al could return to performing, at least in the short run. Many factors needed to be considered. Canceling the rest of the tour might effectively end Al's performing career, since venues would be hesitant to hire a septuagenarian with a fragile health condition. Of course, Al wanted to go on. But even he was not sure he was well enough to perform the first concert after his collapse, which would be in Frankfurt. Luckily, fate stepped in.

Earlier in the tour, Al had stopped in Milan and attended a recording session of the Brazilian composer-arranger Eumir Deodato. Deodato, who established himself in the music industry of his native Brazil as a teenager, eventually worked with Brazilian legends Milton Nascimento, Antônio Carlos Jobim, and many others. He made a big and unexpected splash in the United States in 1973 with the jazzy-disco arrangement of the opening of Richard Strauss's *Also Sprach Zarathustra*, which had entered pop culture through Stanley Kubrick's influential film *2001: A Space Odyssey*. The album Deodato was recording in Italy, *The Crossing*, was being made with mostly Italian musicians, largely from the band Novecento. While in Milan, Al heard an instrumental track (with no vocals) they had completed. Within thirty-six hours of leaving the studio, Al had written a lyric for the song. The day before Al's "return" concert was to take place, brothers Pino and Nino Nicolosi flew to Frankfurt, rented a studio, and had Al overdub the vocals on "Double Face." Al had considerable trepidation about how his voice would work and about facing a microphone and audience after his heart crisis. Yet, he recovered his confidence at the session and was able to perform live the next day, just two weeks after his collapse.

Later in the year, Al clarified, to some degree, what had happened in France in an interview with Lee Mergner for *JazzTimes*. Not surprisingly, given his general outlook on life, as well as his concern for his career, Al put as positive a spin on the incident as possible. Mergner wrote:

> Sometimes a story is just too good, or even too bad, to be true. Recently, many jazz fans and insiders were shocked to read reports from Europe that singer Al Jarreau had collapsed on stage and was

in critical condition in a hospital in France. To paraphrase Twain, rumors of his demise were slightly exaggerated. "Well, it seemed like a juicy story to folks," Jarreau said, speaking by phone from his home in California. Much of the initial coverage emanated from a French newspaper and was picked up by Reuters and then virally by other outlets . . . and words like "collapsed" and "critical condition" virtu-ally jumped out of the articles. . . .

Jarreau was in the midst of a European tour, when he found him-self short of breath on the day of a performance in the Marseille area of France. He decided to seek medical attention at a nearby hospital, where he was diagnosed with the relatively common and treatable condition of heart arrhythmia (ironic given his own impeccable sense of time). He was hospitalized for a few days and had to cancel a few shows, which he found perhaps most upsetting of all. "I said to my-self, 'Wait a minute, this doesn't feel right.' I never cancel a show but I was short of breath and I thought I should err on the side of caution and get myself checked out." Certainly high altitude didn't help mat-ters. "Right, I need to be careful about doing that. While I was there [at the hospital], I got a new Ten Commandments written just for me, from the doctors. A lot of 'Don't do this, don't do that.' I need to be more conscious of salt intake and other healthy heart things." All in all, he said he's feeling good now, if a little humbled. "I'm doing pretty okay here. I did decide to go in and get myself checked out. I think that was important. There were some things that I didn't know were going on with me."[20]

Al understated the "few days in the hospital" and the "few concerts" he had to cancel. And while he made it seem as though he had calmly recog-nized a problem and asked for help, Joe Gordon remembered the event as much more of a crisis. A few months later, Al told the *Toronto Star* about a few lifestyle changes he had finally made after this scare. "I'm eating a little different and resting a little different," he said. "I was never a heavy smoker, but I'm a non-smoker now, that's a serious change. I cold-turkeyed that bad boy. Certainly my lungs are happier, my whole cardiovascular [system] is happier."[21]

Regardless of how long it took Al to recover from this incident, Joe Turano felt it was remarkable that he came back from this setback to tour again—he referred to Al as "Superman" and a "road dog." By early 2011, Al was performing more regularly again, and he soon made trips to Moscow and Minsk, Belarus. The next summer, he performed in England and Germany, and at the Marciac Festival in France.

Everyone who was close to Al knew that touring was the heart and soul of his career. Even after he resumed touring, his health could no longer be taken for granted. Yet, Al Jarreau was in no way finished with his career.

LOVE SONGS
Rhino Records, 2008

The songs that appear on this album are "We're in This Love Together" and "Teach Me Tonight" from *Breakin' Away*, "So Good" from *Heart's Horizon*, "After All" from *High Crime*, "Wait for the Magic" from *Tenderness*, "Heaven and Earth" from *Heaven and Earth*, "Through It All" from *Tomorrow Today*, "Let It Rain" from the *Givin' It Up* album done with George Benson (the track is a vocal duet by Al and Patti Austin, with Benson on guitar), "Not Like This" from *Jarreau*, "Brite 'N' Sunny Babe" from *All Fly Home*, "Secrets of Love" from *All I Got*, "My Foolish Heart" from *Accentuate the Positive*, and "Goodhands Tonight" from *Best of Al Jarreau*.

Some may be surprised that Al was cocomposer on only three of these selections and sole composer of just one ("Brite 'N' Sunny Babe"). Probably many fans would have made some different choices for love songs sung by Al, but these were his choices—or, at least, his choices influenced by members of his marketing team. The album rose to number eleven on the jazz albums chart, where it spent twenty-two weeks.

CHRISTMAS
Rhino, 2008

Dan Higgins, one of the busiest saxophone and reed players on the West Coast, is an unsung star on this record. Although his major contribution is all of the clarinets and flutes on Clare and Brent Fischers' arrangement of "Have Yourself a Merry Little Christmas," he also adds the delightful touch of penny whistle and wood flute on Larry Williams and Al's arrangement of "Hark the Herald Angels Sing."

The old favorite "Hark" is done in a meter of five. It is also notable for Williams's decision to have Lenny Castro play udu, essentially a hollow water jug used as a drum, and have Larry Tuttle play "stick," a ten- or twelve-stringed instrument popularized in the 1970s that can effectively cover guitar and bass parts simultaneously.

Larry Goldings, one of the most respected organists in jazz, is almost indistinguishable on "The Christmas Song," but his funky style is immediately noticeable on Al and Larry Williams' composition "Gloria in Excelsis."

One other bit of music business trivia related to the making of this album: Take 6 performed as part of a music business barter. In exchange for the group's appearance on *Christmas* (their track was delivered to Williams's house at the very last minute of production), Al performed on their album *The Standard*, singing on the Miles Davis classic "Seven Steps to Heaven."[22]

The *Christmas* sessions were also bittersweet. Dave Carpenter, who plays acoustic bass on three tracks, died in the interval between the recording and the issuing of the album. And guitarist Ross Bolton, who had been a fixture with the touring band for almost a decade, made his last recorded appearance with Al on "The Christmas Song." Bolton passed away in 2013.

LATER GUEST APPEARANCES

Take 6. *The Standard.* **Heads Up, 2008.**
Al's participation on this album was done in exchange for Take 6's contribution to his *Christmas* album. Al sang on the group's version of Miles Davis's "Seven Steps to Heaven," with lyrics by Jon Hendricks (who makes a brief appearance on the track). As Take 6 wrote in their album notes, "The vocalist with the flexibility to sing lyrics at this incredible speed is the peerless Al Jarreau." According to Larry Williams, it was quite a challenge to get this jaw-dropping performance recorded. Marrying Hendricks's words to the original Miles Davis trumpet solo lines was nearly impossible.

Benny Golson. *New Time, New 'Tet.* **Concord Jazz, 2009.**
Al's reading of Golson's superb composition "Whisper Not" is quite straightforward—something he probably considered necessary on such a beautifully crafted piece that was originally conceived as an instrumental. Al stays close to the melody, with a little understated inflection here and there. Eddie Henderson follows the vocal with a half chorus of tasty muted trumpet, leading into a bluesy piano spot for Mike LeDonne. Then, Al returns with the "instrumental interlude." His last half chorus features some deviation from the melody. Finally, Al becomes an instrument with a brief improvised solo over a repeated progression near the end. Leonard Feather's lyrics about reigniting a love affair are moving, but they are overshadowed by the melodic and harmonic genius of this compositional gem.

Eumir Deodato. *The Crossing.* **Soul Trade (Italy); issued in the United States on SMC Entertainment, 2010.**
Al is featured on the album's opener, "Double Face." He scats over the intro—a signature Deodato groove and sound—before going into the verse. It's a love song, but his lyrics speak of a risky love that could

be doomed from the start. After the last chorus, Al scats again, leading into Deodato's Fender Rhodes solo. The album ends with a shorter, radio-friendly version of "Double Face."

Al's other cocomposer track, "I Want You More," features vocalist Dora Nicolosi. Al has a brief spot that sounds like an improvisation, doubled by Nicolosi singing an octave higher. Nicolosi was the lead singer of the Italian band Novecento, which also featured her husband, Lino Nicolosi, and his siblings Pino and Rossana Nicolosi, all of whom are featured as instrumentalists on numerous tracks on *The Crossing*.

THE VERY BEST OF: AN EXCELLENT ADVENTURE
Warner/Reprise/Rhino, 2009

This album's one new track, "Excellent Adventure," was written by Al and his former pianist Freddie Ravel. It was produced by The Randy Watson Experience, which was James Poyser and Ahmir "?uestlove" Thompson (better known as Questlove). Right around the time of *Excellent Adventure*'s release, Poyser and Thompson became well known throughout the country as members of the hip-hop-based band The Roots. The Roots went on to become the house band for NBC's *Late Night with Jimmy Fallon*, which transitioned into *The Tonight Show* in 2014.

The funky "Adventure" is contemporary, hip, and heavily produced. Some of Al's singing is almost spoken in a hip-hop style. A section in the middle is, in fact, rapped. But there are touches of Jarreau's earlier style present here and there throughout the track. For much of the tune, he sings at the very bottom of his vocal range (often with a higher vocal track overdubbed); his low range was featured more often in the latter stages of his career.

24

———— ✳-✳-✳ ————

FINALE

The year 2011 finally saw the release of the songs Al had recorded at San Francisco's Half Note jazz club during his time there with the George Duke Trio in 1965. Al and Duke had performed together occasionally in the years immediately preceding this release, including a couple of trips to Russia.[1] The release was stimulus for some special performances in 2011, with a particularly noteworthy appearance of several nights at the Blue Note in New York City.[2] There, the two legendary musicians performed tunes that they used to do back in the 1960s ("Moanin'" and "Come Rain or Come Shine"), songs that they had collaborated on in the years since ("Roof Garden" and "Cold Duck"), and even a couple of Duke originals that would reappear in Al's recorded work just a couple of years later ("Backyard Ritual" and "Brazilian Love Affair").[3]

Video of the two old friends both on and off stage makes clear the long-standing and deep bond between them, as well as the great fun they had just hanging out together and making music so many years after their relationship began. Perhaps, at seventy-one and sixty-five, they sensed that their time left together was running out.

When asked by an interviewer in 2012 about whether he was the same person at seventy-one years old that he had been fifty years earlier, Al answered with his characteristic thoughtfulness and humility:

> We all change every moment, so probably not. I am changing and I am closer to "getting it right" now than I was before. And what I mean by "getting it right" is making the most and the best of your life that

you ought to be committed to doing, and in some ways I am a lot the same and in some ways I am changing. I have some New Year's resolutions that I am better at keeping this year than last year [*laughs*]. Just doing some things differently in my life, because it's important. I have some doctors these days that I didn't have ten years ago, and they are shaking that finger in my face and saying "stop this and stop that," and I am still putting too much salt in my food, and I like my cocktail in the evening. So in some ways I am changing and doing things better, and being honest with myself and my wife and those around me, but this is all stuff and a side of me that you wouldn't know unless I talk about it, but it's in the songs. Things that I knew that are important, like living a good, honest, clean, responsible life. The little life we all want to do when we sit and look at ourselves and then look at the man in the mirror. It's part of the answer, and maybe the most important part of what it is all about as I go into my 72nd year.[4]

In response to the question "What do you think is your biggest accomplishment in life?" Al answered: "I really think it's managing such a long career that's still going, and having a family that's pretty happy, you know? My wife hasn't left me, and my son is not in jail or doesn't do drugs or smoke. He just joined me on tour and he is loving it. Last summer he said, 'Okay, let's do it,' and it's working out great."

In 2012, Al made another highlight album, *Live*. When he recorded *Givin' It Up* with George Benson in 2006, the initial business arrangement had been for a single album with Concord Records. A few years later, Al signed a deal with Concord for three more albums. According to Al's manager Joe Gordon, everyone at Concord was very kind, as they had a great deal of respect for Al, and the intention was that Al would finish his career as a Concord artist. *Live* was the first product of this contract.

Live was a collaboration between Al and the Metropole Orkest, an orchestra founded in 1945. When the Dutch government and royal family had returned from their World War II exile in London, they decided that their country needed "an orchestra to bring pleasure and hope to the Dutch people." The Orkest, which came to be funded by the Dutch Broadcasting Corporation, was made up of musicians from around Europe and "developed a reputation as a full symphony orchestra with an integrated big band."⁵ Since 2005, the Metropole had been led by the American Vince Mendoza, who had built a sterling reputation as a composer and arranger in jazz, pop, and music for film.

When it was determined that Al would do a project with Metropole, negotiations about repertoire began. Al's music director, Joe Turano, who was ultimately credited as coproducer of the album, described the process: "[I was] consulting with Vince Mendoza . . . about what tunes he wanted, what he thought Metropole would be suited to do, what he liked. So we would go back and forth about that, then I'd bring that back to Al, and Al would go, 'Well, that's great; what about this?'. . . So Vince and I settled between ourselves—with Al in an advisory role—what the tunes would be, and Vince shared his ideas about how he might treat them."⁶ Once the preliminaries were over and rehearsals began, Al and Joe Turano agreed that everything Mendoza wrote "was absolute, sheer brilliance," but they both felt that his compositions needed some editing. Mendoza was not dogmatic about his arrangements and was willing to make any adjustments needed to make Al comfortable.

Four of the tunes on *Live* came from *Accentuate the Positive*: two jazz standards, "I'm Beginning to See the Light" and "Midnight Sun," and two jazzy "grooving" tunes, "Cold Duck" and Al's composition with Russell Ferrante, "Scootcha-Booty." *Live* also included two of the modern jazz classics to which Al had added lyrics, creating his own classics: "Something That You Said" and "Spain (I Can Recall)." The hit "We're in This Love Together" probably seemed like a necessary inclusion. Rounding out the program were Al's lesser hit, the romantic "After All"; a showcase for Al's love of Brazilian music, "Agua de Beber"; Larry Williams's beguiling "Flame"; and the group band composition "Jacaranda Bougainvillea." While all of these songs had convincing settings in their original recordings, the inspired Mendoza arrangements for this huge, outstanding ensemble gave Al a musical vehicle unlike any he'd had before. Joe Gordon confirmed that Al was "very proud" of, in fact "thrilled" with, the result. And, while it did not win, *Live* was nominated in 2012 for a Grammy in the Best Jazz Vocal Album category.

All was not well, though, as was reported in many outlets; in another health "hiccup," Al had to cancel several concert dates in France in 2012 due to a bout of pneumonia.⁷

In 2013, Al made a guest appearance on an album by another important jazz singer from Milwaukee, Tierney Sutton. Sutton, whose stellar career led to an amazing nine Grammy nominations (at the time of this book's publication), was just spreading her jazz wings and learning the ropes in the early 1980s when she sat in at a gig by another important Milwaukee jazz artist, pianist Lynne Arriale.[8] As Sutton told the story, after singing a tune or two, bassist Al Anderson confronted her.

> He said, "You sing pretty good. But you need to learn to swing. I want
> you to come to my house tomorrow, at noon." . . . So I go over to
> his house, and he puts a record on, and he says, "Guess who this is?"
> And it's this really swingin' voice, . . . and I'm guessing like, "Is that
> Carmen McRae?" . . . And I couldn't figure out who it was, and I said,
> "Are you sure I know this person?" He said, "I'm positive you know
> this person." . . . It was Al Jarreau.

The recording was Al's "Iowa record," from years before he became an international figure. Sutton listened over and over to these tracks and learned precisely how eighth notes need to be swung. She says, "If I can swing, it's because of that record."[9]

Al sang on Sutton's Joni Mitchell tribute album *After Blue*, released by BFM Jazz in 2013. While most of the album is devoted to the reflective melodies and lyrics that Mitchell is famous for, the one real swinging tune on the album is "Be Cool," originally on Mitchell's 1982 album *Wild Things Run Fast*. Sutton said that when she decided which songs would appear on her album, she immediately thought of Al for this one. As it turned out, Al owed her a "free" session, as they had agreed to trade dates after she had recorded a duet with him for a Jarreau album, which regrettably was never used.

Al's dear friend George Duke died of chronic lymphocytic leukemia in August 2013. Upon hearing the news, Al was so upset that he called his sister Rose Marie from Russia, waking her in the middle of the night.[10] Al wanted to honor his longtime companion in a meaningful musical way. That desire led to Al's next album—and, sadly, the last one he would release—*My Old Friend: Celebrating George Duke*, released in 2014. According to an article in *Billboard*, the chief creative officer of Concord Records, John Burk, came up with the idea. Al admitted that the suggestion "scared the crap out of [him]." "Of course, I had to say yes," he continued. "But doing George Duke is a serious undertaking. I picked areas where I thought it was important for people to hear his work—but also wanted to represent what he did in my own way and have it be real."[11]

It was decided that the album would feature Duke's songs, notably excepting the title track, which had appeared on Al's 1981 hit album *Breakin' Away*.[12] "My Old Friend" was written by Richard Page. Its touching and bittersweet lyrics poignantly expressed Al's feelings about George.

Performing the ten Duke compositions for the album were many guest stars: Dianne Reeves, Stanley Clarke, Gerald Albright, Boney James, Marcus Miller, Jeffrey Osborne, Lalah Hathaway, Kelly Price, and even Dr. John. While Joe Gordon handled most of the logistics of making the record, John Burk was the driving force behind bringing these outstanding talents together.

The mix of tunes runs the gamut of Duke's work. Three selections from Duke's brilliant 1979 *A Brazilian Love Affair* are particularly outstanding on *My Old Friend*: "Some Bossa (Summer Breezin')," and the medley of "Brazilian Love Affair" and "Up from the Sea It Arose and Ate Rio in One Swift Bite." Al loved Brazilian music, performing it even before his so-called Brazilian period with Julio Martinez in the late 1960s and early 1970s. On this record, Al performs these strongly Brazilian-influenced tunes with style and spirit. The composition Duke wrote for Miles Davis's *Tutu* album, "Backyard Ritual," which becomes "Churchyheart" with Al's new lyrics, was a bold musical choice.

My Old Friend, like *Live*, was an excellent representation of Al's skills; it would have been a fine album at any point in his career. And, while the Duke album was the last official album release of Al's career, it was not the last album he made. NDR Bigband leader Jörg Achim Keller approached Al with the idea of revisiting the Duke Ellington Songbook with Al performing as vocalist with the NDR Bigband. It was a proposal Al could not resist. He came up with his ideas of how he wanted to sing the Ellington classics and sang those ideas into a recorder; Joe Turano then crafted rhythm arrangements and those went to the NDR for Keller's orchestrations.[13] An announcement about Al's forthcoming tour dates with the NDR claimed: "Keller's new take on Ellington's body of work by combining the qualities of Al Jarreau and the NDR Bigband through new arrangements, managed to create something really excitingly brand new—Ellington 2.0, if you will. Also, his collaboration with Keller managed to provide Jarreau, who grew up with the music of the greats like Ellington, Fitzgerald and so on, with a totally new perspective of Ellington's music than the few songs he already had in his live repertoire."[14]

Although Al toured with the band performing this material in the fall of 2016, regrettably, due to a combination of legal and business considerations, this album has never been released.

Al's last performance in his hometown was at the Northern Lights Theater at the Potawatomi Casino in August 2015. In a review titled "Al Jarreau Puts On a Joyful Homecoming Concert at Potawatomi," the *Milwaukee Journal Sentinel*'s Piet Levy described a virtual lovefest:

It's common to feel a special energy at a homecoming show for a Milwaukee artist who's done good.

But the affection expressed at Al Jarreau's return to Milwaukee Friday . . . was on a whole other level.

Not so much from the admiring audience, which was rightfully gracious toward the seven-time Grammy-winning jazz, pop and R&B singer. I'm talking about from Jarreau himself.

"I'm so happy. I'm so blessed," the 75-year-old proclaimed at one point.

And if that reads like Sally-Field-at-the-Oscars-style melodrama, that's nothing compared to his over-the-top outpouring of love.

Jarreau's exuberance rivaled Ebenezer Scrooge on Christmas morning, his banter and behavior bordering on lunacy, but undeniably infectious all the same. The California resident spoke with great pride about his upbringing, his time at Lincoln High School, his appreciation of the snow here. (Like I said, he seemed a little cuckoo.)

And he called out to individual friends by name and responded to strangers like long-lost relatives. The coziness of the near-capacity, 500-seat theater helped with that intimacy—"I can smell your per-

fume, girl," he cheerfully told an audience member—and he strayed
from the 14-song set list to perform zealous snippets of "Across the
Midnight Sky" and "Alonzo" a cappella, upon request.

"We know some things that are very valuable and important because we come from Milwaukee," Jarreau said at one point.

Statements like these seemed too sincere to be pandering. And
Jarreau and his five-piece band didn't really need to butter up the
crowd.[15]

Levy went on to praise the band, singling out Joe Turano, a native
of Milwaukee's suburb West Allis, and Turano's arrangements of "High
Crime" and Harry Belafonte's "Day-O (The Banana Boat Song)." And Al did
not disappoint, either. Levy wrote that "his signature scat-style vocal riffing was as swift as ever during the buttery blues of 'Great City,' a new track
yet to be recorded, and he could still hit those pleasurable high notes on
'My Old Friend.' . . . Jarreau infused every note with childlike glee—even
gargling water at one point while scatting on 'Easy.'" Levy concluded his
review by describing an interaction with a crowd member that perfectly
encapsulated Al's generosity of spirit that night. "'We love you, Al,' the fan
who requested 'Sky' later yelled. 'I love you more,' Jarreau replied back.
There was no doubt about that."

Al showed up in the *Milwaukee Journal Sentinel* again several months
later when his opinion piece "We're All in the Arts Together" was published
in March 2016. In it, Al related his history as a youth in Milwaukee, including his experience playing music at Lincoln High School. He addressed
what he considered a crisis: "I am very concerned that, today, children in
my hometown of Milwaukee, and across our country, are not getting the
same exposure to arts that I had." He talked about how arts programs had
been cut and how 2008 data showed that "African-American and Hispanic
students were only half as likely to have access to art programs in school as
their white peers." As he encouraged readers to support the arts through
organizations like the United Performing Arts Fund, he expressed his long-
held belief that "for the sake of our own sane and healthy survival here on
Earth, we must learn to understand each other better. And the arts are a
common language for communicating toward this goal."[16]

Just a few months later, Al would put his money where he saw it was

The Wisconsin Foundation for School Music presented Al with a Lifetime
Achievement Award at a grand ceremony at the Pfister Hotel in Milwaukee in 2016.
ILLUSTRATOR, ZACH BARTEL

needed. In October, he returned to Milwaukee—for what would be the last time—for a special event at the grand downtown Pfister Hotel. He was presented with a Lifetime Achievement Award from the Wisconsin Foundation for School Music.[17] At the same time, attendees celebrated the scholarship fund Al had established for music students in the Milwaukee Public Schools, crystallizing his commitment to arts education.

It was a magical night. Mayor Tom Barrett spoke, as did other local luminaries. Al's high school teacher Ron DeVillers and his old partner from the Indigos Ann Hassler made special remarks during the presentation. Joe Turano delivered the keynote address. Al exhibited visible delight in the performances of young musicians from the Milwaukee High School for the Arts. There was also a presentation of a commemorative video, a shorter version of the Wisconsin Public Television film *Al Jarreau: Coming Home* that would be released in 2017. Al's brief talk was inspiring, filled with the spirit of what all people owe one another in attempting to make the world a better place, with a focus on the importance of music and education. Among his remarks were these:

> When we teach our kids about [the arts], we teach our kids that sensitivity training. We need more sensitivity training. We're getting to have a world [in which we are] not sensitive to each other. We've moved away from each other and so part of the answer that we have to find as people who are going to school is to fix some things like that. And so, it's just so wonderful to be here with some people that are educators. God, I love teachers, my goodness, I love teachers.[18]

On a personal note, I was honored and blessed to represent Ripon College at this event, along with two of my students. When we spoke with Al there, he encouraged the students to sing the college's alma mater with him. Afterward, the students and I were in complete agreement that what we had seen and heard at this event was clearly what the United States, in the midst of a very ugly presidential campaign, seriously needed.

Al's remarks about a world in which people are not sensitive toward one another was, at least in part, a reaction to the election coming at the end of President Barack Obama's eight years in office. Just five months earlier, Al had been invited to the White House by President Obama to celebrate

International Jazz Day on April 30, 2016. During the interview with Wisconsin Public Television, Al told producer Steve Doebel what an honor it was to be there—how he was able to "stand there next to Michelle [Obama] and she has her arm around me. 'Hi Al . . .' That's an amazing thing and I have her little note to me."[19]

Among the other jazz artists present were Chick Corea, Herbie Hancock, Diana Krall, Christian McBride, Wayne Shorter, Pat Metheny, and Dianne Reeves, as well as non-jazz artists Aretha Franklin, Sting, and Buddy Guy.[20] The international contingent was represented by Chucho Valdés, Paquito D'Rivera, and Lionel Loueke. The *New York Times* reported that the singers "mostly tackled standards from their working repertory, delivering quick distillations of their personae," with Al's delivery being "wily and pliable."[21] Al later spoke of how "wonderful" it was to "go there and sing [and] play with these other jazz greats, and there's the first family and a lot of the cabinet sitting there front row center. Pretty amazing stuff. Amba-jazz-dors."[22]

In a *JazzTimes* article accompanied by a photograph from the White House performance featuring Al with other notable jazz singers—Dee Dee Bridgewater, Kurt Elling, and Esperanza Spalding (singing John Lennon's "Imagine")—Al shared some additional thoughts about that day with Lee Mergner. It was one of the few times in his career that he spoke directly in public about politics and race, acknowledging, even if briefly, the prejudice and discrimination Obama had experienced during his time as president. "It was wonderful that the Obamas, almost by executive order, welcomed International Jazz Day to the White House lawn," Al said. "We're only about five years into International Jazz Day, which is celebrated on April 30 in [195] countries, sending out this joyful thank you and appreciation and playing of jazz. It was just perfect that it took place there. I was so glad that I was a part of it."[23] And when asked if the trip to the White House held any special significance for him, Al responded:

Yes, being at the White House . . . has a lot of significance that Republicans have not been able to tarnish. They tried to assassinate this administration and have done a pretty good job of killing the country in favor of their selfish ideas. Shut the government down and all that. It's obvious why we don't talk about it. You are not going to hear it from corporate radio, press and television. "Wrong color. He cannot be my commander-in-chief."

Besides the tensions playing out across the nation in the lead-up to the 2016 election, Al was also experiencing some personal hardships. His wife, Susan, was battling esophageal cancer and her health was beginning to deteriorate. Then, an incident occurred in September, as Al prepared to travel for a single concert in Curaçao. The show was sponsored by the North Sea Jazz Festival, which had been a great supporter of Al's career over the years.[24] He planned to go to the island a couple of days early to relax before the concert. Driving to the airport, Al did not feel well. Apparently, as he had been home taking care of Susan, who was particularly ill then, Al had not been taking care of himself. He went directly to Thousand Oaks Hospital, where he was treated for exhaustion. But after just a couple of days, he was released, caught a red-eye flight to Curaçao, walked directly onto the stage upon arrival, and performed the concert without even a sound check.

Although Al's health was poor during the last years of his life, he continued to perform, giving dozens of concerts a year. To stop performing

Al continued to perform with his longtime bassist, backup singer, and music director Chris Walker very late into Al's career. COURTESY OF CHRIS WALKER

was not a viable option to Al. Years later, Joe Gordon said, "He always explained that that's not him. And if he sat home, it would be his downfall. So we went out [during those final years], and took him around the world, and he had a tougher time walking out onto the stage. He would sing a whole concert sitting on a stool. But he sang a wonderful concert, and people loved it."[25]

According to Al's son, Ryan, in the *Unsung* documentary, "He wanted people to see that, 'I'm going strong; I'm not quitting.' My dad always said, 'The day that I stop performing is when I can no longer physically make it onto that stage.'" As Al himself put it in the interview with Wisconsin Public Television in 2016, "You can't cut me out of the game [*laughs*]. A lot of people . . . have left the game because they're too tender and soft. Hey, I've got my lunch pail. I'm comin'. And if I've got an audience, I'll do it."[26]

In the late fall of 2016, Al was scheduled for a six-week tour with the NDR Bigband. Prior to heading for Europe, he was again attending to Susan and again not taking care of himself. Joe Gordon reported, however, that once Al was on tour, he felt good, and performing seemed to be healing, both spiritually and physically, for him.

He and the band played some of the usual high-class venues in Vienna, Frankfurt, Zurich, Monte Carlo, and Amsterdam, as well as numerous other dates around Germany, Norway, and elsewhere. They performed Ellington and Billy Strayhorn selections from the unreleased album, as well as some Gershwin from the earlier *Porgy and Bess* project. Amateur videos from the tour show Al singing well, with his usual ebullient onstage persona, but appearing somewhat fragile sitting on his stool at the performances. At the penultimate concert of the tour, in Monte Carlo on November 29, he talked to the crowd about Ripon College, jokingly suggesting that the audience must have known all about this little college in Wisconsin. He went on to say that the very first song his group at Ripon, the Indigos, had learned was Ellington's "Mood Indigo," which he then performed.

After the last show of the tour, in Zurich on December 2, he returned to the United States. His last public performance was a duo with Joe Turano at the One World Theatre in Austin, Texas, on December 9. The duo had been opening their shows with a song called "Jarreau" by singer-songwriter Brenda Russell, who was in the audience that night.

Early in 2017, Al was scheduled to take part in one of the jazz cruises that had become popular among fans and musicians alike. The tour was scheduled to crisscross the Caribbean from January 28 to February 4. Al's presence on the cruise for the first time was used in the marketing of that year's tour. "We wanted to make our 'Sweet Sixteen' anniversary an unforgettable party for our guests," said Michael Lazaroff, the executive director of Entertainment Cruise Productions, LLC. "Having Al Jarreau onboard to help us celebrate is a dream come true for all of us at The Jazz Cruise and is a gift to all of our amazing guests."[27]

In a 2016 visit with his frequent interviewer Lee Mergner at *JazzTimes*, Al talked with enthusiasm about doing the cruise, about his recent recording project with NDR, and the voice-piano duo with Joe Turano, which he tentatively and jokingly called JoeReau.[28] During the second half of 2016, that duo had played at the Montreux Jazz Festival, Ronnie Scott's club in London, and some other venues on both sides of the Atlantic.

The week before the cruise was to take place, Al spoke with his older sister, Rose Marie Freeman.[29] She asked Al how he was feeling, and his response—"Not bad"—was not comforting to Rose Marie. Not wishing to listen to Rose Marie's reservations about him doing the cruise, Al cut off the conversation, saying that Susan needed him. Rose Marie asked Al to call her back that night. Yet, she did not hear from him for days, so she left a message on his phone urging him not to go on the tour.

As it turned out, a situation unfolded that was very similar to what had happened before the Curaçao concert the previous September. On the way to the airport to fly to rehearsals for the cruise, Al felt ill and went directly to Thousand Oaks Hospital. This time, the situation was much more serious. Shortly thereafter, Joe Gordon called Rose Marie, informing her that Al had been transferred to Cedars-Sinai Medical Center. Al would be there for the rest of his life.

During his hospitalization, Al's team announced that he was retiring from touring. A preliminary Facebook post optimistically reported that he was "recovering slowly and steadily." According to *Rolling Stone*, his son, Ryan, had reported that he "caught his dad singing 'Moonlighting' to one of the nurses."[30] Joe Turano said that Al was still talking about "his baby"—the Ellington project—during these last days.[31]

Al's second cousin Sandra Moss, having been alerted by Rose Marie of

Al's admission to the hospital, became a daily visitor during his last days. "That was a priority of what I should be doing," she said.[32] As a health care professional, Sandra was familiar with the setting. But because of their age difference (she was twelve years younger than Al) and different stations in life, she had not spent a great deal of time with Al prior to this. "He stayed in that wonderful personality that he had," she remembered. "He was always welcoming and loving to everyone that came to see him." But Sandra also clearly saw that Al was very weak, uncomfortable, and in pain. Did Al know that he was near death? Sandra said, "I think a part of him knew . . . [but there was] a certain amount of denial. [Al was a] spiritually very deep man . . . that's why I say part of him absolutely knew."

During one of her visits to Al's room, Sandra remembered Al asking, "Can you hear that? . . . I hear a choir." When she said she didn't hear anything, he responded, "Well, listen really intently, because it's coming from down the hall." After she listened again and heard only hospital sounds, Al was incredulous that she couldn't hear what he did. He said: "I do. I hear a full choir." It was a sign for Sandra.

She recalled another moving story from those last days:

At one point, he wanted to get up. [The] therapist came. [Al] was so weak, he couldn't walk very far, even a few steps from the bed. . . . Then, one day he showed me the power of his lungs. I never thought about it, because I'm not a professional singer, but to think about the music and the sound that came from those lungs and that body. And one day he demonstrated [by singing]. . . . It was like he called from another power to exhibit to me the power of his lungs, which he didn't have for sitting up, standing up, and moving. But he still had that power. . . . It was extraordinary. I can't tell you that I've ever seen that power. . . . I was a bit surprised, but not shocked, that even in that state that he was in, which was by this time getting very close, that he could demonstrate that to me. I said to him . . . "I can't believe what I'm seeing, because you're so weak. . . . In some ways you're weak; in another way you're not at all weak." And he just smiled.

Larry Williams, who had been working with Al on and off since the early 1980s, tearfully related a deeply meaningful moment he experienced in the hospital: "[Al] was coming in and out of consciousness at the end. His heart was failing and we knew it, knew his time was limited. And one time I was in the room alone with him, in ICU, and he says, 'Larry, do you think I did enough? You think I did enough?' 'Yeah, Al, you did enough [*laughs ruefully*]. You did more than enough. [You] changed music, Al.' He seemed okay with that."[33]

When the end was very near, Al's brother Marshall made one last phone call to the hospital. "'[I know] you can't answer, man, but we've always loved you,' I said. And he was gone. He was gone."[34]

Al died on the morning of February 12, 2017, at the Cedars-Sinai Medical Center in Los Angeles.

Some months later, Ryan explained that Al's death was devastating for him and Susan. "It was very hard," he said. "My mom is in remission with esophageal cancer, so for her, it's been a lot harder. Just 'cause she doesn't have her best friend. And I know they were inseparable."[35] Nearly two years after her husband's death, Susan died of cancer on January 31, 2019.

AL JARREAU AND THE METROPOLE ORKEST — LIVE
Concord Records, 2012

While Al, Joe Turano, and Metropole Orkest leader Vince Mendoza all put a considerable amount of effort into determining which songs to perform and making sure the songs' compositions would showcase the strengths of both Al and the orchestra, the group faced the additional challenge of creating this album from just two nights of live performance. With the large number of players and the vagaries of live situations—including Al's career-long penchant for "going for it" live, both musically and vocally, rather than playing it safe—there was some apprehension for all involved. According to Joe Turano, the orchestra could be counted on to be "spot-on," but they still wanted to get the best solos from the band members—and Al's best takes. Those things don't always line up.

There's only so much that can be done with live tracks in postproduction, but Turano put in considerable work and the final product is superb—a fitting major project for Al's late career.

The highly skilled European artists featured included guitarist Peter Tiehuis; saxophonists Leo Janssen, Marc Scholten, and Paul van der Feen; trumpeter Ruud Breuls; synthesizer player Ronald Kool; and, prominently, trombonist Bart van Lier.

Christopher Loudon's *JazzTimes* review of the album addressed Al's waning abilities at this point in his career: "While Jarreau's trademark nasality remains as distinctive as ever, there's no question that his vocal power has diminished. He is, however, canny enough to pace himself accordingly." Loudon also wrote that the album "serves as a testament to the septuagenarian's indefatigable panache."[36]

This album peaked at number twelve on the *Billboard* contemporary jazz chart and at number twenty-seven on the jazz albums chart on July 7, 2012. It spent eleven weeks on both charts.

MY OLD FRIEND: CELEBRATING GEORGE DUKE
Concord Records, 2014

Almost all of the guest artists on this album had professional—and personal—connections to Duke. Dianne Reeves, the celebrated jazz singer who won a National Endowment of the Arts Jazz Masters award in 2018, was George Duke's cousin. He produced and performed on a number of her recordings. Duke and Stanley Clarke formed the Clarke/Duke Project in the 1980s, recording three albums. The first included the hit "Sweet Baby," which on *My Old Friend* features vocalist Lalah Hathaway. Multiple Grammy Award winner Hathaway was on Duke's final album, *Dream Weaver*.[37] Jeffrey Osborne sings the only non-Duke song besides the title track; the original version of "Wings of Song" was produced by Duke for

Osborne's self-titled debut album in 1982. Saxophonist Gerald Albright also performed with Duke, who produced one of his albums as well. Duke and Al had both worked and recorded with Boney James. Marcus Miller had worked with Al many times before, in addition to collaborating with Duke.

While John Burk coproduced most of the tracks, Clarke, Miller, and James were also producers or coproducers of many tracks. "Bring Me Joy" and "You Touch My Brain" were originally on Duke's 2010 album *Déjà Vu*. On "Bring Me Joy," through the miracle of modern recording technology, Duke actually plays the keyboards on the track. Dr. John was an inspired choice to interpret "Brain."

George Duke wrote and produced "Backyard Ritual" for Miles Davis's famous 1986 *Tutu* album, one of only two tracks on that album not written (at least in part) and produced by Marcus Miller. On *My Old Friend*, Miller produced a new version of the tune, "Churchyheart (Backyard Ritual)," with Al's lyrics including Christian references and a nod to Davis's "Bitches Brew."

My Old Friend peaked at number sixty-nine on the *Billboard* top 200 on August 23, 2014, a very respectable accomplishment for a seventy-four-year-old artist. It reached number one on both the contemporary jazz and jazz album charts that same week, spending thirty weeks and twenty-one weeks on those charts, respectively. The album received the 2015 NAACP Image Award for Outstanding Jazz Album.

25

LEGACY

fter Al's death was reported through dozens if not hundreds of media
outlets and social media sites, tributes poured in from throughout
the entertainment community, as well as from myriad fans. Among the
prominent names of those reacting to the loss were singers and instrumental musicians covering a wide swath of styles and even generations. Some
had worked directly with Al, while many others had just been inspired by
him. A sample of the long list of admirers includes such widely diverse
figures as Bootsy Collins, Lenny Kravitz, Chaka Khan, Marcus Miller, BeBe
and CeCe Winans, Angélique Kidjo, Najee, Dave Koz, Jody Whatley, John
Legend, Dianne Reeves, Tierney Sutton, Jill Scott, Robert Glasper, Lalah
Hathaway, Boney James, Jane Monheit, Joey DeFrancesco, Herb Alpert,
Audra McDonald, Paula Abdul, and Questlove. Among nonmusicians,
the Reverend Jesse Jackson; actors Billy Dee Williams, LeVar Burton, and
Octavia Spencer; director Ava DuVernay; and supermodel Naomi Campbell weighed in.

Down Beat posted this summary quote from Al's record label: "'We
feel very fortunate to have worked with Al, one of the most distinctive
and extraordinary vocalists in the music,' said Concord Records president,
John Burk. 'He was truly a force of nature and a beautiful human being that
will be fondly remembered and deeply missed by us all.'"[1]

Countless numbers of Al's fans reacted, and they have continued to
express their gratitude for his music daily on YouTube, Facebook, Twitter,
and other sites, even years after his death.

What was it about this man and his music that inspired the love and

Al's grave marker in Forest Lawn Memorial Park in Hollywood Hills, California, features a quote from his song "Mornin'." PHOTO BY THERESA ROBINSON, COURTESY OF ROSE MARIE FREEMAN

respect of so many, from all walks of life? Al's accomplishments, his life's journey, and many of his own words have been recounted throughout this book, but what else can be said about this exceptional figure?

There are many who might buy into the picture put forth in the 1989 *Jazziz* feature, which referred to Al as both "lucky" and "good." Al's career, despite small setbacks, was going very well at that time. He was lucky to have been born into a strong, loving, musical family and that his own musical gift was nurtured early. He was also lucky to have found a sympathetic manager, signed with a record company that believed in him, and connected with musicians with whom he could develop his very personal style of music. These bits of good fortune, combined with his incredible work ethic, exceptional musicality, and fantastic musical instrument—his voice—led Al to stardom. Yet many people don't realize, or tend to forget, that Al did not get his big professional break until he was thirty-five years old. In the fickle and youth-centered entertainment business, even during the glory years of the music business in the 1970s, that was rare indeed. Beyond his outsized talent, Al's youthful appearance, spirit, and outlook allowed him to succeed despite his late start. Onstage, Al was not just dynamic but also exceedingly easy to like, and he seemed eminently approachable. Audiences not only loved his talent, they loved him.

And musicians loved playing with Al—because of his playfulness, versatility, and raw talent, among other things. Chris Walker, Al's longtime touring bassist, explained that Al's band members felt they always had the freedom to explore new ideas. "Al loved that," he said. "Most people don't give you that type of flexibility, but Al was totally different in that regard."[2] And Joe Turano echoed the sentiment: "[Onstage], he'd let you go; I love him because he always let me go, on saxophone, whatever, 'Just do your thing, man, don't worry about the record.' He encouraged complete creativity. But he also knew what he wanted."[3]

Of course, Al's high standards sometimes posed a challenge for the musicians who worked with him. Drummer Mark Simmons recalled an incident when he came up against the limits of Al's flexibility:

He wasn't an intense person to work with, but he could be very particular in what he wanted to hear. I remember very fondly at one show I decided that I was going to experiment a bit with the song. I played some new patterns we had not rehearsed. Being the class act he was, Al did not want the audience to see him frustrated and upset with my experimentations. Instead, he turned around, holding the mic to his back, looked at me and said, "Don't fuck with the singer!" and went back to singing. I knew immediately to stick to the patterns we had practiced. The next day, Al, the band, and I all had a good laugh about that one.[4]

Especially in his later years, manager Joe Gordon said, "When Al got fatigued doing shows, he got angry. Because he was very open and clear about what wore him out. And how much he could tolerate and what was abusive and excessive. And if managers scheduled too many shows or musicians didn't do a full thirty-two-bar solo when they were supposed to, versus sixteen, he would get pissed off. Because [during] those sixteen bars, Al had to carry the load instead of a guitar player. And again, it's all on the vocal cords."[5] Chris Walker mentioned that dealing with Al was sometimes "quite a task, you know, keeping him on point, and suggesting musical things for him to do. Even just putting a set list together sometimes used to take two hours." Larry Williams also talked about the challenge of being

onstage with Al: "He'd like you to follow him, when possible. And I don't
know ten thousand songs. He can sing the lyrics, the bass line, and the
chords—he can sing every note in the chord to all these songs. He has
some kind of a perfect recall for this. He can't find his car keys [*laughs*],
but he knows things."⁶

Obviously, Al's inimitable vocal abilities were another reason why musicians loved playing with him. "Al was a pure genius," Mark Simmons said.
"He was like a human percussionist with his vocals. The way he interpreted
melodies and how he wrote and arranged his lyrics were simply brilliant.
He had a special kind of style. He could go from jazz to pop to R&B to
bluegrass to folk or whatever he was inspired to sing."⁷ Similarly, Marcus
Miller noted, "People notice when he's imitating a horn or a bass, but he's
also singing like water, like rain, singing like a piece of wood, or like a plate
cracking on the floor. . . . These are all available to him. All these sounds,
because he's just always aware. . . . In life, he's always observing things.
[And] he doesn't just see everything. He hears everything."⁸

Almost all of Al's colleagues had very personal relationships with him.
Bill Darlington, Al's manager from 1996 to 2006, admitted there were issues in their working relationship, but said, "Overall my relationship with
Al—I always think about it in a warm way. He'd call me in the middle of the
night and we'd talk about random, crazy things. I mean it made me laugh.
We always would laugh together."⁹ Chris Walker said he stayed with Al for
the better part of two decades because "he was an easy guy to be around.
When you find somebody who is so full of joy, and so encouraging, and
just brilliant at what he does . . . you just want more of it, and you can
never get enough of it."

Al's family members also admired his charismatic and generous personality. "He just had that leadership ability to do things," his older brother
Alphaeus said. "He'd draw people to him, you know. And he would help
you if he could."¹⁰ Al's cousin Sandra Moss said that no one ever seemed
to have anything bad to say about him. The only complaint that family
members had was that they didn't see enough of him. They sometimes
expressed this frustration, said Moss, "not because they were mad, but
because . . . he would bring so much light, so much wisdom, so much
sunshine whenever he would come into your home. . . . It would always

be a special event. Always. It would be the most ordinary circumstance, like coming for lunch, but it would turn into being always special, always edifying. You know he always had a message—to sing about or to bring."[11]

Al's son, Ryan, traveled to Ripon College in May 2017 (his first visit to Wisconsin) to accept the college's Medal of Merit for his late father. Among Ryan's brief remarks to the college's graduating class and guests were these:

> I just want to say that I'm very proud to have had Al Jarreau as a father. Most people always ask me, "How does it feel to have a Grammy-winning award winner as a father?" My answer always was, "How did you grow up with your father?" He was just a normal man when he was in the house. He wasn't "Al Jarreau," he didn't go around requesting or demanding that people respect him. He was someone who loved people, who loved interactions with people. He wanted to change people's lives. He wanted to improve. He believed in education. He believed that a mind is a horrible thing to waste—and he reminded me throughout my whole life. And he would talk about Ripon a lot, about everything this college had done, what it meant to him, and just what Wisconsin was to him.[12]

An adjective that comes up frequently in conversations about Al is *spiritual*. Jerry Levin, who lived with Al and toured with him through the late 1970s and 1980s, reflected on the the spiritual side of the man:

> He was really, really a spiritualist. . . . To take it a bit further, he was really a healer. That's one of the things that he could do in life, and I saw it over so many years. He would take so much time talking with people that he barely knew, and within minutes they were telling him their darkest secrets and all the things that were going wrong in their life, and he would just kind of walk them through different scenarios of what they could do to improve . . . and it was unbelievable. He was just that kind of guy.[13]

Bassist and producer Marcus Miller, who worked with Al on many projects over many years, said, "He was truly one of the most giving, beautiful people that you could ever meet. And I know you say that about everybody, but, man, it's really true about him. And I'm sure anybody you talk to will tell you the same thing."[14] Chris Walker played for almost twenty years with Al. He explained that his boss, a dear friend and father figure, was defined by "the loving light that he carried around, onstage and off stage." Joe Turano said that Al "was brilliant musically and thoughtful in his innate level of intelligence and insight and everything; he was tremendous. And his insights, from his heart, from his soul, and from his intellect—intellect into the state of the world. . . . Conversations with him were inspiring, stimulating, [and] thought-provoking."[15]

During one 2012 interview, when a reporter told Al, "You are a very spiritual person. What you say is always positive, in a world like this," Al responded by saying,

> Maybe there's such emotion and passion gathered around spiritual beliefs that [they] must be really important for people. Well, yes, we will have to fight wars, but spiritual beliefs, such as who we are, where we came from, what we are doing, what we ought to be doing, and where we are going, these are the questions that get answered and we seek out and we search out and we hold on to, that define what we do and help us define where we are going and help us define what is important to be doing in the morning. So thank you, Mom and Dad.[16]

Saxophonist Michael Paulo, who spent ten years touring with Al, talked about one special performance as indicative of Al's spiritual nature:

> I remember a particular concert in Italy on top of Roman ruins. It was a surreal experience as it seemed like Al was actually channeling the souls of many that probably lived and died there. It's hard to explain but I know all in the band felt it. He sang with so much passion and depth with every concert. It wasn't an exercise in popularity but a genuine love and expression of his music, and he put every bit of his soul into it. I have performed with many artists and singers and most at times go through the motions because they have to. I never felt that with Al.[17]

One of Jerry Levin's favorite shows took place at Graham Chapel at Washington University in St. Louis, in November 1978, when Al's career was just starting to bloom. Halfway through the concert, a severe thunderstorm materialized, and the power in the venue went out. Although crew and concert organizers went out to see about cranking up a generator and salvaging the concert, the power had gone out in that entire part of the city. As the promoters and Levin began negotiating about refunding ticket prices to the audience, Al started singing all alone on the stage. The band's percussionist passed out instruments to band members. Audience members got out lighters and flashlights from their purses and backpacks, bathing the room with a kind of a warm glow. Al finished the set, singing seven or eight songs a cappella. At one point, he sat on the edge of the stage. Several rows back, there was a couple with a small child. The youngster was brought up to the stage, where he sat on Al's knee, and Al sang directly to the boy. Levin finished the story by saying, "I don't think anybody that was there will [ever] forget it."

Al's cousin Sandra Moss told a somewhat similar story about a 1991 concert in Los Angeles. It was the fifth annual John Coltrane Festival, put on by Coltrane's wife, Alice, and it featured multiple bands.[18] The sound system had been a problem throughout the concert. When it went out at one point, Moss remembered that Al went out and did an a cappella set, even tap dancing to hold the audience. The *Los Angeles Times* reported that he did "an energetic, completely impromptu solo rendering of 'Take Five'" and, due to all of the riffing he did to keep the crowd entertained, the reporter called him a "guest speaker." Moss claims that Al saved the concert.

A late-career feature in the *International Musician* in 2014 also highlighted Al's ability to connect to his audiences:

No matter who is onstage with Jarreau, he is a charismatic and gracious performer who manages to deliver an energetic and unique show every time. He says that the key is to get the audience involved in the performance.

"Find something that they can sing with you," he says. "It becomes something else when people join in and get involved in the music. I love that kind of communication, and talking to people in the audience and feeling it together. Something happens when that occurs and people go home with that experience."[19]

Yet, while being a public figure and giving openly of himself night after night onstage, Al was in many ways a private person as well. Even those closest to him don't pretend to have completely understood him.

Peter Bock, who sang with Al in the Indigos at Ripon College and remained Al's close friend throughout his life and career, described Al for a piece in the *Milwaukee Journal* in 1989. First, he echoed the familiar praise about Al's magnetism, saying: "Al has an electric charm and has always been able to win the hearts of people instantaneously. . . . It's something I've never seen to that extreme in any other person. That is what I think has paved the road for him: his ability to capture people's hearts." However, he also described Al as "at the same time gregarious and shy." And, despite his charming demeanor, Bock stated:

Al is in a lot of pain—has been since the mid-'60s. He allows it to flow through him freely. He has all the characteristics of the tortured souls—the Mozarts, the Schuberts, the German Romantics. That's what he has to be. When he started taking his art seriously, on a full-time basis, it opened the floodgates. That was during the hippie era when that sort of thing was encouraged. It was a confluence of things that just allowed him to open . . . his heart and dive in. . . . Part of him is off in art space—feeling, shaping, turning [things and experiences] into a representation of reality."[20]

In a tribute to Al on the occasion of his death, Jerry Levin wrote, "Al Jarreau wasn't a saint and he certainly had his demons, but his spirit was magical and oh so soulful. He made everyone feel special . . . that is an amazing quality."[21] Similarly, Larry Williams, who toured with Al for longer than anyone, said, "There are no saints in the business." He specifically described Al as "a very complex individual with many different sides. It would take a team of psychologists to uncover all the stuff in there. And no one book would even do it justice from that standpoint." Like many world-traveling musicians, Al faced temptations throughout his career.

And not all of his personal relationships, including with those closest to him, were comfortable or easy. He was lauded as a great artist by many fans and critics, but he was also denigrated for the artistic choices he made. His life was not all glamour and ease.

While racism and racial inequality remain huge and troublesome social issues in the United States in 2023, Al rarely addressed these topics when speaking for the public record. African American bassist Chris Walker, who played with Al from the late 1990s until Al's death, said that Al "never, never" talked with him about race. Yet, Al and his family almost certainly encountered racial discrimination that he chose not to publicize. Al's father chose to come north after his marriage, not wanting to raise a family in the South. But, of course, racism also existed in the North, and Milwaukee has been considered one of the most racially segregated metro areas in America for many decades.

In one 1989 *Milwaukee Journal* article, reporter Mary Kane seemed to be prodding Al into talking about his experiences with racism. (This was only months after he deflected a question about race in a *Jazziz* feature.) Al did not allow himself to be baited; he turned the question sideways, shifting an answer that could have been personal into something more general about his professional career. Kane wrote:

> Despite the acclaim he has received, to say that Jarreau has led a charmed existence would be far wide of the mark. Yet he still finds it unbecoming to give in even far enough to acknowledge that there might have been indignities along the way.
>
> "I mean, that's maybe strange to some, disturbing for others. But a curiously wonderful thing for me is that the indignities, if anything, they are not personally suffered; they . . . have to do with so much great music that gets unheard, gets lost, gets cut from the team.
>
> "So, personal indignities . . . are no different than what some people with something a little different to say have gone through. And so I'm not especially crying the blues for my own case. I am, in fact, one who's sort of broken through and who can be pointed to by others who are making the effort and finding a little difficulty and saying, 'Hey, there's a late bloomer.'"[22]

The comments Al made in his very late interview with Lee Mergner about his visit to the Obama White House in 2016 were an exception to his usual reluctance to talk directly about social issues. He told Mergner:

I hope you get to watch the Muhammad Ali funeral service and see people of every stripe saying eloquent things that haven't even been said about dead presidents, about a guy named Muhammad Ali who came from nothing and stuck to his principles and his religious beliefs. Which is who we are and what we are as Americans. Freedom of religion. They shut him down because of it, took away his money, his position. And he still became King of the World. The Greatest. That's the message in his funeral today. If we watch it and listen to it, it might cut through the Donald Trump bullshit and the selfishness of Wall Street's greed and all of it that just denies that we're in this world together.[23]

Mergner asked, "What is that phrase about history bending toward the truth? That well described Martin Luther King, and probably does Muhammad Ali." And Al responded, "The phrase is 'The arc of the [moral universe] is long, but it bends toward justice.'"

Al's sister Rose Marie Freeman, who forged a pioneering path as a Black woman in corporate America, communicated her sense of why Al did not talk about racial matters more publicly. Indeed, she may have explained her brother's position as well as anyone. It was her "sisterly belief/assessment," she wrote, that Al avoided fully disclosing his thoughts on issues related to race because that "would expose intense and hurtful areas at the central core of his being (i.e., family interracial marriages, including his own)." Not only had both of Al's marriages been with white women, but his brothers Emile and Marshall had also entered into interracial marriages. Additionally, there were interracial marriages in the family's next generation. Rose Marie speculated that "avoiding those exchanges [about race] allowed [Al] complete, full concentration on his career" and that his evasions were "efforts to survive and succeed. . . . All he really wanted to do [was] sing! [He left] global racial harmony to others [who were] perceived to be more qualified."[24]

More than two years after Al's death, the *Milwaukee Independent* presented an article titled "The Case for Renaming a Milwaukee Street in Honor of Hometown Jazz Legend Al Jarreau." Alderman Khalif J. Rainey made the suggestion in June of 2019, African American Music Appreciation Month. "Such a high honor would be a major step toward ensuring that Mr. Jarreau's music, generosity and impact on Milwaukee and the world will be remembered for generations," Rainey argued.[25] Although he made a substantial case for renaming a street in the area near where Al grew up—which already had streets named in honor of Martin Luther King Jr. and Vel R. Phillips, the pioneering Black woman judge, politician, and civil rights activist—apparently, the idea has not gained significant traction.

What about Al's place in history? All pop music is a product of its time, and as such, its so-called shelf life sometimes only lasts for as long as the life span of the generation who heard it when it was new. Those who still consider themselves diehard Al Jarreau fans at the time of this book's publication are not typically a young demographic, and they are obviously not getting any younger. Yet original fans have passed along their love of Al Jarreau's music to their children and grandchildren, keeping the music alive. Through YouTube, Apple Music, Spotify, and other sites, niche music has survived and likely will continue to thrive through whatever music service succeeds them. And Al's music, though it continually crossed boundaries, is probably considered "niche" today.

In the long run, will Al be considered an important jazz artist? For those who hold to a very narrow or limited definition of jazz, the answer is probably no. Yet Jon Hendricks, a musician considered central to jazz singing, saw Al as the next step beyond Hendricks himself in the evolution of jazz vocalization. In 2011, Hendricks—who was being interviewed along with Al and another prominent jazz singer, Kurt Elling—said about Al: "When I first met him, he came to see me six nights straight. And he'd sit right in front. And so I'm going to find out who this guy is. He looks like me, and he looks like Harry Belafonte. So I've got to find out. Well, he asked me a question. He says, 'How do you scat?' Now I've never been asked that question before, in my whole life. . . . I said to him, 'Well, you know the melody; scat the chords.' . . . And he came back about three nights later, and kicked my butt."

Elling joked, "And you've regretted telling him ever since."

"That's right," Hendricks said, playfully. "I should have kept my mouth shut."[26]

Although Al's early career featured him taking what might have been the next evolutionary step forward in scat singing, it was a unique and very personal step. In the end, it did not lead a movement of young jazz singers in a certain direction. Al insisted on satisfying his inner need to sing R&B and pop, as well as jazz, which placed him in a singular position in American music. Certainly, there have been fans of R&B and pop who never quite warmed up to Al's music because they were baffled by the jazz sensibility that was a part of everything he did.

As Larry Williams put it, a big part of Al's musical life was an attempt "to break down musical barriers and create something new that would reach more people than a 'traditional jazz album.' And the popularity of Al's best records shows that he succeeded magnificently."[27]

"I don't know what else I am beyond what I sing about and do as an artist," Al said in 2012. "I have had the chance to live the artist life, to create, and make my living creating, and also to be celebrated as an artist, and to enjoy that."[28]

ACKNOWLEDGMENTS

Thanks to all of the generous people whose recollections, contributions, and help have made this book what it is:

Jarreau family members: the late Alphaeus Jarreau; Rose Marie (Jarreau) Freeman; the late Marshall Jarreau, who died in the late stages of the book's completion; Ryan Jarreau; Arthur "Chuckie" Lee; and Sandra Moss.

Jarreau family friends Maxwell Carter and Theresa Robinson.

The musicians, from the beginning of Al's career to the end: the late Ron DeVillers, Jack Carr, Kaye Berigan, the late Les Czimber, Julio Martinez, Rich Dworsky, Tom Canning, Michael Paulo, Larry Williams, Chris Walker, Joe Turano, and Mark Simmons.

Those on the business side of things: Patrick Rains, Jerry Levin, Abe Totah, the late Bill Gillan (Gilkowski), Kaiyoti Pesante, and, at the last minute, Bill Darlington and Glen Broomberg.

Al's last manager, Joe Gordon, who continues to tend to Al's affairs. Joe connected me with many of the others mentioned here, facilitated arrangements with Warner Music Group, and negotiated permissions for the quoting of Al's lyrics. He remained patient and extraordinarily helpful throughout the process, and he supplied valuable history about Al's last years.

Al's Ripon College (and lifelong) friends Peter Bock, Donna Oberholtzer, and Ann Hassler, as well as his Twin Cities friend Marilyn Goodman.

PBS Wisconsin producer Steve Doebel, for access to the unused footage and interviews for the Wisconsin Public Television documentary *Al Jarreau: Coming Home*.

Steve Schaffer, Kevin Abing, and especially Ben Barbera, at the Milwaukee County Historical Society.

At Ripon College: Andrew Prellwitz and Karlyn Schumacher at Lane

Author Kurt Dietrich (right) and his wife, Maria Kaiser Dietrich (left), with Al Jarreau after his concert at Ripon College in October 2006. PHOTO BY JIM KOEPNICK, COURTESY OF KURT DIETRICH

Library (thanks also to Andy for help with German translations); Director of Creative and Social Media Ric Damm; for logistical support, Vice President and Dean of Faculty John Sisko; and former Director of Charitable Gift & Estate Planning Bill Neill, Ripon College class of 1967.

University of Iowa archivist David McCartney and Beth Fisher at the Iowa City Public Library.

Jazz journalist Bill Milkowski, for his perceptive reading of the manuscript. Rose Marie Freeman, Tim Schaid, Julio Martinez, Rich Dworsky, Pat Rains, Tom Canning, Jerry Levin, Larry Williams, Joe Turano, and Joe Gordon, who each read various chapters and made helpful corrections, clarifications, and suggestions.

Carolyn Sturm, for help with German, and David Ginsburg, for some sleuthing.

My wife, Maria, who hung in there with me throughout the journey and also did a close reading of the manuscript, making valuable small improvements throughout.

Kate Thompson, director of the Wisconsin Historical Society Press, for her enthusiasm and support for the project, from beginning to end. Katherine Pickett, for her meticulous copy editing of the manuscript. WHSP production editor John Ferguson, for his great skill in turning words and images into a physical book. My fabulous editor at WHSP, Liz Wyckoff, who improved this book in so many ways. And beyond her brilliant editing skills, Liz tirelessly negotiated agreements with photographers and record labels, duties that were certainly way above and beyond the call.

And the greatest thanks to Al's sister Rose Marie (Jarreau) Freeman. Rose Marie supplied invaluable information about the family and Al's early life, but the relationship that we built over the several years of the project through our frequent phone conversations goes deeper than I can describe. I will always treasure it.

NOTES

Introduction

1. Rose Marie Freeman, interviews with the author, 2019–2022.
2. The footage is not available to the public. WPT graciously allowed me to watch the video and take notes.
3. For at least some of this time, the Blahowskis' tavern was known as Cozy Corner. (Thanks to Ben Barbera at the Milwaukee County Historical Society for some history of this establishment.)
4. Al told me this same story in 2012. On that occasion, he sang some of "Too Fat Polka."
5. After earning a master's degree in counseling at the University of Iowa, Al was a rehabilitation counselor during the early part of his adult life, before his music career took off. See chapter 6.
6. This is a paraphrase from Al's lyrics for his 1983 hit song "Mornin'."

Chapter 1

1. Many of the recollections and a considerable amount of the information in this chapter were supplied to me by Al Jarreau's older sister, Rose Marie Freeman, in our phone conversations and email exchanges during 2019–2022. By this time, Rose Marie was considered the head of the Jarreau family. Her memory is excellent, she had valuable documentation related to the family, and she was most generous with everything. In 2020, I was also able to speak with Al's younger brother Marshall and his older brother Alphaeus for more family background. All quotes from Alphaeus and Marshall are from my conversations with them.
2. The family has never traced this ancestry, and I didn't think it was my place to do so.
3. Rose Marie Freeman, interview with the author, July 8, 2022.

4. The school was renamed Oakwood College in 1943 and Oakwood University in 2008.

5. All information about Oakwood is from the school's website. "Mission & History," Oakwood University, https://oakwood.edu/our-story/mission-history/.

6. *Al Jarreau L'enchanteur: Un Documentaire Musical de Thierry Guedj*, directed by Thierry Guedj (France: Portrait & Company, aired January 1, 2016, on French O).

7. This nugget of information appeared in the obituary "Rev. Jarreau Mourned," *Milwaukee Courier*, October 1, 1977. The article was kindly supplied to me by Rose Marie Freeman.

8. Rose Marie Freeman, interview with the author, July 3, 2020.

9. Rose Marie Freeman, interviews with the author, 2019–2022.

10. These dates came from the obituary printed in the Obsequies (funeral service) program for her father that Rose Marie found in her family documents.

11. Rose Marie Freeman, interview with the author, July 8, 2022.

12. According to Milwaukee city directories, the Jarreaus lived at 1708 North Fifth Street, apartment 15, until 1944. However, both Rose Marie and Al always referred to 336 West Reservoir as their childhood home. It was only a few blocks from the Fifth Street address. Rose Marie told me that they rented at 332 West Reservoir for a brief period before purchasing the home at 336.

13. Maxwell Carter's recollection was that while he regularly set pins and became a serious bowler, he remembers Al setting pins only once, "and he didn't care for it." It is possible, though, that Al set pins more often before the Carters moved in with the Jarreaus.

14. Geiser's was a Milwaukee brand from the 1930s through the 1980s, when it was bought by Borden. Its slogan was "Be Wiser, Buy Geiser's." Ambrosia, another Milwaukee brand, was founded in 1894. Its downtown plant was finally abandoned in 1992, when it moved to the city's northwest side.

15. The background information and all quotes in this paragraph are from John Gurda, *Milwaukee: City of Neighborhoods* (Milwaukee: Historic Milwaukee, Inc., 2015), 197–202.

16. Gurda, *Milwaukee*, 199.

17. In 2020, Alphaeus recalled one other Black family that owned their home

living in the area, but Rose Marie believes that these close neighbors, the Taylors, bought their house after the Jarreaus purchased theirs.

18. Rose Marie wondered in 2020 whether the commonality of names of the two Emiles, as well as the fact that they were both from New Orleans, made them more like brothers than just employer and employee.

19. Rose Marie Freeman, interviews with the author, 2019–2022.

20. *Al Jarreau: Coming Home* (Wisconsin Public Television, 2017), unused footage.

21. Lee Underwood, "Al Jarreau," *Down Beat*, October 1976.

22. A. O. Smith also manufactured the giant blue Harvestore silos seen all over Wisconsin and the Midwest.

23. *Coming Home*, unused footage.

24. All quotes from Maxwell Carter are from our 2020 conversation.

25. *Coming Home*, unused footage.

26. Peter Bock, phone interview with the author, September 2019.

27. Peter Bock, phone interview with the author, September 2019.

28. *Coming Home*, unused footage.

29. On another occasion, Rose Marie told me that her mother "always ended up getting her way." Freeman, interviews with the author.

30. Freeman, interviews with the author.

31. Maxwell Carter, interview with the author, April 30, 2020.

32. *Coming Home*, unused footage.

33. *Coming Home*, unused footage.

34. *Al Jarreau L'enchanteur*.

35. Steve Bloom, "Al Jarreau: Breaking Away," *Down Beat*, February 1982, 26.

36. Alphaeus Jarraeau, phone interview with the author, May 11, 2020.

37. *Coming Home*, unused footage.

38. The author contacted the keepers of the Bowes/Mack archives; they had no record of Emile Jarreau being involved in any national broadcasts. It's possible, however, that he took part in regional competitions of the organization.

Chapter 2

1. *Al Jarreau: Coming Home* (Wisconsin Public Television, 2017), unused footage.

2. *Coming Home*, unused footage.

3. This and the remaining quotes in this chapter from Rose Marie Freeman are from one of my numerous conversations with her from 2019 to 2022 unless otherwise noted.

4. *Unsung*, Season 9, Episode 6, "Al Jarreau," produced by Jason B. Ryan, aired April 12, 2020 on TVOne, https://tvone.tv/video/watch-unsung -al-jarreau/

5. "Bio by Photo: Al Jarreau," in-house publication from WEA (Warner- Elektra-Asylum Records), 1986.

6. The recollections are from Rose Marie's remarkable memory.

7. Both Rose Marie and Marshall say that their brother Emile had a beautiful voice, but unlike Al, Emile "was not committed to seek music as a profes- sion," according to Rose Marie.

8. Bill Milkowski, "Superstar Has Soft Spot in Heart for Milwaukee," *Milwau- kee Journal*, July 7, 1978.

9. Mary Kane, "Complex Melody: The Joy and Pain of Al Jarreau," *Milwaukee Journal*, July 30, 1989.

10. Freeman, interviews with the author, 2019–2022.

11. Alphaeus Jarraeau, phone interview with the author, May 11, 2020.

12. *Al Jarreau: Coming Home* (Madison, WI: Wisconsin Public Television, 2017), https://pbswisconsin.org/watch/wpt-documentaries/al-jarreau -coming-home-0sqziq/.

13. Freeman, interviews with the author, 2019–2022.

14. Steve Bloom, "Al Jarreau: Breaking Away," *Down Beat*, February 1982, 26.

15. Leonard Feather, "Life with Feather: Milwaukee's Al Jarreau Finally Get- ting Attention," *Milwaukee Journal*, March 16, 1977.

16. *Coming Home*, unused footage.

17. After Al graduated, Marshall took his place in the small vocal group that sang for the Follies.

18. Alphaeus Jarraeu, phone interview with the author, May 11, 2020. Sister Rose Marie also remembers the oldest Jarreau brother, Emile, taking part in the Follies shows when he was a student at Lincoln.

19. *Coming Home*, unused footage.

20. *Coming Home*, unused footage.

21. *Coming Home*, unused footage.

22. In *Cream City Chronicles* (Wisconsin Historical Society Press, 2007), Mil- waukee historian John Gurda writes about the annual Christmas parade

sponsored by Schuster's Department Stores. Me-Tik, "a real Alaskan Eskimo . . . remained a fixture in the parade for years." This parade, which wound for a convoluted seven miles (past all three Schuster stores) on the rails of the Milwaukee streetcar system, drew a crowd of three hundred thousand in 1947. John Gurda, *Cream City Chronicles* (Madison: Wisconsin Historical Society Press, 2016), 279–280.

23. Maxwell Carter, phone interview with the author, April 30, 2020. James Catania, the father of young Jim Catania, became a well-known "character" in the Milwaukee nightlife scene. Known as Jimmy Mortell, he sometimes sang in the tavern, often impersonating Jimmy Durante, a famous national entertainer, whom he resembled. The Internal Revenue Service assessed an entertainment tax on Mortell, claiming that his act was a cabaret act. The case went to court in 1963. Mortell won. In 1968, Mortell/ Catania was shot and killed in the bar, in a holdup gone wrong. Chris Foran, "A Milwaukee Nightlife Legend Dies in a Gun Battle—In His Own East Side Bar," *Milwaukee Journal Sentinel*, March 6, 2018 (original article published 1968).

24. This is Carter's recollection. Marshall also recalls that the boys were paid for this service with a significant amount of money for that era.

25. Marshall Jarreau, interview with the author, April 20, 2020.

26. Maxwell Carter, phone interview with the author, April 30, 2020.

27. With that entry is also a poem: "Often-times shy, but a pretty nice guy. Yet his mind's in a whirl 'cause he can't find a girl." *The Quill*, 1958 Lincoln High School Yearbook, Yearbook Collection, Mss-1865, Milwaukee County Historical Society.

28. *Milwaukee Journal*, photo, April 28, 1958.

29. "Bio by Photo: Al Jarreau."

30. Kane, "Complex Melody."

31. Much of this paragraph comes from Kurt Dietrich, *Wisconsin Riffs: Jazz Profiles from the Heartland* (Madison: Wisconsin Historical Society Press, 2018), 103.

32. Marshall earned a track scholarship to Marquette University, but he left the school after a year after suffering an injury that limited his ability to run. This and the remaining quotes from Marshall in this chapter are from his phone interviews with the author, April 2020.

33. Marshall Jarreau, phone interviews with the author, April 2020.

34. Maxwell Carter, phone interview with the author, April 2020. Carter went
    on to play minor league ball in Eau Claire, where Hall of Famer and Mil-
    waukee hero Hank Aaron had begun his career. Carter played there with
    Aaron's brother Tommie, a future major leaguer.
35. "Al Jarreau Featured Singer," *Oshkosh Daily Northwestern*, April 4, 1963.
36. In the *Coming Home* unused footage, Al said that at Ripon he couldn't keep
    up with taking part in two sports, singing, and academics. After his "schol-
    arship" was replaced with a campus job by the basketball coach, it was clear
    that he had to stick to that one sport (see chapter 3).
37. *Coming Home*, unused footage.

Chapter 3

1. Jean Grant, "Jarreau by Any Name," *Ripon Magazine*, Summer 1993, 7.
2. *Ripon College Days*, November 4, 1958.
3. Al Jarreau, interview with the author, June 22, 2012.
4. *Al Jarreau: Coming Home* (Wisconsin Public Television, 2017), unused
   footage.
5. *Coming Home*, unused footage.
6. *Coming Home*, unused footage.
7. Dave Shogren, "Grammy Winner Al Jarreau Returns for Homecoming,"
   College Days, November 5, 1982.
8. Rose Marie states that their father strongly impressed upon the Jarreau
   children that they should not hitchhike. Al might have been hitchhiking at
   times, not to get home, but to do music jobs in Milwaukee.
9. *Ripon College Days*, January 12, 1960.
10. *Ripon College Days*, March 1, 1960.
11. *Ripon College Days*, December 8, 1961.
12. This section is based on Bock's article and a long phone conversation I had
    with him in September 2019. Quotes are from the article unless noted
    otherwise. Peter Bock, "The *Indigos* . . . Then and Now," *Ripon Magazine*,
    Summer 1993.
13. Coincidentally, Ellington's great alto saxophone soloist Johnny Hodges
    worked briefly in "early 1958" with a small group called the Indigos, which
    also included Ellington's alter-ego Billy Strayhorn. Con Chapman, *Rabbit's
    Blues: The Life and Music of Johnny Hodges* (New York: Oxford University
    Press, 2019). Peter Bock says that the Ripon Indigos were unaware of this.
    Peter Bock, email to the author, November 6, 2019.

14. The Ripon College *Crimson 1960* (Ripon, WI: Ripon College, 1960), x, https://issuu.com/ripon_college/docs/crimson_1960.

15. Peter Bock, phone interview with the author, September 2019.

16. The Ripon College *Crimson 1961* (Ripon, WI: Ripon College, 1961), 69, https://issuu.com/ripon_college/docs/crimson1961.

17. Bock, Peter. "The *Indigos* . . . Then and Now," *Ripon Magazine*, Summer 1993.

18. *Ripon College Days*, November 3, 1961.

19. *Ripon College Days*, February 24, 1959. According to the exhaustive study by Klaus Stratemann, *Duke Ellington: Day by Day and Film by Film* (Copenhagen: JazzMedia, 1992), the band had disbanded for a short period as Ellington worked on the film score for the movie *Anatomy of a Murder*. Part of that time he spent not too far from Wisconsin in Michigan's Upper Peninsula, where the action of the movie took place. Ellington himself came to the campus to receive an honorary degree from the college in May of 1973.

20. Information about the festival comes from my phone conversation with Bock, September 2019.

21. Higgins went on to become a jobbing bassist in the Chicago area.

22. *Ripon College Days*, April 20, 1962.

23. Bock went to graduate school at Purdue University, where he got his master's degrees in engineering and theater. He worked for the NASA Apollo program and eventually joined the faculty of George Washington University, becoming a pioneer in the area of artificial intelligence. Ashley-Farrand earned a master's degree, served three years in the army in Korea, was ordained as a minister, and became a health care marketing and management consultant. He died in 2010. Oberholtzer earned degrees in English and, eventually, psychotherapy. Years after the Indigos, she and Bock reconnected and were married in 1990. Jensen went on to a distinguished career with the American Chamber Ballet Company in New York. Ann Hassler worked in radio and television production, real estate, and junior high and high school teaching. After not seeing Al for over fifty years, she spoke at his Lifetime Achievement Award ceremony in Milwaukee in 2016.

24. Joan Howard, *Ripon College Days*, May 18, 1962. The quoted section from the article is edited; some of the lines in the article were transposed; and some comments that Jarreau made about Ray Charles were too garbled in the mix-up of lines to be sorted out so have been omitted.

Chapter 4

1. Unless noted otherwise, the information presented here is from my phone conversations with Les Czimber in 2020 and the notes to his 1996 CD *Someday My Prince Will Come*, Miracle Records.

2. There is a photo of an advertisement for Czimber at the Driftwood in Joey Grihalva's *Milwaukee Jazz* (Charleston, SC: Aracadia Publishing, 2019), 44.

3. Abe Totah, phone conversation with the author, May 22, 2020. Czimber confirmed this to me as well. Other quotes from Totah are also from this conversation. Some of this information also was elucidated when I met with Totah and Gillan in July 2021.

4. Czimber set this record playing in conjunction with the release of the movie *Song Without End*, a biography of nineteenth-century classical piano giant Franz Liszt (who was part Hungarian). A year later he broke the record by an hour in Beloit, in a furniture store. The ad noted in note 2 above billed Czimber as the "World's Champion Marathon Pianist."

5. Zan Stewart, "Jazz Emigre Finds Voice in America: Pianist: After secretly performing in Soviet-ruled Hungary in the 1950s, Les Czimber came to the U.S., where luck has been on his side ever since," *Los Angeles Times*, November 23, 1991.

6. Czimber believes that Al was working at Schlitz Brewing at the time, so it probably would have been during a summer break, after Al started at Ripon College. The stories I heard from Czimber and Totah conflicted somewhat; with further information from Gillan, I have made my best informed guess about the timeline.

7. While there is no definitive documentation about when Al started, in our conversation of July 2021, Gillan, Totah, and I came to the conclusion that Al probably began at the Driftwood in 1959. Soon thereafter Totah left for California; Gillan ran the club until 1962.

8. Abe spent a considerable amount of time with McRae during her residency in Milwaukee, but he refused her invitation to go on the road with her. His involvement with her stirred up some resentment from people who, during the 1950s, did not appreciate mixed-race relationships. This included members of his own family.

9. Kaye Berigan, email correspondence with the author, 2021.

10. Czimber, CD notes.

11. Bill Gillan always entertained suspicions that the Driftwood was "torched," at the direction of a competitor, possibly someone with Mafia connections. Nothing of that nature was ever proved, however, as was usually the case in such incidents. Bill Gillan, conversation with the author, summer 2021.

12. *Coming Home*, unused footage.

13. Jack Carr, email correspondence with the author, 2020–2021.

14. Jack Carr, email correspondence with the author, April 13, 2020.

15. Ron DeVillers, phone interview with the author, April 3, 2020.

16. Marshall Jarreau, phone interview with the author, April 30, 2020. Marshall sang to me at that time some of "Something's Coming." The next quote is also from this conversation.

17. *Coming Home*, unused footage.

18. *Perspektiven* 5, no. 3 (Summer 2006): 6. Goethe House Wisconsin is a nonprofit German American cultural institute. Founded in 1958, it was still active in 2023.

19. All quotes related to the pageant are from an unsigned article, "Al Jarreau Featured Singer in Miss Wisconsin Pageant," *Oshkosh Daily Northwestern*, April 4, 1963.

Chapter 5

1. Sometime shortly after Pearl's death (but probably after Al had graduated from Ripon College), Emile moved to 1728 West Capitol Drive.

2. Peter Bock, phone interview with the author, September 2019.

3. "Al Jarreau Featured Singer in Miss Wisconsin Pageant," *Oshkosh Daily Northwestern*, April 4, 1963.

4. *Al Jarreau L'enchanteur: Un Documentaire Musical de Thierry Guedj*, directed by Thierry Guedj (France: Portrait & Company, aired January 1, 2016, on French O).

5. "Al Jarreau Speaks at the University of Iowa—September 18th, 2014," YouTube, September 22, 2014, https://youtube.com/watch?v=bLx4qXbZBrs.

6. "Al Jarreau Speaks at the University of Iowa."

7. Al stated that Joe Abodeely, who ran the club, "was just in love with Frank Sinatra music." "Bio by Photo: Al Jarreau," in-house publication from WEA (Warner-Elektra-Asylum Records), 1986.

8. One such ad is in the November 12, 1964, edition of *The Daily Iowan*.

9. David McCartney, "Old Gold: 1962 Campus Concert Featured Both Al

Jarreau and Simon Estes: UI Archivist Recalls Early Performance by Acclaimed Singers," *Iowa Now*, March 3, 2017, https://now.uiowa.edu/2017/03/old-gold-1962-campus-concert-featured-both-al-jarreau-and-simon-estes.

10. Larry Hatfield, "Better Than Amateur Hour," *The Daily Iowan*, December 1, 1962.

11. McCartney, "Old Gold."

12. Hatfield, "Better Than Amateur Hour."

13. The documentation for the date is difficult to find; however, the album is *Live at the Tender Trap* by the J. R. Monterose Quartet. The recording was rereleased on the Spanish label Fresh Sound in 1993. The original release was apparently *J. R. in Action*, on the Studio 4 label. A 1993 CD rerelease is Fresh Sound (Sp)FSCD1023 [CD].

14. "Al Jarreau speaks at the University of Iowa."

15. Mark Gardner, "J. R. Monterose Speaks to Mark Gardner," *Jazz Monthly*, March 1968, 5. A few years later, in 1975, Monterose said that being in Iowa was "just what I needed. . . . Sometimes it was okay musically too!" John Jeremy, "J. R. Monterose—Something with Music in It," *Coda* XII, no. 3 (January 1975): 3.

16. Before his work on *Glow*, Oehler had contributed arrangements to jazz trumpet great Freddie Hubbard's *High Energy* album. This and *Glow* were early entries in Oehler's significant list of credits in jazz.

17. Diana Nollen, "Al Jarreau Returning to Corridor Roots for Iowa Soul Festival," *The Gazette* (Cedar Rapids, IA), 2014, https://hooplanow.com/articles/1685-al-jarreau-returning-to-corridor-roots-for-iowa-soul-festival.

18. Sanborn immediately followed Al at Iowa, beginning the fall after Al received his degree and left. "Bio by Photo," WEA.

19. *Al Jarreau L'enchanteur*.

20. Neither the archivist at the University of Iowa nor a helpful librarian at the Iowa City Public Library were able to find a record of the wedding.

21. As of 2021, this record can be seen and heard at https://youtube.com/watch?v=ioHduXoNKgE.

22. Jarreau was presented with a Distinguished Alumni Award from the University of Iowa in 2005.

23. After working as a member of Joe Abodeely's trio in the mid-1960s,

Bezemer went on to a varied career on the West Coast, being skilled and
versatile enough to make a living for decades before his death in 2020.
Bezemer's biographical information was put together from various websites, including https://afm47.org/press/homegoing-and-repass-for-cal
-bezemer/, http://musicangels.biz/Pages/services.html, https://linkedin
.com/in/cal-bezemer-00146171, and https://facebook.com/calbezemer.
24. Based on the information on some bootleg copies, the album may have
    been produced by Jim and Tony Sotos, who were running a club in Moline,
    Illinois, at the time.
25. Marshall Harlene, "Legal," Chords and Discords (letters to the editor),
    Down Beat, August 1989.
26. Patrick Rains, email to the author, September 12, 2022.
27. Tierney Sutton, interview with the author, fall 2011. A fuller version of
    this story appears in Kurt Dietrich, *Wisconsin Riffs: Jazz Profiles from the
    Heartland* (Madison: Wisconsin Historical Society Press, 2018), 113. See
    also chapter 24 in this book.

Chapter 6
1. Les Czimber, phone conversations with the author, 2020.
2. *Al Jarreau: Coming Home* (Wisconsin Public Television, 2017), unused
   footage.
3. From interview notes from Jean Grant (edited by the author), for her articles that appeared in *Ripon Magazine*, summer 1993.
4. Grant interview notes.
5. *Al Jarreau L'enchanteur: Un Documentaire Musical de Thierry Guedj*, directed
   by Thierry Guedj (France: Portrait & Company, aired January 1, 2016, on
   French O).
6. Notes to *Al Jarreau and the George Duke Trio, Vol. 1: Live at the Half Note*,
   BPM Records, BPM 0212.
7. "Al Jarreau and Julio Martinez, 1968–2017," *From the Vault* 559, Pacifica Radio Archives, March 17, 2016, http://fromthevaultradio.org/
   home/2017/03/21/ftv-559-al-jarreau-and-julio-martinez-1968-2017/.
8. *Unsung*, Season 9, Episode 6, "Al Jarreau," produced by Jason B. Ryan,
   aired April 12, 2020 on TVOne, https://tvone.tv/video/watch-unsung
   -al-jarreau/.

9. Biographical information on George Duke is from a variety of online and print resources, including standard encyclopedias and his website, http://georgeduke.com/biography.html.

10. Elizabeth Pepin, "Swing the Fillmore," The Fillmore, PBS, https://pbs.org/kqed/fillmore/learning/music/swing.html.

11. *Al Jarreau L'enchanteur.*

12. *Al Jarreau L'enchanteur.*   ·

13. Diana Nollen, "Al Jarreau Returning to Corridor Roots for Iowa Soul Festival," *The Gazette* (Cedar Rapids, IA), 2014, https://hooplanow.com/articles/1685-al-jarreau-returning-to-corridor-roots-for-iowa-soul-festival.

14. Duke may have mixed up his timeline in this quote, as Malo was not active in San Francisco until a few years later.

15. *Al Jarreau L'enchanteur.*

16. Scott Yanow, "George Duke: Dukin' Out the Hits," *Down Beat*, November 1984, 18.

Chapter 7

1. "Al Jarreau and Julio Martinez, 1968–2017," *From the Vault* 559, Pacifica Radio Archives, March 17, 2016, http://fromthevaultradio.org/home/2017/03/21/ftv-559-al-jarreau-and-julio-martinez-1968-2017/.

2. Information in this and the following five paragraphs are from Julio Martinez, phone interview with the author, August 20, 2020.

3. The show for which Julio did the music, *High Mass*, was written by John Alioto; Alioto's father, Joseph, was about to become mayor of San Francisco.

4. This and the following quote are from "Al Jarreau and Julio Martinez, 1968–2017."

5. Years later, Al referred to this time with Julio as his "Brazilian period." Mark Ruffin, "Full Circle: Al Jarreau Attempts to Reinvigorate His Jazz Love Affair," *Down Beat*, October 2004, 45–47.

6. *Al Jarreau L'enchanteur: Un Documentaire Musical de Thierry Guedj*, directed by Thierry Guedj (France: Portrait & Company, aired January 1, 2016, on French O).

7. Information and quotes in this paragraph from Julio Martinez, phone interview with the author, August 20, 2020. Julio suggested that Al coached Phyllis to prepare her for the exams she needed to pass to qualify for the job.

8. *Al Jarreau: Coming Home* (Wisconsin Public Television, 2017), unused footage.

9. Dino's became well known nationwide due to its being featured on the popular television show *77 Sunset Strip*. More history can be found in Kliph Nesteroff, "The Rise and Fall of Dino's Lodge," *WFMU's Beware of the Blog: A Radio Station That Bites Back*, July 24, 2011, https://blog.wfmu .org/freeform/2011/07/dining-at-dinos-lodge.html.

10. Unless otherwise noted, information and quotes in this and the following three paragraphs are from "Al Jarreau and Julio Martinez, 1968–2017."

11. Martinez has explained the challenge of getting Fleming to skate rhythmically to a song like this; previously she had only skated "out of rhythm." Martinez, phone interview.

12. Gayle had opened at the Los Angeles Playboy Club in 1964. Best known for standup, he later got into television and films, becoming known for his work on *Tin Men* and Woody Allen's *Broadway Danny Rose*, in which he played a fictionalized version of himself.

13. Unless otherwise noted, information and quotes in this and the following three paragraphs are a combination of accounts from Patty Farmer, *Playboy Swings: How Hugh Hefner and Playboy Changed the Face of Music* (New York: Beaufort Books, 2015), and Julio Martinez, phone interview with the author, August 20, 2020. Long quotes in this section are all from the book. Al supplied one of the blurbs, praising the book in its introductory pages.

14. Martinez describes an incident or two in Farmer, *Playboy Swings*.

15. *Al Jarreau L'enchanteur*. Duke goes on to relate an entertaining story about Al and women at the Half Note in the documentary.

16. "Al Jarreau and Julio Martinez, 1968–2017" and Julio Martinez, phone interview with the author, August 2020.

17. While Martinez's comment is an overstatement, the band was filled with top New York pros and included longtime Basie saxophonist Frank Wess.

18. Julio Martinez, phone interview with the author, August 2020.

19. Julio also laughingly told me about the duo working earlier at what may have been the Voom Voom Room in Milwaukee. At that time it would have been on its way to becoming what it became infamous as—a strip joint. Ben Barbera of the Milwaukee County Historical Society reports that many of these clubs doubled as music venues and strip clubs, and were usually run

by the Mafia. It is possible, however, that Julio was referring to the Boom Boom Room noted in chapter 4.

20. Michael H. Drew, "Singer Al Jarreau Displays New Skills," *Milwaukee Journal*, July 21, 1970. All quotes in this and the next two paragraphs are from this article.

21. Jacobs's father, Irwin, became among the richest men in Minnesota, running the Northwestern Bag Company and other businesses.

22. This and the quotes in the next three paragraphs are from "Al Jarreau and Julio Martinez, 1968–2017."

23. "Bio by Photo: Al Jarreau," in-house publication from WEA (Warner-Elektra-Asylum Records), 1986.

24. Richard Dworsky, "Bio," https://richdworsky.com/bio.

25. "Al Jarreau and Julio Martinez, 1968–2017."

26. Richard Dworsky, interview with the author, September 2020.

27. Marilyn Goodman, phone interview with the author, February 2022.

28. In 1968, Paulsen had launched a well-documented semiserious bid for the US presidency.

29. Information about the concerts is from Twin Cities Music Highlights, "Jarreau: 1970," http://twincitiesmusichighlights.net/concerts/jarreau-1970/; Richard Dworsky, interview; Julio Martinez, interview; and Jon Bream, "Jarreau's Parading Home with Breakthrough Punch," *Minneapolis Star*, June 2, 1977. Husney shares his story of the Canned Heat concert in Winnipeg in his memoir, *Famous People Who've Met Me* (Los Angeles: Rothco Press, 2018).

30. The song "Window Well" is available at https://facebook.com/AlJarreau Official/videos/the-jarreau-band-window-well/1766822456806195/, with a wonderful video showing life in the early 1970s in California. The film was produced by Thierry Guedj, who produced the documentary *Al Jarreau l'Enchanteur* in 2016. "Window Well," "The Fawn" (a stunning ballad performance), "Seasons," and "Full Measure" are at Richard Dworsky's YouTube channel: https://youtube.com/channel/UClORwf HDUHRGehmHvh4LV4Q.

31. "Bio by Photo," WEA.

32. Patrick Rains related to me that the managers who set up this arrangement were paying for the Laurel Canyon house with money from their other business—making porn movies. When their movie business went bad,

they could no longer afford the house in the Canyon. Rains, interview with the author, October 22, 2020.

33. Richard Dworsky, interview with the author, September 2020.

34. Bream, "Jarreau's Parading Home."

35. Bream, "Jarreau's Parading Home."

Chapter 8

1. All Rains quotes in this and the next five paragraphs are from Patrick Rains, interview with the author, October 22, 2020.

2. Patrick Rains, interview with the author, October 22, 2020.

3. This and subsequent quotes from Dworsky in this chapter, unless otherwise noted, are from Richard Dworsky, interview with the author, September 2020.

4. Julio Martinez, phone interview with the author, August 20, 2020.

5. "Al Jarreau and Julio Martinez, 1968–2017," *From the Vault* 559, Pacifica Radio Archives, March 17, 2016, http://fromthevaultradio.org/home/2017/03/21/ftv-559-al-jarreau-and-julio-martinez-1968-2017/.

6. Biographical information is from Canning's website (https://tomcanning music.com/biography), and from our phone conversation of October 2020. Quotes are also from that conversation unless noted otherwise.

7. Many years later, Canning found out that *Amahl* was also a favorite of Al's. Al had seen it many times and could sing some of its themes to Tom.

8. One cut from this performance appears on the 1974 compilation album *Impulse Artists on Tour* from ABC Impulse Records.

9. *Al Jarreau L'enchanteur: Un Documentaire Musical de Thierry Guedj*, directed by Thierry Guedj (France: Portrait & Company, aired January 1, 2016, on French O).

10. Larry Williams, phone interview with the author, April 2021.

11. Rains told me a remarkably similar story to the one described in *Unsung*, Season 9, Episode 6, "Al Jarreau," produced by Jason B. Ryan, aired April 12, 2020 on TVOne, https://tvone.tv/video/watch-unsung-al-jarreau/.

12. Rich Dworsky reports that he and Al had done some sort of private showcase at the Troubadour a couple of years earlier. Richard Dworsky, phone interview with the author, 2020.

13. Lee Underwood, "Al Jarreau: The Amazing Acrobat of Scat," *Down Beat*, March 23, 1978.

14. In March 2021, Tom spoke very frankly with me about this particular chapter in his professional relationship with Al. Happily for Canning, Al was glad to welcome him back into the fold after the record deal was signed, and he became an integral part of Al's musical formula for the next seven years, including on Al's first seven albums.

15. Jerry Levin, phone interview with the author, December 2020.

16. Patrick Rains told me that at this time LiPuma had recently been promoted to a vice president position. But it is stated quite clearly in LiPuma's biography that he was still in A&R at this time, never becoming a VP before leaving the label in 1978. Ben Sidran, *The Ballad of Tommy LiPuma* (Madison, WI: Nardis Books, 2020), tracks 5 and 6.

17. Patrick Rains, phone interview with the author, October 22, 2020.

Chapter 9

1. Patrick Rains, phone interview with the author, October 22, 2020. All quotes in this chapter from Rains are from this interview.

2. Canning was helping Al get his songs together at this point, but cocomposing didn't really happen until the *All Fly Home* album; see next chapter.

3. "We Got By," Words and Music by Al Jarreau, Copyright © 1975 AL JARREAU MUSIC, Copyright Renewed, All Rights Administered by SONGS OF UNIVERSAL, INC., All Rights Reserved, Used by Permission, *Reprinted by Permission of Hal Leonard LLC*.

4. *Unsung*, Season 9, Episode 6, "Al Jarreau," produced by Jason B. Ryan, aired April 12, 2020 on TVOne, https://tvone.tv/video/watch-unsung-al-jarreau/.

5. Julio Martinez, interview with the author, August 20, 2020.

6. Richard Dworsky, interview with the author, September 2020.

7. Jim Gosa, review of *We Got By* by Al Jarreau, *High Fidelity and Musical America* 25, no. 12 (December 1975): 119–120.

8. "Spirit," Words and Music by Al Jarreau, Copyright © 1975 AL JARREAU MUSIC, Copyright Renewed, All Rights Administered by SONGS OF UNIVERSAL, INC., All Rights Reserved, Used by Permission, *Reprinted by Permission of Hal Leonard LLC*.

9. In 1976, *Down Beat* referred to the Nachwuchskünstler prize as "the German music Academy's Award for Outstanding Male Vocalist." Lee Underwood, "Al Jarreau," *Down Beat*, October 7, 1976.

10. All quotes from Canning in this chapter are from Tom Canning, interviews with the author, late 2020.

11. "Start bie Onkel Pö," *Der Spiegel*, November 15, 1976, https://spiegel
.de/kultur/start-bei-onkel-poe-a-65006f0b-0002-0001-0000
-000041069518.

12. All quotes in this section are from Charles Mitchell's review of *Glow* by Al
Jarreau, *Down Beat*, November 4, 1976, 25.

13. Joan Downs, "Music: Tops in Pops," *Time*, August 23, 1976, 38.

14. Lee Underwood, "Al Jarreau: The Amazing Acrobat of Scat," *Down Beat*,
March 23, 1978.

15. I do not necessarily agree with this theory, but I believe it is worthy of
consideration.

16. "Start bie Onkel Pö."

17. Underwood, "Al Jarreau."

18. All quotes from Jerry Levin in this and the next three paragraphs are from
Jerry Levin, phone interviews with the author, 2020–2021.

19. In our interviews, Jerry Levin remembered it as the first show of the tour,
but according to Levin's own tour itinerary, the Hamburg date was about
halfway through the tour. Nonetheless, his recollection of the audience
response at the concert is probably accurate.

20. Levin, phone interviews, 2020–2021.

21. Spheeris has made many films of different sorts but is best known for
the huge 1992 hit *Wayne's World*, starring *Saturday Night Live* stars Mike
Myers and Dana Carvey.

22. Mikal Gilmore, review of *Look to the Rainbow* by Al Jarreau, *Down Beat*,
October 6, 1977.

23. In addition to a raft of television scores, Grusin wrote the scores for such
distinguished films as *Three Days of the Condor*, *The Graduate*, *On Golden
Pond*, *Tootsie*, and *The Fabulous Baker Boys*. He won an Oscar for the score
for *The Milagro Beanfield War*. He also recorded a number of jazzy instrumental albums under his own name. "Dave Grusin," *Wikipedia*, February 28, 2023, https://en.wikipedia.org/wiki/Dave_Grusin.

24. Tom Canning, phone interview with the author, October 2020.

25. Esther Berlanga-Ryan, "Al Jarreau: Simple and Necessary Happiness,"
All About Jazz, March 12, 2012, https://allaboutjazz.com/al-jarreau-simple
-and-necessary-happiness-al-jarreau-by-esther-berlanga-ryan.php.

26. Tom Canning, phone interview with the author, March 2021.

27. Levin recalls Blessing as being "completely different from all the rest of
us. . . . His hobby was collecting vintage first-edition books. . . . He was

really quiet, kept to himself, never went out. . . . What he did was so subtle and so amazing and so inspirational. It just added something different that nobody else in the jazz world was doing at that time." Jerry Levin, phone interview with the author, 2020.

Chapter 10

1. Gail Buchalter, "Scat's New King, Al Jarreau, Says He Got By Thanks to Religion and His Second Wife," *People*, January 18, 1982.

2. Sandy Ross, *A Place Called the Bla-Bla Café* (Tarzana, CA: SLR Productions, 2006).

3. In his review of this movie, famed film critic Roger Ebert said, " 'Invasion of the Bee Girls' is the best schlock soft-core science fiction movie since maybe '*The Vengeance of She.*' " Roger Ebert, review of *Invasion of the Bee Girls*, RogerEbert.com, June 20, 1973, https://rogerebert.com/reviews/invasion-of-the-bee-girls-1973.

4. Interestingly, from the late 1970s through most of the 1980s, Al shared living quarters with his road manager Jerry Levin; he did not live with Susan. Jerry Levin, interviews with the author, 2020–2021.

5. This and the following long quote are from Lee Underwood, "Al Jarreau," *Down Beat*, October 7, 1976.

6. Lee Underwood, "Al Jarreau: The Amazing Acrobat of Scat," *Down Beat*, March 23, 1978.

7. Patrick Rains, phone interview with the author, October 2020.

8. Tom Canning, phone interview with the author, October 2020.

9. Joe Reagoso's notes to *Live in London*, Deluxe Edition (Friday Music, 2010).

10. Reprise, founded by Frank Sinatra in 1960, was a subsidiary label of Warner at this time, and many new Warner artists were released on Reprise. Al's first two albums were on Reprise; in 1976, the label was discontinued, and his subsequent records were released on Warner Bros.

11. *Unsung*, Season 9, Episode 6, "Al Jarreau," produced by Jason B. Ryan, aired April 12, 2020 on TVOne, https://tvone.tv/video/watch-unsung-al-jarreau/.

12. Tom Canning, interview with the author, October 2020.

13. Douglas Clark, review of *All Fly Home* by Al Jarreau, *Down Beat*, February 8, 1979.

14. *Unsung*, "Al Jarreau."

15. Underwood, "Acrobat of Scat."
16. Larry Williams, interview with the author, April 8, 2021.

Chapter 11

1. Tom Canning, phone interviews with the author, October 2020 and March 2021. All subsequent quotes from Canning in this chapter are from these interviews unless noted otherwise.
2. Patrick Rains, interview with the author, October 2020.
3. Kellock became a well-known studio keyboard player on the West Coast. Around the time that *This Time* was recorded, he had done some tours with Al's band as the second keyboard player. Tom Canning remembers "Your Sweet Love" as evolving during sound checks on a tour. Tom Canning, interviews with the author, October 2020 and March 2021.
4. Tom Canning, interview with the author, March 2021.
5. Williams was called in at the last minute to play keyboards on the song when Chick Corea's track proved unsatisfactory (see album sidebar at the end of this chapter). Fortunately, Williams had been playing the song night after night with his band, Seawind. Williams, phone interview with the author, April 2021.
6. "Alonzo," Words and Music by Al Jarreau, Copyright © 1980 AL JARREAU MUSIC, All Rights Administered by SONGS OF UNIVERSAL, INC., All Rights Reserved, Used by Permission, *Reprinted by Permission of Hal Leonard LLC.*
7. Tom Canning says of "Alonzo": "That's like a personal favorite. . . . We cut it very quickly; I think that was a first or second take, just as a trio. Myself and Abe [Laboriel] and Ralph Humphrey . . . And, it's a fantastic song. And just one of Al's really great compositions."
8. *Al Jarreau L'enchanteur: Un Documentaire Musical de Thierry Guedj*, directed by Thierry Guedj (France: Portrait & Company, aired January 1, 2016, on French O).
9. Tom Canning, interview with the author, October 2020, and Jerry Levin, interview with the author, December 2020.
10. Quotes from Roger Murrah, Jay Graydon, Steven Ivory, and Marcus Miller in the discussion of "We're in This Love Together" are from *Unsung*, Season 9, Episode 6, "Al Jarreau," produced by Jason B. Ryan, aired April 12, 2020 on TVOne, https://tvone.tv/video/watch-unsung-al-jarreau/.
11. Tom Canning, interview with the author, October 2020.

12. Visa, the credit card company, used a vocal version of "Blue Rondo" that was very close to Al's version on an advertisement that aired throughout the 2020 Tokyo Olympic Games (which took place in 2021). It turns out that it is a remake of a remake, "released by Universal Music Group [and] called 'Jarreau of Rap (Skatt Attack).' The 2019 song is by Nas and features Al Jarreau and Keyon Harrold." Kate Hagan Gallup, "This Is the Song in Visa's New Meet Visa Commercial," *The List*, November 29, 2021, https://thelist.com/475304/this-is-the-song-in-visas-new-meet-visa-commercial/?utm_campaign=clip.

13. This and further quotes from this article are from Steve Bloom, "Breaking Away," *Down Beat*, February 1982.

14. James Borders, review of *Breakin' Away* by Al Jarreau, *The Black Collegian*, December 1981/January 1982. This journal is little known in mainstream America. It is described as "a career and self development magazine targeted to African-American students and other students of color." "The Black Collegian," IMDiversity, https://imdiversity.com/channels/eon/the-black-collegian-online/

15. Both quotes are from *Unsung*, "Al Jarreau."

16. Patrick Rains, interview with the author, October 2020.

17. Canning told me, "[George Duke] spent quite a bit of time with Al, translating what Al [was] sort of singing his way through 'Alonzo,' and kind of humming some notes that he thought should be in the chords, and George kinda transcribed all that and brought his own expertise into organizing it. And so it sounded good. But I mean the chords are very sophisticated in 'Alonzo.' And in a more mercenary world, somebody that had spent as much time as George did putting that together might have wanted to ask for a cowriter [credit]. But George did not. He just thought it would be a way to help Al get the song across the finish line." Al's later musical director Joe Turano speculates that Duke had some real input on the ending section in particular.

Chapter 12

1. Steve Bloom, "Breaking Away," *Down Beat*, February 1982.

2. All information and quotes about touring, unless otherwise noted, are from Jerry Levin, interview with the author, December 2020.

3. Craig Modderno, "Al Jarreau Scats His Way Up Sales Charts," *USA Today*, August 1983.

4. Jerry Levin, interview with the author, January 2021.

5. All quotes related to this performance are from Bill Milkowski, "Jarreau Woos, Wins Hometowners," *Milwaukee Journal*, September 18, 1980.

6. All quotes related to this show are from Kevin Lynch, "Al Jarreau's Inner Electricity Charges Crowd," *Milwaukee Journal*, November 4, 1981.

7. All quotes related to the Summerfest show are from Divina Infusino, "Jarreau Thrills Hometown Crowd," *Milwaukee Journal*, July 3, 1982.

8. This quote and the quote from Levin in the following paragraph are from Jerry Levin, interview with the author, December 2020.

9. Jill Warren, "Jarreau Concert Shines Despite the Rain," *Indianapolis Star*, July 23, 1982.

10. Rose Marie Freeman talked to me about the Rodman Center visit on several occasions during our conversations of 2019–2021.

11. The information about Al's October 1962 visit to Ripon, unless otherwise noted, is from a variety of written communications in the Jarreau archive, Ripon College.

12. I attended this event with my wife and a number of my students.

13. Mary Kane, "Al Jarreau: Ripon Class of '62," *Oshkosh Daily Northwestern*, October 30–31, 1982.

14. Dave Shogren, "Grammy Winner Al Jarreau Returns for Homecoming," *Ripon College Days*, November 5, 1982. As a student, Shogren played bass in the school's jazz band.

15. The author's wife has carefully guarded her signed copy of the *This Time* album since that night.

16. Modderno, "Al Jarreau Scats."

17. The Brewers, then in the American League, won the game from the St. Louis Cardinals to take a 3–2 lead in the Series; unfortunately, the hometown heroes lost the next two games and the Series in St. Louis in the team's only World Series appearance in team history.

18. Jon Bream, "Jarreau's Parading Home with Breakthrough Punch," *Minneapolis Star*, June 2, 1977.

19. Jon Bream, "Jarreau Combines All the Pop Elements," *Minneapolis Star and Tribune*, June 18, 1984.

Chapter 13

1. The quotes in this paragraph are from *Unsung*, Season 9, Episode 6, "Al Jarreau," produced by Jason B. Ryan, aired April 12, 2020 on TVOne, https://tvone.tv/video/watch-unsung-al-jarreau/.

2. "Mornin'," track 1 on Al Jarreau, *Jarreau*, Warner Bros. Records 1-23801, 1983, 33⅓ rpm.

3. As of January 2021, the official video of "Mornin'" on YouTube had been viewed more than 5.6 million times. One of the comments left by a viewer said, "The fact that over 500 [out of 5.6 million] people disliked this video makes me weep for humanity." Al Jarreau, "Al Jarreau – Mornin' (Official Video)," YouTube video, https://youtube.com/watch?v=kzXNdLVZs3k&ab_channel=RHINO.

4. Omartian had already played on *This Time* and *Breakin' Away*. He had also produced Christopher Cross's self-titled 1980 album, which won multiple Grammy Awards, including Album of the Year.

5. The quotes in this paragraph are from *Unsung*, "Al Jarreau."

6. The quotes in the paragraph and the next are from Craig Modderno, "Al Jarreau Scats His Way Up Sales Charts," *USA Today*, August 1983.

7. All of the following quotes from Canning in this chapter, unless otherwise noted, comes from Tom Canning, phone conversation with the author, 2020.

8. Al's tour manager and housemate Jerry Levin told me that he and Al would go hear Weather Report anytime they performed within a hundred miles of wherever they might be. Alex Acuna, the drummer on *Heavy Weather*, later played several tours with Al.

9. Joe Reagoso, notes to *Live in London: The Deluxe Edition* (Friday Music, 2010).

10. Toshiki Narada, notes to Japanese CD release of *High Crime*, 2014. There is conflicting evidence about the release date of this CD, and therefore the date of the interview, but 2014 seems most likely.

11. Narada, notes to *High Crime*.

12. An odd scene in this video shows the woman briefly reading D. H. Lawrence's *Lady Chatterley's Lover* with wide-open eyes. As of early 2023, this video could be seen at https://youtube.com/watch?v=PA0tEe91-_E.

13. Information and quotes in this and the next three paragraphs are from

Michael Paulo, phone conversation and subsequent emails with the author, February 2021.

14. This review appeared in a recurring column called Listen Up! in the *Milwaukee Journal*, December 2, 1984.

15. Reagoso, notes to *Live in London*.

16. Larry Williams, phone interview with the author, April 8, 2021.

17. These three songwriters would collaborate with Graydon on "Let's Pretend" on the *High Crime* album of 1984. Page and George had previously done some of the background vocals on *Breakin' Away*.

18. Tom Canning, phone interview with the author, 2020.

19. Tom Canning, phone interview with the author, 2021.

20. This and the following quotes from Turano are from Joe Turano, email correspondence with the author, March 2021.

21. There is a credit given on the album for "additional recording at Bill Schnee studio."

Chapter 14

1. Gary Graff, "Setbacks Aren't Roadblocks for Jazz-Pop Artist Al Jarreau," *Orlando Sentinel*, September 1, 1985.

2. Quotes about the Rio Festival are from Jerry Levin, interviews with the author, 2020–2021.

3. Jerry Levin, email correspondence with the author, February 2021.

4. The history of the possible making of the Nat King Cole film is pieced together from the articles cited; Patrick Rains, email correspondence with the author, November 2021; and Jerry Levin, phone interview, December 2020.

5. While Cole's life story is well known and widely available, particularly recommended is the recent biography by Will Friedwald, *Straighten Up and Fly Right: The Life and Music of Nat King Cole* (New York: Oxford University Press, 2020).

6. "Al Jarreau to Star in Nat 'King' Cole movie," *Jet*, April 8, 1985.

7. Marilyn Beck, "Jarreau to Film Nat King Cole Story in Debut," *Chicago Tribune*, December 19, 1985.

8. Tidyman, who was white, created one of the signature Black action heroes of the 1970s, John Shaft.

9. Quotes about the demise of the Cole project, unless otherwise noted, are from Jerry Levin, interviews with the author, 2020–2021.

10. "Ernest Tidyman," *Wikipedia*, October 1, 2022, https://en.wikipedia.org/wiki/Ernest_Tidyman.

11. Levin, email correspondence with the author, November 8, 2022.

12. Graff, "Setbacks Aren't Roadblocks."

13. *Unsung*, "Al Jarreau."

14. Susan Stevens, "Al Jarreau and His Music Grow with Changing Times," *Fort Lauderdale News/Sun-Sentinel*, December 27, 1985. This article was also distributed through Tribune Media Services, appearing under different titles (e.g., "Jarreau takes over New Year's party").

15. Smoking was a habit that Jarreau shared with Nat King Cole. It was lung cancer that killed Cole at age forty-five.

Chapter 15

1. Nile Rodgers, *Le Freak: An Upside Down Story of Family, Disco, and Destiny* (New York: Spiegel & Grau, 2011). Rodgers's life story is at times almost beyond belief. The autobiography is a fascinating document of a man and an era.

2. "Bio by Photo: Al Jarreau," in-house publication from WEA (Warner-Elektra-Asylum Records), 1986.

3. Besides the artists that Rodgers had produced before working with Al, he later produced hit albums for the Rolling Stones, Christina Aguilera, and Lady Gaga; he won three Grammy Awards and was inducted into the Rock and Roll Hall of Fame and the Songwriters Hall of Fame.

4. By his own admission, Rodgers was deep into his addiction to alcohol and cocaine at this time.

5. David Marchese, "The Deep Hidden Meaning of Nile Rodgers," *Vulture*, July 26, 2015.

6. The internet provides conflicting information on "Moonlighting," making it difficult to discern what is and is not true.

7. Jerry Levin, interview with the author, 2022.

8. The Jarreau theme was not used at the beginning of the very first episode.

9. "Moonlighting" is on expanded CD versions of the original album.

10. Patrick Rains, interview with the author, October 2020.

11. Joe Reagoso, notes to the 2011 release of *L Is for Lover*.

12. Jerry Levin, interview with the author, 2020.

13. Tina Maples, "Warm Reward: Jarreau's Voice Turns up Heat for Those Who Braved Cold," *Milwaukee Journal*, November 13, 1986.

14. Kris Kodrich, "Al Jarreau Brings Jazzy Voice Back to Home State," *Wisconsin State Journal*, November 15, 1986.

15. Martha Southgate, "Star Quality," *Essence*, May 1989. Two of the founders of *Essence* once described it as a "lifestyle magazine directed at upscale African American women." "*Essence* (magazine)," Wikipedia, https://en .wikipedia.org/wiki/Essence_(magazine). A significant portion of Al's fan base might fit this demographic.

16. *Al Jarreau L'enchanteur: Un Documentaire Musical de Thierry Guedj*, directed by Thierry Guedj (France: Portrait & Company, aired January 1, 2016, on French O).

17. The rest of the *Tutu* album was produced by Marcus Miller, who would, in a few years, produce Al's album *Tenderness*.

18. *Al Jarreau L'enchanteur*.

19. "Carolina in the Morning" has been done by so many artists over the years that Al undoubtedly knew it in several different versions.

20. Southgate, "Star Quality."

21. All quotes in this and the following eleven paragraphs, unless otherwise noted, are from Wayne Lee, "Jarreau," *Jazziz* 6, no. 2 (February/March 1989). The title on the cover of the magazine is "Al Jarreau: The Fate of a Natural Winner," but the title is different inside the issue.

22. Elizabeth Chur, "3rd Time's a Charm: Al Jarreau Makes R&B Statement with 'Heaven and Earth,'" *Chicago Tribune*, July 30, 1992.

23. Robin Tolleson, "Al Jarreau: A Troubadour's New Tones," *Down Beat*, April 1989.

24. Data from Don Heckman's notes to *The Very Best of Al Jarreau*.

25. Mary Kane, "Complex Melody: The Joy and Pain of Al Jarreau," *Milwaukee Journal*, July 30, 1989.

26. Joe Turano, email correspondence with the author, March 2021.

27. Robin Tolleson, "Al Jarreau: A Troubadour's New Tones," *Down Beat*, April 1989.

Chapter 16

1. *Body Heat* rose to number one on the R&B chart and as high as number six on the pop chart.
2. The lyrics to "Hot News Blues" are printed on the inner sleeve of the *Secret Agent* album.
3. Gail Buchalter, "Scat's New King, Al Jarreau, Says He Got By Thanks to Religion and His Second Wife," *People*, January 18, 1982.
4. I find it interesting—and contradictory—that Hubbard was slammed for making albums like *The Love Connection* that had beautiful string writing, yet only five years later jazz wunderkind Wynton Marsalis would make a "string album" (*Hot House Flowers*) that was praised as being the successor to Clifford Brown's classic album of the 1950s, *Clifford Brown with Strings*.
5. Charles Waring, notes to *Bundle of Joy, Super Blue* and *The Love Connection*, rerelease on BGO Records, 2013.
6. Mainieri was performing under his own name, but along with other members of the collective band Steps Ahead, of which Mainieri was a founder and probably the mastermind. He did record one album for Warner Bros. under his own name in 1981.
7. The song "That's What Friends Are For" became a monster hit three years later, when Dionne Warwick, who had recorded many of Bacharach's biggest hits, put it out as a single, with contributions by three other hitmakers, Stevie Wonder, Elton John, and Gladys Knight. That single won a Grammy and was the top-selling single of 1986 in the US. Its profits were donated to AIDS research.
8. "Girls Know How" was probably recorded during the same time period that resulted in the album *Breakin' Away*.
9. *We Are Family* was produced by Bernard Edwards and Nile Rodgers, of Chic fame. See chapter 15 for Al's interaction with Rodgers. For baseball fans, "We Are Family" became the theme song of the Pittsburgh Pirates, who won the World Series in 1979.
10. Background information on the film and the music is largely from Jim Lochner's notes to the 2016 rerelease of the soundtrack. Quotes here are from those notes.
11. Richard Sandomir, "Lennie Niehaus, Who Set Eastwood's Films to Music, Dies at 90," *New York Times*, June 10, 2020, https://nytimes.com/2020/06/10/movies/lennie-niehaus-dead.html.

12. There is considerable information about "We Are the World" in a variety of places on the Internet, including the soloists listed in order. In February 2022, the official video was listed as having been viewed on YouTube more than 86 million times.

13. *We Are the World: The Story Behind the Song*, directed by Tom Trbovich, written by Mikal Gilmore (Los Angeles, CA: Golin-Mally Productions and Ken Kragen Productions, 1985), on YouTube, https://youtube.com/watch?v=p5Va0VrFK7s&ab_channel=JamesJames.

14. As noted in chapter 2, Al's sister Rose Marie Freeman identified Belafonte as a Jarreau family favorite back in the siblings' youth.

15. This was presented with its companion, *Miles at Montreux*, as part of a *Great Performances* show on public television. This particular performance was probably from the New Orleans Jazz and Heritage Festival of 1986.

16. Dan Oulette, "Miles Davis' 'Rubberband' Finally Arrives," *Down Beat*, December 2019.

17. In a nice touch, Al's longtime touring saxophonist Michael Paulo plays on the remixed version of "Al Jarreau."

18. Joe Marchese, notes to *Melissa Manchester, Ma+hema+ics: The MCA Years*, Geffen Records/Real Gone Music, 2018.

19. Marchese, notes to *Melissa Manchester*.

20. As noted in chapter 7, Bob James had heard Al sing with Ripon College's Indigos at the Notre Dame Jazz Festival in 1962.

21. This category had existed only since 1979. Sanborn also won the award the previous year, for his album *Straight to the Heart*.

22. The machinations behind the making of this album, and this cut, are related in Ben Sidran, *The Ballad of Tommy LiPuma* (Nardis Books, 2020), 225–227.

23. As of January 2022, a performance could be seen at "David Sanborn & Al Jarreau—Since I Fell For You (live, 1985)," Daily Motion, https://dailymotion.com/video/x3054c6.

24. Besides Sanborn, guitarist Eric Gale, bassist Marcus Miller, and drummer Steve Gadd are on this track. All four would appear on Al's 1994 *Tenderness* album and the live album recorded at the Montreux Jazz Festival in 1993.

25. *Al Jarreau L'enchanteur: Un Documentaire Musical de Thierry Guedj*, directed by Thierry Guedj (France: Portrait & Company, aired January 1, 2016, on French O).

26. Kemp Powers's play on which *One Night in Miami* was based was produced

in 2013. It depicted the night of February 25, 1964, when these four major figures gathered in a hotel room, only months before Cooke was shot to death in California. The film was nominated for Oscars in three categories.

27. Later on, "You Send Me" was listed among the five hundred most important rock and roll records by the Rock & Roll Hall of Fame, and came in at number 115 on *Rolling Stone*'s "The 500 Greatest Songs of All Time." "500 Greatest Songs of All Time (2004)," *Rolling Stone*, December 11, 2003, https://rollingstone.com/music/music-lists/500-greatest-songs-of-all -time-151127/sam-cooke-you-send-me-36553/.

28. Franks released his own version of "Somehow Our Love Survives" some years later, in 1995, on his album *Abandoned Garden*, also on Warner Bros. His recording features Al's frequent musical partner David Sanborn.

29. Bill Lee's music was released on one album, as *Do the Right Thing (Original Score)*, on Columbia Records; the music by the other artists was released as *(Music from) Do the Right Thing* on Motown Records.

30. "Fight the Power" utilizes only two musicians—saxophonist Branford Marsalis and turntablist Terminator X—along with a variety of samples and loops.

31. Jones, incidentally, played with the band Chic, the musical brainchild of Nile Rodgers, who produced Al's 1986 album *L Is for Lover*.

32. As Mister Señor Love Daddy, this was one of Jackson's earliest film appearances, at the beginning of his now illustrious career. He also had a small part in Lee's earlier *School Daze*.

33. Jon Hendricks, liner notes to Jon Hendricks and Friends, *Freddie Freeloader*, Denon Records, 1990.

34. The concert was on March 29, 1990. See "Absolut Vocalese: An Evening with Jon Hendricks," Stratta-Philips Productions, Inc., Carnegie Hall, https://carnegiehall.org/about/history/performance-history-search?q= Jon%20Hendricks&dex=prod_PHS&page=2&event=26744.

Chapter 17

1. A collection of photographs of Al's band performing at the Santa Barbara Bowl in Santa Barbara, California, on June 30, 1989, can be found at https://sbbowl.com/photos/concert_detail/1986_06_30_al_jarreau/2175. Paulo identified the "summer" band from these photos.

2. Reed also sang backup vocals on one track of *Heart's Horizon*.

3. Information about Vonda Shepard from the bio page of her website, http://vondashepard.com/bio/, and "Ally McBeal," IMdB, https://imdb.com/title/tt0118254/.

4. As of early 2023, this concert was posted online at https://youtube.com/watch?v=RziF-gz_L5w.

5. Mary Kane reported that the concert raised half a million dollars. Mary Kane, "Complex Melody: The Joy and Pain of Al Jarreau," *Milwaukee Journal*, July 30, 1989.

6. This set list is compiled from various sources, mostly the list at https://setlist.fm/search?query=al+jarreau.

7. Stephen Holden, "The Sunny Personality of Al Jarreau," *New York Times*, April 24, 1989.

8. Diane Patrick, "Al Jarreau at Radio City Music Hall, New York," *JazzTimes*, August 1989, https://musiclistenersjournal.wordpress.com/2013/04/15/al-jarreau-at-radio-city-music-hall-jazztimes-august-1989/.

9. Larry Nager, "Jarreau Digs Roots of R&B," Playbook, *The Commercial Appeal*, June 26, 1992.

10. All quotes from here to the end of the chapter are from Don Heckman, "Jazz Review: Jarreau Pulls Crowd Right into His Comfy Musical Living Room," *Los Angeles Times*, July 3, 1989.

Chapter 18

1. Kevin Allman, "Singing Praises to Writers of the Songs," *Los Angeles Times*, May 1, 1991.

2. Al's honorary degree from Berklee was reported widely; the notice I saw was in the *Oshkosh (WI) Northwestern*, May 5, 1991.

3. All quotes in the next four paragraphs are from Michael Paskevich, "Al Jarreau Speaks Out for Singers: Vocalist Laments Lack of Interest in the Art," *Las Vegas Review-Journal*, October 11, 1991.

4. All quotes in this paragraph are from Elizabeth Chur, "3rd Time's a Charm: Al Jarreau Makes R&B Statement with 'Heaven and Earth,'" *Chicago Tribune*, July 30, 1992. This syndicated article reappeared in *The Sacramento Bee*, November 27, 1992.

5. All quotes in this and the next four paragraphs are from "RIP Al Jarreau 1992 Interview with Donnie Simpson," YouTube, April 9, 2017, https://youtube.com/watch?v=p8exgDrJovg.

6. Walden opened his Tarpan Studios in San Rafael, California, in 1985.

7. Al also expressed his admiration for Miles's later cutting-edge "fusion" album *Bitches Brew* (1970): "It taught people that you can do the thing of using the framework of contemporary music, contemporary-sounding music of the time, as he did in *Bitches Brew*, and bring your thing to it. And just open the minds of people, you know." "RIP Al Jarreau 1992 Interview with Donnie Simpson."

8. Davis won for the album *Doo-Bop*. Produced by Easy Mo Bee, who is best known for producing the rap artists Notorious B.I.G., Tupac (2Pac) Shakur, and LL Cool J, *Doo-Bop* might just as easily have been classified as rap.

9. This is an interesting comment, given that Al's next album, *Tenderness*, only a year away, included a number of his early hits.

10. Chur, "3rd Time's A Charm."

11. As the interviews were both conducted when Al was in Rome and the content is quite similar, one might even wonder if the two reporters were in on the same phone call. See Keith Spera, "A Renaissance for Al Jarreau," Lagniappe, *Times-Picayune* (New Orleans), June 26, 1992; and Larry Nager, "Jarreau Digs Roots of R&B," Playbook, *The Commercial Appeal*, June 26, 1992.

12. Mathieson was the keyboard player for the famous 1975 gig at The Troubadour in Los Angeles that led to Al's signing with Warner Bros. Mathieson also made contributions to *All Fly Home, This Time, Jarreau*, and later on, *Tomorrow Today*.

13. "Album of the Week: Al Jarreau: *Heaven and Earth*," *BRE Music Report*, June 26, 1992.

14. Gordon Chambers, "Music Review: *Heaven and Earth*," *Entertainment Weekly*, August 7, 1992.

15. Achy Obejas, "Jarreau Covers All the Angels: Singer's Voice out of This World at Chicago Theatre," *Chicago Tribune*, September 24, 1992.

16. Stephen Holden, "Al Jarreau's Night of Equal-Opportunity Joie de Vivre," *New York Times*, November 16, 1992.

17. The lyrics Al wrote for Chick Corea's "Spain," on *This Time*, also showcased impressionistic images; a similar style would show up in Al's lyrics to the Weather Report tune "A Remark You Made" ("Something That You Said") on his 2000 *Tomorrow Today* album.

Chapter 19

1. All quotes in this and the next three paragraphs, unless otherwise noted, are from Thor Christensen, "2 Milwaukee Singers, 2 Paths," *Milwaukee Journal*, March 14, 1993.
2. "RIP Al Jarreau 1992 Interview with Donnie Simpson," YouTube, April 9, 2017, https://youtube.com/watch?v=p8exgDrJovg.
3. The quotes from Miller in this and the next few paragraphs are from *Al Jarreau: Tenderness*, directed by Alan Carter (1993; Los Angeles, CA: Rhino Entertainment, 2021), DVD.
4. Al's quotes in this and the next few paragraphs are from *Al Jarreau: Tenderness*.
5. *Al Jarreau: Tenderness*. The song "Go Away, Little Girl" was first released by Bobby Vee. Crooner Steve Lawrence's 1962 version reached number one on the *Billboard* Top 100 for a couple of weeks, and teen idol Donny Osmond's 1971 remake reached number one years later.
6. Probably the most famous jazz version of "Summertime" is the 1959 Miles Davis/Gil Evans interpretation.
7. James T. Jones IV, "Al Jarreau's 'Tenderness' Brings Back His Jazz Feeling," *USA Today*, June 8, 1994.
8. On the fairly comprehensive website allaboutmusic.com, Urbanos's only listing is for this song, which also appeared on Al's 2008 *Love Songs*: https://allmusic.com/artist/todd-urbanos-mn0003201980?16679419 56867.
9. All quotes in the following paragraphs are from Don Heckman, "Live Wire. Al Jarreau," *Jazz Times*, September 1994, 47–48, 104–105.
10. The one member missing from the *Tenderness* band, who saw only limited duty on the album, was keyboardist Neil Larsen.
11. Eagle Records has released many live performances from the Montreux Festival, with the cooperation of the festival. They approached Al's manager Joe Gordon asking for permission to release this concert recording. One would presume that Sanborn's name is not listed because of some contractual issues.
12. Al Jarreau July 6, 1993 Setlist, Setlist.fm, https://setlist.fm/setlist/al -jarreau/1993/auditorium-stravinski-montreux-switzerland-63f42a23 .html.

13. Jones was the nephew of jazz vocal icon Betty Carter. He had started writing for *USA Today* in 1988 and, during his time with the paper, interviewed a wide range of prominent African American artists. He died at the age of thirty-six in 1996. "James T. Jones IV," Wikipedia, August 8, 2021, https://en.wikipedia.org/wiki/James_T._Jones_IV.

14. Jones, "Al Jarreau's 'Tenderness'."

15. Unsigned review of *Live at Montreux 1993*, by Al Jarreau, *JazzTimes*, July/August 2016.

Chapter 20

1. Don Heckman, "Al Jarreau: Song Salesman," *Los Angeles Times*, May 29, 1997.

2. Patrick Rains, interview with the author, October 22, 2020.

3. Patrick Rains, interview with the author, October 22, 2020.

4. Theresa Robinson, interview with the author, August 5, 2020.

5. All quotes in this paragraph are from Alan Sculley, "Al Jarreau: I'll Be Smokin' After Career 'Halftime,'" *Morning Call* (Allentown, PA), August 16, 1997.

6. Heckman, "Al Jarreau: Song Salesman."

7. This quote and the others from Al in the following three paragraphs are from Sculley, "Al Jarreau: I'll Be Smokin'."

8. Mike Joyce, "Jarreau and the NSO: A Symphony of Styles," *Washington Post*, November 30, 1998. While Al and Gil Goldstein continued to do these concerts together for a number of years, no evidence has been found to suggest that they had worked together prior to the symphony concerts. Perhaps the *Washington Post* was incorrect to use the word "longtime" in the sentence. Bill Darlington, interview with the author, August 15, 2022.

9. Joyce, "Jarreau and the NSO."

10. Sculley, "Al Jarreau: I'll Be Smokin'."

11. Wolfgang Spahr and Ellie Weinert, "Getting Priorities Straight: The Region's Major and Indie Labels Focus on Artists That Could Be the Next Big Thing at Home and Abroad," Billboard Spotlights Germany, Switzerland and Austria, *Billboard*, December 6, 1997.

12. Sculley, "Al Jarreau: I'll Be Smokin'." A big band album never happened

(although he performed several tours with the NDR Bigband of Germany), but eventually Al recorded a jazzy album of mostly standards, with support of a superb jazz combo. See chapter 22.

13. Information in this paragraph comes from *"Grease* (musical)," Wikipedia, November 19, 2022, https://en.wikipedia.org/wiki/Grease_(musical); "Jody Watley Throwback Thursday in 1996 on Broadway in The Hit Musical GREASE!," Official Jody Watley Website, July 16, 2020, https://jody watley.net/tag/chubby-checker/; and "Chubby Checker," Wikipedia, October 27, 2022, https://en.wikipedia.org/wiki/Chubby_Checker.

14. Sculley, "Al Jarreau: I'll Be Smokin'."

15. Stephen Holden, "Jazz Festival Review: Al Jarreau, Happy and Ready to Prove It," *New York Times*, July 4, 1995; and Frank Scheck, "Jarreau Borders on Excess; O'Day Directs Energies to Style," *Christian Science Monitor*, July 20, 1995. Scheck wrote: "Jarreau's voice is, to be sure, an impressive instrument, and he can do amazing things with it. In just the opening minutes of his concert, he had it swooping and swirling, going from a high falsetto to a deep bass rumble, and he made sounds that resembled gargling, far-off explosions, and the noise of heavy machinery operating at various speeds."

16. Mayo, like so many Jarreau sidemen, went on to a distinguished career, and is perhaps best known for his work with Earth, Wind & Fire, Sergio Mendes, and more recently, John Legend.

17. This concert is posted at various places on the internet. Several of those incorrectly list the date as 2004. It has been posted on the Al Jarreau Facebook page: https://facebook.com/AlJarreauOfficial/videos/al-jarreau-live-at-newport-1996/307668464002572/.

18. Information about Ravel comes from "About," Life in Tune with Freddie Ravel, https://lifeintune.com/about; "Freddie Ravel," Wikipedia, February 8, 2023, https://en.wikipedia.org/wiki/Freddie_Ravel; and the interesting interview posted at Lis Lewis, "A Chat with Musical Director Freddie Ravel," The Singers Workshop, https://thesingersworkshop.com/a-chat-with-musical-director-freddie-ravel/.

19. "Ross Bolton," Guitarinstructor.com, https://guitarinstructor.com/product/viewinstructor.action?biographyid=1201.

20. "Jota Morelli," Sonor, https://sonor.com/artists/jota-morelli/.

21. Some of this information comes from "About Chris Walker," Chris Walker Music, https://chriswalkersmusic.com/about-chris-walker/, but most comes from Chris Walker, interview with the author, August 21, 2020.

22. Joe Gordon, interview with the author, October 2021.

23. Heckman, "Al Jarreau: Song Salesman."

Chapter 21

1. Larry Williams, phone interview with the author, 2021.

2. Jim Abbott, "Al Jarreau Outlasted a Lot of Fads," *Orlando Sentinel*, January 19, 2001.

3. Jerry Levin, phone interview with the author, December 2020.

4. Paul MacArthur, "Backstage with . . . Al Jarreau," *Down Beat*, August 2000. Quotes in the next three paragraphs are also from this article.

5. Abbott, "Al Jarreau Outlasted a Lot of Fads."

6. As noted in chapter 19, "Puddit" was performed and recorded at Montreux in 1993.

7. Abbott, "Al Jarreau Outlasted a Lot of Fads."

8. Jonathan Widran, review of *Tomorrow Today* by Al Jarreau, AllMusic.com, https://allmusic.com/album/tomorrow-today-mw0000260652.

9. John Sharpe, review of *Tomorrow Today* by Al Jarreau, AllAboutJazz.com, August 1, 2000, https://allaboutjazz.com/tomorrow-today-al-jarreau -grp-records-review-by-john-sharpe.php.

10. "The Pop Dose Guide to Al Jarreau," Pop Dose, March 4, 2008, https:// popdose.com/the-popdose-guide-to-al-jarreau.

11. MacArthur, "Backstage with . . . Al Jarreau."

12. Joe Gordon, interview with the author, August 2021.

13. Information about Turano's life is from my various talks (phone calls and in person) with Joe in 2020 and 2021.

14. Joe's story includes living in the young women's mansion in an exclusive neighborhood, getting to be friends with actor Dan Blocker (Hoss on *Bonanza*), getting funding for a demo tape, and other good "midwesterner moves to La-La-Land" stories.

15. As of early 2022, this concert could be viewed at https://youtube.com/ watch?v=jlaRiwPujAQ.

16. "Al Jarreau Setlist," July 10, 2000, https://setlist.fm/setlist/al-jarreau/ 2000/auditorium-stravinski-montreux-switzerland-3f575ab.html.

17. As of 2023, this performance can be heard at https://youtube.com/ watch?v=7VWO6029T2w.

18. Mark Simmons, email correspondence with the author, January 2020.

19. In fact, for every song up until the last two, "Jacaranda" and "Route 66," the beat range is between 66 and 88 per minute (except for the long beats divided in three in "Oasis," which are slower yet).

20. While I have a real fondness for "Jacaranda Bougainvillea," that reaction is not universal. Maurice Bottomley of PopMatters.com wrote about it, "The music is completely bogus at one level but the piece is carried off with much aplomb and an agreeable romanticism." Bottomley, review of *All I Got* by Al Jarreau, *PopMatters*, January 9, 2003.

21. Ron Miller, "Al Jarreau: All I Got," Artist Interview, *Jazz Review*, https:// web.archive.org/web/20060106110300/http://jazzreview.com/article details.cfm?ID=1037. It is unclear exactly when this first appeared, but from the content, it must have been in late 2002. Thanks to David Ginsburg for help in determining this.

22. Miller, "Al Jarreau: All I Got."

23. Bottomley, review of *All I Got*.

24. Gail Mitchell, "Al Jarreau: Read All About It," *Billboard*, October 26, 2002, 78. There was also a notice about the reading program on the back of the CD package.

25. Mitchell, "Al Jarreau: Read All About It."

26. Miller, "Al Jarreau: All I Got."

27. Ricardo was the television alter ego of actor-musician Desi Arnaz on the wildly popular *I Love Lucy*, the 1950s hit show that starred Arnaz alongside his wife, Lucille Ball. Arnaz, both on the show and in real life, led a big Latin band.

28. Williams, phone interview with the author, 2021. Hey also arranged "Flame" on this album.

29. Jim Newsom, "Recordings: Jazz Reviews," review of *Man in the Air* by Kurt Elling, *PortFolio Weekly*, November 4, 2003, http://jimnewsom.com/ PFW-JazzReviews1003.html.

30. Abbott, "Al Jarreau Outlasted a Lot of Fads."

31. Chris Walker, email correspondence with the author, 2022.

32. Paula Edelstein, review of *All I Got* by Al Jarreau, AllMusic.com, https:// allmusic.com/album/all-i-got-mw0000227460?1629572595680.

Chapter 22

1. All of Williams's quotes in this long section about *Accentuate the Positive* are from Larry Williams, phone conversations with the author, April and November 2021.

2. An example of a song Al edited was "Cold Duck." Williams says, "I think I had two more sections that I had to 'Cold Duck' that I took into a thing; and he made it a separate tune that we recorded that didn't make the record. But that was okay." Williams also described some of the songs that were cut as "really cool tracks. One of them was a 'Stella by Starlight' arrangement that was a Freddie Ravel idea that was a 6/8, a very cool thing that came off great. [And] actually a couple things I played piano solos on didn't make the record [*chuckles*]. Which . . . eh . . . whatever."

3. In today's extraordinarily broad range of what many refer to as jazz, the labels "avant-garde," "free," and "experimental" are not as meaningful as they once were.

4. All quotes in this and the next two paragraphs are from John McDonough, review of *Accentuate the Positive* by Al Jarreau, *Down Beat*, September 2004, 60–61.

5. John Corbett, Jim Macnie, and Paul de Barros, "The Hot Box," reviews of *Accentuate the Positive* by Al Jarreau, *Down Beat*, September 2004, 60–61.

6. All quotes in this and the next six paragraphs are from Mark Ruffin, "Full Circle: Al Jarreau Attempts to Reinvigorate His Jazz Love Affair," *Down Beat*, October 2004.

7. Turano, interview with the author, September 2021.

8. Larry Williams, email correspondence with the author, November 2021.

9. All quotes in this and the next three paragraphs are from John Murph, "Accentuate the Swing: Al Jarreau Moonlights with Jazz," *JazzTimes*, September 2004. The article's subtitle might seem to be a little swipe at Jarreau, suggesting that jazz is only a sidelight for him. However, it might also just be a reference to Al's big 1980s hit "Moonlighting."

10. Jim Trageser, "Al Jarreau Holds Forth on the Art of Singing, the Decline of Radio and the Glory of he Great American Songbook," AllAboutJazz.com, https://allaboutjazz.com/al-jarreau-holds-forth-on-the-art-of-singing-the-decline-of-radio-and-the-glory-of-the-great-american-songbook-al-jarreau-by-jim-trageser.php. Joe Turano reports that when he joined

the band in 2000, Al was treated like "royalty" in Europe. Turano, interview with the author, 2020.

11. Trageser, "Al Jarreau Holds Forth."

12. Bill Darlington, interview with the author, August 15, 2022.

13. Andrew Gilbert, "Total Inspiration: The Many Voices of Al Jarreau," *Jazz-Times*, August 2006.

14. Jim Santella, "A Romantic Evening in Central Park 2004," AllAboutJazz.com, September 15, 2004, https://allaboutjazz.com/a-romantic-evening-in-central-park-2004-al-jarreau-by-jim-santella.php.

15. Janine Coveney, "A Long Time Coming," *JazzTimes*, December 2006.

16. Michael Jackson, review of *Givin' It Up* by George Benson and Al Jarreau, *Down Beat*, December 2006.

17. Brian Soergel, review of *Givin' It Up* by George Benson and Al Jarreau, *JazzTimes*, December 2006.

18. Larry Williams, phone interview with the author, April 8, 2021.

19. Joe Turano, phone interview with the author, November 17, 2020.

Chapter 23

1. Jerry Levin, interviews and email correspondence with the author, 2020 and 2021.

2. Manager Joe Gordon reports that Al did a number of other similar gigs in Moscow and St. Petersburg around this time. Gordon, interview with the author, October 27, 2021.

3. All information and quotes in the next three paragraphs are from Kaiyoti Pesante, phone interview with the author, December 2021.

4. The following story appears in Kurt Dietrich, *Wisconsin Riffs: Jazz Profiles from the Heartland* (Madison: Wisconsin Historical Society Press, 2018), 110.

5. Although Al contributed his services for free, given that his whole band had to be paid and equipment had to be rented, the college probably did not make a great deal of money from the concert. However, no one associated with the event would ever suggest that it was not an inspiring moment in the history of the institution.

6. "The NDR Bigband—An Ensemble of Soloists," NDR, https://ndr.de/orchester_chor/bigband/bigbandvitaeng101.html.

7. R. J. Deluke, "Al Jarreau: Christmas Time at Last," AllAboutJazz.com, De-

cember 15, 2008, https://allaboutjazz.com/al-jarreau-christmas-time
-at-last-al-jarreau-by-rj-deluke.

8. All quotes from Williams in this chapter are from Larry Williams, interviews with the author, April and November 2021.

9. Williams now says, "That was one hundred thousand dollars; but I thought
that couldn't do it. [But] that's like an extravagance today." In the world of
music in the 2020s, he says, "I would kill for that."

10. All quotes from Turano in this chapter are from Joe Turano, interview with
the author, September 2021.

11. Turano especially appreciated the kudos he got from Jorge Calandrelli for
the "Bells" arrangement.

12. Alfred Burt (1920–1954) is known almost exclusively for his fifteen Christmas carols.

13. The background to these and other lyrics can be found at "Wihla Hutson,"
http://alfredburtcarols.com/burt/Web%20Pages/Wihla.htm.

14. There are stories about the book and Al's involvement with it around the
internet, including at the author's website, https://carmenrubin.com/.

15. This peak occurred three years after Al's death.

16. Thanks to Joe Gordon for supplying most of this information.

17. Joe Gordon told me the details of Al's collapse in the fall of 2021. Gordon
choked up while telling the story, reflecting the gravity of the situation at
the time.

18. Associated Press, "Al Jarreau Stable, Changes Hospitals in France," *Billboard*, July 24, 2010.

19. "Al Jarreau in Critical Condition in France," *Billboard*, July 23, 2010; "Al
Jarreau Getting Better, Hopes to Resume Touring Soon," *Associated Press*,
July 26, 2010.

20. Lee Mergner, "Al Jarreau: Feelin' Pretty Good. Singer Set for Performances at
Wolf Trap and Other Venues in U.S. and Japan," *JazzTimes*, August 15, 2010.

21. Ashante Infantry, "Al Jarreau Lives (Still) to Sing," *Toronto Star*, May 5,
2011.

22. In 2021, Larry Williams told me of sweating out the white-knuckle timing
of producing *Christmas*. Also, Take 6 honored their friend Al Jarreau after
his death with an arrangement of his song "Roof Garden" on their 2018
album, *Iconic*.

Chapter 24

1. Esther Berlanga-Ryan, "Al Jarreau: Simple and Necessary Happiness," *All About Jazz*, March 12, 2012, https://allaboutjazz.com/al-jarreau-simple-and-necessary-happiness-al-jarreau-by-esther-berlanga-ryan.php. Other dates from 2009–2011 are mentioned on George Duke's website.
2. Up-and-coming bassist Esperanza Spalding played a couple of the nights.
3. A list of songs was found at "Al Jarreau Setlist: Blue Note Jazz Club," Setlist.fm, May 14, 2011, https://setlist.fm/setlist/al-jarreau/2011/blue-note-jazz-club-new-york-ny-4384dbdf.html.
4. Berlanga-Ryan, "Al Jarreau: Simple and Necessary Happiness."
5. "The Orchestra," Metropole Orkest, https://mo.nl/en/the-orchestra.
6. Joe Turano, interview with the author, September 2021.
7. This is reported at the African American Registry (https://aaregistry.org/story/al-jarreau-born/) as well as numerous other outlets.
8. Arriale was known as Lynne Bernstein at that time.
9. Kurt Dietrich, *Wisconsin Riffs: Jazz Profiles from the Heartland* (Madison: Wisconsin Historical Society Press, 2018), 113–114. In a conversation in November 2021, Tierney repeated this story in almost the exact same words. Lynne Arriale is also profiled in *Wisconsin Riffs*.
10. Rose Marie Freeman, phone interview with the author, October 2021.
11. Gail Mitchell, "Al Jarreau Salutes George Duke on New Star-Packed Album," *Billboard*, August 8, 2014, https://billboard.com/articles/6207037/al-jarreau-salutes-george-duke-my-old-friend.
12. One other non-Duke tune is on the CD, Jeffrey Osborne's "Wings of Love."
13. "Al Jarreau Announces Two 2017 German Dates with NDR Bigband," https://marshall-arts.com/news-articles/al-jarreau-announces-two-2017-german-dates-with-ndr-bigband.
14. Turano described the process to me in February 2022.
15. This long quote and the following paragraph are from Piet Levy, "Al Jarreau Puts on a Joyful Homecoming Concert at Potawatomi," *Milwaukee Journal Sentinel*, August 22, 2015.
16. Al Jarreau, "We're All in the Arts Together," *Milwaukee Journal Sentinel*, March 18, 2016.
17. This was just the fourth time the award was given; Les Paul received the first award in 2004.

18. Short excerpts from Al's talk appear in the film *Coming Home* from Wisconsin Public Television.

19. Marcus Miller reported that he had previously done International Jazz Days with Al in Paris and Istanbul. Scott Yanow, "Remembering Al Jarreau," *Performances Magazine*, June 2017.

20. "2016 All-Star Gobal Concert," International Jazz Day, https://jazzday .com/global-concert-2016/.

21. Nate Chinen, "Global Flavors and Asides to Obamas at White House Jazz Gala," *New York Times*, April 30, 2016.

22. *Al Jarreau: Coming Home* (Wisconsin Public Television, 2017), unused footage.

23. Lee Mergner, "Never Givin' Up: A No-Holds-Barred Conversation with Al Jarreau," *JazzTimes* 46, no. 7 (September 2016).

24. Information in this paragraph from Joe Gordon, interview with the author, 2021.

25. Gordon's quotes and the quote from Ryan Jarreau in the next paragraph are from *Unsung*, Season 9, Episode 6, "Al Jarreau," produced by Jason B. Ryan, aired April 12, 2020 on TVOne, https://tvone.tv/video/ watch-unsung-al-jarreau/.

26. This clip appeared in *Unsung*, but it had previously appeared in the WPT film *Coming Home*.

27. "The Jazz Cruise 2017 Celebrating Its 16th Sailing Welcomes Al Jarreau," AllAboutJazz.com, July 12, 2016, https://allaboutjazz.com/news/ the-jazz-cruise-2017-celebrating-its-16th-sailing-welcomes-al-jarreau/.

28. Mergner, "Never Givin' Up."

29. Rose Marie Freeman, phone conversation with the author, October 2021.

30. The retirement announcement was made due to a number of complicated and delicate business considerations. *Rolling Stone* quoted Ryan in its obituary of Al, which also listed the "recovering" statement. Despite conflicting information about the last days, I assume that *Rolling Stone*'s sources were correct. Daniel Kreps, "Al Jarreau, Grammy-Winning Jazz Singer, Dead at 76," *Rolling Stone*, February 12, 2017, https://rollingstone .com/music/music-news/al-jarreau-grammy-winning-jazz-singer-dead -at-76-191952/.

31. Joe Turano, phone interview with the author, February 2022.

32. Sandra Moss, phone interview with the author, July 2020.

33. *Unsung*, "Al Jarreau." Joe Turano and Joe Gordon had very similar experiences in the hospital. Joe Turano, interviews with the author, 2021; Joe Gordon, interview with the author, December 2021.

34. *Unsung*, "Al Jarreau."

35. *Unsung*, "Al Jarreau."

36. Christopher Loudon, review of *Al Jarreau and the Metropole Orkest: "Live,"* *JazzTimes*, September 2012.

37. An inspired performance by Al and Hathaway of the standard "Summertime" with George Duke's trio can be seen and heard at https://youtube .com/watch?v=xeOAb2DlarE.

Chapter 25

1. Bobby Reed, "Singer Al Jarreau Dies at 76," *Down Beat*, February 13, 2017, https://downbeat.com/news/detail/singer-al-jarreau-dies-at-76.

2. All Walker quotes in this chapter are from Chris Walker, phone interviews with the author, August 2020 and December 2021.

3. Joe Turano, interview with the author, September 2021.

4. Mark Simmons, email correspondence with the author, January 29, 2022.

5. Joe Gordon, phone interview with the author, 2021.

6. *Al Jarreau L'enchanteur: Un Documentaire Musical de Thierry Guedj*, directed by Thierry Guedj (France: Portrait & Company, aired January 1, 2016, on French O).

7. Mark Simmons, email correspondence with the author, January 29, 2022.

8. *Al Jarreau L'enchanteur*.

9. Bill Darlington, interview with the author, August 15, 2022.

10. Alphaeus Jarreau, phone conversation with the author, May 11, 2020.

11. Sandra Moss, phone interview with the author, July 2020.

12. I had the privilege of being Ryan's host for the weekend. The quoted passage of Ryan's talk is from an in-house recording.

13. All Levin quotes in this chapter, unless otherwise noted, are from Jerry Levin, phone interviews with the author, December 2020 and January 2021.

14. *Unsung*, Season 9, Episode 6, "Al Jarreau," produced by Jason B. Ryan, aired April 12, 2020 on TVOne, https://tvone.tv/video/watch-unsung -al-jarreau/.

15. Joe Turano, interview with the author, June 2021.

16. Esther Berlanga-Ryan, "Al Jarreau: Simple and Necessary Happiness," *All About Jazz*, March 12, 2012, https://allaboutjazz.com/al-jarreau-simple -and-necessary-happiness-al-jarreau-by-esther-berlanga-ryan.php.

17. Michael Paulo, email correspondence with the author, February 2021.

18. While most of this story came from Sandra Moss, there was a brief concert review in the *Los Angeles Times*. Don Heckman, "Jazz Review: A Long, Slow Haul at the 'Trane Festival," *Los Angeles Times*, October 3, 1991, https:// latimes.com/archives/la-xpm-1991-10-03-ca-4500-story.html.

19. "Al Jarreau: Ceaseless Creator of Fresh Sounds in Music," *International Musician*, June 5, 2014.

20. Mary Kane, "Complex Melody: The Joy and Pain of Al Jarreau," *Milwaukee Journal*, July 30, 1989.

21. Jerry Levin, email correspondence with the author, December 16, 2020.

22. Mary Kane, "Complex Melody."

23. Lee Mergner, "Never Givin' Up: A No-Holds-Barred Conversation with Al Jarreau," *JazzTimes* 46, no. 7 (September 2016).

24. Rose Marie Freeman, email correspondence with the author, September 2021.

25. "The Case for Renaming a Milwaukee Street in Honor of Hometown Jazz Legend Al Jarreau," *Milwaukee Independent*, June 24, 2019.

26. This exchange appears in the documentary *Al Jarreau L'enchanteur*.

27. Larry Williams, email correspondence with the author, November 2021.

28. Berlanga-Ryan, "Al Jarreau: Simple and Necessary Happiness."

INDEX

Note: Page numbers in *italics* refer to illustrations.

A. O. Smith Corporation, 2, 10
Abbott, Jim, 254, 256, 257
Abodeely, Joe, 41–42
Abramov, Jan, 286
academics, 23, 24–25, 32, 137
Accentuate the Positive (album), 270–278, 280, 283–284
acting career, 139, 166–167, 246–247
Adams, Bernard, 137
Adams, Oleta, 249, 251
African Americans, Jarreau family as, 5
"After All" (song), 147, 148, 151, 158, 159, 297
After Blue (Sutton Joni Mitchell tribute album), 304
aging, on, 301–302
Ahmad Jamal Trio, 30
Airmen Of Note (service jazz band), 159
Al Jarreau, 1965 (album), 44
Al Jarreau and the Metropole Orkest – Live (album), 302–303, 315–316
Al Jarreau: Coming Home (2017 video), 309
"Al Jarreau" (Davis song), 195, 202
Al Jarreau in London (video), 154, 161
Al Jarreau L'enchanteur (2016 French documentary), 1, 49
Al Jarreau Live in London (album). *See In London* (album)
Al Jarreau: The Very Best Of: An Excellent Adventure (retrospective collection). *See The Very Best Of: An Excellent Adventure* (compilation album)
album sales, 107; *Accentuate the Positive*, 283; *Al Jarreau and the Metropole Orkest – Live*, 316; *All Fly Home*, 103–104; *All I Got*, 265; *Best of Al Jarreau*, 251; *Breakin' Away*, 116; *Givin' It Up*, 285; *Glow*, 85, 88; *Heart's Horizon*, 183; *Heaven and Earth*, 217, 225–226, 235; *High Crime*, 151, 163, 167; *Jarreau* album, 140, 155; *L is Lover*, 173; *In London*, 170; *Look to the Rainbow*, 87–88, 94; *Love Songs*, 289; *My Old Friend: Celebrating George Duke*, 317; *Tenderness*, 234; *This Time*, 112–113; *Tomorrow Today*, 258; *The Very Best Of: An Excellent Adventure*, 293; *We Got By*, 78, 81
albums, compilation. *See* compilation albums
albums, delayed release of: *Al Jarreau, 1965*, 44; in Germany, 80–81; *Live at Montreux 1993*, 112, 234, 237–238; *Live at the Half/Note 1965, volume 1*, 47, 50, 301; *Tomorrow Today*, 253, 258
albums, deluxe editions of: *Heart's Horizon*, 185; *L Is for Lover*, 163, 173, 183, 203; *In London*, 100, 152–154, 161–162
albums, unreleased, 219, 306, 312
Ali funeral, 327
All About Jazz website, 257, 278
All Fly Home (album), 102–106, *103*
All I Got (album), 261–266, 269
"All or Nothing at All" (song), 176, 183, 185, 186
Allen, Steve, 58
Allis-Chalmers Manufacturing Company, 2

Allman, Kevin, 213
AllMusic.com, 257, 269
Ally McBeal (TV show), 206
"Alonzo" (song), 112, 124, 206, 238, 307
Alsou (Alsou Ralifovna Abramova), 286
Anderson, Al, 304
Arrested Development (band), 224–226
arts education, 307–309
Ashley-Farrand, Thomas "Duffy," 26, 27, 28, *28*
Ashti Meets Birdman Al (Rubin book), 292
Asian Americans, 151
athletics, Al and, 21–23, 24, 26, *27*
Aunt Fanny's Cabin (soul food restaurant), *114*
Avedon, Richard (photographer), 112, 113
Azinger, Marshall "Gus," 37, 39

Bacharach, Burt, 191–192
Badger Boys State, 20–21, *21*, 24
Bainbridge Records, 44
Baird, Larry, 293–294
Barrett, Tom, 309
Barros, Paul de, 273
baseball, 22–23
basketball, 24, 26, *27*
Battle, Kathleen, 230–231
beauty pageants, 37
Beduhn, Bob, 18
Belafonte, Harry, 17, 60, 194–195
Bell, Bill, 40
The Beltones (quintet), 19
Benjamin, Richard, 193
Benson, George, 53, 129, 144, 164, 200–201, 208, 265, 280–283, *281*, 285, 286
Bergen-Belsen concentration camp, 131
Berigan, Kaye, 35
Berklee School/College of Music (Boston), 70, 213, 252
Berlin, Germany, 86
Best of Al Jarreau (album), 239, *240*, 250–251
Bet Cha Say That to All the Girls (Sister Sledge album), 192, 202
big-band album idea, 246
Billboard, 137, 267, 294. *See also* album sales

Bla Bla Café (Los Angeles club), 56, 66–68, *68*, 71–73, 78, 95, 96
The Black Collegian, 122–123
Blessing, Lynn, 85, 94, 102, 105, 154
Bloom, Steve, 120–122, 127, 134, 135
"Blue in Green" (Davis/Evans song), 216–217, 219, 221, 223
Blue Note (New York City club), 301
"Blue Rondo à la Turk" (Brubeck song), 118, 293
Bock, Peter: on Al's character, 325; on Emile Jarreau, Jr., 12; and the Indigos, 26–27, 28, *28*, 29, 31, 138; on Pearl Jarreau's death, 39
Body Heat (Jones album), 187, 201
Bolton, Ross, 248, 249, 258, 261–262, 298
"Boogie Down" (song), 140, 142–143, 156, 157, 160–161, 162, 235, 251, 278
Boom-Boom Room (Red Carpet Inn, Milwaukee), 38
Borders, James, 122–123
Bortolussi, Dick, 60, *61*, 63
Bottomley, Maurice, 264, 274
Brazilian album idea, 246
BRE Music Report, 219
Breakin' Away (album), 113–120, *117*, 125–126, 143–144
Bream, Jon, 138–139
Breeden, Leon, 70
Bremen, Germany, 131
Broadway, music of, 17, 19, 49, 94, 230, 244–245. *See also West Side Story* songs
Broomberg, Glen, *263*
Brown, Paul, 250, 254, 257, 261
Brubeck, Dave, 87, 94, 118, 206, 260. *See also* Dave Brubeck Quartet
Bullock, Hiram, 197–198, 203
Burk, John, 318
Burnett, T-Bone, 70

cabasa/shekere, 71, 206
Caesars Palace (Las Vegas, NV), 213–214
Calandrelli, Jorge, 291
Calderon, John, *279*
California, Al's move to, 45
California, State of, Al's work for as rehabilitation counselor, 45–46, 54

Calvary Baptist Church (Milwaukee), 16, 17
Canning, Tom, *110*; on album producers, 107; and *All Fly Home*, 103–104, 105, 106; on *All I Got*, 261; and *Breakin' Away*, 125–126; childhood and history, 69–71; on Ertegun, 73; and *Glow*, 92–93; on Graydon, 108–109; on *Jarreau*, 156–157; on larger venues, 99, 100; and *Look to the Rainbow*, 93–94; at Montreux Jazz Festival, 84–85; on music of late 1970s and early 1980s, 144; and music videos, 118–119; on need for change in mid-1980s, 145–146; performances with Al, 79–80; as producer, 126, 140; roles on *We Got By*, 90–91; on "Roof Garden," 116; and *This Time*, 110, 111, 124; and Warner Bros. contract, 76; on *We Got By* lyrics, 78; and "We're in This Love Together," 115
Carlton, Larry, 92
Carnegie Hall (New York City), 247
Carpenter, Dave, 298
Carr, Jack, 35–36
Carry On (Purim album), 189–190, 202
"Carry On" (Purim song), 189–190
Carter, Maxwell, 10–11, 12, 19, 20, 22–23, 59
Casino Lights (album), 191, 202
Catania, Jim, 20
CBS New Year's Eve show, 168
Cecchi, Al, 48
Cedars-Sinai Medical Center, 313, 315
Central Park (Huntington Beach, CA), 280
Chambers, Gordon, 219–220
Checker, Chubby, 246
Cheeks, Thomas, 20, 25
Chic (band), 170
Chicago Theatre (concert venue), 220
Chicago Tribune, 166, 180, 215–216, 220
choir membership, at Lincoln High School, 18
choir room at the Rodman Center for the Arts (Ripon College), 136–137, *137*
Chong, Robbie, *171*, 172

Christensen, Thor, 224–226
Christian Science Monitor, 247–248
Christmas (album), 290–292, *290*, 298
Chur, Elizabeth, 180, 215–216
Circle Star Theatre (San Carlos, CA), 213
City Heat (film), 192–193, 202
City Rhythm (Shakatak album), 195–196, 202
Clark, Douglas, 104–105
Clarke/Duke Project (band), 316
Clayton, Kenton, 142
clothing for performances, 130
Cocker, Joe, 261
Cole, Nat King, 17, 164–167, 169, 184, 233, 262
Coleman, Ornette, 249
Collins, Felicia, 205
Collins, Phil, 213
Coltrane, John, 230
Columbia Records, 30, 31
Commercial Appeal (Memphis newspaper), 219
compilation albums. See *Best of Al Jarreau* (album); *Love Songs* (compilation album); *The Very Best Of: An Excellent Adventure* (compilation album)
Concord Records, 280–281, 289, 302, 318
Conover, Willis, 33
Cooke, Sam, 197–198
Corbett, John, 273
Corea, Chick, 71, 111–112, 125, 188, 201
Correro, Joe, 64, 66, 74, 85, 90, 92, 94, 102, 105
Costa Mesa, CA, 210–211
Counts of Rhythm (quartet), 16
cover photos. See *specific album names*
Crawford, Randy, 191
Crimson (Ripon College yearbook), 29
The Crossing (Deodato album), 295, 299–300
crowds, performing for, 99–100
Crown Room (Pfister Hotel), 58, *59*
Cuban Missile Crisis, 52
Cunningham, Isabella, 5
Curaçao concert, 311
CYO bowling alley, 3
Czimber, Lazlo "Les," 29, 33–36, 37, 44, 45, 260

Da Costa, Paulinho, 105, 185, 227, 230, 234, 269

The Daily Iowan (Iowa City), 40, 42

Dane County Coliseum (Madison), 175

Dangerfield, Rodney, 57–58

Darlington, Bill: end as manager, 283; as manager, 242–243, 250, 253, 256, 271, 275, 278–279, 321

Dave Brubeck Quartet, 30. *See also* Brubeck, Dave

Dave Kennedy Studios (Milwaukee recording studios), 43

Davenport, N'dea, 205

Davis, Debbie, 259, 280

Davis, Miles, 47, 49, 64, 195, 200, 202, 216, 223

"Day by Day" (song), 196

Daylie, Daddy-O (Chicago deejay), 17

demo recordings, 55, 62, 64, 68–69, 72, 164, 231

Deodato, Eumir, 295, 299–300

The Depot (Minneapolis club), 60, 62, 63

Der Spiegel, 83–84

Deutscher Schallplattenpreis (later the Echo Award), 78

DeVillers, Ron, 18, 36–37, 309

Dick Tracy (film), 199–200, 203

Die Philharmonie (Berlin, Germany), 287–288

Dietrich, Kurt (author), 331

Dietrich, Maria Kaiser (author's wife), 331

Dino's Lodge (Los Angeles club), 55

"Dinosaur" (song), 231

disco music, 279

divorce, from Phyllis Hall, 42

Do the Right Thing (film), 198–199, 203

"Do What You Do" (Moran song), 189

Doebel, Steven, 2, 310

Doky Brothers 2 (Doky Brothers album), 249, 252

doo-wop, 17, 18

Dorothy Chandler Pavilion (Los Angeles), 212

Dorough, Bob, 273

Double Six of Paris (band), 28

Double Vision (Sanborn/James album), 169, 196–197, 203, 250

Douglas, Mike, 58

Down Beat: 1982 Bloom profile, 127, 134, 135; on "Al Jarreau" tune, 195; on albums, 44, 81, 88–90, 104–105, 272–275, 282; feature articles on Al, 82–83, 97–99, 120–122, 182, 185, 276; interviews in, 10, 49, 105, 255–256; on performances, 74; record label quote about Al's death, 318

Downs, Joan, 82

Drew, Michael, 58–60

Driftwood Lounge (Milwaukee club), 29, 32, 33–36, 34

drum machine sounds, 115, 145, 146, 158, 261

Drysdale, Don, 34

duck sounds, 22

Duke, George, 47; on Al and women, 57; and album release in 2011, 301; and "Alonzo," 124; childhood and history, 46–47; death of, 304; on the Half Note, 49; on improvisation, 53; *My Old Friend* (2014 tribute album), 118, 304–305, 316–317; as producer, 176, 185, 189–190, 192, 239; and "Roof Garden," 116–117. *See also* George Duke Trio

Dworsky, Richard "Junior," 60–64, 61, 66–67, 71, 76–77, 96

earthquake, 239–240

East, Nathan, 140, 146, 148, 154, 158, 160, 161

Eastman School of Music, 69

Eastwood, Clint, 193

Ebsen, Kiki, 206

Edelstein, Paula, 269

education, as important focus, 11, 19

Edwards, Bernard, 170

Edwards, Blake, 192–193

Elfman, Danny, 199–200

Elling, Kurt, 268, 328–329

Ellington, Duke, 27, 305–306

Entertainment Weekly, 219–220

Epic Records, 72, 73

Erkilla, Jack, 38, 43

Ertegun, Ahmet, 73, 213

Essence magazine, 176, 178

Estes, Simon, 40
Eugene O'Neill Theatre (New York
    City), 246
European tours: 1976, 80; 1977, 84–85,
    86, 131; 1989, 206–207; 2000,
    258, 260; 2007, 287–288; 2010,
    294–296; 2012, 288; and NDR
    Bigband, 306, 312; and support of
    international audience, 278
Evans, Bill, 216, 223
"Excellent Adventure" (song), 300
exercise regimen, 130–131

Fargo, ND, showcase, 62
Farmer, Patty, 56, 57
Feather, Leonard, 18
female fans, 59–60, 135–136, 230
Festival International de Jazz de
    Montréal, 258
Fingerhut, Allan, 60
Fischer, Clare and Brent, 291
Flack, Roberta, 86
Fleming, Peggy (figure skater), 55
Floyd, George, 199
The Follies, 18–19
Forest Lawn Memorial Park (Hollywood
    Hills, CA), 319
Fort Lauderdale News/Sun-Sentinel, 168
Foster, David, 107–108, 147, 156
Freddie Freeloader (Hendricks album),
    200–201, 203
Free Speech movement, 52
Freeman, Rose Marie (née Jarreau),
    5, 17, 266; on Al and music, 16;
    and Al's health, 313; birth of, 7;
    on birth of Ryan, 168; on female
    fans, 135–136; on Jarreau family
    economic situation, 12; on Pearl's
    death, 39; phone call to, 304; on
    racial issues, 9, 327
Frost, David, 58
"Fun and Fancy" (1957 Follies show), 18
fusion (musical genre), 49, 143,
    196–197, 251, 272

Gadd, Steve, 124, 125–126, 144, 219,
    227, 228, 234, 237
Gale, Eric, 227, 237
Gassama, Malando, 154, 161

Gatsby's (Sausalito, CA, club), 53, 54, 55
Gayle, Jackie, 56
George Duke Trio, 47, 48, 49, 50, 301.
    See also Duke, George
Germany, Al in, 83–84
Gibbs, Leonard "Doc," 205, 206, 210
Gillan, Bill, 33
Gilmore, Mikal, 88–90
"Girls Know How" (song), 192
Give It What U Got (Bullock album),
    197–198, 203
Givin' It Up (album), 280–281, 285
Glatman, Bruce, 62–63
Glow (album), 79–82, 81, 84, 86,
    92–93, 107
'Go Away, Little Girl' (song), 229
"God's Gift to the World" (song), 256,
    257
gold record, Al's first, 110
Gold Star Studio, 55
Goldings, Larry, 298
Goldstein, Gil, 245, 249, 293–294
Golson, Benny, 292, 299
Goodman, Marilyn, 62
Goodwin, Penny, 18
Gordon, Joe, 294, 302, 303, 312, 313,
    320
Görg, Galyn, 148
Gosa, Jim, 77
Graff, Gary, 163–164, 167
Grammy Awards: for All Fly Home,
    103, 105; for Breakin' Away, 117,
    119–120, 120; for Givin' It Up,
    282; for Heart's Horizon, 177, 185;
    for Heaven and Earth, 215, 217,
    224–225; Live nomination, 303;
    for Look to the Rainbow, 86, 87; for
    "We Are the World," 194
grave marker, 319
Gray, Wardell, 28
Graydon, Jay, 110; and Al as jazz singer,
    113, 182; and albums, 111, 113, 117,
    124, 144, 147, 157; as producer,
    108–110, 125, 140, 145, 164, 171,
    176, 185; and songs, 115–116;
    venues, large, compared to smaller
    clubs, 90
Grease revival, 246
Greek Theatre (Los Angeles venue), 101

Green Point Stadium (South Africa), 262

Grier, Rosey, 58

GRP/Arista (record label), 253

GRP/Verve (record label). *See* Verve Records

Grusin, David, 90–91, 253

guest appearances, 187–203, 244, 249–250, 251–252, 299–300

Gurda, John, 9

Haight-Ashbury (San Francisco), 48, 229

Half Note (San Francisco club), 47, *47*, 48–50, 57, 301

Hall, Phyllis, 42, *43*, 54, 95

Halyard Park (Milwaukee neighborhood), 8, 9

Hancock, Herbie, 206

Harrison, Lou, 244

Hassler, Ann, 27, 30, 31, 309

Hatfield, Larry, 40

Heard, John, 48

Heart's Horizon (album), 175–178, *177*, 182, 185–186

Heaven and Earth (album), 214–223, *215*, 224

Heckman, Don, 210–211, 231–233, 239–242, 250

Hedlund, Dik, 60, *61*, 63

Hefner, Hugh, and jazz music, 56

Hendricks, Jon, 200–201, 203, 255, 269, 281, 299, 328–329

Henry L. Palmer School, 3, 19

Henry Maier Festival Park (Milwaukee), 133

Hey, Jerry, 124, 126, 155, 156, 158, 268

The Hi Fis (quintet), 18

Higgins, Dan, 298

Higgins, Jim, 30–31

High Crime (album), 146–151, *149*, 158–159, 163–164

High Fidelity, 77

hip-hop and rap music, 213–214, 218, 224, 235, 279, 300

Holden, Stephen, 208, 220–221, 247

Holdridge, Lee, 172

Holiday House (Milwaukee club), 36

Hollywood Walk of Fame star, 260

"The Hot Box" (*Down Beat* feature), 273

"Hot News Blues" (Corea song), 188–189

Howard, Joan, 31–32

Hubbard, Freddie, 103, 106, 190–191, 202

Husney, Owen, 62

"I Keep Callin'" (song), 157

"I Love What We Make Together" (song), 195

I Loved You Then . . . I Love You Now (Moran album), 189, 202

Imboden, Tris, 205

Improv comedy club, 58

improvisations: on *All I Got*, 269; on *Breakin' Away*, 125; on Corea *Secret Agent*, 188; on European tours, 206, 207; on *Heaven and Earth*, 222; Holden on, 208, 221; on *Jarreau* album, 156; on *Live at Montreux 1993*, 237; on *Look to the Rainbow*, 86–87, 94; on *Tenderness*, 236; on *This Time*, 124; on *Tomorrow Today*, 267–268

In London (album), 147, 152–154, *153*, 160–162

Indianapolis Star, 135, 209

The Indigos, 26–31, *28*, 32, 52, 138, 312

Infusino, Divina, 133–134

International Jazz Day, 310

International Musician, 324–325

Internationales Congress Centrum (Berlin venue), *128*

interracial marriages, 327

Iowa, University of, 1, 35, 36, 39–44

"Iowa record" (album), 44, 50, 304

"Jacaranda Bougainvillea" (song), 261–262

Jackson, Michael (musician), 118, 154, 188, 193, 205, 259, 261

Jackson, Michael (reviewer), 282

Jacobs, Jay, 127

Jacobs, Sheldon "Shelly," 60, 62–63

James, Bob, 52, 196–197, 203

James, Boney, 249–250, 252

Jarreau (album), 140–144, *144*, 155–157

Jarreau (band), 60–61, *61*, 62–65, *63*

Jarreau, Al: on aging, 301–302; in album cover photos, 77, *81*, *87*, *113*, *117*, *144*, *149*, *153*, *171*, *215*,

228, 240, 289, 290, 293; athletic
endeavors of, 21–23, 27; birth of,
7; complex nature of his character,
325–326; in concert photos, 56, 63,
68, 101, 128, 141, 279, 281, 288, 311;
death of, 315, 318, 319; difficulty
categorizing, 1, 72–73, 82, 84, 221,
272, 276–277, 328–329; family
of, 5–17, 17, 43, 218, 266; health
problems of, 267, 291, 294–296,
303, 311; musical knowledge of,
28–29; musical style of, 179–180,
182–183, 219–220, 264–265, 269,
270–276, 321; in photos, 7, 11, 17,
21, 27, 28, 43, 61, 110, 114, 120,
137, 139, 181, 194, 218, 263, 266,
331; positive attitude of, 2, 20, 140,
142, 179, 208, 224–226, 233, 284,
306–307, 321–322; spirituality
of, 3, 97–98, 322, 323–324; vocal-
instrumental sounds of, 20, 58,
59, 89, 132, 133, 175, 211. See also
album sales; single sales; and specific
album and song titles
Jarreau, Alphaeus, 7, 9, 10, 12, 14, 17,
218, 321
Jarreau, Edythe, 6, 6, 13
Jarreau, Emile Alphonse "Emile the
First," 5
Jarreau, Emile, III, 7, 12, 17, 39–40, 218
Jarreau, Emile, Jr. "Emile the Second,"
5, 6, 6, 7, 9–10, 13–14, 16, 17
Jarreau, Ida Perry, 5
Jarreau, Joyce, 7, 17
Jarreau, Marshall, 17, 218; on Al's death,
315; birth of, 7; on family economic
situation, 12; on father, 10, 14; on
running with Al, 22; on "We Got
By" song, 76; on West Side Story
songs, 37
Jarreau, Pearl Walker, 5, 6, 6, 7, 13–14,
16, 17, 39
Jarreau, Rose Marie. See Freeman, Rose
Marie (née Jarreau)
Jarreau, Ryan, 168, 181, 184, 312, 313,
315, 322
Jarreau, Susan Player, 181; and Al's
female fans, 135–136; and Al's
health, 315; and Al's singing, 288;
background and marriage to Al,

95–97, 96; birth of Ryan, 168;
and Christmas, 290; Chur on, 180;
and Darlington, 283; death of,
315; and esophageal cancer, 311;
Robinson on, 243
Jarreau family, 5–17, 17, 43, 218
jazz critics, on pop music, 82
jazz cruises, 313
jazz fusion, 49, 143, 196–197, 251, 272
Jazz Review, 262, 263–264
The Jazz Singer skit, 121
jazz singers and jazz singing, 82, 179; Al
as, 18, 182–183, 235, 269, 272–273,
276, 280; Al on, 16, 275; Bloom on,
121; Clark on, 104; Gilmore on, 89;
Golson on, 292; Rains on, 83; and
Warner Bros., 102–103
jazz vocalist competition, Al as judge
for, 260
Jazz West, 64
Jazziz, 178, 319
JazzTimes: articles in, 231–233, 279; on
International Jazz Day celebration,
310; interviews in, 281, 295–296,
313; "Opening Chorus" feature,
277–278; reviews in, 208–209,
238, 282–283, 316
Jensen, Gail, 27, 30, 31
Jet (magazine), 166
Jewish Community Center (Milwaukee),
18, 22
jogging, 130–131
John Coltrane Festival (Los Angeles),
324
Johnson, Buddy, 197, 231
Johnson, Charles "Icarus," 154, 160, 248
Johnson, Jimmy, 35
Jones, James T., IV, 230–231, 234–235
Jones, Quincy, 30, 187–188, 201
Joyce, Mike, 245
JVC Jazz Festival, 247

Kane, Mary, 183, 326
Keller, Jörg Achim, 305–306
Kelley, David E., 205–206
Kennedy, John F., 34, 52
Kennedy Center (Washington, DC), 245
Kermit the Frog, 168
Kiev, Ukraine, 279
Kilbourn Reservoir Park (Milwaukee), 19

"Killer Love" (song), 186
Klemmer, John, 71
Klugh, Earl, 112, 124, 177, 180, 185
Koch, Robert, 246
Kodrich, Kris, 175
Krall, Diana, 254, 271

L Is for Lover (album), 170–174, 171,
    183–184
"L is for Lover" (song), 171, 173, 183, 184
LA Free Press (underground newspaper),
    73
The Labor Temple (Twin Cities club), 62
Laboriel, Abraham "Abe," 85–86, 94,
    124, 125–126, 185
Lambert, Hendricks & Ross (vocal
    group), 27–28, 50, 83–84, 255
Larsen, Neil, 191, 204–205, 207, 227,
    248
Las Vegas Review-Journal, 213, 224
Laurel Canyon (Los Angeles), 63–64
Lazaroff, Michael, 313
Lee, Bill, 199
Lee, Leslie, 113–114
Lee, Peggy, 55
Lee, Spike, 198–199
Lee, Wayne, 178–181
Leviev, Milcho, 118
Levin, Jerry, 114; on albums, 94, 148,
    164; on Al's character, 134–135,
    322, 325; and Alsou, 286; on
    concert power outage, 324; and
    Laboriel, 85–86; as lighting
    designer at the Troubador, 74–75;
    on new musicians, 174; on songs,
    113–115, 172; as tour manger, 103,
    129–131, 136
Levy, Piet, 306–307
Levy, Ramon, 18
Lewis, James, 114–115
Lewis, Jerry, 34
"Like a Lover" (song), 239, 250–251
Lilies of the Field (Poitier film), 91
Lincoln Center of the Arts (middle
    school), 4
Lincoln High School, 3, 18, 20, 132
LiPuma, Tommy: about reunion with
    Al, 253–254, 257, 258; and Ostin,
    75; as producer, 92, 93, 107, 162,
    271, 275, 284; and We Got By, 91

literacy issues, 265–267
Live (highlight album), 302–303,
    315–316
live albums. See In London (album); Look
    to the Rainbow (album); Tenderness
    (album)
Live at Montreux 1993 (album), 234,
    237–238
Live at the Half/Note 1965, volume 1
    (album), 47, 50
Live in London (2010 deluxe CD), 162
Live in London (album). See In London
    (album)
live performances, 127–139, 204–211,
    212, 235, 259–260, 262, 278–280,
    286–288
live performances vs. studio recordings,
    152, 153, 184, 207, 232, 236–237,
    242
Look to the Rainbow (album), 86–90, 87,
    93–94, 107, 131, 154
Los Angeles Times, 210, 213, 239–242
"Lost and Found" (song), 261
Lou Harrison: A Portrait (album), 244,
    251
Loudon, Christopher, 316
The Love Connection (Hubbard album),
    190–191, 202
Love Songs (compilation album),
    288–290, 289, 297
Lubbock, Jeremy, 157
Lucas, Arno, 258–259, 261–262
Lyle, Bobby, 148, 154, 160
Lynch, Kevin, 133

MacArthur, Paul, 255–256
Mack, Ted, 14
Macnie, Jim, 273
Madison Square Garden (New York
    City), 220–221
Mahavishnu Orchestra (band), 214
Manchester, Melissa, 196, 202
Mancini, Henry, 30, 178, 186
Mandela, Nelson, 262, 263
Mandela, Zindzi, 263
Manhattan Transfer, 86, 108, 168
Maples, Tina, 174–175
Marcus family, 35
Marshall, Harlene, 44
Martin, Dean, 55

Martinez, Julio: on Al's David Frost appearance, 58; in band Jarreau, 60, *61*, 65; at the Bla Bla Café, *56*, 66–67; "Brazilian period," 305; childhood and history, 51–52; on Duke, 46; and *Glow* songs, 79; musical history with Al, 53–57; on Playboy Bunnies' interest in Al, 57; on rock clubs, 60

"Mas Que Nada" (song), 229–230

Mathieson, Greg, 74, 124, 143, 219

Mathis, Johnny, 17, 34, 44, 208, 221, 265

McBride, Christian, 271, 273, 310

McBride, Reggie, 102, 105

McCann, Les, 73, 74

McCartney, David, 40

McDonough, John, 272–273, 276

McFerrin, Bobby, 176–177, 180, 200, 207, 262–263, 268, 282

McRae, Carmen, 34–35

Mecca Lounge (Santa Clara, CA), 45

Meir, Golda, 9

Mel Marcus Trio, 18

Mendoza, Vince, 303, 315

Mergner, Lee, 295–296, 310–311, 313, 327

Metropole Orkest (Dutch orchestra), 302–303, 315–316

Mike Blahowski's Polka Tavern, 3, 8

Miles Ahead documentary, 195

Milkowski, Bill, 132

"Millennium Bug," 253

Miller, Marcus: on Al's musical style, 123, 321; and *Live at Montreux*, 234, 237, 238; and *My Old Friend*, 305, 317; on songs, 116, 142, 228; and *Tenderness*, 226, 227, 228, 230, 231; and unreleased album, 219; on working with Al, 322–323

Miller, Mulgrew, 274

Miller, Ron, 262, 263–264

"Million Dollar Baby" (song), 193

"Milwaukee" (song), 92

Milwaukee, WI, 1–4, 7–8, 33–36, 58, 132–134, 224–226, 306–307

Milwaukee Braves, 23, 173

Milwaukee High School for the Arts, 4

Milwaukee Independent, 328

Milwaukee Journal: articles in, 38, 224–226, 325, 326; photo from national anthem performance, 138, *139*; reviews in, 58–60, 132, 133–134, 151, 174; and sports, 23

Milwaukee Journal Magazine, 183

Milwaukee Journal Sentinel, 306–307

Milwaukee Magazine, 37

Milwaukee Public Schools, 309

Milwaukee Sentinel, 23, 38

Minneapolis Star, 64, 138

Minneapolis Star and Tribune, 138–139

Minor, Rickey, 205, 206–207, 209, 211, 248

The Minstrel Show (San Francisco Mime Troupe), 53

Mississippi Burning (film), 180–181

Mitchell, Chuck, 81–82

Mitchell, Gail, 265–266

Modderno, Craig, 143

Monk, Thelonious, 200

Monterose, J. R., 40–41

Montréal concert, 259–260

Montreux Jazz Festival (Switzerland), 71, 84–85, 191, 212, 234, 260

"Moonlighting" (song), 164, 172–173, 183, 203, 250, 293, 313

Moonlighting (TV soundtrack), 172–173, 203, 250

moonwalk, 154, 161

Moran, Gayle, 188, 189, 202

Morelli, Jota, 248, 249, 258, 261–262

Moriera, Airto, 190

"Mornin'" (song), 140–142, *141*, *319*

Morning Call (Allentown, PA), 244

Moss, Sandra, 313–314, 321–322, 324

Mountain Winery (Saratoga, CA), 212

MTV music videos, 88, 118

Murph, John, 277–278

Murrah, Roger, 114, 115

music as ministry, 3, 10, 99

"The Music of Goodbye" (song), 196, 202

music videos, 87–88, 118–119, 142–143, 148–150. *See also specific video names*

musical saw, 13–14, 16

Musikhalle (Hamburg, Germany), 86

"My Favorite Things" (song), 230, 236

My Old Friend: Celebrating George Duke (album), 305, 316–317

Nachwuchskünstler prize, 78
Nager, Larry, 219
The Nat King Cole Story (film), 164–167, 169
national anthem performances, 138, *139*, 287
National Symphony Orchestra, 245
NDR Bigband, 287–288, 305–306
NDR radio (Norddeutscher Rundfunk), 80
"Never Explain Love" (song), 199
New Orleans, Louisiana, 5
New Time, New 'Tet (Golson album), 292, 299
New York City concerts, 120–121, 207–209, 220–221, 247, 301
New York Times, 208, 247, 310
Newport Jazz Festival, 248
niche music, 49, 163, 328
Niehaus, Lennie, 193
"Night on the Town" event, the Indigos at, 29
Night Shift (film), 191–192, 202
Norddeutscher Rundfunk (NDR) Bigband, 287–288, 305–306, 312
Norddeutscher Rundfunk (NDR) radio, 80
North Sea Jazz Festival, 212, 260, 311
North Texas State University (NTSU), 70
Northern Lights Theater (Potawatomi Casino in Milwaukee), 306
Northrop Auditorium (Minneapolis), 138–139
Notre Dame Collegiate Jazz Festival (1962), 30–31, 39, 52
Novecento (band), 295, 300

Oakwood Junior College (Huntsville, AL), 5–6
Obama, Barack and Michelle, 309–310
O'Bee, Emile, 9
Obejas, Achy, 220
Oberholtzer, Donna, 27, 28, *28*
Oehler, Dale, 41, 92
Offenburg, Germany, 206
Ogerman, Claus, 190
On Broadway Theater (San Francisco), 51, 53
One Night in Miami (film), 198

One World Theatre (Austin, TX, venue), 312
Onkel Pö (Hamburg, Germany, venue), 80
Orlando Sentinel, 163–164, 254, 256
Oshkosh, WI, 37, 38, 136
Oshkosh Daily Northwestern, 23, 37, 39, 136
Oslo, Norway, 131
Ostin, Mo, 75
Out of Africa (film), 196, 202

Pabst Theater (Milwaukee), 6
Page, Richard, 108, 118, 147, 156, 162, 184, 305
Palais des Sports (Paris venue), *141*
Palazzo dello Sport (Rome venue), 206
Paskevich, Michael, 213–214, 224
Patrick, Diane, 208–209
Paulo, Michael, 150–151, 160–161, 204, 205, 206, 211, 323
Paulsen, Pat, 62
People magazine, 95, 96–97, 180
performance anxiety, 99–102, 137
Pesante, Kaiyoti, 286–287
Pfister Hotel (Milwaukee), 1–2, 35–36, 37, 38, 58–60, 308, 309
Pierson, Matt, 240, 241
Playboy Club circuit, 56–57
Playboy Jazz Festival, 235
Playboy Swings (Farmer), 56
Player, Susan Elaine. *See* Jarreau, Susan Player
politics, Al on, 310–311
Ponti, Carlo, 96
PopMatters.com, 264, 274
Prächt, Gregor, 245–246
A Prairie Home Companion, 61
Prince (musician), 62
"Puddit (Put It Where You Want It)" (song), 237–238, 256
Purim, Flora, 189–190, 202

R&B albums, *Heaven and Earth* as, 218
racial equality, in songs, 256, 292
racial issues: Al on, 181–182, 310–311, 326, 327; Al's lyrics and, 78; and car choices, 287; Cole and, 165; a concern for Al's father, 21; in *Do the Right Thing*, 199; in Milwaukee, 9,

36, 117; and radio stations, 143; in "Raging Waters" video, 149–150; as student at Ripon College, 25–26
racial makeup of concert audiences, 35, 134, 220
Radio City Music Hall (New York City), 207–209
"Raging Waters" (song), 147, 162
"Raging Waters" video, 149–151, 154, 205
Rainey, Khalif J., 328
Rains, Patrick: on album producers, 107–108, 173; and albums, 44, 78, 85, 94, 110, 120, 226; on Al's musical style, 83, 84, 123; and Al's tours, 127; on larger venues, 99–100; as manager, 67–69, 72, 147, 242–243; and *The Nat King Cole Story* film, 164–165; on promotion of Al's career, 78–79; and public relations, 182; on record companies, 73, 75–76; and videos, 118, 151; and "We're in This Love Together," 115
Randy Watson Experience (band), 300
rap music and hip-hop, 213–214, 218, 224, 235, 279, 300
Ravel, Freddie, 248, 249, 254, 258, 259, 261–262, 267, 273, 274, 284, 285, 300
Raynard (record label), 43
Reagoso, Joe, 173–174
record companies, artists and, 240, 241–242
recordings released much later. *See* albums, delayed release of; singles, delayed release of
Redding, Otis, 230
Reed, Gene, 205
Reeves, Dianne, 316
rehabilitation counselor, career as, 3, 45–46, 54
religion, Al's education in, 131
religious experience, performing as, 232–233
religious feeling about life, 97–98, 99, 112
Reservoir, Inc. (publishing company), 19
Reynolds, Burt, 193

Rhino Records (record label), 289, 290, 292–293
"Rhythm-a-ning" (song), 200–201
Rimson, Jerome, 80
Ripon, WI. *See* Badger Boys State; Ripon College
Ripon College: Al as student at, 1, 24–32, 35; Al on, 312; author's representation of, 309; awards granted by, 136–138, 322; benefit concert at, 287, *288*; sports at, 23, 27
Ripon College Days, 24, 25, 26, 31–32
Ritenour, Lee, 249, 251
Robinson, Theresa, 243
Rock in Rio Festival, 164
Rodgers, Nile, 170–171, 172, 173, 174, 184
Rolling Stone, 313
"Rompin' and Stompin'" (song), 200
"Roof Garden" (song), 116, 117, 118–119, 125, 162, 211, 251
roomers, in Jarreau family home, 12
Ross, Annie, 28
"(Round, Round, Round) Blue Rondo à la Turk" (song), 118, 125, 293
Rubin, Carmen, 292
Ruffin, Mark, 274, 275, 276
running, 130–131
Russell, Brenda, 312

Saifer, Lorne, 73–74
Saisse, Philippe, 174, 177–178, 180, 183–184, 185, 227, 234, 238
Salle Pleyel (Paris venue), 86
Sample, Joe, 92, 198, 203, 219, 227, 234, 236, 238, 257, 288
San Francisco, CA, 46, 48, 51–53
San Francisco Mime Troupe, 52–53
Sanborn, David, 42, 129, 174–175, 176, 180, 182, 191, 196–197, 203, 227, 228, 234
Santa Barbara Bowl (CA), 210
Santa Monica Civic Auditorium, 100
Santella, Jim, 280
Sardino's (Milwaukee club), 36
Sargeant, Stan, *279*
Saturday Night Live (TV show), 79–80
"Save Your Love for Me" (song), 231
"Says" (song), 184

scat singing: in Al's early life, 16, 35, 55, 63; Jon Hendricks on, 201, 328–329; critics' and reviewers' comments on, 82–83, 88, 104, 132, 138, 175, 209, 220, 235, 272–273, 307; on "Spain (I Can Recall)," 111–112; on *Tenderness*, 236
Schaid, Tim, 2
Scheck, Frank, 247–248
Schlitz brewery, 2
Schmitt, Al, 72, 75, 90, 91, 92, 93, 105, 107
Schnitzer, Bobby, 60, 61, *61*, 62, 63, 64
scholarship, loss of, 24–25
Schuster's Department Store (Milwaukee), 2
Scientology, 189
Scotch Mist (Twin Cities venue), 62
Scott, Jill, 282
SCTV Network 90 (NBC late-night show), 121
Sculley, Alan, 243, 244, 245–247
Seawind (band), 150, 155
Secret Agent (Corea album), 188, 201
Seventh-day Adventists, 5, 7, 9–10, 15, 121
Severinsen, Doc, 57
Shakatak (band), 195–196, 202
Shankman, Ned, 63
Sharpe, John, 257
shekere/cabasa, 71, 206
Shepard, Vonda, 205–206, 208, 209
Shepherd, Cybill (actress), 172
"She's Leaving Home" (song), 104, 106, 229, 236, 237
sideman, Al as. See guest appearances
Simmons, Mark, 260–261, 272, *279*, 284, 291, 320, 321
Simpson, Donnie, 216–218, 224
"Since I Fell for You" (song), 197, 251
single sales: "Boogie Down," 140; "Moonlighting," 173; "Mornin,'" 140; songs from *High Crime*, 147; songs from *Jarreau* album, 140; "We're in This Love Together," 119
singles, delayed release of, 164, 173
SIR studios, 86, 227
Sister Sledge (band), 170, 192, 202
smoking habit, 168–169

smooth jazz, 196–197, 249, 252, 254, 261, 265, 267, 272
"Some Children See Him" (song), 292
"Somehow Our Love Survives" (song), 198
"Something That You Said" (song), 255–256, 260, 268
songwriting, 89–90, 103–104, 106, 122–123
South Africa, 262, *263*
Southgate, Martha, 176, 178
"Spain" (Corea song), 87, 111–112, 124–125, 189
"Spain (I Can Recall)" (song), 111–112, 118, 124–125, 189, 207, 208, 251, 270, 274, 303
Spanish flu (1918), 13
Spellbound (Sample album), 198, 203
Spera, Keith, 218
St. Catherine's Residence (Milwaukee), 22
St. Francis Church (Milwaukee), 8
St. Louis performance, 324
stage fright, 99–102, 137
Stallworth, Paul, 74, 90–91, 92
Stan Kenton Orchestra (band), 29
The Standard (Take 6 album), 299
Stevens, Danny, 60
Stevens, Susan, 168–169
Stewart, Michael "Patches," 154, 160, 161, 205, 207, 227, 234, 236, 237
The Strand (Redondo Beach, CA), 213
Straw, Bill, 55
Studer, James, 154, 161
studio recordings vs. live performances, 152, 153, 184, 207, 232, 236–237, 242
Summerfest (Milwaukee), 133–134
"Summertime" (song), 230
"superdisc" as part of CD package, 282, 285
Sutton, Tierney, 44, 304
Sweet Thing (Boney James album), 249–250, 252
swing era, 117
symphony concerts, 112, 244–245, 258, 276, 293–294
synthesizer sounds, 92, 110, 146, 148, 158–159, 185–186, 192, 291

"Take Five" (Desmond song), 84, 87, 89, 94, 154, 206, 251, 260, 274, 324
Take 6 (vocal group), 199, 292, 298, 299
talent contests, 14
The Tender Trap (Cedar Rapids, IA, club), 40–42, *41*
Tenderness (album), 221, 226–235, *228*, 236, 237
Tenderness (video), 227–228, 229, 233
"10K Hi" (song), 185–186
This Time (album), 110–113, *113*, 122, 124–125, 126, 156, 160, 163
Thomann, Don, 25
Thomas, Todd "Speech," 224–226
Thousand Oaks Hospital, 311, 313
"Three Coyote Stories" (from *Lou Harrison: A Portrait*), 244, 251
Three Dog Night (band), 63
Tidyman, Ernest, 166–167
Time, 82, 85
Times-Picayune (New Orleans), 218–219
Timmons, Bobby, 28
Tolleson, Robin, 182, 185
Tomorrow Today (album), 253–258, 261, 267–268, 269, 272
"Tomorrow Today" (song), 254, 257, 260
The Tonight Show, 57, 58
Toronto Star, 296
Totah, Abe, 33, 34–35, 45
touring activities, 127–139, 204–211, 212, 235, 278–280, 286–288. *See also* live performances vs. studio recordings
touring bands, 204–205, 248–249, 258–259, 260–262, *279*
trio album idea, 246
The Troubadour (Los Angeles venue), 73–74, 76, 253
"Try a Little Tenderness" (song), 230
Turano, Joe, *279*, *288*; and albums, 262, 269, 285, 291, 292, 303, 305–306, 315–316; on Al's health, 294, 297, 313; on Al's reaction to criticism, 277; on Al's relations with other musicians, 320; and concerts, 307, 312; with JoeReau, 313; keynote address at Milwaukee event, 309;

on working with Al, 71–72, 159, 184, 259, 320, 323
Tutu (Davis album), 47
A Twist of Jobim (Ritenour album), 249, 251
"Two on the Aisle" (1958 Follies show), 18–19

Uihlein Hall (Milwaukee), 132–133, 134
Underwood, Lee, 10, 74, 82, 97–99
United Performing Arts Fund, 307
University of Iowa, 1, 35, 36, 39–44
unreleased albums, 219, 306, 312
Unsung (2020 documentary), 113, 115, 117, 123, 142, 312
Uris Theatre (New York City venue), 120–121
USA Today, 138, 143, 230–231, 234–235

venues, large, compared to smaller clubs, 99–102
Verizon Reads literacy program, 265
Verve Records, 253–254, 270–271, 272, 276
The Very Best Of: An Excellent Adventure (compilation album), 210, 293, *293*, 300
Video Soul (BET TV show), 216–218, 224
videos, music, 87–88, 118–119, 142–143, 148–150. *See also specific video names*
vocational rehabilitation, master's degree in, 39, 44

Wahlers, Roberta J., 151
"Wait for the Magic" (Urbanos song), 231
Walden, Narada Michael, 214–216
Walker, Chris, *311*; and albums, 262, 267–268, 269, 284, 291; and Al's health problems, 294; on Al's positivity, 321; on Al's relations with other musicians, 320; on "Boogie Down" lyrics, 142; on Duke, 46; musical background of, 248–249; on racial issues, 326; in *Unsung* documentary, 117; on working with Al, 320, 321, 323

Walker, Pearl. *See* Jarreau, Pearl Walker
Warner Bros. Records: Al's concern
    over relationship with, 80–81; and
    Al's tours, 127; and *Casino Lights*
    album, 191; contract expiration and
    negotiations, 239, 240, 242; and
    LiPuma, 107; and music videos, 118;
    recordings, 85, 102, 250; signing
    with, 75–76
Washington Post, 245
We Are the World documentary, 194–195
"We Are the World" (song),
    168, 193–195, *194*, 202
We Got By (album), 76–79, *77*, 80, 81,
    85, 86, 87, 90–91, 94, 102, 107,
    152, 217
"We Got By" (song), 12, 76, 80, 88, 92,
    132–133, 228, 236
WEA (Warner Bros. parent company),
    154
Weather Report (band), 144, 255, 268
Weber, Lowell, 24
Weiske, Kermit "Doc," 24
Wembley Arena (London), 100–102,
    152, 161, 207
"We're All in the Arts Together" (Al
    Jarreau opinion piece), 307
"We're in This Love Together" (song),
    113–116, 119, 125, 153, 161–162, 237
"We're in This Love Together" video, 34,
    119, 142
West Side Story songs, 34, 37, 245
Weyenberg Shoe Factory, 3
White House performance, 309–311
Whittinghill's Restaurant (Sherman
    Oaks, CA), 55–56

Whittington, "Sweet" Dick, 56
Widran, Jonathan, 257
Wiener Stadthalle (Vienna), 206
Wilkinson, Nigel, 80
William Morris Agency, 127
Williams, Larry, *279*; and albums,
    105–106, 112, 124, 162, 270–272,
    275–276, 278, 284, 285, 290–292,
    299; on Al's character, 325; on Al's
    death, 314–315; on Al's musical
    style, 123, 329; on Al's reaction to
    criticism, 277; on first meeting with
    Al, 72; on "Mornin'" video, 142; on
    working with Al, 320–321
Williams, Vanessa, 256, 257
Willis, Allee, 111
Willis, Bruce (actor), 172
Wilson, Bob, 72
Wisconsin Foundation for School
    Music, 1, 308, 309
Wisconsin Public Television
    documentary, 2, 8, 22, 310, 312
Wisconsin Roof Ballroom/Garden, 117
Wisconsin State Journal, 175
World Series, 138, *139*
WTMJ (Milwaukee), 33, 35

"Yo' Jeans" (song), 176–177
"You Don't See Me" (song), 228
"You Send Me" (song), 198
"Your Song" (John song), 80–81, 92,
    229, 236, 248, 289

Zarathustra (band), 60, 61–62